D0857166

The Rhythm of Being
A Study of Temporality

The Rhythm of Being
A Study of Temporality

by

Howard Trivers

Philosophical Library
New York

Library of Congress Cataloging in Publication Data

Trivers, Howard.
  The rhythm of being.

  1. Time.   I. Title.
BD638.T75   1985· 115   84-20680
ISBN 0-8022-2466-0

To
the Radcliffe graduate student
of philosophy in the green sweater
at Rosenstock-Huessy's seminar on the
Philosophy of History,
Harvard fall semester, 1934

CONTENTS

ACKNOWLEDGMENTS   xi

PART I
THE TEMPORALITY OF THE UNIVERSE
Chapter 1 Clocks   3
Chapter 2 Development of the Time Concept in Modern
            Science   6
Chapter 3 Relativity   16
Chapter 4 Einstein's Views on the Time Concept   20
Chapter 5 Space-Time   25
Chapter 6 From Special to General Relativity   28
Chapter 7 The Physical Structure of the Universe   32
Chapter 8 The Origin of the Universe   35
Chapter 9 Quantum Theory   41
Chapter 10 Time's Arrow   47
Chapter 11 Galaxies   51
Chapter 12 Stellar Evolution   54
Chapter 13 Geology   59
Chapter 14 Evolution   65
Chapter 15 The Origins of Life   71
Chapter 16 Irreversibility of Time in Evolution   82

PART II
THE TEMPORALITY OF THE SELF

Chapter 1 The Psychogenetic Development of the
            Consciousness of Time   87
Chapter 2 Succession and Duration   94
Chapter 3 The Perceived Present   99
Chapter 4 Individual and Social Aspects of the
            Experience of Time   105
Chapter 5 The Subjective Experience, Self-Awareness,
            of Animals   116
Chapter 6 Biological Rhythms   128
Chapter 7 The Self and Time   138

PART III
TIME AND HISTORY

Chapter 1 History of Nature vs. History of Man   145
Chapter 2 Prehistory: The Temporal Span   149
Chapter 3 Time, History, and Culture   166
Chapter 4 Rhythms in History: Hegel, Spengler,
            and Toynbee   227

AFTERWORD   313

NOTES   315

INDEX   337

ACKNOWLEDGMENTS

Ralph Place, a physicist, and Dwight Hoover, an historian, both Professors at Ball State University, were mentors from the inception of this work. Dr. Place made many valuable suggestions and textual improvements for Part I. Dr. Hoover provided me with materials from his course on historiography and has afforded me sound advice on critical issues during the preparation of the manuscript. Both Drs. Place and Hoover read the whole manuscript, as did Don C. Roberts, a learned engineer, whose sage advice has always been helpful to me with respect to this work as well as other matters.

Professor David Layzer of Harvard sent me a syllabus of a pertinent course he conducts as well as reprints and a personal manuscript. Ruth Howes, Professor of Physics at Ball State, argued with me and thereby enlightened me on the subject of relativity. Dr. Eric Johnson of the Ball State Chemistry Department read the section on "The Origins of Life," and made many valuable suggestions. Professor B.K. Swartz of the Anthropology Department suggested readings for the section "Prehistory" and made corrections and improvements of the text.

My friend James H. Breasted, Jr. guided me to the fine books on Egypt and Mesopotamia of the Oriental Institute, University of Chicago. At his suggestion I consulted his neighbor, John H. Finley, Jr., retired Harvard Classics Professor, on the Greeks, and in a telephone conversation he listed for me the excellent readings cited. Dr. E.F. Campbell, Vice President of the American Schools of Oriental Research made useful suggestions as to books on the

Hebrews, as did Rev. Lawrence Martin, First United Presbyterian Church here. Professors J.K. Fairbank, Harvard, and Frederick K. Mote, Princeton, led me to the sources on China. At Professor Mote's suggestion, I called Professor S.Y. Teng of Indiana University, who sent me a copy of his article on Herodotus and Ssu-ma Chien. Professor Frank Klingberg, Southern Illinois University, gave me copies of his original seminal articles on rhythms in history. My former colleague and friend Martha Mautner of the State Department sent me the material on cycles in the USSR prepared by Dr. Sid Ploss.

I am greatly indebted to Ball State University for logistic support during all these years of work on this book. The excellent facilities of the Bracken Library have afforded me not only a habitat but also positive assistance. In particular, Neil Coyle and Alice Hoover of the Reference Section have rendered me countless services of great help and value. Dr. Richard Kelly, Chairman of Business Education, and Liz Lewis, the Departmental Secretary, have continuously aided me over the years by permitting use of their transcribing machine as well as by arranging a succession of student assistants to do the transcribing: Barbara Cain, Julie Moore, Sandy Layman, and Theresa Mote.

The final manuscript was typed by Lisa Keener, a young lady of matchless diligence, competence, and intelligence.

The author also wishes to gratefully acknowledge permission to quote from the following sources:

Clark, Grahame, *Aspects of Prehistory*. Berkeley, Calif.: University of California Press, 1970.

Cottle, Thomas J., and Klineberg, Stephen L., *The Present of Things Future*. New York: The Free Press, 1974. Reprinted with permission of The Free Press, a Division of Macmillan, Inc. Copyright © 1974 by The Free Press.

Dawson, Raymond, *The Chinese Experience*. New York: Charles Scribner's Sons, 1978. Copyright © by Raymond Dawson. Reprinted with permission of Charles Scribner's Sons.

De Romilly, Jacqueline, *Time in Greek Tragedy*. Ithaca, N.Y.: Cornell University Press, 1968.

Einstein, Albert, *Ideas and Opinions*. New York: Crown Publishers, 1954. Copyright © 1954, 1982 by Crown Publishers, Inc.

Fraisse, Paul, *The Psychology of Time*. New York: Harper & Row, Publishers, Inc., 1963.

Frankfort, Henri; Frankfort, Mrs. H.A. (Groenewegen-); Wilson, John A.; Jacobsen, Thorkild; and Irwin, W.A., *The Intellectual Adventure of Ancient Man: An Essay on Speculative Thought in the Ancient Near East*. An Oriental Institute Essay. Chicago: The University of Chicago Press, 1946.

Frankfort, Henri, *Kinship and the Gods: A Study of Ancient Near Eastern Religion as Integration of Society and Nature*. An Oriental Institute Essay. Chicago: The University of Chicago Press, 1948.

Griffin, Donald R., *The Question of Animal Awareness*. New York: Rockefeller University Press, 1976. Reprinted by permission of Professor Donald R. Griffin.

McGraw-Hill Encyclopedia of Science and Technology. New York: McGraw-Hill, 1977.

Minkowski, Eugene, *Lived Time*, tr. Nancy Metzel. Evanston, Ill.: Northwestern University Press, 1970.

Orgel, L.E., *The Origins of Life: Molecules and Natural Selection*. New York: John Wiley & Sons, Inc., 1973. Reprinted by permission of Professor L.E. Orgel.

Saslow, W.C., and Jacobs, K.C., eds., *The Emerging Universe*. Charlottesville, Va.: The University Press of Virginia, 1972.

Simpson, George G., *The Major Features of Evolution*. New York: Columbia University Press, 1953. Copyright © 1953, Columbia University Press. Reprinted by permission of the publisher.

Spengler, Oswald, *The Decline of the West*, tr. C.F. Atkinson. New York: Alfred A. Knopf, Inc., 1926, 1928, and renewed 1956 by Alfred A. Knopf, Inc. Reprinted by permission of the publisher.

Toulmin, Stephen, and Goodfield, June, *The Discovery of Time.* New York: Harper & Row, Publishers, Inc., 1965.

Toynbee, Arnold J., *Civilization on Trial.* New York: Oxford University Press, 1948.

Toynbee, Arnold J., *A Study of History,* abridgement of Vol. I-VI by D.C. Somervell. New York and London: Oxford University Press, 1947.

Toynbee, Arnold J., *A Study of History,* abridgement of Vol. VII-X by D.C. Somervell. New York: Oxford University Press, 1957.

Verhoogen, John, et al., *The Earth.* New York: Holt, Rinehart & Winston, 1970.

Weinberg, Steven, *The First Three Minutes.* New York: Basic Books, Inc., 1977. Copyright © 1977 by Steven Weinberg. Reprinted by permission of Basic Books, Inc., Publishers.

Whitehead, Alfred North, *Science and the Modern World.* New York: Macmillan, 1925. Copyright 1925 by Macmillan Publishing Co., Inc., renewed 1953 by Evelyn Whitehead.

Whitrow, G.J., *The Natural Philosophy of Time.* London: Thomas Nelson & Sons, 1961. By permission of Oxford University Press.

Whitrow, G.J., *The Nature of Time.* New York: Holt, Rinehart & Winston. Copyright © 1972 by Thames and Hudson Ltd. Reprinted by permission of Holt, Rinehart & Winston, Publishers.

Wilson, John A., *The Burden of Egypt.* Chicago: The University of Chicago Press, 1951.

Wright, G. Ernest, *God Who Acts.* Chicago: Henry Regnery Co., 1952.

"It is impossible to meditate on time and the mystery of the creative passage of nature without an overwhelming emotion at the limitations of human intelligence."

—Alfred North Whitehead

PART I
THE TEMPORALITY OF THE UNIVERSE

Chapter 1
Clocks

In Jonathan Swift's *Gulliver's Travels*, first published in 1726, the inventory of the content of Gulliver's pockets, which was prepared by a Royal Commission for the Lilliputian Emperor, contained the following passage: "There were two pockets which we could not enter: These he called his fobs;... Out of the right fob hung a great silver chain with a wonderful kind of engine at the bottom. We directed him to draw out whatever was fastened to that chain; which appeared to be a globe, half silver, and half of some transparent metal; for, on the transparent side, we saw certain strange figures circularly drawn, and thought we could touch them, till we found our fingers stopped by that lucid substance. He put this engine to our ears, which made an incessant noise like that of a water-mill. And we conjecture it is either some unknown animal, or the god that he worships; but we are more inclined to the latter opinion, because he assured us (if we understood him right, for he expressed himself very imperfectly), that he seldom did anything without consulting it. He called it his oracle and said it pointed out the time for every action of his life."[1]

Jonathan Swift understood very well the role of the mechanical timekeeper, the clock and the watch, in the life of modern Western man. There were many factors in the development from the 17th century on of the specific concept of linear, continuous, advancing time which is intrinsic to modern science and modern Western man. There can be little doubt, however, that the invention of the

3

mechanical clock played a significant role in the development of this concept.

The earliest timekeepers that have survived to the present are sundials and waterclocks of ancient Egypt, from about 1500 B.C. Sundials and waterclocks continued to be the only timekeepers available in classical Greece and Rome, and sundials continued to be used in Medieval Europe. Sandglasses, originating in Europe in the 14th century, were used merely to measure small intervals of time. Waterclocks with an escapement mechanism were developed in China between about the 8th and 11th century A.D., the best known of which is described and illustrated in a Chinese text written by Su Sung in 1092. It has been suggested that the idea of an escapement mechanism was transmitted to Europe from China.

The first all-mechanical clocks were made around 1300 in Europe, with an escapement mechanism, wheels, gears, and weights. These first mechanical clocks were designed not to indicate the time on a dial, but to drive dials that gave astronomical indications, and to sound the hour by ringing bells. Mechanisms for ringing bells, made of toothed wheels and oscillating levers, may have played a role in the invention of mechanical clocks.

According to Lewis Mumford, the mechanical clock may have arisen in part out of the orderly routine of the monasteries in medieval times. The bells in monasteries were rung regularly at specified times calling for the devotions of the day. In the 13th century, the bell towers spread outside the monastery into the cities bringing an orderly routine and a new regularity to the lives of merchants and working men. In the 14th century the new clocks not only rang bells but also had a dial and a hand that showed the time by its movements. In Mumford's words, "The clock, not the steam-engine, is the key-machine of the modern industrial age."[2]

Springs were first used instead of weights for the driving power of clocks in the second half of the 15th century. The first watch, spring-driven, was built in Nuremberg, Germany in 1504 by Peter Henlein, a young locksmith; it was a drum-shaped timepiece, six inches in height, which took two years to build. In 1525 Jacob Zech, a Swiss clockmaker in Prague, invented the first effective main spring control. In the second half of the 16th century and in the 17th century, watchmaking was developed on a broad industrial scale, particularly in Switzerland and England. By 1704 all the basic mechanism in a quality standard watch of today had been invented. Swift's Gulliver, whose travels were reported in 1726, must have been carrying a quality watch.

Greater accuracy in time measurement was first made possible when the pendulum was applied as a regulator in clocks. Galileo's discovery in 1582 of a natural periodic process that can be repeated indefinitely and counted—namely, the swinging pendulum—is regarded as the origin of modern precise timekeeping. In that year, Galileo noted that, as timed by his pulse, a swinging lamp in the cathedral of Pisa seemed to have the same time of swing for large as for small arcs. Later after experimentation with swinging pendulums, Galileo concluded that each simple pendulum has its own period of oscillation depending on its length. In his old age Galileo attempted to apply the pendulum to clockwork so as to record mechanically the number of swings. However, he died in 1642, before the clock he designed was constructed.

Working independently in Holland, the Dutch scientist Christiaan Huygens completed a preliminary model of a spring-driven pendulum clock in 1656, which was built in the following year by his clockmaker. Huygens' pendulum clock opened up the era of precision timekeepers, which were able to measure physical time with an accuracy of about ten seconds a day. In Whitrow's words, "The invention of a mechanical clock which could, if properly regulated, tick away continually for years on end greatly influenced belief in the quasi-geometrical homogeneity and continuity of time."[3]

The invention of the mechanical clock also played a significant role in the formulation of the mechanistic conception of nature that prevailed from Descartes to Lord Kelvin at the end of the 19th century. Early in the 17th century Kepler affirmed that the universe was similar to a clock, as did Robert Boyle and others. The most extreme claim for the influence of the mechanical clock has been expressed by Lewis Mumford, stating that it "dissociated time from human events and helped to create the belief in an independent world of mathematically measurable sequences: the special world of science."[4]

Chapter 2
Development of the Time Concept in Modern Science

In the "Dialogues and Mathematical Demonstrations concerning Two New Sciences," published in 1638, Galileo treats time like a spatial dimension. Discussing the velocity of a falling body, he states, "The time of fall may be represented by any limited straight line."[5] Although Galileo may not have been the first to represent time by a geometrical straight line, nevertheless his tremendous scientific achievements and his prestige led to the effective propagation of this idea through his theory of motion set forth in this book on "Two New Sciences." However, Galileo only used straight line segments ("any *limited* straight line") to represent definite time-intervals). He never related time to a straight line of unlimited extension.

About thirty years later, Isaac Barrow, Newton's predecessor in the Lucasian chair of mathematics at Cambridge, delivered his *Geometrical Lectures*, which contained the first specific discussion of the general concept of linear, mathematical time. His views on the nature of time are not only important in themselves, but also significant because of their influence on Newton. Newton was a student at Cambridge during the time of Barrow's mathematical lectures, and he attended Barrow's lectures. In 1669 Newton revised and edited Barrow's *Geometrical Lectures*.

In answering the question whether there was time before the creation of the world, Barrow states: "Just as there was space before the world was founded, and even now there is an infinite space beyond the world (with which God co-exists)...so before the world and together with the world (perhaps beyond the world) time was, and is; since before the world arose, certain beings were able continually to remain in existence (God and the Angels presumably), so now things may exist beyond the world capable of such permanence."[6]

He goes on: "Time denotes not an actual existence but a certain capacity or possibility for a continuity of existence; just as space denotes a capacity for intervening length. Time does not imply motion, as far as its absolute and intrinsic nature is concerned; not any more than it implies rest; whether things move or are still, whether we sleep or wake, Time pursues the even tenor of its way."[7] Here is clearly the origin of Newton's well-known definition of time: "Absolute, true, mathematical time, of itself, and from its own nature flows equably without relation to anything external." Barrow goes on, "Time implies motion to be measurable; without motion we do not perceive the passage of Time. We evidently must regard Time as passing with a steady flow; therefore, it must be compared with some handy steady motion, such as the motion of the stars, and especially of the sun and moon..." To the question of how one knows that the sun is carried by an equal motion and that days or years are of equal duration, Barrow replies, "...if the sundial is found to agree with motions of any kind of time-measuring instrument, designed to be moved uniformly by successive repetitions of its own peculiar motion, under suitable conditions, for whole periods or for proportional parts of them; then it is right to say that it registers an equable motion. It seems to follow that strictly speaking the celestial bodies are not the first and original measures of Time; but rather those motions, which are observed round about us by the senses and which underlie our experiments, since we judge the regularity of the celestial motions by the help of these. Not even is Sol himself a worthy judge of time, or to be accepted as a veracious witness, except so far as time-measuring instruments attest his veracity by their votes."

As to the ultimate relation of time and motion, Barrow states: "Time may be used as a measure of motion; just as we measure space in some magnitude, and then use this space to estimate other magnitudes commensurable with the first; i.e., we compare motions with one another by the use of time as an intermediary." Barrow regarded time as essentially a mathematical concept with many analogies to a line "for time has length alone, is similar in all its parts and can be looked upon as constituted from a simple addition of successive instants or as from a continuous flow of one instant; either a straight or a circular line."[8] Although Barrow believed that "there is a great affinity and analogy between space and time,"[9] he did not identify time with a line, and criticized Hobbes for doing so. In Barrow's view, time was "the continuance of anything in its own being."[10]

Barrow was not only a mathematician, but also a theologian. In the case of both space and time, Barrow accepted Henry More's religious approach: space and time are nothing but the omnipresence and the eternal duration of God. Time is not for him a metaphysically independent entity. "Barrow never forgot that there was an infinite and everliving God, whose existence beyond the world involved space, and whose continued life before the creation of things in motion involved time. It was just because they were caught up in the unchangeable divine nature that space and time possessed that clarity and fixity which made it possible to compare with exactness by their aid sensible magnitude and motion." The religious reference is implicit when Barrow speaks of time as "flowing in its even tenor," as "independent of motion as far as its absolute and intrinsic nature is concerned," as "an absolute quantity, independent of all reference to measure,"[11] and in other references.

Newton's view of time follows directly that of Barrow's. In explaining his definitions of absolute time, absolute space, and absolute motion, which appear at the beginning of Newton's "Mathematical Principles of Natural Philosophy" of 1687, Newton states in a *Scholium*, following the *Definitions*: "Hitherto I have laid down the definitions of such words as are less known, and explained the sense in which I would have them to be understood in the following discourse. I do not define time, space, place, and motion, as being well known to all. Only I must observe that the *vulgar* conceive those quantities under no other notions but from the relation they bear to sensible objects. And thence arise certain prejudices for the removing of which, it will be convenient to distinguish them into absolute and relative, true and apparent, mathematical and *common*" (my emphasis). These comments are directed against Descartes' conception of the relative, or relational, character of these ideas.

Newton's famous *Definition* of time is as follows: "Absolute true and mathematical time, of itself, and from its own nature flows equably without regard to anything external, and by another name is called duration: relative, apparent, and common time, is some sensible and external (whether accurate or unequable) measure of duration by the means of motion, which is commonly used instead of true time; such as an hour, a day, a month, a year."[12] Thus time and duration are only two names for the same absolute entity, contrary to Descartes' view that time is something subjective and distinct from the duration which Descartes relates to the amount of reality of the created being. Furthermore, contrary to the view of Aristotle that "time is the measure of motion," Newton does not recognize a necessary link between time and motion, stating, "It may be that there is no such thing as an equable motion whereby time may be accurately measured. All motion may be accelerated and retarded, but the flowing of absolute time is liable to no change. The duration or perseverance of the existence of things remains the same; whether the motions are swift or slow, or none at all: and therefore it ought to be distinguished from what are only sensible measures thereof."[13]

It may seem curious that the view of absolute space and time set forth by Newton in contrast to the "vulgar" and "common" has now become the common view of ordinary people if they try to think about time: time seems to exist in its own right, it is something without beginning or end, and continues independently of whatever happens. This is really not something curious, though; it is more a residue in modern Western man of the successful development of mechanics and physics on the basis of Newton's conceptions and subsequent scientific accomplishments.

It would not serve our purpose to discuss here the many philosophical criticisms of Newton's idea of absolute time, flowing uniformly without relation to anything else in the universe. Newton was not merely a scientist, he was also a theologian like Barrow. There was a religious source of his views on space and time; they were not merely entities derived from mathematico-experimental science. The religious source became quite clear when Newton added his *General Scholium* to the second edition of the *Principles* in 1713, which states as follows: "From his true dominion it follows that the true God is a living, intelligent, and powerful Being; and from his other perfections, that he is supreme, or most perfect. He is eternal and infinite, omnipotent and omniscient; that is, his duration reaches from eternity to eternity; his presence from infinity to infinity...He is not eternity or infinity, but eternal and infinite; he is not duration or space but he endures and is present. He endures forever and is everywhere present; and by existing always and everywhere, he constitutes duration and space..."[14]

During the 17th century the new concept of a homogeneous, continuous, linear advancing time began to replace the ancient cyclical view of time and the universe. In 1602, Francis Bacon set forth the concept of linear progress in time in an early work, entitled "The Masculine Birth of Time." Bacon declared that the advancement of "the happiness of mankind" was the direct purpose of all his work. He believed that the proper aim of knowledge is the improvement of human life, the increase of happiness and the mitigation of suffering. He regarded the real goal of the sciences as "the endowment of human life with new inventions and riches";[15] for him the end of knowledge was utility. When we look back to antiquity, we must realize that in the meantime knowledge has been increased by a tremendous number of observations and experiments. "Time is the great discoverer, and truth is the daughter of time, not of authority."[16] As to the future, Bacon affirmed that if the errors of the past are avoided there is every hope of steady progress in the modern age. However, he did not really turn his mind to the possibilities of a remote future, despite his recognition of "the inseparable propriety of time which is ever more and more to disclose truth."[17] His view of living in the old age of the world suggests that he did not expect a vast amount of time before the end of mankind, nor did he envisage an indefinite advance in the future.

It is strange that Newton as theologian supported the cyclical view; he was convinced that the world was soon coming to an end. However, the concept of linear progress in time was affirmed by Barrow, Locke, and Leibniz, among others in the 17th century. To Locke is attributed one of the clearest statements of the scientific concept of time developed in the 17th century: "...*duration is but as it were the length of one straight line*, extended in *infinitum*, not capable of multiplicity, variation, or figure; but is one common measure of all existence whatsoever, wherein all things, whilst they exist, equally partake. For this present moment is common to all things that are now in being, and equally comprehends that part of their existence as much as if they were all but one single being; and we may truly say, they all exist in the same moment of time."[18] For Locke, time also had a moral and social function. In contrast to Hobbes, who believed that individual strife and conflict were the natural state of man, Locke believed in the fundamental goodness of man, in the social character of man in the state of nature, and in the perfectibility of human nature. Locke's philosophy has thus been termed "the austere philosophy of an age inspired wholly by one great hope, that of progress."[19]

Leibniz was another great 17th century thinker who espouses the view of linear advance and progress in time. Voltaire ridicules

Leibniz because of his affirmation that God, having considered all possible worlds, had chosen the best. According to Leibniz, God had to consider the interests of the whole universe, of which the earth with humanity is only a minor part. The evils of our small world he regarded as negligible in comparison with the perfection of the whole cosmos. Leibniz does not argue that at any given moment the universe is as perfect as it could be; it is endowed with potentiality and "will develop towards perfection throughout infinite time." Leibniz's optimism thus concerns the universe as a whole, not the earth, and his view would be consistent with a pessimism as to human destiny. However, he does point to the possibility that "in the course of time the human race may reach a greater perfection than we can imagine at present."[20]

The key to the Newtonian concept of time is that time is independent of events, that there exists an infinite series of temporal moments, and that events are distinct from them but can occupy some of them. "Thus temporal relations between events are complex relations formed by the relation of events to the moments of time which they occupy and the before-and-after relation subsisting between distinct moments of time."[21] Newton's views were opposed vigorously in his own lifetime by Leibniz, who formulated the theory that events are more fundamental than moments, a theory known as the relational theory of time.

Leibniz believed that we derive time from events, that time is not an entity in itself, but merely the order in which events occur. For him, temporal moments are merely abstract concepts, being classes of events defined by simultaneity. Two events are simultaneous according to Leibniz, not because they occupy the same moment of absolute time but because each occurs together with the other. Just as Newton's theory, Leibniz's view of time was founded on certain metaphysical and theological conceptions, namely, "on his principles of sufficient reason, identity of indiscernibles, and pre-established harmony."[22] The differences between Newton and Leibniz on metaphysical and theological issues, including the problem of time, were set forth in an exchange of letters in the years 1715 and 1716 between Leibniz and Dr. Samuel Clarke. Dr. Clarke, who was Rector of St. James, Westminster, was a philosophical theologian and an intimate friend of Newton. Newton, who personally strongly disliked public controversy and polemics, evidently entrusted to his friend Dr. Clarke the task of replying to Leibniz's letters. We cannot deal here with this fascinating correspondence in much detail; there are few, if any, exchanges of correspondence in any way comparable. Though on a much higher level of philosophical thought, to my mind in its polemical style it is reminiscent of the exchange of letters in 1963-1964 between the Communist Party of the Soviet Union and the Chinese Communist Party.

In his first letter Leibniz wrote:

"Sir Isaac Newton says that *Space is an Organ* which God makes use of to perceive Things by. But if God stands in need of any Organ to perceive Things by, it will follow that they do not depend all together upon him, nor were produced by him."

"Sir Isaac Newton and his followers have also a very odd Opinion concerning the Work of God. According to their Doctrine, God Almighty wants to *wind up* his Watch from Time to Time: Otherwise it would cease to move. He had not, it seems, sufficient Foresight to make it a perpetual Motion. Nay, the Machine of God's making is so imperfect, according to these Gentlemen, that he is obliged to *clean* it now and then by an extraordinary Concourse, and even to *mend* it, as a Clockmaker mends his Work; who must consequently be so much the more unskillful a Workman, as he is often obliged to mend his Work and to set it Right. According to *My* Opinion, the same Force and Vigor remains always in the World, and only passes from one part of Matter to another, agreeably to the Laws of Nature, and the beautiful pre-established Order."[23]

In his third letter Leibniz applied the principle of sufficient reason to time in the following well-known passage: "Suppose someone asks why God did not create everything a year sooner; and that the same person wants to infer from that that God did something for which He cannot possibly have had a reason why He did it thus rather than otherwise, we should reply that his inference would be true if time were something apart from temporal things, for it would be impossible that there should be reasons why things should have been applied to certain instants rather than to others, when their succession remained the same. But this itself proves that instants apart from things are nothing and that they only consist in the successive order of things; and if this remains the same, the one of the two states (for instance that in which the Creation was imagined to have occurred a year earlier) would be nowise different and could not be distinguished from the other which now exists." Leibniz deduced from his principle of sufficient reason the principle of the identity of indiscernibles, according to which it is impossible that two things, differing only in number, but otherwise completely similar, can exist. In his fourth letter to Clarke he wrote: "To suppose two things indiscernible is to suppose the same thing under two names. Thus the hypothesis that the universe should have originally had another position in time and place from which it actually had, and yet all the parts of the universe should have had the same position with regard to one another as that which they have in fact received, is an impossible fiction."[24]

In Leibniz's Monadology, the Monads are "the true atoms of nature, and in fact, the Elements of things."[25] They are each in varying degrees percipient. Although the Monads are mutually independent, having "no windows through which anything may come in or go out,"[26] nevertheless each mirrors the whole course of the universe from its own point of view and the states of all Monads at every instance correspond with each other. In accordance with the principle of pre-established harmony, the Monads have been so perfectly constructed that they remain in accord through change without either mutual influence or external assistance. Thus according to Leibniz, "neither space nor time can exist in their own right independently of bodies, except as ideas in the mind of God. Space is the order of coexistences, and time is the order of succession of phenomena. This order is the same for all Monads, for since each of the latter mirrors the whole universe they must necessarily keep pace with one another. Consequently, in so far as the temporal aspect of the universe is concerned, Leibniz's principle of harmony is equivalent to the postulate of universal time."

Leibniz's thinking on the question of the temporal origin of the universe is made clear in the following passage: "It is a similar, that is to say an impossible fiction, to suppose that God had created the world several million years sooner. Those who incline towards such kinds of fiction will be unable to reply to those who are in favor of the eternity of the world. For since God does nothing without a reason, and since there is no reason assignable why He did not create the world sooner, it will follow either that He created nothing at all, or that he produced the world before any assignable time, which is to say that the world is eternal. But when we show that the beginning, whatever it was, is always the same thing, the question of why it was not otherwise ceases to exist. If space and time were something absolute, that is to say if they were something other than certain orders of things, what I am saying would be a contradiction. But since this is not the case, the hypothesis is contradictory, that is to say it is an impossible fiction."[27]

It would not be germane to discuss Leibniz's theory of time further here. Suffice it to say, while the Newtonian point of view was dominant throughout the 18th and 19th centuries and constituted the basis for the great advances in mechanics and physics, nevertheless Leibniz's is nowadays more in accord with contemporary thought on the nature of time.

As we have said earlier, the concept of linear advance in time was supported by the eminent 17th century thinkers Leibniz, Barrow, and Locke. John Locke had a profound influence on the 18th century French philosophers of the Enlightenment. They affirmed also the new progressive view of time which led them to discard the Bible-based story of natural creation. In 1721 Montesquieu wrote: "Is it possible for those who understand nature and have a reasonable idea of God to believe that matter and creative things are only 6,000 years old?" In the middle of the century, Diderot wrote in terms of "millions of years." Immanuel Kant believed that the universe may be hundreds of millions of years old.[28]

Descartes is acknowledged as the originator of the idea of cosmic evolution. Believing that originally the world was filled with matter distributed as uniformly as possible, he set forth a theory of successive formation of the sun and the planets by natural processes of separation and combination. In his "Universal Natural History and Theory of the Heavens," published in 1755, Kant applied Newtonian concepts to the problems of cosmic evolution. He also began with the idea that in the beginning matter was in a gaseous state spread throughout the universe, but not spread uniformly. Through this lack of uniformity, a giant cloud of gas, contracting under its own gravitation, begins to rotate, producing eventually a star as a result. Thus the universe has become less homogenous with the passage of time. He believed that we live in an evolutionary, or developing, universe in the sense that the present is essentially more complex than the past. In 1778 the geologist James Hutton in his "Theory of the Earth" expressed the view that the Earth has required enormous periods of time to have reached its present condition, and from his study of sedimentary and igneous rocks he concluded that "we find no vestige of a beginning—no prospect of an end."[29]

The final benchmark in the modern view of time as linear continual progression without cyclical repetition came in 1859 with Darwin's *Origin of Species*. While the notion of biological development and organic evolution was, as it were, in the air at the time, *The Origin of Species* laid a sound basis for this conception by disproving definitively the dogma of the fixity of species and by explaining the evolution of species by transformations through natural selection. Darwin's ideas were reinforced by the growing science of paleontology and the accumulating material evidence of the great antiquity of man. Man's perspective in time was revolutionized by the contemporaneous advances in geology and biology, just as the heliocentric theory of Copernicus had revolutionized his perspective in space.

Jonathan Swift's Gulliver told the Lilliputians that his watch "pointed out the time for every action of his life." Swift was a very prescient thinker. Two hundred and fifty years later, in a world dominated by Western science, human life generally is regulated chronometrically so that even elementary functions such as eating and sleeping are more apt to be induced by the clock than by feelings of hunger or fatigue. Such chronometric control can be burdensome, and the burden is sometimes revealed in psychopathic individuals: one such put a bullet through his watch in order to "stop time." At any rate, the conception of a linear, continual, advancing time has become a dominant feature in human society and in human conceptions throughout most of the world today.

Chapter 3
Relativity

The Newtonian conception of absolute space and absolute time prevailed in the natural sciences until the first decade of the 20th century. It was definitively challenged, and relegated to the status of an outdated past theory, by a new insight, namely the Principle of the Relativity of Uniform Motion. Einstein was not the first to put forward this principle. In 1904 Poincare described the principle and even named it the "Principle of Relativity." Einstein's formulation of the special theory of relativity was published in 1905, under the title, as translated in English, "On the Electrodynamics of Moving Bodies."

To outline the innovation of the special theory of relativity, we will use Einstein's own words as follows: "In classical physics, we had one clock, one time flow, for all observers in all coordinate systems. Time, and therefore such words as 'simultaneously,' 'sooner,' 'later,' had an absolute meaning independent of any coordinate system. Two events happening at the same time in one coordinate system happened necessarily simultaneously in all other coordinate systems." According to the relativity theory, "Two events which are simultaneous in one coordinate system may not be simultaneous in another coordinate system."[30]

Describing his efforts leading to the special theory of relativity, Einstein set down in his autobiographical notes:

By and by I despaired of the possibility of discovering the true laws of

16

mechanics and thermodynamics by means of constructive efforts based on known facts. The longer and more despairingly I tried, the more I came to the conviction that only the discovery of the universal formal principle could lead us to assured results.... How then, could such a universal principle be found? After ten years of reflection such a principle resulted from a paradox upon which I had already hit at the age of sixteen: If I pursue a beam of light with the velocity c (velocity of light in a vacuum), I should observe such a beam as a spatially oscillatory electromagnetic field at rest. However, there seems to be no such thing.... From the very beginning it appeared to me intuitively clear that, judged from the standpoint of such an observer, everything would have to happen according to the same laws as for an observer who, relative to the earth, was at rest.[31]

The famous Michelson-Morley interferometer experiment of 1887 played a significant role in connection with the special theory of relativity. It was believed that the velocity of light through the ether in the direction of the motion of the earth should differ from the velocity of light in an opposite direction. By this experiment and many other subsequent ones, "no dependence of the speed of light on direction could be found." Einstein terms this result as a "verdict of 'death' to the theory of a calm ether-sea through which all matter moves."[32] While Michelson's experiment influenced Einstein's work by strengthening his conviction concerning the validity of the principle of the special theory of relativity, he wrote in a letter that he was "pretty much convinced of the principle"[33] before he knew this experiment and its result.

The relativity theory begins with two assumptions:
1. The velocity of light in vacuo is the same in all coordinate systems moving uniformly, relatively to each other.
2. All laws of nature are the same in all coordinate systems moving uniformly, relative to each other.

In Einstein's words, "The law of the constant velocity of light in empty space, which has been confirmed by the development of electrodynamics and optics, and the equal legitimacy of all inertial systems (special principle of relativity), which was proved in a particularly incisive manner by Michelson's famous experiment, between them made it necessary...that the concept of time should be made relative, each inertial system being given its own special time.... According to the special theory of relativity, spatial coordinates and time still have an absolute character insofar as they are directly measurable by stationary clocks and bodies. But they are relative insofar as they depend on the state of motion of the selected inertial system. According to the special theory of relativity the four-dimensional continuum formed by the union of space and time (Minkowski) retains the absolute character which, according to the earlier theory, belonged to both space and time separately. The influence of motion (relative to the coordinate system) on the form of bodies and on the motion of clocks, also the equivalence of energy and inert mass, follow from the interpretation of coordinates and time as products of measurement."[34]

The difference between classical physics and relativity theory is revealed when we consider two coordinate systems moving relatively to each other. The classical physicist splits the four-dimensional continuum into three-dimensional spaces and the one-dimensional time continuum; he bothers only about space transformation, as time is absolute for him. For relativity theory, "time as well as space is changed by passing from one coordinate system to another, and the Lorentz transformation considers the transformation properties of the four-dimensional time-space continuum of our four-dimensional world of events."[35] The Lorentz transformation group may be defined "as a group of linear transformations which leave a particular value of the velocity—the velocity of light—invariant. These transformations hold for the transition from one 'inertial system' to another which is in uniform motion relative to the first. The most conspicuous novel property of this transformation group is that it does away with the absolute character of the concept of simultaneity of events distant from each other in space. On this account it is to be expected that all equations of physics are covariant with respect to Lorentz transformations."[36] Einstein summarized the content of the special relativity theory in one sentence: "All natural laws must be so conditioned that they are covariant with respect to Lorentz transformations." It follows from this, he states, that "the simultaneity of two distant events is not an invariant concept and that the dimensions of rigid bodies and the speed of clocks depend upon their state of motion."[37]

The four-dimensionality of reality is not new in the special theory of relativity. In classical physics, an event is localized by four coordinates, three spatial, one temporal: "...the totality of physical 'events' is thus thought of as being imbedded in a four-dimensional continuous manifold. This four-dimensional continuum breaks objectively into one-dimensional time and three-dimensional spatial sections, the latter of which contain only simultaneous events. This resolution is the same for all inertial systems. The simultaneity of two definite events with reference to one inertial system involves the simultaneity of these events in all inertial systems." Thus time is absolute. In the special theory of relativity, however, the sum total of events simultaneous with the selected event exist in relation to a particular inertial system, but no longer independently of the choice of the inertial system. "The four-dimensional continuum is now no longer observable objectively into sections, which contain all simultaneous events; 'now' loses for the spatially extended world its objective meaning."[38]

In the special theory of relativity, "if we imagine matter and field to be removed, inertial space or, more accurately, this space together with the associated time remains behind. The four-dimensional structure (Minkowski-space) is thought of as being the carrier of matter and of the field. Inertial spaces with their associated time are only privileged four-dimensional coordinate systems that are linked together by the linear Lorentz transformations. Since there exists in this four-dimensional structure no longer any sections which represent 'now' objectively, the concept of happening and becoming are indeed not completely suspended, but yet complicated. It appears therefore more natural to think of physical reality as a four-dimensional existence, instead of, as hitherto, the evolution of a three-dimensional existence."[39]

Chapter 4
Einstein's Views on the Time Concept

Einstein has some interesting remarks about the nature and origins of temporality. In an article published in 1936, he writes: "An important property of our sense experiences and more generally of all our experiences, is their temporal order. This kind of order leads to the mental conception of a subjective time, an ordering scheme for our experience. The subjective time leads then via the concept of a bodily object and of space to the concept of objective time,...."[40] In a book published in 1938, introducing the question of "What is a clock?" he writes: "The primitive subjective feeling of time flow enables us to order our impressions, to judge that one of them takes place earlier, another later."[41] The "primitive subjective feeling of time flow" does not help us much. However, in a book published in 1954, Einstein discusses the psychological origin of the concept of time in the following terms: "This concept is undoubtedly associated with the fact 'calling to mind,' as well as with the differentiation between sense experiences and recollection of these. Of itself it is doubtful whether the differentiation between the sense experience and recollection (or a mere mental image) is something psychologically directly given to us. Everyone has experienced that he has been in doubt whether he has actually experienced something with his senses or has simply dreamed about it. Probably the ability to discriminate between these alternatives first comes about as the result of an activity of the mind creating order."[42] How prescient is this last sentence in the light of the views of Fraisse and other psychologists to be discussed later in Part II, "The Temporality of the Self." Einstein continues: "An experience is associated with a 'recollection', and it is considered as being 'earlier' in comparison with 'present experiences.' This is a conceptual ordering principle for recollected experiences, and the possibility for this accomplishment gives rise to the subjective concept of time, i.e., that concept of time which refers to the arrangement of the experiences of the individual."[42]

How does Einstein proceed from "subjective" time to "objective" time? After referring "to the primitive subjective feeling of time flow" in the earlier discussion of "What is a clock?" he writes: "But to show that the time interval between two events is ten seconds, a clock is needed. By the use of a clock the time concept becomes objective. Any physical phenomenon may be used as a clock, provided it can be exactly repeated as many times as desired. Taking the interval between the beginning and the end of such an event as one unit of time, arbitrary time-intervals may be measured by repetition of this physical process. All clocks, from the simple hour glass to the most refined instruments, are based on this idea."[43]

In his later discussion of "the psychological origin of the concept of time," after discussing "the subjective concept of time," he poses the question: "What do we mean by rendering objective the concept of time?" He gives as an example: "A person A ('I') has the experience 'it is lightning.' At the same time the person A also experiences such a behavior of the person B as brings the behavior of B into relation with his own experience 'it is lightning....' For the person A the idea arises that other persons also participate in the experience 'it is lightning.' 'It is lightning' is now no longer interpreted as an exclusively personal experience, but as an experience of other persons (or eventually only as a 'potential experience'). In this way the interpretation that 'it is lightning,' which originally entered into the consciousness as an 'experience,' is now also interpreted as an (objective) 'event.' It is just the sum total of all events that we mean when we speak of the 'real external world.'"[44] In order to arrive at the idea of an objective world, Einstein adds, "An additional constructive concept still is necessary: the event is localized not only in time, but also in space." Furthermore, Einstein adds another comment. He had previously linked up the concept of space with experiences using boxes and the arrangement of material objects in them. The persons "who had to be introduced for the formation of an objective concept of time, also play the role of material objects in this connection." He expresses the view, therefore, that "the formation of the concept of the material object must precede our concepts of time and space."[45]

In the 1936 article cited above, Einstein discussed the transition from subjective to objective time in the following way: "Ahead of the notion of objective time there is, however, the concept of space; and ahead of the latter we find the concept of the bodily object. The latter is directly connected with complexes of sense experiences. It has been pointed out that one property which is characteristic of the notion 'bodily object' is the property which provides that we coordinate to it an existence, independent of (subjective) time, and independent of the fact that it is perceived by our senses. We do this in spite of the fact that we perceive temporal alterations in it." Einstein then derives the concept of space from the 'contact' of 'practically rigid' bodily objects. "The totality of all conceivable quasi-rigid continuations of a body B_0 is the infinite 'space' determined by it...the fact that every bodily object situated in any arbitrary manner can be put into contact with the quasi-rigid continuation of some given body B_0 (body of reference), this fact is the empirical basis of our conception of space."[46]

According to Einstein, the following two postulates, independent of each other, are involved in the introduction of objective time:

1. The introduction of the objective local time by connecting the temporal sequence of experiences with the readings of a "clock," i.e., of a periodically recurring closed system.
2. The introduction of the notion of the objective time for the events in the whole space, by which notion alone the idea of local time is extended to the idea of time in physics.

Einstein adds the following note concerning the first postulate: "...it does not mean a 'petitio principii' if one puts the concept of periodic occurrence ahead of the concept of time. Such a conception corresponds exactly to the precedence of the concept of the rigid (or quasi-rigid) body in the interpretation of the concept of space."[47] To my mind this is one of the most significant and revealing thoughts in all of Einstein's discussion of time. Before considering it further, let me set down Einstein's note concerning the second postulate: "The illusion which prevailed prior to the enunciation of the theory of relativity—that, from the point of view of experience, the meaning of simultaneity in relation to spatially distant events and, consequently, that the meaning of physical time is *a priori* clear—this illusion had its origin in the fact that in our everyday experience we can neglect the time of propagation of light. We are accustomed on this account to fail to differentiate between 'simultaneously seen' and 'simultaneously happening'; and, as a result, the difference between time and local time is blurred."[48]

Let us return to Einstein's note to the first postulate. In considering the origin and the empirical content of the concept of time, he puts the concept of periodic occurrence ahead of the concept of time. In discussing in Part II the connection between the self and time, we will point out that rhythms are an intrinsic characteristic of the natural universe and of human life. A "periodic recurrence" is a reiteration, and as such, it is also a rhythm. When Einstein puts the concept of periodic occurrence ahead of the concept of time, he is testifying that rhythm is the primordial ground of time. He is also testifying that the common view of periodic recurrence or rhythm as necessarily presupposing time is not correct in a fundamental sense. To be sure, once the concept of objective time has been elaborated, we can interpret rhythms in a temporal way, and we can measure their temporal intervals. However, this common usage neither reveals nor corresponds with the fundamental conceptual relation.

In the chapter on "Relativity" in *Science and the Modern World*, Alfred North Whitehead sets forth a viewpoint pertinent to our discussion. He states: "An event is the grasping into unity of a pattern of aspects.... If the pattern endures throughout the successive parts of the event, and also exhibits itself in the whole, so that the event is the life history of the pattern, then in virtue of that enduring pattern the event gains an external effectiveness.... It is in this endurance of pattern that time differentiates itself from space. The pattern is spatially *now*; and this temporal determination constitutes its relation to each partial event. For it is reproduced in this temporal succession of these spatial parts of its own life. I mean that this particular rule of temporal order allows the pattern to be reproduced in each temporal slice of its history."[49] The pattern, you will note, is "reproduced," i.e., reiterated, repeated, in the succession of the parts of the event. In a subsequent passage, Whitehead extends this interpretation of repetition to the relation between successive events. "Endurance is the repetition of the pattern in successive events. Thus endurance requires a succession of durations, each exhibiting the pattern." Earlier, he describes the duration as "the field for the realized pattern constituting the character of the event." He also termed a duration, "as the field of the pattern realized in the actualization of one of its contained events," an epoch. "Time is sheer succession of epochal durations. But the entities which succeed each other in this account are durations. The duration is that which is required for the realization of a pattern in the given event. Thus the divisibility and extensiveness.is within the given duration. The epochal duration is not realized *via* its *successive* divisible parts, but is given *with* its parts."[50]

In an earlier passage in this same chapter, Whitehead refers to the process of realization in the actual universe, "which is the adjustment of the synthetic activities by virtue of which the various events become their realized selves." He states: "This adjustment is what introduces temporal process...time, in its character of the adjustment of the process of synthetic realization, extends beyond the spatio-temporal continuum of nature."[51] Temporal process in this sense is not necessarily one single series of linear succession; in fact, Whitehead finds that temporal process of realization can be analyzed into a group of linear serial processes, each of which is a space-time system.

Chapter 5
Space-Time

Let us return to Einstein's special theory of relativity. According to this theory, as already quoted, "spatial coordinates and time still have an absolute character in so far as they are directly measurable by stationary clocks and bodies. But they are relative in so far as they depend on the state of motion of the selected inertial system."[52] This means that measuring rods and clocks at rest in a particular inertial system can determine coordinates of space and time and make measurements which are of a precise and absolute nature for that particular inertial system. However, other inertial systems may be moving uniformly with respect to that particular inertial system. From the viewpoint of the other inertial systems, the measuring rods of the selected inertial system are contracted and its clock runs slow. This is a reciprocal relation. From the viewpoint of the selected inertial system, the measuring rod of the other inertial systems are contracted and their clocks run slow. Are the changes "real" or "apparent"?

According to the special theory of relativity, there are no privileged inertial systems, and hence it can be argued that the measuring rods and clocks are in each case really as measured. However, this does not seem to me persuasive. Even if one were to argue that to be "real" is to be measurable, measurement is not the exclusive and exhaustive characteristic of reality, even in physical science. A measuring rod is a material object; it is a rigid or quasi-rigid body. A clock is a material entity, embodying and perpetuating a rhythm.

25

The real material structure of a body is determinate in its own inertial system. Hence the changes are merely "apparent," that is, changes relative to the observer. "It was one of the great merits of Einstein's approach...that he circumvented the problem of the structure of matter and turned his attention to the theory of measurement. Instead of assuming that there are *real*, that is, structural, changes in length and duration owing to motion, Einstein's theory involves only *apparent* changes; and these are independent of the microscopic constitution and hidden mechanisms controlling the structure of matter."[53] However, while there may not be real internal structural changes, there may be real changes in external characteristics, for instance, the relativistic increase in mass of a rapidly moving physical particle.

When Einstein in an earlier citation stated, "It appears, therefore, more natural to think of physical reality as a four-dimensional existence, instead of, as hitherto, the evolution of a three-dimensional existence"[54] he was influenced by the famous mathematician Hermann Minkowski. In a lecture in 1908, three years after Einstein's original article on the special theory of relativity, Minkowski set forth the conception of a new absolute world, later called *space-time*, which replaced Newton's absolute time and space. He termed a point of space at a point of time a "world-point," and he termed the totality of all world-points the "world." A particle of matter or electricity enduring for an indefinite time he called a "world-line," the points of which can be found by successive reading of the time that would be shown by a clock (if there were such) carried by the particle. According to Minkowski, "The whole universe is seen to resolve itself into similar world-lines," and "physical laws might find their most perfect expression as the reciprocal relations between these world-lines."[55] Following Einstein's special relativity, Minkowski's absolute world gives different "projections" in space and time for different observers in uniform motion.

Minkowski's concept of space-time has had a tremendous influence in physics, cosmology, and philosophy. In his oft-quoted assertion, Minkowski claimed: "Henceforth space by itself and time by itself are doomed to fade into mere shadows, and only a kind of union of the two will preserve an independent reality."[56] Minkowski's world is like the "block universe," a term of William James, where events do not happen but we merely become aware of them. The great mathematician Hermann Weyl expounded this view thus:

The scene of action of reality is not a three-dimensional space, but rather a *four-dimensional world in which space and time are linked together indissolubly*. However deep the chasm may be that separates the intuitive nature of space from that of time in our experience, nothing of this qualitative difference enters into the objective worlds which physics endeavors to crystallize out of direct experience. It is a four-dimensional continuum which is neither "time" nor "space." Only the consciousness that passes on in one portion of this world experiences the detached piece which comes to meet it and passes behind it as history, that is, as a process that is going forward in time and takes place in space.[57]

According to this view, the passage of time is a feature of consciousness that has no objective counterpart.

Pierre Janet made the observation that "philosophers have a special horror towards time; they have done everything in order to suppress time."[58] This remark is, of course, not true in its full generality, although there has been a profound philosophical tradition which has sought to eliminate or subordinate the passage of time. It should not be surprising that mathematicians, even very great ones, think along the lines of this philosophical tradition.

Chapter 6
From Special to General Relativity

Immediately after setting forth the special theory of relativity in 1905, Einstein moved on to the considerations which led eventually to the general theory of relativity. In his own account of this, he states: "When by the special theory of relativity I had arrived at the equivalence of all so-called inertial systems for the formulation of natural laws, the question whether there was not a further equivalence of coordinate systems followed naturally,... To put it in another way, if only a relative meaning can be attached to the concept of velocity, ought we nevertheless to persevere in treating acceleration as an absolute concept? From the purely kinematic point of view there was no doubt about the relativity of all motions whatever; but physically speaking, the inertial system seemed to occupy a privileged position, which made the use of coordinate systems moving in other ways appear artificial.... I attempted to deal with the law of gravity within the framework of the special theory of relativity.... I tried to frame a *field-law* for gravitation, since it was no longer possible, at least in any natural way, to introduce direct action at a distance owing to the abolition of the notion of absolute simultaneity."[59] Einstein points out that in classical mechanics, the vertical acceleration of a body in the vertical gravitational field is independent of the horizontal component of its velocity and hence works out independently of its internal kinetic energy. In his thinking "the acceleration of a falling body was not independent of its horizontal velocity or the internal energy of a system." Thus he was led to the

28

principle of the equality of inertial and gravitational mass. He then abandoned the attempt to treat the problem of gravitation within the framework of the special theory of relativity, since it failed to do justice to the most fundamental property of gravitation. He formulated the principle of the equality of inertial and gravitational mass as follows: "In a homogeneous gravitational field all motions take place in the same way as in the absence of a gravitational field in relation to a uniformly accelerated coordinate system." This principle he called the "principle of equivalence," and it indicated to him that "the principle of relativity needed to be extended to coordinate systems in non-uniform motion with respect to each other, if we were to reach a natural theory of the gravitational fields."[60] He recognized the need to frame a theory whose equations kept their form in the case of non-linear transformations of the coordinates.

In the general theory of relativity, Einstein also introduced the principle of *general covariance*, according to which all possible frames of reference in all possible kinds of motion are assumed to be on an equal footing and the laws of nature can be expressed in the same mathematical form for all possible observers in *all* types of motion.

In seeking the non-linear transformations of the coordinates required for a theory of gravitation, Einstein found the answer in the mathematical investigations of Riemann in the middle of the 19th century, namely, "the group of all continuous (analytical) transformations of the coordinates. Under these transformations the only thing that remains invariant is the fact that neighboring points have nearly the same coordinates; the coordinate system expresses only the topological order of the points in space (including its four-dimensional character). The equations expressing the laws of nature must be covariant with respect to all continuous transformations of the coordinates."[61] The Riemannian metric utilized had the property that the metric of the special theory of relativity is still valid for small regions in the general case as well, i.e., in regions where the gravitational field is negligible. While in special relativity, the motion of a particle moving with uniform velocity is represented by a straight-line path in Minkowski's space-time, in general relativity the world-line of a particle in a gravitational field is a geodesic in the space-time associated with this field, a geodesic corresponding in Riemannian geometry to a straight-line in ordinary geometry. The applicable Riemannian metric is the metric of a space of constant curvature, since this is the only type of space, everywhere homogeneous, isotropic, continuous, and locally Euclidean. In 1928 H.P.

Robertson deduced the mathematical form of the space-time metric of a homogeneous and isotropic world-model, involving the line-element of a space of constant curvature.

In the general theory of relativity space-time coordinates are stripped of all independent reality. In Einstein's words, "The metrically real is now only given through the combination of the space-time coordinates with the mathematical quantities which describe the gravitational field."[62] Einstein also points out that "according to general relativity, the concept of space detached from any physical content does not exist. The physical reality of space is represented by a field whose components are continuous functions of four independent variables—the coordinates of space and time. It is just this particular kind of dependence that expresses the spatial character of physical reality."[63] In another formulation of the same issue, Einstein states that, according to the general theory of relativity, "space as opposed to 'what fills space,' which is dependent on the coordinates, has no separate existence.... There is no such thing as an empty space, i.e., a space without field. Space-time does not claim existence on its own, but only as a structural quality of the field."[64]

Einstein mentions two weaknesses of the general relativity theory: "In the first place, the total field appears in it to be composed of two logically unconnected parts, the gravitational and the electromagnetic. And in the second place, this theory, like the earlier field theory, has not up till now [1940] supplied an explanation of the atomistic structure of matter. This failure has probably some connection with the fact that so far it has contributed nothing to the understanding of quantum phenomenon."[65]

While for Newton time was independent of the universe and for Leibniz it was an aspect of the universe, in Einstein's relativity theory time becomes an aspect of the relationship between the universe and the observer. In special relativity, each observer, at rest or in uniform relative motion, has his own time system and there exists a multiplicity of time systems associated with different observers. Although in special relativity there is no privileged observer, there is a privileged *class* of observers, namely, those at rest or in uniform relative motion. In the general theory of relativity all possible frames of reference in all possible kinds of motion are on an equal basis and there are no privileged observers. As a result of relativity theory, what then has happened to the concept of linear advancing time? Has it been eliminated, must we abandon it? How shall we date an event, if there are a multiplicity of time systems dependent on observers? Is there no *objective* sequence in temporal passage?

To answer these questions, we must look to cosmology, namely the science of the structure of the physical universe. The relativity theories are concerned with the nature of physical laws and not with the pattern of events occurring in nature and the actual distribution of matter in the universe. Even if time is an aspect of the relationship between the universe and the observer, it does not necessarily follow that it is not an intrinsic feature of the universe with objective significance, due to the general structure of the universe.

In a paper published in 1917, Einstein applied his General Theory of Relativity to cosmology, in which he put forth the idea of *cosmic time*. "Associated with this idea was the concept of a homogeneous spatial substratum determined by the distribution of matter in bulk throughout the universe, local irregularities being regarded as 'smoothed-out.' "[66] Whitrow finds a confusion in Einstein's thought resulting from the fact that his theory of local gravitation was developed first and his theory of world gravitation later. "Consequently, the associated theory of cosmic time and space arose as a particular application of his general theory of the fine structure of space-time." Whitrow states that the "smoothed-out" universe should be taken as the ultimate frame of reference and general relativity regarded as "primarily a technique for analyzing local gravitational fields superimposed on the world-gravitational field." He points out that when studying the universe as a whole, Einstein modified his theory by introducing into the field equations a new term, called the "cosmical constant." "The finite homogeneous world-model discovered by Einstein as a consequence of introducing this term was a static system in spherical (or elliptic) space." In 1920 the English physicist A.S. Eddington wrote that universal space and time are restored in this Einstein model for phenomena on a cosmical scale and "relativity is reduced to a local phenomenon."[67] Since 1917 there has been a plethora of world-models.

Chapter 7
The Physical Structure of the Universe

In setting forth current ideas concerning the physical structure of the universe, I shall follow Whitrow's discussion. "...the universe is composed of galaxies, some larger and some smaller, but all, despite certain characteristic differences of structure, roughly comparable with our own Milky Way stellar system. The distribution of these galaxies is somewhat patchy but shows marked signs of general uniformity when considered from a sufficiently large-scale point of view.... In investigations of theoretical models of the universe, hypothetical observers fixed in the different galaxies are called 'fundamental observers.' These observers are 'privileged' in the sense that they are associated with the bulk distribution of matter in the universe... In the models most widely studied the times kept by the fundamental observers fit together to form one universal time, called *cosmic time*. In other words, according to these observers, there are successive states of the universe as a whole which define a cosmic time. In terms of this, all events have a unique time order."[68] He then notes that the anomalies of time-ordering arising in the special theory of relativity are due not to the nature of the events themselves but to the introduction of observers moving through the universe relative to the fundamental observers in their neighborhood. "From the point of view of the fundamental observers there is a common linear time-order for all events that can, in principle, be observed by them."

Whitrow then states as mathematically proven that the existence

32

of cosmic time in a model universe depends on the model being isotropic, namely, that it looks the same in each direction to any fundamental observer, there being no preferential spatial direction. "Moreover, each fundamental observer sees himself at the center of the same world-picture as any other at the same epoch of cosmic time."[69] Strong evidence confirming the isotropy of the universe was discovered in 1965 by the American radio astronomers, Penzias and Wilson, who received a Nobel Prize in physics in 1978. They discovered a microwave radiation of a few centimeters wavelength which is coming to us in more or less equal amounts from each direction of space. The variation in the intensity of this radiation for different directions is less than one percent. This variation is so slight that the possibility of any local origin for the radiation is excluded, since a source in the solar system, the Galaxy, or even the local cluster of galaxies would not appear isotropic to us, located, as we are, far from the center of these systems. "This radiation is therefore believed to be a constituent of the universe as a whole...unless we are at a freak center of isotropy—which seems most unlikely—we must assume that this radiation is isotropic about every fundamental observer in the universe. The evidence for the validity of the concept of cosmic time is therefore now impressive."[70]

The discovery of isotropic microwave radiation with an equivalent temperature of 3° Kelvin had even more important implications with respect to the nature and origin of the universe and of time. Before proceeding along these lines, it may be pertinent to recall the pregnant thought of St. Augustine concerning the origin of the universe and the origin of time. In Book XI of his Confessions, St. Augustine poses the question, evidently current at this time: *"What was God doing before he made heaven and earth?"*[71] He declines to answer, as some do, that God was preparing hell "for pryers into mysteries," saying, "It is one thing to answer questions, another to make sport of the questioners.... rather had I answered, 'I know not,' what I know not, then so as to raise a laugh at him who asketh deep things and gain praise for one who answereth falsely." He then answers "boldly," "that before God made heaven and earth, He did not make anything."[72] "If before *heaven and earth* there was no time, why is it demanded, what thou then didst? For there was no 'then', when there was no time...At no time then hadst thou not made any thing because time itself thou madest."[73] Finally, he tells those who ask this question to understand "that time cannot be without created being."[74]

To avoid here theological discussion of creation doctrine, let us understand here "created being" as physically existent being. Thus, time does not exist on its own, but coexists and is coextensive with the universe. If the universe is infinite, then time is infinite; if the universe is finite, then time is finite, with an origin and an end corresponding to the origin and end of the universe.

Chapter 8
The Origin of the Universe

Astronomers are able to measure quite accurately the motion of a luminous body in a direction along the line of sight by a property of wave motion, called the Doppler effect. This property was first discovered in 1842 for both light and sound waves by Johann Christian Doppler, a professor of mathematics in Prague. If a source of a sound or light wave is at rest in relation to an observer, the time between the arrival of wave crests at the observer's instruments is the same as the time between crests as they leave the source. However, if the source is moving away from the observer, the time between arrivals of successive wave crests is increased, and the wave will appear to have a longer wave length; if the source is moving toward the observer, the time between arrivals of wave crests is decreased, and the wave appears to have a shorter wave length.

The great importance of the Doppler effect to astronomy began in 1868, when applied to the study of individual spectral lines. It had been discovered earlier that "when light from the sun is allowed to pass through a slit and then through a glass prism, the resulting spectrum of colors is crossed with hundreds of dark lines, each one an image of the slit...the dark lines were always found at the same colors, each corresponding to a definite wave length of light. The same dark spectral lines were also found...in the same positions in the spectrum of the moon and the brighter stars.... These dark lines are produced by the selective absorption of light of certain definite wave lengths as the light passes from the hot surface of a star through its cooler outer atmosphere. Each line is due to the absorption of light by a specific chemical element, so it became possible to determine that the elements on the sun, such as sodium, iron, magnesium, calcium, and chronium, are the same as those found on earth."[75]

Sir William Huggins found in 1868 that "the dark lines in the spectra of some of the brighter stars are shifted slightly to the red or the blue from their normal position in the spectrum of the sun. He correctly interpreted this as a Doppler shift, due to the motion of the star away from or toward the earth."[76] Through the Doppler shift, it was also possible to measure accurately the velocities of the stars and to calculate the distances of nearby stars.

Immanuel Kant in 1755 was the first to propose that some of the nebulae are galaxies like our own. Nebulae are extended astronomical objects with a cloudlike appearance; some are galaxies, others are clouds of glowing dust and gas within our galaxy. Kant suggested that a certain type of nebulae is really a circular disk about the same size and shape as our own galaxy. The idea of a universe filled with galaxies like our own was widely accepted by the beginning of the 19th century. However, it was only in 1923, with the use of a new 100-inch telescope at Mt. Wilson, that Edwin Hubble was first able to discern the separate stars in the Andromeda Nebula. It became clear at that time that the Andromeda Nebula and the thousands of similar nebulae are galaxies like our own spread out in the universe in great distances in all directions. Examination of the spectral shift of these galaxies reveals that, "aside from a few close neighbors like the Andromeda Nebula, the other galaxies are generally rushing away from our own"; indeed, "every galaxy is rushing away from every other galaxy."[77] Thus it seems "that the universe is in a state of violent explosion, in which the great islands of stars known as galaxies are rushing apart at speeds approaching the speed of light."[78] In 1929 Hubble discovered "that the red shifts of galaxies increase roughly in proportion to the distance from us...just what we should predict according to the simplest possible picture of the flow of matter in an exploding universe."[79]

Believing that there was a proportional relationship between velocity and distance for galaxies with velocities ranging up to 20,000 kilometers per second, Hubble in 1931 estimated that velocities increase by 170 kilometers per second for every million light years distance. With improved astronomical observations, the relation between velocity increase and distance, called the "Hubble Constant," is now estimated to be about 15 kilometers per second per million light years. This figure "is the same for all galaxies at a given time, but...the Hubble Constant changes with time as the universe evolves."[80]

The discovery of the recession of distant galaxies led to interest in cosmological models that are homogenous, isotropic, and expanding. The Friedmann models, set forth by the Russian mathematician Alexandre Friedmann in 1922, provide the mathematical background for most modern cosmological theories. "The Friedmann models are of two very different types. If the average density of the matter of the universe is *less* than or equal to a certain critical value, then the universe must be spatially infinite. In this case the present expansion of the universe will go on forever. On the other hand, if the density of the universe is *greater* than this critical value, then the gravitational field produced by the matter curves the universe back on itself; it is finite though unbounded like the surface of the sphere.... In this case the gravitational fields are strong enough eventually to stop the expansion of the universe, so that it will eventually implode back to indefinitely large density. The critical density is proportional to the square of the Hubble Constant; for the presently popular value of 15 kilometers per second per million light years, the critical density equals 5 times 10^{-30} grams per cubic centimeter, or about 3 hydrogen atoms per thousand liters of space."[81]

We mentioned earlier the cosmic microwave radiation, corresponding to a temperature of 3°K, discovered by Penzias and Wilson. Weinberg has termed this discovery "the most important cosmological advance since the discovery of the red shifts."[82] Its importance lies in its role in the development and corroboration of a theory of the early universe now called by astronomers "the standard model," or more vulgarly, "The Big Bang" theory. A "Big Bang" cosmological theory setting forth the explosive origin of the present state of the universe was first outlined in the late 1940's and early 1950's. At this time it was even predicted that a radiation background existed which was left over from the early universe with a present temperature of 5°K. However no one at this time sought to find the predicted microwave radiation. Penzias and Wilson were not looking for it in 1964. They sought to use a Bell Telephone Laboratory radio antenna to measure the intensity of the radio waves emitted from our galaxy at high galactic latitudes, i.e. out of the plane of the Milky Way. To their surprise they found that they were receiving microwave noise, independent of direction, which did not vary with the time of the day or the season of the year. This indicated that these radio waves were not coming from the Milky Way, but from the universe itself.

At the time of the publication of the experimental results of Penzias and Wilson, the cosmological interpretation by a group of Princeton physicists was likewise published. Robert H. Dicke, a senior Princeton physicist, had speculated in 1964 that there should be some observable radiation left over from a hot, dense, early stage of cosmic history. He suggested a search for such a microwave radiation background, but he learned of Penzias' results before the Princeton theorist, P.J.E. Peebles, had developed ideas concerning the radiation present in the early universe. "Peebles noted that if there had not been an intense background of radiation present during the first few minutes of the universe, nuclear reactions would have proceeded so rapidly that a large fraction of the hydrogen present would have been 'cooked' into heavy elements, in contradiction with the fact that about three-quarters of the present universe is hydrogen. This rapid nuclear cooking could have been prevented only if the universe was filled with radiation having an enormous equivalent temperature at very short wavelengths, which could blast nuclei apart as fast as they could be formed."[83] This radiation should have survived the subsequent expansion of the universe, with its equivalent temperature falling as the universe expanded, in inverse proportion to the size of the universe. Hence the present universe should also be filled with radiation, with its equivalent temperature lowered to a few degrees Kelvin, corresponding to the expansion of the universe, so that the radiation would now appear as a background of radio noise, coming equally from all directions.

Toward the end of his book *The First Three Minutes*, Steven Weinberg states: "...we have been able to extrapolate the history of the universe back in time to a moment of infinite density. But this leaves us unsatisfied. We naturally want to know what there was before this moment, before the universe began to expand and cool.

"One possibility is that there never really was a state of infinite density. The present expansion of the universe may have begun at the end of a previous age of contraction, when the density of the universe had reached some very high but finite value....

"However, although we do not know that it is true, it is at least logically possible that there *was* a beginning, and that time itself has no meaning before that moment. We are all used to the idea of an absolute zero of temperature. It is impossible to cool anything below -273.16°C, not because it is too hard or because no one has thought of a sufficiently clever refrigerator, but because temperatures lower than absolute zero just have no meaning—we cannot have less heat than no heat at all. In the same way, we may have to get used to the idea of an absolute zero of time—a moment in the past beyond which it is in principle impossible to trace any chain of cause and effect. The question is open, and may always remain open."[84]

The physical universe is expanding. As to whether it will continue to expand indefinitely, the standard model does not give a clear answer: as we have seen before, it depends on whether the cosmic density is less or greater than a certain critical value. If the cosmic density is *less* than the critical density, then the universe is of infinite extent and will go on expanding forever. However, if the cosmic density is *greater* than the critical value, then the universe is finite and its expansion will eventually cease, giving way to an accelerating contraction. Assuming the cosmic density is twice its critical value, and the present value of the Hubble Constant (15 kilometers per second per million light years) is correct, then the expansion phase of the universe has lasted 10 thousand million years until now. This expansion phase will continue for about 50 thousand million years, and then the universe will begin to contract. After 50 thousand million years of contraction, the universe will have returned to its present size, and after another 10 thousand million years it will be approaching a singular state of infinite density.

What will happen when the universe approaches this state of infinite density? Some cosmologists believe that a kind of cosmic "bounce" will take place and the universe will begin again to expand. If the universe does re-expand, its expansion will again be halted and followed by another contraction, followed by another bounce, and so on forever. In their 1965 paper on the cosmic microwave radiation background, Dicke and his colleagues "assumed that there was a previous complete phase of cosmic expansion and contraction and they argued that the universe must have contracted enough to raise the temperature to at least 10 thousand million degrees in order to break up the heavy elements formed in the previous phase."[85] Were this correct, our universe is an oscillating universe, with an endless cycle of expansion and contraction stretching into the infinite past and toward the infinite future. Hence there would have been no beginning and there will not be an end. Thus, expansion and contraction constitute the macroscopic rhythm of the universe. Weinberg notes the philosophic attractiveness of the oscillating model because it "nicely avoids the problem of genesis."[86]

If rhythmicity is intrinsic to the nature of being, then it should not be surprising to us that cosmologists are able to discern a macroscopic rhythm in the constitution of the universe. The attractiveness of the oscillating model then lies in the fact that it expresses in a macroscopic cosmological scale the rhythmicity which permeates all nature, animate and inanimate, down to the elementary physical particles, as we shall now see.

Chapter 9
Quantum Theory

The Lowell Lectures of 1925, delivered by Alfred North White-head, contain a brief discussion of the quantum theory. With his usual prescience, Whitehead makes this statement: "There are certain indications in modern physics that for the role of corpuscular organisms at the base of the physical field, we require vibratory entities."[87] Over fifty years have passed since this statement, and there has been meanwhile a tremendous development in quantum theory and in microphysics, the study of atoms and of their sub-atomic constituents. In the past twenty-five years, in particular, perhaps the major field of physics has been the study of the behavior of the subatomic components of matter, the field called particle physics. Great advances have been made in the understanding of the subatomic world; indeed one enthusiastic particle physicist believes that "this will stand as the major intellectual accomplishment of mankind in the 20th century."[88]

It is remarkable that Whitehead's statement quoted above still remains pertinent, still remains true, through the advance in our detailed knowledge of the atomic and subatomic microworld. When I recently asked a distinguished particle physicist whether Whitehead's statement still had any relevance, he replied, "Why, yes, of course; after all, a particle is a wave, and a wave is a particle." This view of the contemporary physicist did not arise spontaneously, but as a result of a historic process of experimentation. In the case of light there has been an alternation of view. On the basis of the evidence available at the time, Newton declared light to be a stream of particles. Newton's particle theory prevailed, until Thomas Young in 1801 demonstrated the wave nature of light by his interference experiment, which revealed a diffraction pattern characteristic of wave phenomena. About one hundred years later, to explain the photoelectric effect, first observed by Hertz in 1887, Einstein argued in 1905 that light consists of particles. While his special theory of relativity was presented in the same year, he won the Nobel Prize, not for his relativity theory, but for his explanation of the photoelectric effect. Einstein argued that quanta of energy reaching the surface of the photocathode were knocking electrons out of their atoms, causing the photoelectric current. This current appears almost instantly, which it would not do if light were merely a wave phenomena. Hence light must consist of particles, arriving in highly localized quanta of energy. These quanta of radiation energy came to be called photons. In Young's experiment light acts like a wave, in the photoelectric effect analyzed by Einstein it behaves like a particle; in Compton scattering (discovered by the American physicist in 1923 when he passed a beam of X-rays through a thin piece of metal foil) it displays both wave and particle properties simultaneously.

In his doctoral dissertation in 1924, de Broglie argued that if light, known to be a wave, can under certain circumstances display the properties of a particle, then perhaps particles, such as electrons, can likewise in certain circumstances exhibit the properties of waves. In 1924, experimental evidence for the diffraction of particles had not yet been discovered, but it was soon thereafter. In the Davisson-Germer experiment in 1927 electron beams were directed against the surface of a nickel crystal, with the diffraction of the particles being then observed. In the original experiment the electrons were reflected from the surface; in later versions, electrons were passed through a thin polycrystalline foil, with interference fringes being observed. Other particles, like neutrons, have also been used in similar experiments with the same results. Moreover, the same interference phenomenon exists when the particles, with low beam intensity, pass through the apparatus one at a time. Thus a single particle is simultaneously squeezing itself through all the available openings, a process normal for waves. "If in the electron interference experiments we use as the detector a device known as the *scintillator*, which flashes every time a charged particle strikes it, there can be no doubt that the electron can be localized, i.e., that they are particles. They produce distinct flashes whenever they hit,... But the pattern of hits made by a large number of strikes is the wave interference pattern. The individual electron arrives as a particle, but the place where it lands is determined by the behavior of a wave which has passed through the equipment. The wave makes its way through all available apertures in the barrier...but what arrives at the detector is intact as a particle."[89] This is not a particular property of electrons. This same wave-particle duality is observed in all the particles of nature, whose mass is small enough to produce visible fringes.

It is noteworthy that 20th century physics had found it necessary to fuse together certain physical concepts, such as space and time, wave and particle. There has been considerable discussion since Bohr's time of complementarity; the wave and the particle have been regarded as complementary aspects of physical reality. Are space and time *complementary* in the same sense? Whether complementary or not, space and time are *conjoint* in space-time. Similarly, wave and particle are *conjoint* in the wave-particle. Both space-time and wave-particle are conjoint in the contemporary conceptual framework of physical reality. "Conjoint" seems to me a more expressive term than complementary, because it means that the one term, e.g., space, wave, cannot be adequately comprehended separately, and that, except as an abstraction, the one term has no conceptual or physical reality without the other.

It is obvious that a wave phenomenon is a form of rhythmic periodicity. If a particle is also a wave, then a particle also partakes of rhythmic periodicity. We have seen earlier how contemporary astrophysics and cosmology have discovered in the oscillating model of the universe a macroscopic rhythm. Now in the great advances of recent decades in microphysics, we find microscopic rhythms in all the elementary physical entities at the base of the material universe. The wave-particles are oscillating entities, and this oscillation is an intrinsic constituent of the wave-particle. Thus evidence of the rhythm of being in the physical universe is revealed both on the macroscopic and the microscopic level.

Einstein based his analysis of the photoelectric effect on the work of Planck, who had analyzed the spectrum of light radiated from bodies as a result of their temperature, a phenomenon called black body radiation. Planck had discovered that by assuming the walls of the radiator to contain oscillators with discrete values of energy, rather than the continuous range of possible energies, he could compute exactly the radiated spectrum being observed. For every frequency in the electromagnetic spectrum, Planck assumed that oscillators could have only those energies which were whole number multiples of a particular *quantum*. Planck proposed that oscillating energies came only in integral multiples of the quantity hν where ν is the frequency of the oscillation in cycles per second, and h is a universal constant of nature, which came to be known as Planck's constant. "In other words, the elementary oscillators which radiate electromagnetic waves of a given frequency were conceived to be charged particles moving back and forth a particular number of time's per second (the frequency), but having only energies 0, hν, 2hν, 3hν, 4hν...and so on."[90] When Planck introduced this assumption, he obtained an equation for total energy radiated by a body at all its various frequencies which was in precise accord with what had been observed experimentally. He was thus able to compute the magnitude of the constant h by relating it to the data on black body radiation. The value of h turned out to be a very small number, h = 6.6 x 10^{-34} joule-seconds.

Rhythmicity in the microworld has been exploited recently by scientists to devise the most accurate timekeeping device currently known. The natural period of electromagnetic waves produced by a vibrating atom has been used for this purpose. These electromagnetic waves are of very precise frequency and form sharp lines in the spectrum; optical spectral lines are unsuitable for time measurements since we cannot measure their frequencies directly. However, certain atoms produce radio frequencies which can be measured directly. On the basis of this knowledge the British physicist, Dr. L. Essen, was able in 1957 to devise a caesium atomic clock. Atoms of caesium produce radio waves of about 9,200 megacycles a second, with a corresponding wavelength of about 3 centimeters. In the caesium clock, "the magnetic field produced by an oscillating electric current is synchronized with certain specific vibrations of caesium atoms. These atoms have a single electron in their outermost electronic shells..."[91] and the interaction between this electron and the nucleus produces energy released as radio waves with the frequency of 9,200 megacycles a second. The accuracy of the caesium clock has been perfected to two parts in 10 million million, corresponding to a clock error of only one second in 150,000 years. This time measurement is, of course, entirely independent of astronomical determinations of time and is more accurate than any astronomical source of time measurement. In 1967, therefore, a new definition of the second was introduced, defined as the duration of 9,192,631,770 periods of the caesium-133 radio waves. In 1968, an astronomical source of radio waves with great regularity was discovered, namely the pulsars. Pulsars are believed to be rapidly rotating neutron stars. The radio waves, emitted by the first pulsar discovered, had a regularity that exceeded one part in a hundred million, the period being precisely 1.33730113 seconds. This regularity is still decidedly less accurate than that of the caesium clock, two parts in 10 million million.

It should be noted here that there is another type of modern scientific clock used for dating geological and archeological deposits. This clock is based on the discovery of radioactivity by Henri Becquerel in 1896. Rutherford and Soddy discovered in 1902 that the number of atoms of a radioactive element disintegrating in a unit of time is proportional to the number of atoms of the element that are present. This discovery was based on the fact that radioactivity is due to instabilities in the structure of nuclei, and not to any external environmental causes, such as temperature, pressure, etc. The rates of radioactive decay are determined by the structural nuclear instabilities, characteristics of the particular isotope of an element. Thus the rate of radioactive decay of a given isotope can be used to measure time; it has been termed "the outstanding example in nature of a non-cyclic linear clock."[92]

It is customary to use the half-life as the unit of measurement, namely, the time required for one-half of any given amount of the element to decay. This is a fixed interval of time for a particular radioactive isotope, since it is independent of the amount present. Hence although this linear clock may be non-cyclic, there is a periodicity involved and the temporal measurement is based on this periodicity.

The type of a decay clock, most used, is based on carbon-14, an element produced in the upper atmosphere by cosmic ray bombardment which produces some neutrons along with other nuclear particles. These neutrons are absorbed by the nitrogen-14 in the atmosphere which, emitting a proton, then changes into carbon-14. This radioactive isotope of ordinary carbon has a half-life of about 5,700 years. Carbon-14 is incorporated into the carbon dioxide of the atmosphere and thus enters into the carbon cycle, so that any organism absorbing carbon dioxide receives a proportional share of this radioactive carbon. When the organism stops absorbing carbon dioxide, e.g., at death, the carbon-14 clock begins to tick, because the proportion of radioactive carbon to ordinary carbon steadily diminishes according to the decay law. Radio-carbon dating can be used effectively up to about 50,000 years, and has given a new tool to archaeologists which has produced important results, e.g., the dating of the wrappings of the Dead Sea scrolls.

Another type of nuclear clock used for geological measurements is based on the accumulation of some element produced by the decay of a radioactive element. It is assumed that the number of atoms of the by-product element at a given time is equal to the number of atoms of the radioactive element that have disintegrated, and the duration of the radioactive decay can then be calculated on the basis of the Rutherford-Soddy law. Although there are many long-lived radioactive elements, scientists have used accumulation clocks based only on uranium, potassium, and rubidium. Helium and lead are the final stable end-products of uranium decay. Efforts to measure the ages of minerals from their uranium-helium proportion have not been successful. However, the ages for many minerals based on the uranium-lead proportion have been determined more successfully, so that it is believed a fairly reliable scale of geological time has been constructed by means of the uranium-lead accumulation clock. This success has been due to the long half-life, 4,500 million years, of uranium-238. Moreover, the knowledge of geological time obtained by the uranium-lead clock has recently been confirmed by use of potassium-argon and rubidium-strontium clocks.

Chapter 10
Time's Arrow

There is a direction in temporality, a before and an after, a succession—to what extent and in what way is this discerned in the physical world? Physical laws, in general, it has been observed, are compatible with the reversal of temporal direction: a dictum which applies to the laws of motion, of gravitation (both Newton's and Einstein's), of electromagnetism, and to the other laws governing the forces and interactions in physics. This does not mean that time does not have a direction, but merely that the laws of physics, or the abstractions of physics, do not disclose a direction in time. In microphysics it has been found that the "strong" interactions between protons and neutrons in atomic nuclei exhibit time-reversal invariance. In the case of the "weak" interactions, an exception has been found to this time-reversal invariance, in the decay of the particles known as neutral K mesons, which seems to "define a preferred time-direction, albeit very weakly."[93] However, there is some question as to whether the time-reversal symmetry in particle physics really relates to time. For example, Gerald Feinberg states as follows: "Time reversal does not imply a literal reversing of the direction of time. Instead, it is a comparison between two physical processes that are related by having all velocities and spins reversed in direction and the objects in the initial state interchanged with those in the final state. For example, in the decay of a positive pion into a muon and neutron, the time-reversed process would be the combination of a muon and neutrino to produce the pion. The rule of changing momenta and spins is such that the handedness of the

47

particles is unchanged between the two processes being compared. Hence the time-reversed process of pion decay is a possible physical process, and the symmetry implies that it would occur in the same way as the decay if the particles would be brought together."[94]

It may well be that there are very fundamental reasons why we are unable to discern directional time in the world of microphysics. In the introduction to his book entitled *Space and Time in the Microworld*, the Russian physicist D.I. Blokhintsev wrote in 1970 as follows: "The concepts and methods which are useful in the macroworld may only indirectly be carried over into the microworld and they require a high degree of abstraction.... It is shown in this monograph that if elementary particles have a structure it is doubtful whether the coordinates of elementary particles x, y, z, t can even be defined exactly, let alone the coordinates of the elements which make up these particles (if they do not exist only in our imagination). This important fact is revealed even in the most favorable gedanken experiments.... From this fact doubt arises about the logical validity of using the symbols x, y, z, t as the space-time coordinates to describe phenomena inside elementary particles. This allows theoreticians a certain freedom of choice of space-time and causal relationships within elementary particles; in other words, an arbitrariness of choice of the geometry in the small."[95]

Perhaps Blokhintsev's comments provide the proper conceptual background for the understanding of the famous fanciful Feynman diagram in which the two world-lines of an electron and a positron meeting and annihilating each other are re-interpreted as the worldline of a single electron traveling forward and backwards in time. Is this not a precious example of "arbitrariness of choice of the geometry in the small"?

If the direction of time is not to be found in the microworld of physics, we must seek it in the macroscopic physical phenomena. We shall find it there. For over a hundred years, evidence of the direction of time has been sought in the statistical aspects of the macroworld of physics. The most important physical law in this connection has been the second law of thermodynamics. The second law of thermodynamics is clearly statistical; it deals with the behavior of large numbers of particles and has no meaning for individual particles or systems containing few particles. In the middle of the 19th century Clausius stated as axiomatic that heat passes from a hot body to a cold body and not in the reverse direction. As a generalization of this statement, Clausius formulated the second law of thermodynamics in terms of entropy, affirming that the entropy of a closed physical system never diminishes. Entropy is an abstract concept, signifying the measure of the disorganization of a physical system. According to the second law of thermodynamics, in a closed physical system (one that neither gains energy from nor loses energy to its environment), entropy automatically tends to increase. Thus there is a tendency of orderly arrangements of molecules to break down into disorderly arrangements. "A familiar example from everyday life is the effect of stirring when cream is poured into a cup of coffee. In a short while we obtain a liquid of uniform color, and however long we stir we never find the contents of the cup reverting to their original orderly state in which coffee and cream were clearly separated."[96]

The Austrian physicist Ludwig Boltzmann interpreted the second law as meaning that any closed system tends to a condition in which the distribution and motion of its constituent parts are completely random, since this is the most probable arrangement for a large number of parts. He believed that this statistical interpretation of the second law accounted for the directional character of time. This view was very soon attacked by other physicists on several grounds. Whitrow summarized its unsoundness thus: "For, owing to the symmetry of the laws of motion with respect to both directions of time, it follows that for any arbitrarily chosen state that shows some degree of ordering there is not only a large probability that it will lead to a less orderly state, but equally there is a large probability that it itself arose from a disorderly state. It would therefore seem to be highly likely that at the time of the chosen orderly state the system is undergoing a fluctuation from disorderliness."[97] Sir Arthur Eddington used the expressive phrase "time's arrow" in referring to the second law of thermodynamics. However, it is unlikely that the arrow of time will ever be found in any physical law. To find it, we must look to the physical constitution of the universe.

We have set forth earlier the cosmological conception of the current expansion of the universe. The British physicist E.A. Milne was one of the first to relate this idea to the concept of time. According to Milne, while the Newtonian universe *has* a clock, the expanding universe *is* a clock, and "time's arrow" is unequivocally determined by the recession of the galaxies. This conception of the relation of the expanding universe to time's arrow is not to my mind incompatible with the previously mentioned conception of the oscillating universe. The expansion of the universe indicates that time has in itself a direction. If the universe were to enter subsequently a contracting phase, it would not necessarily mean that the direction of time had been reversed. The contracting universe would indicate that time has an arrow just as well as the expanding universe. Time is born of rhythmicity. A macroscopic cosmological rhythmicity would point to, and give expression to, this ultimate derivation of time.

According to the current interpretation of the red shifts, the expansion of the universe must have begun less than 20 billion years ago. Is there any other evidence that the present expanding state of the universe is that old? Indeed, there is considerable evidence that our galaxy is about 10-15 billion years old. "This estimate comes both from the relative abundance of various radioactive isotopes in the earth (especially the uranium isotopes, U-235 and U-238) and from calculation of the evolution of stars. There is certainly no direct connection between the rates of radioactivity or stellar evolution and the redshift of distant galaxies,..."[98] Hence it is generally believed that the beginning of the expansion of the universe as deduced from the Hubble Constant is correct.

Chapter 11
Galaxies

In his book, Weinberg briefly extends his account beyond "The First Three Minutes." After 34 minutes and 40 seconds have elapsed from the Big Bang the temperature of the universe is now 300 million degrees Kelvin. The processes of cosmic nucleosynthesis have stopped. "The nuclear particles are now for the most part either bound into helium nuclei or are free protons (hydrogen nuclei), with about 22 to 28 percent helium by weight. There is one electron for each free or bound proton, but the universe is still much too hot for stable atoms to hold together." After 700,000 years, with the universe continuing to expand and cool, the temperature will fall to the point where electrons and nuclei can form stable atoms. The absence of free electrons will make the contents of the universe transparent to radiation; "and the decoupling of matter and radiation will allow matter to begin to form into galaxies and stars."[99]

One consequence of the "big bang" theory is that the material left over from the first three minutes, out of which the galaxies and stars must originally have been formed, consisted of 22-28 percent helium, with almost all the rest hydrogen. Physicists made this calculation of the cosmological helium production, based on the 3°K temperature of the present cosmic microwave radiation background and on the assumption that there is a huge ratio of protons to nuclear particles. This calculation corresponded to independent estimates that the sun and other stars started their existence as mostly hydrogen, with about 20-30 percent helium. These estimates of the primordial helium content of the universe "are based on comparisons of detailed calculations of stellar evolution with statistical analysis of observed stellar properties plus direct observation of helium lines in the spectra of hot stars and interstellar material."[100]

A galaxy is a gravitationally bound conglomerate of many stars. A hundred thousand stars is regarded as the likely minimum number. Our own galaxy, the Milky Way Galaxy, is a flat, rotating, disk-like stellar system 100,000 light-years in diameter, containing about 100 billion stars, with "spiral arms" in the disk, a large "central bulge," and a "halo" of old stars and globular clusters. Our solar system is located some 30,000 light-years from the center of our galaxy. About 5-10 percent of the mass of our galaxy is in the form of gas and dust between stars; in addition, the interstellar space is permeated by starlight, cosmic rays, and weak magnetic fields. Although as early as 1750 Thomas Wright, and five years later Immanuel Kant, set forth the view that our universe contains many galaxies, it was not determined until 1923 that the universe contains other galaxies as well as our Milky Way Galaxy (see p. 36).

Over the past half century, and particularly after World War II, considerable progress has been made in our knowledge of the galaxies. A large number of galaxies have been discovered, with very diverse structural forms and characteristics. Despite this advance in our knowledge, there is no clear understanding of how galaxies are formed. "The theory of the formation of the galaxies is one of the great outstanding problems of astrophysics, a problem that today seems far from solution."[101] Newton suggested that the origin of the sun and stars might be due to the gravitational clumping of matter into separate fragments. As mentioned earlier, applying Newtonian ideas, Kant set forth the view that originally all matter was in a gaseous state, spread throughout the universe, but not spread uniformly. Through this lack of uniformity, giant clouds of gas, contracting under their own gravitation, begin to rotate, and thus stars are born. In the case of our solar system, the sun in this process has shed matter from its center to form the planets by further gravitational contraction.

The contemporary sketch of galaxy and star formation in the standard Big Bang cosmology is not very different. When the temperature of the expanding universe has cooled sufficiently for the decoupling of matter and radiation, then, in the account of a recent text: "Small density fluctuations in the cooling gas began to self-gravitate and grow, until they overcame the cosmic expansion and collapsed into proto-galaxies; this galaxy formation occurred about 100 million years after the initial big-bang event."[102]

"Within each forming galaxy, another new activity was also beginning. Smaller clouds of gas, pulled together by gravity, were contracting faster than the overall galaxy. As these small clouds contracted, their temperature began to rise. And when their temperature reached several million degrees, atoms of hydrogen crashed into each other with such force that they fused together to become deuterium and helium. In the fusion process energy was released, and these thermonuclear reactions became self-sustaining. The small clouds of gas had become stars, and the galaxies began to shine."[103]

What does our knowledge indicate as to the temporal nature of galaxies? According to Morton S. Roberts: "Theories, or viewpoints at least, have been proposed suggesting a temporal relation among the different galaxy types. Different theories have different sequences of aging; in some the ellipticals are the oldest, in others the irregulars are the oldest. A third possibility is that all galaxies form at the same time, with differences of type reflecting differences in initial conditions of formation. This list is not complete; there are variants of these possibilities. In defining the problem it is important to distinguish two types of age: chronological and evolutionary.... Various astronomers subscribe to one or another of the above evolutionary schemes. In my opinion the present data are not sufficient to favor any particular theory. We see galaxies of different structural types—elliptical, spiral, and irregular—all of which contain stars we believe to be old. This would imply that they have the same chronological, but different evolutionary, ages."[104]

Our knowledge of galaxies thus seems to indicate that galaxies are not constant and unchanging in time, that they undergo evolutionary processes, but that we are not at present able to correlate these evolutionary processes with the diverse type of galaxies.

Chapter 12
Stellar Evolution

During the past one hundred years, the astronomical study of stars has led to theories of stellar evolution, namely the correlation of the changes in stellar phenomena with a temporal sequence of evolution (formation, aging, decline, and perhaps even death). In 1865 Zoellner suggested that a star's color indicated its temperature, red stars being relatively cool and white stars the hottest. A few years later Vogel and others proposed that this indicated an evolutionary process, with the hot, white stars being very young and the cooler, red stars very old. In 1887 Sir Norman Lockyer set up a theoretical basis for such an evolutionary sequence. The classification of stars by temperature was further developed by the Draper Catalogue published by Harvard in 1890. In 1905 E. Hertzsprung discovered that while the absolute magnitude of the nearer stars arranged in order of spectral types according to the Harvard-Draper sequence diminished progressively from Class B (white) to M (red), the more distant orange and red stars were much more luminous, and were moreover less constant in magnitude whatever their spectral class. Hertzsprung termed the former type *dwarfs* and the latter *giants*. The Princeton astronomer H.N. Russell made the same discovery independently and in 1913 published the first Hertzsprung-Russell diagram in which the stars are plotted by spectral type against absolute magnitude. Russell concluded that the giant and dwarf stars differed in density rather than mass, and he proposed an evolutionary sequence which later was found incompatible with some of the observed data. Later Baade discovered that stars exist in two distinct "populations," population I stars being mainly blue-white stars of spectral types O and B situated mostly in the arms of spiral galaxies, and population II being the cooler, redder stars found in the nuclei of spiral galaxies and in elliptical galaxies. It was found that globular clusters consisted mostly of population II stars and galactic clusters mostly of population I stars.

There is considerable uncertainty about the early phases in the formation of a star. It is generally conjectured that protostars are cool, distended, randomly formed, gaseous condensations of interstellar matter. A protostar contracts rapidly in a process of gravitational compression, which constitutes the first stage in the history of a newly formed star and leads to the establishment of a quasi-equilibrium state. For the Sun this initial period of rapid contraction is estimated to have lasted about twenty years. When a star first reaches the quasi-equilibrium state, it is as a whole in a state of convective equilibrium. "During the subsequent contraction, its luminosity decreases while its apparent temperature remains approximately constant. At a certain stage in the contraction, which occurs early the more massive the star, and which does not occur at all in stars whose mass is less than one-quarter that of the Sun, a nonconvective core appears and begins to grow at the expense of the convective envelope. Once the nonconvective (radiative) core contains a substantial fraction of the mass of the star, the luminosity stops decreasing with further contraction but the apparent temperature begins to increase. During this phase of contraction through a series of quasi-equilibrium states, the energy radiated by a star is supplied by contraction.... Ultimately the central temperature of the star becomes so high that thermonuclear reactions occurring there release enough energy to make up for the energy lost by radiation. At this point the contraction ceases and the star settles down to a quiet period of middle age during which its luminosity and apparent temperature remain almost constant while the supply of hydrogen in the core is gradually depleted. During this evolutionary phase of middle age, a star belongs to the main sequence of the Hertzsprung-Russell diagram."[105] This phase lasts a few million years for the most luminous upper-main-sequence stars to more than a hundred billion years for lower-main-sequence stars. The main-sequence phase ends when the hydrogen in the core of the star has been all converted to helium so that the core consists entirely of helium and heavy elements.

From this phase there is considerable theoretic uncertainty as to the evolutionary course. While the helium core contracts, growing hotter and denser, the envelope expands perhaps a hundred times the initial size. At this *red giant* stage, it is believed that a star can follow either of two separate evolutionary paths dependent on stellar mass. If the stellar mass is less than a certain value (slightly more than the mass of the Sun), the contraction of the helium core leads to a stable configuration due to a degeneracy in the core increasing the pressure so that the contraction practically ceases. The star meanwhile becomes increasingly brighter and redder as the hydrogen-burning shell works its way outward. If the stellar mass is much greater than that of the sun, the onset of degeneracy in the helium core does not halt the contraction which continues until the temperature in the core is high enough to induce helium-burning reactions to a considerable extent. "These reactions require exceedingly high densities and temperatures in the region of 100 million degrees K. The reactions convert helium into carbon, oxygen, neon, and magnesium. Further contraction, following the exhaustion of helium, leads to still higher temperatures and densities and to a series of intricate nuclear reactions in which the production and capture of neutrons is thought to play an important part. These reactions release energy so rapidly that the star may explode, thus becoming a supernova."

Another line of evolution of stars considerably more massive than the sun leads to white dwarfs. This evolutionary course, however, is not well understood. In the final stage, the white dwarf is a star "that is all core and that is neither burning nuclear fuel nor contracting but simply growing progressively cooler." If the mass of the star is less than a critical value, not much greater than the mass of the sun, "there is a unique value of density (and hence of stellar radius) at which the pressure forces just balance the gravitational ones; this is the equilibrium configuration of a white dwarf.... If the mass exceeds the critical value, equilibrium can never be obtained; very massive stars probably end catastrophically."[105]

From the standpoint of human dimensions, the timescale of stellar evolution is very long. For example, it is estimated that about 5 billion years after the formation of our galaxy, our small sun contracted from an interstellar gas and dust cloud in a spiral arm about 30,000 light-years from the center of the galaxy. This contraction is believed to have taken place in a few million years, with the result that the sun became a main-sequence star. Its lifetime in its middle age as a main-sequence star is about 10 billion years. At the present time it has been a main-sequence star for 5 billion years. It is estimated that the planetary system accreted from the residue of the solar formation about 4.6 billion years ago. In 5 more billion years the sun will have exhausted its central hydrogen and will become a red giant. Its expansion in the red giant stage may be so great that for some time the earth will orbit the solar center within its tenuous outer reaches. The lifetime of the sun as a red giant is estimated at a few million years.

It should be noted from the foregoing account of stellar evolution that the nuclear transformations responsible for the continual radiation from the sun and stars are essentially irreversible and cannot continue indefinitely. Eventually all stars cease to shine in the way the sun now does and become either white dwarf stars or neutron stars or even possibly black holes. Whatever their final condition, the fact that stars as radiating bodies cannot continue in the same state forever is evidence for the unidirectional temporality of the universe.

As mentioned above, it is generally believed that the sun and all the bodies of the solar system are products of contraction or condensation from a dispersed interstellar gas and dust cloud. The earth and other smaller planets differ in composition from the sun and the larger planets, because they lacked strong enough gravitational fields to retain their hydrogen and helium. According to one theoretical variant, the earth was formed originally by coagulation of cold particles in a turbulent gas cloud. The earth may have been uniform in composition at first, but as its size increased, the temperature of the interior rose as a result of compression and radioactive decay, and iron separated from the silicate to form the core. The bulk of the elements, particularly the light and the radioactive elements, was concentrated outward in the mantle, the plastic inner and the solid outer mantle, and the crust. It is believed that this process is still going on. Since the conductivity of the earth is so low, it is possible that the earth's interior may still be warming, contrary to the 19th century view that the earth must be cooling and therefore was hotter in the past. After the discovery of radioactivity in 1896, Lord Rayleigh calculated the heat generated by radioactive minerals in the earth's crust, showing that it explained the flow of heat at the surface. The changes in the earth's crust and its surface features are explained by radiogenic heat and gravitational forces. Some geologists believe that the rate of change of the earth's surface features has been accelerating throughout its history, "In any case the earth is still undergoing change, and can be expected to evolve for some time to come."[106]

The age of the earth, the time that it has existed with approximately its present mass and density, is about 4.6 billion years, according to the best contemporary estimate. This estimate uses the uranium-lead accumulation clock, mentioned earlier; specifically, it is based on the meteorite-lead method, an extension of the uranium-lead accumulation method to include meteorites. When the different isotopic composition of the leads isolated from various iron and stone meteorites are compared, a simple pattern emerges, with the ratios of the isotopes being found equal to a constant. The ratio of radiogenic lead^{207} and lead^{206} formed during a period of uranium decay is time-dependent and the age of any closed system containing uranium is easily determined by measuring this ratio. With the constant ratio or composition found in meteorites, the age of meteorites is calculated to be 4.6 billion years; this has been confirmed by other radioactive-decay methods. Meteorites may be considered as separate little planets, all formed at the same time, all containing the same kind of primordial lead, and all having varying proportions of radiogenic lead. "These meteoritic leads constitute only a very small fraction of the total of every possible kind of lead, so that if the lead from an object of an unknown age fits the description of a meteoritic lead it is probably safe to conclude that the object has the age calculated for meteorites. This is the case for the earth. Samples of common lead are obtained from the oceans which contain mixtures of lead derived from all lands, and these leads fit the description of meteoritic lead. One therefore may conclude that the earth has the same age as meteorites, namely 4.6 billion years."[107]

Chapter 13
Geology

We have been outlining the temporal history of the natural universe from the standpoint of contemporary physical science. However, the conceptual presuppositions for this interpretation were established, not by astronomy or physics, but by two other sciences, geology and biology, roughly in the period from 1750 to 1860. The geologists led the way.

Geology was the first branch of natural science to establish a conceptual framework based on ordered temporal change. The geologists discovered that the earth had a temporal development; the earth had in its structure and configurations, as it were, a "history." The enlargement of the temporal horizon of Western man from the limited scale of Biblical chronology to a new, vaster time-scale was an achievement of the geologists who, between 1750 and 1850, studied and interpreted the rock strata and fossils of the earth's crust.

By 1750 geologists were already beginning to recognize that the rock-strata and fossils as found at the time provided information about the past conditions of the earth's surface. By detailed study of rocks and fossils they sought to reconstruct the successive stages by which the earth arrived at its present structure and form. The first numerical estimates of past time involved in the development of the earth were published in the 1770's by Comte de Buffon. The first three volumes of his *Natural History* were published in 1749 and the series was not complete at the time of his death in 1788. "Buffon had

59

aimed to produce a scientific encyclopedia dealing in succession
with the planetary system, the Earth, the human race and the different kingdoms of living creatures..."[108] However, his early hypothesis
about the origin of the solar system was attacked by Sorbonne
theologians so that, like Galileo, he was obliged to make a formal
retraction. For twenty-five years he carried on his work without
publishing the results. In 1774, however, he felt free to publish his
Introduction to the History of Minerals. In the opening words of this
book, he gave elegant expression to his general purpose as follows:
"...so in natural history one must dig through the archives of the
world, extract ancient relics from the bowels of the earth, gather
their fragments, and assemble again in a single body of proofs all
those indications of the physical changes which can carry us back to
the different Ages of Nature. This is the only way of fixing certain
points in the immensity of space and of placing a number of mile-
stones on the eternal path of time. The past is like distance: our view
of it would shrink and even be lost entirely, if history and chronology had not marked the darkest points by beacons and torches....
Natural history...embraces in its scope all regions of space and all
periods equally, and has no limits other than those of the universe."[109]
    To Buffon, the earth's present condition was very different from
its original one, and since then it had passed through several other
phases, the temporal periods of which he called *epochs*. "The surface of the earth has taken different forms in succession; even the
heavens have changed, and all the objects in the physical world
are...caught up in a continual process of successive variations..."[110]
The problem for him was to reconstruct the past epochs by use of
"facts" and "relics": "facts" were those physical properties on which
he based his arguments about the cooling of the planets; "relics"
were such things as fossils, shells, and mammoth-bones. Buffon's
calculations of the time-span of the earth and the other planets were
far too short; for the earth he estimated 168,000 years, at least. While
the details of Buffon's calculations and his figures were all wrong, he
achieved the essential point of breaking the time-barrier of scriptural chronology.
    James Hutton is generally recognized as the father of modern
geology. His *Theory of the Earth* was published in 1788. Hutton
rejected the theory of catastrophes previously used to explain the
stratification of rocks, the origin of mountains, the deposition of
oceans, and other geological phenomena. He sought to understand
all geological phenomena—mountain ranges, deep-canyon and
integrated-valley systems, the soil, the strata, the rocks themselves—

on the basis of processes which we can observe in operation today. For Hutton, in geology the present is the key to the past. To understand geologic phenomena, we must extrapolate into the past the natural observable processes of the present; thus we come to understand geologic development as an orderly succession of changes based on actual causes. For example, Hutton writes in opposition to the theory of catastrophes as follows: "From the top of those decaying pyramids [Mt. Blanc and surrounding peaks] to the sea, we have a chain of facts which clearly demonstrate this proposition [against catastrophism]. That the materials of wasted mountains have traveled through the rivers; for in every step of this progress, we see the effect, and thus acknowledge the proper cause. We may often be witness to this action; but it is only a small part of the whole progress that we may thus perceive, nevertheless it is equally satisfactory as if we saw the whole; for throughout the whole of this long course we may see some part of the mountain moving some part of the way. What more may we require? Nothing but time. It is not any part of the proofs that will be disputed; but after allowing all the parts, the whole will be denied; and for what?—only because we are not disposed to allow that quantity of time which the ablution of so much wasted mountains might require."[111] Hutton concluded that vast periods of time were required for the earth to have reached its present state. Hutton is credited also with freeing geology from the scriptural chronology, limiting the span of time to some 6,000 years.

This emphasis on time continued to animate the research of geologists in the generations following Hutton. The British geologist Charles Lyell in his *Principles of Geology* in 1830 wrote as follows: "It was not until Descartes assumed the indefinite extent of the celestial spaces and removed the supposed boundaries of the universe, that a just opinion began to be entertained as to the relative distances of the heavenly bodies; and until we habituate ourselves to contemplate the possibility of an indefinite lapse of ages having been comprised within each of the more modern periods of the earth's history, we shall be in danger of forming most erroneous and partial views in Geology...." Earlier, the French geologist George Scrope, excited by the profusion of the geological remains in the *Massif Central*, exclaimed: "The leading idea which is present in all our researches, and which accompanies every fresh observation, the sound which to the ear of the student of Nature seems continually echoed in every part of her works, is—Time!—Time!—Time!"[112] This emphasis on the role of time in geology has remained to the present. An excellent contemporary textbook in the field of physical geology states as follows: "Geology is a historical science. It deals with successions of events in *time*, and with geological processes whose roles are determined by their *rates*.... Geology owes its peculiar and singular flavor to the pervasive role of time, whose total span, compared to that of written history, is vast."[113]

Hutton made famous the strata at Siccar Point, on the southeastern coast of Scotland, where almost undisturbed sedimentary strata lie nearly horizontally across folded beds of an older sedimentary series. Hutton was the first to recognize here the record of a sequence of events covering an immense interval of time: (1) accumulation; (2) folding and elevation above sea level; (3) partial erosion of the lower series of sediments; (4) deposition of the upper series; (5) uplift of both above sea level. Moreover, this is only part of the span of time, for the accumulation of the lower strata was a result of the erosion of a yet older rock mass with its own unrecorded history.

Stratigraphy was born in England. Its chief inventor was William Smith, a self-made craftsman, who worked as a surveyor and became well known as a practical engineer. From his youth on he was intensely interested in geologic observation. In his travels he carefully noted the succession of the strata and collected the organic fossils in each layer. In 1794 he found similar sequences of strata recurring right across England. Subsequently he recognized that the corresponding strata in any part of England always contained the same characteristic fossils. Smith came to realize that the surest means of recognizing a geologic formation was through its distinctive fossils, and this made possible the systematic development of stratigraphy. Beginning in 1799, by 1815 he achieved the famous five-miles-to-an-inch systematic geological map of England and Wales. The gross features differ hardly at all from those that appear in modern textbooks. "...Smith's work convinced geologists that the strata in all parts of the earth's crust belonged in the single common sequence—Cambrian, Ordovician, Silurian, Devonian, and so on—and that this sequence was not merely a fact of geology but reflected the temporal order in which the rocks had been laid down. Only a few members of the whole sequence were present at any one location but, among those that were represented, the lower ones were also the older.... Moreover, this common sequence of strata was confirmed by the common sequence of fossil species found within them: in fact, the fossil contents of two strata provided an even better basis for comparing their relevant positions—and so their relative ages—than their mineralogical contents."[114] While Steno a hundred years before had recognized a general association between different fossils and strata, as had other geologists subsequently, William Smith demonstrated convincingly that the sequence of fossil forms could be used to identify the sequence of the strata in their order of superposition.

While the British proceeded with the mapping of the stratigraphic record, French effort in the first decades of the 19th century was directed primarily to the successive faunas themselves, as displayed in the younger rock series of Northern France. Thus arose modern paleontology, associated especially with the names of Cuvier and Lamarck. Paleontological studies came to play a fundamental role in geology, making it possible to estimate the comparative age of rock formations in different regions and countries.

In his *Elements of Geology*, 1839, Charles Lyell set forth the essential stratigraphic principles: superposition of strata in order of decreasing age; use and limitations of lithology and of fossils in identification and correlation of stratigraphic units; the significance of unconformities. His generalized column of "fossiliferous strata" was adopted throughout Britain, France, and Germany and includes names still retained in modern geological chronology. In ensuing years additions and modifications were made which reflected the knowledge that certain geological systems are more fully developed in other areas than Britain. By 1880 a stratigraphic column was achieved, which is still universally accepted as the basis of a corresponding geological time scale.

Against the view that catastrophic upheavals and accompanying annihilation of preexisting life were events to be used for geologic correlation on a regional scale, Lyell set forth "the principle of uniformitarianism." The term "uniformitarianism" is misleading: it does not mean that uniformity is a characteristic of geological phenomena in general, nor that the rates of natural processes have necessarily been uniform throughout geological time. It does signify that to understand the past development of the earth up to the present configuration, we must rely on physical agencies known to us today. Hence he sought to show how the formation of known geological features could be explained by the action of weathering, volcanic upthrust, sedimentation, erosion, and similar processes. "He recognized that even major unconformities used to delimit stratigraphic systems have local rather than transcontinental significance. Faunal change in time he regarded as slow and spontaneous,... he also appreciated the role of migration in the abrupt upward changes in fauna so commonly observed in stratigraphic sections. Lyell taught that worldwide implementation of a stratigraphic time scale could become possible only through patiently piecing together mutually overlapping data of many local records. To this principle most geologists adhere today. There is little support for the idea that alternating periods of continental uplift and submergence on a global scale provide the basis for continental or worldwide correlation by orogeny (mountain formation) and unconformity."[115]

During the century after Lyell's work, a worldwide stratigraphic time scale has been achieved, based on the Western European scale. It has been found that certain events, such as faunal innovations, extinctions, and evolutionary trends, that mark the fossil record from Cambrian times (600 million years in the past) onward in Europe are paralleled in distant continents. Their relative order everywhere is identical. The accumulated evidence has shown that certain worldwide faunal events are valid indices of the stratigraphic order and thus of time. Since Precambrian rocks are for the most part unfossiliferous, it has been as yet impossible to set up a corresponding worldwide time scale on the basis of stratigraphy for the Precambrian period. Repeated episodes in the Precambrian period of orogeny, metamorphism, emplacement of granitic plutons, and prolonged erosion have made it more difficult to establish the Precambrian sequence; nevertheless, it has been possible by conventional and radiometric means to reconstruct the broad sequence of local events in the Precambrian time-span.

Chapter 14
Evolution

Charles Lyell's *Principles of Geology* set forth in 1830 the geological account of the development in time of the earth's crust. It took nearly thirty years, until the publication of Darwin's *Origin of Species* in 1859, before the similar giant step was taken in biology by Darwin's zoological account of the development in time of organic species. There was a direct connection between Lyell and Darwin, a direct connection between geology and biology in this critical stage of the development of the temporal history of the natural universe. Darwin was greatly influenced by Lyell's *Principles of Geology*, a copy of which he took with him on H.M.S. Beagle in 1831 on the advice of his teacher, Professor Henslow, who had arranged his appointment as chief naturalist on the Beagle. Subsequently he served as Lyell's scientific assistant, being able to confirm by his own geological observations the soundness of Lyell's uniformitarian principles. The evolutionary explanation of the origin of species appeared to Darwin as a natural continuation in biology of Lyell's uniformitarian principles in geology. Henslow, an orthodox catastrophist opposing Lyell's views, although advising Darwin to take along a copy of Lyell's *Principles*, told him at the same time "on no account [as Darwin reported] to accept the views therein advocated."[116]

The voyage on the Beagle lasted nearly five years. Reading Lyell soon turned Darwin into a Uniformitarian. "From that time on, Darwin was to look at living nature with the same eye that Lyell had brought to geology—an eye for continuities and likenesses both between present species and their fossil predecessors. At last he had found a task worthy of his intellect; to discover an explanation of the 'succession of organic types,' both in space and in time, as natural and 'uniformitarian' as that which Lyell had given to geological development.... 'geological distribution and geological relations of extinct terrestrial inhabitants in South America first led me to the subject.' Travelling southward down the Argentine coastline, he was impressed 'by the manner in which closely allied animals replace one another'—just as though they were not entirely distinct populations, but rather so many varieties derived from a common original stock. As the environment varied, so too the same structure might be put to different uses—the wings used by most birds for flying served the ostrich as a sail, and the penguin as a flipper. As for South American geology: the giant fossil armadillos recovered from the Pampas showed extraordinary anatomical resemblances to present-day species barely one-tenth their size."[117]

Thus far the general pattern had been one of steady variation in organic form coinciding with gradual changes in the environment. Like his predecessors, Buffon and Lamarck, Darwin was led to seek a mechanism by which the environment itself might change a single original population into many different species. His observations at the Galapagos Islands obliged him to change his views. The Galapagos Islands, 600 miles west of Ecuador, are some 200 small volcanic islets, forming a collection of micro-environments, all subject to the same physical influences and composed of the same black lava. Nevertheless each separate island seemed to have its own distinct flora and fauna.

Darwin wrote: "I never dreamed that islands of about fifty or sixty miles apart, and most of them in sight of each other, formed of precisely the same rocks, placed under a quite similar climate, rising to nearly equal height, would have been differently tenanted." Thus Darwin learned that "identical physical conditions could provide a setting in which a dozen distinct species might be formed, whose differences could not possibly be explained by climate and geography alone."[118] He was thus led to seek a theory to explain how species close in time and space could be so different in characteristics. Darwin maintained a journal of observations and thoughts during his five years on the Beagle. As Darwin wrote: "On my return home in the autumn in 1836, I immediately began to prepare my Journal for publication, and then saw how many facts indicated the common descent of species." Puzzled by this organic evolution by descent, he began to keep notes on the "transmutation of species... facts which bore in any way on the variation of animals and plants under domestication and nature."[119] Lyell had cited the view of de Candolle, a Swiss botanist, on the importance of competition between species: "All the plants of a given country are at war with one another. The first which established themselves by chance in a particular spot tend, by the mere occupancy of space, to exclude other species—the greater choke the smaller; the longest livers replace those which last for a shorter period; the more prolific gradually make themselves masters of the ground, which species multiplying more slowly would otherwise fill."[120] Lyell had generalized this view into a "universal struggle for existence" in which "the right of the strongest eventually prevails; and the strength and durability of the race depends mainly on its prolificness—every species which has spread itself from a small point over a wide area must...have marked its progress by the diminution or the entire extirpation of some other and must maintain its ground by a successful struggle against the encroachment of other plants and animals." Lyell understood how this struggle might as a selection process destroy existing species. "Darwin's genius was to see how that same selection might *create* new species."[121]

Darwin soon realized that he had to explain both how new, variant forms of animals and plants appeared and also why certain of them were able to survive at the expense of rivals. Malthus's *Essay on the Principle of Population*, first published in 1795, was read by Darwin in October 1838. Malthus had argued that human population tends to increase "geometrically" while the means of subsistence increases at best "arithmetically." Whatever the efforts of human beings, population will thus always outrun the food supply. Measures to increase social welfare will enhance fertility, and so augment the pressure of population on resources. While de Candolle and Lyell had noted the competition among plants and animals, Malthus described the same phenomenon with respect to man so lucidly and vigorously that it profoundly affected Darwin's thinking. As Darwin wrote: "Being well prepared to appreciate the struggle for existence which everywhere goes on from long-continued observation of the habits of animals and plants, it at once struck me [on reading Malthus] that under these circumstances favorable variations would tend to be preserved, and unfavorable ones to be destroyed. The result of this would be the formation of new species. Here then I had at last got a theory by which to work."

By the end of 1838, Darwin realized, "*If* variant forms capable of being inherited by later generations occurred sufficiently often, and *if* such variant individuals lived in an environment where that particular variation enhanced their chances of multiplying at the expense of their fellows (without the effects of the variations being submerged in cross-breeding), *then* a Malthusian theory would explain why the animals actually surviving the struggle for existence would consist predominantly of the 'best-adapted' forms. Furthermore, given *sufficient time*, populations originating from the same parent-groups, but exposed to different physical conditions and competitors, might end with characteristics quite as different from one another as those produced by the deliberate contrivance of animal-breeders and pigeon-fanciers." Darwin named this process "natural selection" in contrast with the "artificial selection" practiced by stock-breeders.

On Darwin's theory, two sets of factors were operating on any plant or animal population, namely, the *physical* environment (climate, soil and so on) and the *biological* environment (food supply, predators and competitors). The joint action of these two complementary factors explained his South American observations: "The smooth gradation of organic forms (fossil and living) on the mainland reflected the coarser selective action of changing climate and habitat over vast periods of time; the more detailed differences between the finches and tortoises of the various Galapagos Islands reflected the more delicate biological balance, which had favored seed-eating birds on one island, insect-eating birds on another."[122]

Although the basic insights of Darwin's views were achieved by the end of 1839, it took twenty years before Darwin published the *Origin of Species* in 1859. These twenty years had been spent in unrelenting labor to perfect his thoughts and their detailed justification, with a result that his *Origin of Species* was a masterpiece in intellectual organization, detailed arguments, and lucid style. It was thus well able to bear its decisive role in promulgating the idea of evolution in the biological realm. Actually, it took an external stimulus to force the publication of Darwin's work. In 1858, Darwin had received a letter from Alfred Russell Wallace, a botanist studying the orchids of the Malayan archipelago. Wallace knew of Darwin's work on the Beagle and had read Malthus, and the idea of "natural selection"—which had occurred to him independently—was set forth in this letter. He had arrived at a theory essentially identical to Darwin's. Darwin's hand thus forced, by a remarkably fair agreement—not unique nor usual in science—the two men presented joint preliminary papers to the Linneaan Society. As a result of this stimulus, Darwin worked intensively to put together the final text of the *Origin of Species*, which was published in 1859.

It is beyond our purpose to attempt to summarize Darwin's thoughts. Let it suffice, however, to cite certain particularly significant quotations as follows:

> *If* under changing conditions of life organic beings present individual differences in almost every part of their structure and this cannot be disputed; *if* there be, owing to their geometrical rate of increase, a severe struggle for life at some age, season, or year, and this certainly cannot be disputed; then, considering the infinite complexity of the relations of all organic beings to each other and to their conditions of life, causing an infinite diversity in structure, constitution, and habits to be advantageous to them, it would be a most extraordinary fact if no variation had ever occurred useful to each being's own welfare, in the same manner as so many variations have occurred useful to man. But *if* variations, useful to any organic being, *ever do* occur, assuredly individuals thus characterized will have the best chance of being preserved for the struggle for life; and from the strong principle of inheritance, these will tend to produce offspring similarly characterized. This principle of preservation, or the survival of the fittest, I have called Natural Selection. It leads to the improvement of each creature in relation to its organic and inorganic conditions of life; and consequently, in most cases, to what must be regarded as an advance in organization....[123]
>
> But we have already seen how it [natural selection] entails extinction; and how largely extinction has acted in the world's history, geology plainly declares. Natural selection also leads to divergence of character; for the more organic beings diverge in structure, habits, and constitution, by so much the more can a large number be supported on the area,...
>
> On these principles, the nature of the affinities, and the generally well-defined distinctions between the innumerable organic beings in each class throughout the world, may be explained.... all animals and all plants throughout all time and space...[are] related to each other in groups, subordinate to groups,... namely, varieties of the same species most closely related, species of the same genus less closely and unequally related, forming sections and sub-genera, species of distinct genera much less closely related and genera related in different degrees, forming sub-families, families, orders, sub-classes and classes. The several subordinate groups in any class cannot be ranked in a single file but seen clustered round points, and these round other points and so on in almost endless cycles. If species had been independently created, no explanation would have been possible of this kind of classification; but it is explained through inheritance and the

complex action of natural selection, entailing extinction and divergence of character.[124]

Darwin recognized that "our ignorance of the laws of variation is
profound."[125] However, he went on to state: "Whatever the cause
may be of each slight difference between the offspring and their
parents—and a cause for each must exist—we have reason to believe
that it is the steady accumulation of beneficial differences which has
given rise to all the more important modifications of structure in
relation to the habits of each species."[126]

Darwin realized that the existing rocks of the earth's crust were
only a fragmentary set of samples of the actual geological past.
Hence, there were frequent gaps in the fossil remains representing
transitional forms between species of the better-known epochs.
Nevertheless he believed that "the theory of descent with modification through variation and natural selection"[127] gave a convincing
interpretation of the facts of geographical distribution and palaeon-
tology. As a result of Darwin's work, the realms of geology, paleontology, and biology can be comprehended together in one sequential course of temporal development. By Darwin the organic world
was also brought within the system of uniform forces and causes
which Lyell had applied in geology. On the base of uniformitarian
geology, which had assumed an enduring balance between the
constructive and destructive agencies shaping the earth's crust,
Darwin, however, had superimposed a new progressive element
associated with the gradual development of organic species. Darwin's account of the evolution of species by "descent with modification," not only extended the temporal scope of natural science, but
also give it an unequivocal direction.

Chapter 15
The Origins of Life

As discussed earlier, the earth is estimated to be about 4.5 billion years old. Very little is known about the first period of its history, particularly in connection with the origin of life. Fossil remains from the very early periods are few, because most of the oldest sediments have spent periods in the interior of the earth under such heat that no fossils could have survived. In fact, very few sedimentary rocks more than 3 billion years are known. Nevertheless, there is evidence that life appeared at some time during the first billion or so years after the formation of the earth. Microfossils resembling contemporary blue-green algae have been found in rocks 3 billion years old, or slightly older. The best preserved are the microfossils from South Africa (the Fig Tree series) which are about 3.1 billion years old. In 1980 microfossils dating back 3.5 billion years were reported to have been found in Australia. Precambrian microfossils have also been found and thoroughly studied in the Gunflint formation on the north shore of Lake Michigan in Canada, where the rocks are about 1.8 billion years old. Many of the fossils in these rocks resemble species of blue-green algae still living today. Fossil research has shown that the earliest Precambrian fossils are the simplest, and that increasingly complex microorganisms evolved throughout the later Precambrian period. Recent paleontological studies of chemical fossils (organic substances deriving from the original organisms) have found several important biochemicals in association with fossil algae in Precambrian sediments, indicating that the biochemistry of

71

these ancient organisms may have been similar to contemporary biochemistry.

The fossil record from the Cambrian period beginning about 600 million years ago is much more substantial. The temporal sequence gives an account of the direction of the evolution of living organisms on this earth. Marine invertebrates were the first fairly large animal found as fossils from the early Cambrian, about 580 million years ago. Sponges, jellyfish, starfish, and marine worms were all common by the end of the Cambrian period about 500 million years ago. The dominant animals were the trilobites which became extinct, but other Cambrian organisms were clearly related to animals living today.

The first vertebrates to appear were fish, found in deposits more than 420 million years old. A very rapid evolution of a great variety of fishes occurred in the Devonian period about 380 million years ago. The new species included some true fishes, such as the sharks, and also scaly fishes with lungs and limb-like fins, which were the ancestors of the amphibians.

"The first amphibians were quite small, but by 300 million years ago giant salamander-like creatures had already taken to the land. The earliest land plants evolved from seaweed or other algae about 400 million years ago; a hundred million years later the land was covered with ferns and primitive trees. It was in this environment, perhaps 280 million years ago, that the first reptiles appeared and then gradually displaced the amphibians. The earliest remains of modern insects date from about the same time.

"The period from 180 to 60 million years ago was the age of the reptiles. These included the giant dinosaurs and flying pterosaurus as well as more familiar lizards, turtles, and crocodiles. The first mammals evolved from reptiles about 180 million years ago, but they did not become dominant for more than another 100 million years. A quite different evolutionary branch led from the reptiles to the modern birds.

"The mammals began to take over the land a little less than 60 million years ago. All of the modern groups of mammals appeared within the next 25 million years. Thirty-five million years ago, primitive horses, pigs, rodents, and monkeys were already established.

"The mammals continued to evolve and diversify. Paleontological evidence suggests that man's ancestors diverged from other groups of apes about 20 million years ago, but biochemical evidence suggests a much shorter time since the separation, perhaps only 5 million years. Very recently the ice ages, which ended 10-15 thousand years ago, caused the extinction of many plants and of the giant mammals. They also resulted in great changes in the distribution of surviving species. Since then the environment has been comparatively stable, except where it has been transformed by agriculture or other human activities."[128]

According to current biological thinking, all presently existing species are descended, by evolution through natural selection, from bacteria or algae that lived on the earth billions of years ago. How did these bacteria or algae originate? Under what conditions? From what materials, from what sources?

The theory, generally accepted today, of the origin of life, was set forth mainly by the Russian biochemist A.I. Oparin in 1938. He proposed that the primitive atmosphere of the earth was a reducing atmosphere, i.e., with an excess of hydrogen, which contained methane, ammonia, water, and hydrogen. It was quite different from the present atmosphere of the earth which is strongly oxidizing and which contains about 80% molecular nitrogen and about 20% of free oxygen, the small amount of carbon in the atmosphere being present as carbon dioxide. The distinction is important because no bio-organic compounds are synthesized in our present atmosphere, and many of these compounds are susceptible to degradation in the present atmosphere. The synthesis of important biochemical compounds takes place readily, however, in a reducing atmosphere. The earth and the whole solar system are believed to have been formed from cosmic dust and gas clouds, which contained a great excess of hydrogen. The planets Jupiter, Saturn, and Uranus have at present atmospheres of methane and ammonia. Oxidizing conditions have developed on Mercury, Venus, Earth, and Mars as a result of the escape of free hydrogen followed by the production of oxygen through the action of high-energy ultraviolet light from the sun on water molecules in the upper atmosphere. While hydrogen is also produced in this process, the hydrogen escapes from the earth's gravitational field leaving free oxygen behind. Oparin proposed that the organic chemicals on which life depends formed naturally in a reducing atmosphere through the effect of energy provided by sunlight, lightning, and high temperatures existing in volcanos. A similar view of the primitive atmosphere was set forth independently by the British biologist J.B.S. Haldane.

In 1952 H.C. Urey corroborated the reducing-atmosphere theory by showing that methane, ammonia, and water are the stable forms of carbon, nitrogen, and oxygen when hydrogen is present in excess. In the next year, Stanley Miller, then a student of Harold Urey, showed that a mixture of methane, ammonia, water, and hydrogen, when subjected to an electric charge, produced diverse organic compounds including amino acids. Ultraviolet light had the same effect. Miller's experiments have been termed "the beginning of modern work on prebiotic chemistry."[129]

The complex organic compounds produced in the reducing primitive atmosphere accumulated on the earth and were dissolved in the oceans and lakes of the primitive earth. These organic compounds in the primitive atmosphere were formed by lightning, ultraviolet light, intense heat, or some other form of energy. When formed in the primitive atmosphere, these organic compounds would have dissolved in raindrops and then were deposited in the oceans and lakes, or if deposited on the earth were eventually washed into these bodies of water. It is presumed that water was in the primitive atmosphere and may have been released also from the interior of the earth. When the atmosphere became saturated with water vapor, rain fell; at first small lakes were formed, and then as more and more water fell, these lakes were enlarged to form the oceans. The fluid, containing the accumulation of large amounts of dissolved organic material in the oceans and lakes of the primitive earth, is often termed "the prebiotic soup." It is not known how long a time was required for the formation of the prebiotic soup. At any rate the time available for synthesis and accumulation of these organic compounds was evidently long enough. It may have taken nearly a billion years. Bear in mind that we have a gap of 1.1 billion years between the formation of the earth 4.6 billion years ago and the oldest known relic of life, found in Australia, as mentioned before, aged 3.5 billion years. Orgel estimates that the prebiotic soup may well have contained a gram of organic material per liter of water which is about a third as concentrated as Knorr's chicken bouillon.

According to Oparin's theory, the many organic compounds, accumulated in the oceans of the primitive earth, reacted to form structures of greater and greater complexity, until a structure was formed which could be called living. The synthesis of the first living organism would thus involve many nonbiological steps. Such compounds as amino acids, hydrocarbons, and lipids by combination and polymerization gave rise to macromolecules, including proteins and nucleic acids which eventually became capable of catalytic ("instructional") self-assembly into still more elaborate structures. There is some basis in laboratory experiments for the concept that the association of colloids was gathered together into coacervate droplets that became link-grouped in protocaryote non-nucleated unicells, each enclosed with a lipid- or protein-based cell wall. Fission or aggregation then produced multicellular strings, like strings of bacterial growth. The nucleated eucaryote cell of more complex organisms was a much later development. It is believed to have arisen by a concentration of complex compounds (some of them to become chromosomes) in the nucleus of the cell unit within the cytoplasmic envelope and controlled in their growth mainly by DNA. According to the fossil record, bacterial and primitive plant growth were the only kinds of organisms for over 2 billion years; the time and the process of evolutionary divergence of animal from plant protists is unknown. For the geological reasons, already indicated, there is an enormous gap in the fossil record, since the first animal fossils suddenly appeared in many diversified kinds in the rocks about 600 million years ago.

The most striking feature of Miller's pioneering experiment in prebiotic synthesis was the discovery that four of the twenty natural amino acids were formed in substantial amounts: glycine, alanine, aspartic acid, and glutamic acid. Most chemists would have anticipated that an electric discharge acting on a mixture of methane, ammonia, hydrogen, and water would produce small quantities of many different substances; after all, many millions of organic compounds are known, and many thousands have structures no more complicated than the amino acids. However, relatively few substances were obtained, many of which are important biochemical compounds found in all living organisms. Subsequently it was found that whenever a reducing mixture of gases is acted on by a strong enough energy source, similar organic compounds, including amino acids, are formed. In the past twenty-five years nearly all of the naturally occurring amino acids have been obtained as products in one of the many prebiotic synthesis experiments. Moreover, it has been found impossible to obtain amino acids from an atmosphere containing free oxygen or from a mixture of carbon dioxide, nitrogen, and water. This result gives strong support to the Oparin hypothesis that the primitive atmosphere was reducing. "Life could not have got started in an atmosphere of the type that exists today." It must be presumed that most primitive organisms were composed of organic compounds formed by energy acting on a reducing atmosphere. Since modern organisms will have retained many features of their primitive ancestors, it is clear why cells living today contain so many of the compounds found as products of prebiotic synthesis. However, all higher and most other forms of life today are completely dependent on oxygen. "Most organisms presumably began to use oxygen once it was abundant and after a time became absolutely dependent on it. Now, they can no longer survive in an oxygen-free environment."[130] Miller, moreover, showed that heating together hydrogen cyanide and formaldehyde (which were formed by the electric discharge) reacted together to give the amino acid glycine. Subsequently another experimenter found that if he warmed ammonia and hydrogen cyanide, in the absence of formaldehyde, together in an aqueous solution for a few days, amino acids were found, as well as adenine. Adenine is one of the four bases present in DNA and RNA. It is also a component of ATP, the intermediate involved in the storage and utilization of chemical energy in biological systems. Since the structure of adenine is quite complicated, it was surprising to find it produced in large amounts from hydrogen cyanide in so simple a reaction. Thus it is believed that "adenine occupies a central position in biochemistry because it is one of the few organic compounds of this degree of complexity that formed in large amounts on the primitive earth. The evidence that many important biochemicals are formed with surprising ease under prebiotic conditions has continued to accumulate. By now, syntheses of almost all of the monomeric components of the genetic apparatus have been achieved under prebiotic conditions."[131]

Orgel summarizes this aspect of prebiotic chemistry as follows: "Whenever a reducing mixture of gases containing carbon, hydrogen, nitrogen, and oxygen is treated violently enough, a similar pattern of small, highly reactive molecules is formed. These include intermediates, such as formaldehyde, hydrogen cyanide, and cyanoacetylene. In the presence of water and ammonia, the reactive intermediates combine together to form more complicated organic molecules. The products are remarkable in that they include many more of the components in modern biochemistry than can be attributed to chance. To explain this finding it must be supposed that the first organisms evolved from primitive ones without much change in chemical composition."[132]

During the last fifteen or twenty years improved radiotelescopes have made it possible to apply radiofrequency spectroscopy to distant astronomical objects, particularly interstellar dust clouds, believed to be the sites of formation of new stars. The first molecules detected were water and ammonia; the next compounds were hydrogen cyanide, formaldehyde, and cyanoacetylene, a group of reactive organic molecules among the most important prebiotic intermediates formed in the primitive reducing atmosphere of the earth. This has been regarded as confirmation of the foregoing ideas on prebiotic syntheses. Confirmation has also come from another source. In September 1969, a large stony meteorite fell and broke up in Australia near the town of Murchison. Chemical analysis of fragments of this meteorite showed that it contained, in addition to other organic compounds, large quantities of the natural amino acids, glycine, alanine, glutamic acid, valine, and proline. Also, some simple amino acids not occurring in the proteins of living organisms were found in the meteorite. Recent experiments have shown that all of the amino acids found in the meteorite can be produced by the action of an electric discharge on a "prebiotic" reducing atmosphere. "The discovery of large amounts of several naturally occurring amino acids in the Murchison meteorite clearly establishes that these compounds are formed spontaneously somewhere else in the solar system."[133]

The amino acids and other prebiotic compounds are rather small compounds. For further progress toward life these molecules had to combine to form polymers (molecules of many parts). The operation of the genetic apparatus depends on properties of polymers performing functions which small molecules could not accomplish. It has been ascertained by experiment that these polymers are not readily formed from amino acid and nucleotides in dilute solutions. It is believed hence that the prebiotic soup had to thicken or solidify in the next stage toward the origin of life. Some organic compounds instead of forming real solutions in water, disperse into small particles of organic material which cluster together in a colloid. Oparin used the term "coacervates" to designate these droplets in the colloid. Oparin suggested the view that, on the primitive earth, coacervate droplets were the most important site for prebiotic condensation reactions. Recent experiments in Israel have also shown that polymerization of the type important for the origin of life takes place on the surface of simple mineral catalysts, e.g., Montmorillonite, a common clay mineral which absorbs certain activated amino acids and converts them to long polypeptide molecules by combining a number of mineral catalysts.

The prebiotic circumstances are essential for the understanding of the origin of life. Equally, if not more, essential is the phenomenon of the replication of macromolecules, polymers. We have referred earlier to the amino acids; they are the "building blocks" of the proteins, a family of substances with very large molecules. The products of joining amino acids in a particular arrangement with carbon, hydrogen, and nitrogen are called peptides, or polypeptides. Enzymes are proteins; they are catalysts, molecules which speed up chemical reactions without themselves being changed in the process, thus being able to function repeatedly. Proteins cannot replicate directly. The information needed to specify a replicating protein sequence is encoded in the sequence of a very different polymeric molecule, a nucleic acid. In a cell the nucleic acid can replicate directly, with the help of appropriate enzymes. There is evidence suggesting that in prebiotic conditions nucleic acids could have replicated in the absence of enzymes. In every cell there are two kinds of nucleic acids, deoxyribonucleic acid (DNA) and ribonucleic acid (RNA). DNA is the genetic nucleic acid containing all of the information needed to direct the synthesis of new cellular proteins. It takes no direct part in this synthesis; rather it functions as a master-copy from which RNA sub-copies are made, and these sub-copies carry the genetic information to the protein-synthesizing system.

Amino acids and nucleic acids form readily under prebiotic conditions; hence it is believed that polypeptides and polynucleotides were among the most abundant polymers on the primitive earth. It seems likely that the genetic apparatus has always been composed of proteins and nucleic acids. No genetic system has ever been proposed based on polymers other than nucleic acids. Orgel summarizes his chapter on replicating molecules as follows: "One must invoke the principle of natural selection to explain how a biological system could have evolved from a prebiotic soup which contained only families of small organic molecules and the random polymers that could be made from them. It seems most likely that polymers related to nucleic acids were formed in the prebiotic soup and could replicate, even if only inaccurately, under prebiotic conditions. Natural selection would then have allowed the polymers that replicated most efficiently to win out.

"The operation of natural selection would have favored those nucleic acid-like polymers that could improve their competitive position by making use of small molecules in their environment. The amino acids were among the molecules used in this way. The genetic code is the result of an elaborate series of adaptations by means of which polynucleotides come to control their environment by directing the synthesis of structural and catalytically active polypeptides. Virtually nothing is known about the successive steps in this adaptation. This is perhaps the most challenging aspect of the problem of the origins of life."[134]

A traditional definition of life was based on the capability of living organisms to reproduce themselves. If certain macromolecules are able to replicate—that is, to reproduce themselves—then we must seek the definition of life elsewhere. Or perhaps it is wrong even to seek the definition, rather we should seek the transition from a macromolecule to the simplest living organism, namely, the cell.

Biologists envisage a number of stages leading up to the evolutionary development of the cell. First, individual macromolecules were formed and replicated by utilizing material already present in the prebiotic soup. In the next stage, nucleic acids began to direct the synthesis of other polymers, including polypeptides. At this point it became important to keep together aggregates of macromolecules. A structure was required that would absorb or enclose macromolecules, but not so as to be impermeable to small molecules, since such small abiotic molecules might be useful. However, when primitive organisms began making biochemical compounds for themselves, it became important to retain small molecules. Thus a membrane had to be developed that was impermeable to useful molecules made within the cell, but permeable to raw materials from outside. Such a membrane is termed "semipermeable." It is believed that these processes evolved in a predominantly aqueous environment.

The earliest organisms grew in the prebiotic soup by making use of preformed molecules, such as nucleotides and amino acids. Presumably when the supply of essential biochemical compounds began to be used up, organisms learned to synthesize these compounds from simple starting materials. When the most abundant components of the prebiotic soup were exhausted, it would then have become necessary to derive new, water-soluble organic materials from the gaseous components of the atmosphere. "The photosynthetic fixation of carbon dioxide must have evolved at this time. Afterwards photosynthesis became essential for the continuation of life on earth. Organic compounds were constantly being oxidized to carbon dioxide and it was only through photosynthesis that the supply of organic carbon compounds could be replenished. It is likely that, at a still later stage, nitrogen-fixing organisms evolved, in response to a shortage of ammonia in the environment."[135]

The final stage in the evolution of life occurred with the evolution of cells surrounded by semipermeable membranes, capable of carrying out a wide range of biosynthetic reactions. This occurred on the primitive earth at least 3 billion years ago, according to fossil evidence and perhaps even earlier. The evolution of multicellular organisms took a further 2 billion years, while creatures with hard shells appeared in large amounts half a billion years ago.

The origin of life appears then to reside in the transition from replicating macromolecules to reproducing cells. There are many murky aspects to this transition. Since cells are the basic unit of life, however, it is natural to regard their creation as the origin of life. The proliferation, diversification, and complexification of cellular organisms during the past 3 billion years are so grandiose as to be almost incredible and incomprehensible. While bacteria, the least complicated of living organisms, consist of a single cell, higher animals may contain thousands of billions of cells; the human brain, which is a mass of nerve tissue weighing about 3 pounds, contains around 50 billion nerve cells. While bacteria cells are small and simple, animal cells are often large and complicated; nerve cells are sometimes many feet long.

If all modern species are descended through evolution by natural selection from bacteria or algae living on the earth a billion years ago, let us look to the bacterial cell for a rudimentary understanding of processes in living organisms. The bacterium *Escherichia coli* is a much studied unicellular organism. Its cells are rods 2-3 x 10^{-4} cm long and 5×10^{-5} cm in diameter; more than one trillion cells could be packed in a volume of one cubic cm. "The bacterium is enclosed by a rigid cell wall and by a cell membrane which is situated just within the wall. The cell wall serves to protect the membrane from damage.... The role of the membrane is in part passive; it acts as the barrier to keep essential molecules inside the cell and to prevent the entrance of harmful molecules. The cell membrane also plays a more active part in bacterial growth, for it contains a series of 'pumps' which select useful molecules from the outside and concentrate them within the cell. Thus the membrane maintains the correct balance between the contents of the cell and the external environment."[136] Within the membrane a series of some hundreds of coordinated chemical actions take place, the purpose of which is to use nutrients in the environment in order to reproduce more *E. coli*. This reproductive task is carried out with great efficiency, since under proper conditions a complete cycle of reproduction takes only 20 minutes. Thus one such bacterial cell could produce 2^{72} or 4.7 billion trillion descendants in a single day. With such a cellular reproductive capability the marvel of evolution over billions of years seems more comprehensible.

To specify the necessary and sufficient conditions for life, Orgel argues that the living organism must be complex and well specified in information content; it must be able to reproduce; the specific information needed for proper reproduction must be stored in a stable way during the reproductive lifetime of the living organism; it must be a result of natural selection.

Natural selection, whether of replicating macromolecules or of living organisms, is based on mutant variations—in other words, on chance. If the mutant variations are disadvantageous in the struggle for existence they are eliminated, but if they are advantageous they enable the descendants of these variations to outgrow and overcome their competitors. The accumulation of many advantageous variations leads to evolutionary development and the adaptation of living organisms to their environment. According to the theory of natural selection, mutant variations make possible the evolution of complex well-adapted organisms from simpler, less well-adapted ones. The mutant variations are taken to be random events. Thus chance rules the biological world, and chance has been so successful on this planet through the aid of time, the billions of years.

Does it really make sense? Do we acquire real insight into biological phenomena by comprehending them within the abstract conceptual framework of random statistical probabilities? If living organisms were mere molecular aggregates of matter, then from this standpoint perhaps the theory would be unobjectionable. From the philosophical view of materialism, the theory would seem quite proper and adequate. However, living organisms are more than mere material aggregates; in the higher animals, they are clearly experiencing, conscious beings; in the most complex animal called man, even self-consciousness is quite manifest. Are consciousness and self-consciousness products of chance? The concept of mutant variations lies at the base of the operation of natural selection in evolution. In so far as the process of mutant variation is not understood, the concept becomes a code-name for random chance occurrences and as such is too abstract and empty to bear the weight of evolutionary development. Until this process is better understood, or the concept is replaced by a sturdier theoretic structure, all evolutionary theory, it seems to me, will be in a sense like the proverbial house built on sand.

Chapter 16
Irreversibility of Time in Evolution

We have noted earlier that Darwin's account of evolution extended the temporal scope of natural science and also gave it an unequivocal direction. The foregoing contemporary view of the origins of life likewise reveals a clear temporal direction. This clear unequivocal direction is well expressed in the phrase "the irreversibility of evolution." Just as the geologists earlier discovered with the aid of paleontology that the earth had, as I said earlier, a "history," the biologists learned, also with the aid of paleontology, that life on this earth had a "history." The distinguished evolutionary biologist, George Gaylord Simpson, has set down the following admirably lucid statement: "That evolution is irreversible is a special case of the fact that history does not repeat itself. The fossil record and the evolutionary sequences that it illustrates are historical in nature, and history is irreversible.... Historical cause embraces the *totality* of preceding events. Such a cause can never be repeated and it changes from instant to instant. Repetition of some factors still would not be a repetition of historical causation. The mere fact that similar conditions had occurred twice and not once would make an essential difference and...the source of existing organisms...would be sure to be different in some respect."[137] Simpson's statement refers to life on this earth. We may ask if it carries implications arguing against the formation of life on other planets or heavenly bodies. Not directly;

however, it does imply that life forms on other heavenly bodies would undoubtedly be quite different from those on earth, and their evolutionary development likewise different.

The principle of irreversibility of evolution is often called "Dollo's Law" after the Belgian paleontologist of that name. Also involved in Dollo's thought was the complementary principle of the irrevocability of evolution; in this sense the influence of a different ancestral condition is not entirely lost in a descendant group. There has been considerable discussion of the principle of irreversibility, including, for example, whether an adaptive trend in some specific characteristic can be reversed. Simpson points out that it often is, e.g., "the horses that became smaller although their immediate ancestors had a definite trend toward larger size. But they did not become like their still earlier ancestors of their own size. Evolution from fish to land animals was reversed in many functional and anatomical characters when land mammals gave rise to whales, but whales are not fishes, far from it."[138] Simpson recognizes that the analyzably separate factors of evolution do not prohibit reversion. Back mutations occur. Lost combinations can be reconstituted. Selection can reverse its trend. "Evolution is readily reversible for particular features, especially those like size that have a very broad genetic basis not necessarily or probably homologous in different groups. It is also more or less reversible to a condition of the immediate ancestry in which the genetic system was essentially the same. This does not alter the broader fact that evolution does not reverse itself exactly or for the whole organism, that it does not double back on itself and repeat quite the same sequence a second time. The statistical probability of a complete reversal or of essential reversal to a very remote condition is extremely small.... The genetical factors are so complex and so constantly changing that extensive reversion is almost impossible. The same is true of the environment. It has thousands, or more likely millions, of pertinent elements all subject to change in various directions.... For the environment to return to an earlier, distinctly different total condition is virtually impossible."[139]

H.F. Blum has come to the same conclusion, expressed in the following terms: "Environmental change involves factors of chance, and the probability that a particular set of mutations will coincide in time and place with a given environment may be very small indeed. Thus the chances of retracing the steps of evolution over any distance becomes vanishing small as the complexity of organisms and their environment increases. In the long course of evolution there may have been chances for short-term reversals on a small scale..."[140]

But "...the overall course of evolution is irreversible; the Ammonites, the Dinosaur, and *Lepidodendron* are gone beyond recall."[141]

Applied to mankind, evolution does not necessarily mean human or social progress; it is a neutral scientific concept, from which either optimistic or pessimistic prognoses may be derived. Darwin himself was an optimist, suggesting that laws of progress might be found in evolutionary processes. He concluded his *Origin of Species* with the following words:

> As all the living forms of life are the lineal descendants of those which lived long before the Silurian epoch, we may feel certain that the ordinary succession by generation has never once been broken, and that no cataclysm has desolated the whole world. Hence we may look with some confidence to a secure future of equally inappreciable length. And as natural selection works solely by and for the good of each being, all corporeal and mental environments will tend to progress towards perfection.[142]

In recent decades a pessimistic note has entered into the interpretation of evolution. G.G. Simpson wrote in 1953: "Evolution is irreversible because it results from its own past and its past is irrevocable. That irrevocability has conditioned what exists and was the ultimate cause, within our realm the most causal of causes, for the extinction of what no longer exists. It also conditions the fact that evolution can run into blind alleys, from which there is no turning back, and that perhaps someday all will end in a blind alley."[143] Discussing the factor of environmental change in evolution, Blum comments, "In recent times, man in particular has had profound influence on environments, perhaps creating more radical and varied changes in shorter time than has any other organism."[144] As early as 1925, in his Lowell Lectures, Alfred North Whitehead noted that "the key to the mechanism of evolution is the necessity for the evolution of a favorable environment, conjointly with the evolution of any specific type of enduring organisms of great permanence." And perhaps as a prescient warning he continues, "Any physical object which by its influence deteriorates its environment, commits suicide."[145]

PART II
THE TEMPORALITY OF THE SELF

Chapter 1
The Psychogenetic Development of the Consciousness of Time

A perception of time is not something given, immediately present, in human consciousness. Time is a construction of the developing human mind and there is no direct sense of time prior to its construction in human experience. The French thinker Lavelle has written: "We cannot say that the experience of time is a primitive experience.... It is that of the present, it is the experience of Being, and time is merely an order which we introduce among the modalities of Being. But it is an experience which is in itself derived; it is the product of reflection."[1] To set forth the psychogenetic development of the consciousness of time, I shall follow primarily the account given by the French psychologist Paul Fraisse, which is based in considerable part on the work of Jean Piaget, the Swiss psychologist.

A baby is capable at birth only of reflex reactions following immediately on a stimulus; there is no temporal perspective in these reactions. Within a few weeks, however, the first temporal references become evident as a result of respondent conditioning. Very soon, as Piaget has shown, a baby who is hungry will stop crying when lifted up to be fed and his mouth will seek his mother's breast before touching it. Such actions reveal an implicit temporal seriation in the sense that a practical utilization of past experience brings anticipation of the future. One stimulus becomes the signal for another: at two months, a baby will turn his head to look in the direction of a noise. Reaction chains are gradually formed with each event becoming the signal for the next one. At about ten months a child can help his mother dress him showing his adaptation to a more complex temporal series. Later, motivated by anticipation, he will take the initiative by performing the first gestures; for example, he will go find his coat and shoes so that he can be dressed to go out for a walk.

The second stage, operant conditioning, appears after the first with the two then developing simultaneously. In operant conditioning the child must learn, as animals do, the action which will bring him satisfaction. A rat can learn to turn a wheel to get some food; a baby can learn to pull a cord in order to make a rattle rattle. Operant conditioning involves temporal perspectives. The child must reconstitute a succession achieved once perhaps by chance; in Malrieu's words, "It is the wished-for future which organizes the present."[2] These reactions are called by Piaget *subjective series*, which are gradually transformed into *objective series* when the apprehended succession is objectified. For example, a baby at birth will cease to want something if removed from his sight, but gradually the object which has disappeared remains present through memory and the baby continues to demand it when it is removed.

As a result of respondent and operant conditioning, a child of about one year acquires a temporal horizon gradually becoming independent of his own reactions. In Piaget's words, "Time finally overflows the duration inherent in the actual activity; it is applied to things themselves and provides a continuous and systematic link between events in the outside world. In other words, time ceases to be simply the scheme necessary to any action, binding the subject to the object, and becomes the simple background embracing both the subject and the object."[3] As the child learns to speak, there ensues an extension and articulation of the temporal perspective. Take the words of a child of two years and one month, quoted by Decroly and Degand in 1913: "Milk, gone, Mariette," which meant, "I have drunk my milk and now I am going to see Mariette"; these simple words disclose the double perspective, past and future, of the present.

A child does not escape from the domination of reflex reactions, elicited by stimuli, simply by training or through intellectual construction. "The temporal horizon of a child develops at the same time as the unity of his personality."[4] The child must learn to inhibit immediate reactions, especially emotional reactions, in order to take into account the past and future. Emotion tends to enclose us in the present. The emotional stability acquired through the integration of the self permits actions on a broader time scale with reference either to the past or the future.

A child soon learns to envisage temporal series and to act accordingly. A child who reaches for his bottle or his mother's arm is recreating a temporal series which refers at the same time to a past and a future. These early temporal series enrich present experience, but do not create a clear distinction between past and future. The language of a child illustrates this: until the age of three, a child speaks only in the present. If a child says, "Mommy gone," he means that Mommy is not there; essentially he is expressing a present situation, albeit with a reference to the past.

By memory we keep present—or better, can make become present again—what has passed away. Only a small proportion of our past experiences is transformed into memories. Memory is not, in Piaget's words, "the integral and passive recording which many authors have thought it to be, as if it were only necessary to consult the register of one's memories and one would find the pages in the correct order together with a table of contents corresponding in advance to every possible classification." A child's memory confirms this: three or four years old, he places all his memories in a single moment called *yesterday*. According to Piaget, "When a child of between two and four years old wants to retell the story of a walk, a visit to some friends, or his adventures on a journey, a multitude of 'juxtaposed' details tumble forth incoherently; each one is associated with others in couples or little successions,..."5 but overall order is lacking. It is not only words which fail the children; at this age they are unable to arrange in order a series of pictures which form a story. Even adults have difficulty in reproducing the order of memories which do not constitute a natural or logical series.

It is generally agreed that memory is a construction. In our memory every event, every action, is associated with the circumstances which may have accompanied it, or were related to it. It is through the complex of associations that we are often able to remember precisely this particular event or action. These associations are particularly significant in memory when part of a conceptual framework. For instance, the most easily reconstituted associations are those corresponding to a causal relationship. Piaget has stressed the influence of the experience of causal relationship on the development of temporal series. The temporal horizon of man, as individual, group, and species, is constituted by the organization of memories. The importance of experiential and conceptual construction in the constitution of the temporal horizon is evidenced by the fact that the temporal horizon of mental defectives, as of young children, is very limited. Both are unable to assemble their memories to form a past, or to anticipate the future; as often noted, they are captives of the present. In extreme cases of mental deficiency the temporal horizon of the past does not exceed about ten days, this being the maximum duration ascribed to a past event; beyond this, everything is in the same shadow, for mental defectives are unable to order their memories.

While the causal aspects of the cause-effect relationship play an important role in the associational reconstitution of the past, the effect aspect of the cause-effect relationship plays a significant role in the foundation of the future. For a child, through conditioning, a relationship is established between the impulse and the action which brings satisfaction. Experiencing the effect, the child becomes capable of organizing his behavior in accordance with a succession. By observing a signal or taking an action, he anticipates on the basis of past experience what he will do, or what will happen in a moment.

A consciousness of duration is a prerequisite for the estimation of time. For young children the meaning of duration lies in the interval between the awakening of a desire and its gratification. The consciousness of duration appears around the age of three or four, when the child is becoming able to defer gratification or to make a sustained effort to attain some purpose. At age five, the earliest age when a child can be tested on time estimation, durations are estimated sometimes by the work accomplished and sometimes by the changes perceived. However, at this age his impressions are not adequate to measure time in units. Hence his results are often quite incorrect. A five-year-old child is incapable of forming the representation of a duration independent of its content. Measurement requires a unit, a uniform unit serving as a reference; this uniformity is a construction, achieved by abstraction.

Two successive stages now ensue in the development of a child's consciousness of time. First, his intuitions of order and duration become more and more independent of his immediate concrete experience as a result of the development of the corresponding representations. Second, the child develops the ability to relate information concerning order and duration through reversible constructions, or through operations.

At age seven to eight according to Piaget, the child becomes capable of passing from one intuition to the other in a reversible construction, implying a grasp of the relationship between the serial order of events and their duration. In Piaget's words, "Although children see the relationships of succession and those of duration at the beginning of the stage of heterogeneous intuitions, without being aware of their necessary relationship with each other, these end by determining each other in a single comprehensive system which is at the same time differentiated and entirely coherent."[6] Thus the child can relate independent series of changes and understand their temporal relationships as successions of events and intervals of duration, without being misled by the nature of the changes themselves. At this stage the child is able to measure time, by observing the coincidence of the beginning and the end of an interval with those of another interval taken as a unit. This ability of a seven- or eight-year-old child to measure time as acquired through concrete operations does not mean that a child at this age conceptually understands what time, as measured by the clock, represents.

A child of seven or eight who relates experienced changes to one another and establishes coseriations does not yet realize that time is a relationship distinct from, and in a sense independent of, change. This level of abstraction is only slowly attained. Research by the French psychologist Michaud on children between the ages of ten to fifteen shows the gradual development through these years of the number of children able to reach this level of abstraction. Only at fifteen do sixty percent of the children understand that clock time is a convention with no effect on the course of change and that this time is independent of human action. Only at adolescence, the age of logical operations in Piaget's view, is the child able to pass from the homogeneity of clock time to the abstract homogeneity of a duration as the thread linking events without being dependent on them.

Thus we learn that the development of the intelligence and the operational level reached at each age determine the individual's apprehension and comprehension of time. High correlations have been found between general intelligence tests and tests relating to temporal orientation. A study by Gothberg on the mentally defective child's understanding of time has shown a correlation between results of a questionnaire concerning various concepts of time and the mental age as .84, but only .31 between it and the chronological age (with the mental age held constant).

Fraisse sets forth certain differences between his and Piaget's views. Both men agree that at the beginning a child's intuition of time is relative to its content; there is no apprehension of duration on its own. A young child can judge duration either by the work accomplished or by changes subjectively felt. According to Piaget, at a later stage, that of *articulate intuition*, the child becomes capable of an introspective estimation of the duration *during* the action itself; through introspection, an inverse relationship is disclosed between the speed of the action and its duration. Fraisse believes that estimations based on introspective information are also found during the first stage, and hence are not characteristic of the second stage. Fraisse believes that in the second stage intuition is gradually transformed into more and more abstract representation; the order of an event is ascertained by a construction corresponding increasingly to reality. Representation of duration becomes increasingly independent of its content. A progressive differentiation takes place between the intuitions of distance, speed, and duration and these three factors can thus gradually be related to one another. When the child can relate order and duration he achieves a conceptual comprehension of time.

Fraisse agrees with Piaget that in the final state "operational time is reached when the order of successions can be deduced from the interrelation of the durations, and vice versa." However, he thinks that "the *representation* of time exists independently and is apparent before the operational stage."[7]

As the foregoing discussion has shown, in the development of the consciousness of time there are two main experiences, each with various aspects: *succession* and *duration*. As experiences, both of these belong to the present. The experience of succession is characterized by the evanescence of all our perceptions. At an age when we distinguish between our perception and its object, our experience is that of perpetual change of our sensations, emotions, and thoughts. The principal characteristic of this experience of succession is irreversibility: we cannot return to the precise experience which has been succeeded. Thanks to memory, however, through this experience of succession temporal perspectives are developed, composed of memory of past presents and of anticipation of future presents.

The experience of duration is the experience of an interval. "It already exists in the perception of a succession in which the interval between successive stimuli is as much a reality as their order and number."[8] At an early stage of development, we become most conscious of duration by the resistance encountered to realization of our wishes. Later duration is also experienced by the distance and quantity of our memories.

Neither the experience of succession nor the experience of duration constitutes an *experience of time*. However, they combine in one symbolic image: that of a space in which all events are located, with their multiplicity and varying degrees of proximity. Temporal perspectives arising from experiences can be the object of the representation only when events are placed side by side. This spontaneous translation of the temporal to the spatial is natural, since temporal order often coincides with spatial order and distances correspond to durations of movement. When walking in the Swiss mountains, if you ask a peasant, "Is the next village far?" he is more likely to answer "an hour" than "four or five kilometers."

As Bergson has insisted, this image of spatialized time does not, however, correspond to any immediate experience. It provides a practical means of representing or making present past or future events with their twofold aspects, of order and duration. Through this imagery the order of events, or changes, is grasped in thought, not merely in experience; through thought, time becomes reversible and we can pass from a later to an earlier event as well as vice versa. Thus time becomes a uniform and continuous background, a conception in which time is assimilated to a Euclidean space in which everything remains. The representation of time by a continuum in one dimension is not adequate when we have to relate heterogeneous series of events to each other. In this case we have to construct time and locate events in relation to each other, although there is no causal order. This construction of time leads to a single and comprehensive conceptual framework which constitutes the temporal universe.

This concept of time is not the result of a simple abstraction derived from many experiences for temporal experiences are heterogeneous. Also it is clear that time is not a simple idea. Time arises from the activity of the self seeking to reconstruct the events and changes in which it takes part. From a psychological standpoint, with the concept of time and the conceptual consciousness of time, the self, or man, achieves "the most complete adaptation to the successions which form the thread of his existence."[9]

Chapter 2
Succession and Duration

Bergson noted that the perception of succession implies the simultaneous, not successive, perception of *before* and *after*. He thought that it would be a contradiction to suppose a succession which is nothing but succession but which nevertheless takes place in a single moment. This contradiction posed no problem for Bergson, however, because he believed we project time into space, make the end of the first element of the succession coincide with the beginning of the second. But is really a contradiction involved in the simultaneous perception of *before* and *after*? The answer hinges on the nature of the "single moment." If the "single moment" were an instantaneous point, there might be a contradiction. The instantaneous point, however, is a mathematical abstraction, with scant relation to human perception.

Psychologists have shown that we can perceive succession. If the clock strikes four and if you pay attention to the clock, you will perceive the succession of four sounds; in other words, the first sound will still be present in some way when the fourth takes place. As Fraisse avowed, "The perception of a stimulus, however brief, is an action which itself has a certain duration and, as it were, creates a bridge between physically successive stimuli."[10] If the frequency of successive stimuli is high, the individual elements are indistinct; if it is lower, we will perceive a succession of separate elements. The phenomenon called "subjective patterning" throws light on the perception of succession. For example, if we attend to a succession of identical sounds at regular intervals, they will seem to us grouped in twos and threes; to our perception they become successive groups, rather than individual sounds. Through this grouping several elements apprehended simultaneously thus form a unit of perception. This may affect behavior. Listening to jazz, bodily movements are often synchronized to the sounds as they occur periodically; the subjective patterning is revealed by the rhythmic variations in the movements.

To understand the perception of succession, it must be realized that the order of succession is *perceived*. This order is not imposed by the mind on stimuli independent of each other. When a clock makes a "tick-tock" sound, we hear the "tick" and the "tock" directly in that order. For order to be perceived, the successive stimuli must be of the same nature; with a succession of sounds and lights there can be no perception of an organization integrating the two, rather a double series will be perceived, one of sounds and one of lights. The order of succession is inherent in the stimuli and cannot be derived from other means, such as memory. As Fraisse states, "The order is given in the actual organization of succession. One condition is necessary, however; the organization must be *spontaneous* and this happens only if the stimuli are homogeneous and all take place within certain temporal limits." We will discuss these limits later.

At the time that we perceive succession as an ordered multiplicity of elements, we also perceive the intervals separating the individual elements. These intervals are durations. "Duration is, as it were, the measure of succession, the value of the interval."[11] Duration is not perceived independently, but only as a factor of organization of an ordered multiplicity.

There is a distinction to be made between the interval duration of the perception of succession and the individual duration between successive perceptions. Consider the "tick-tock" of a clock. The "tick" and the "tock," organized together, constitute an interval which has a duration. The interval between the "tock" and the "tick" of the next double sound is different; it is perceived as a gap of uncertain duration. Confirming this distinction, psychological tests have shown that persons listening to rhythmic structures repeated identically will be able to reproduce the intervals of the structure accurately, but they cannot grasp with similar accuracy the duration of the interval between the rhythmic groups. Also, other experiments with auditory structures have shown the functional difference between intervals within an organization and those separating one organized group from another. If the duration of an interval within a rhythmic group is changed, the character of the whole unit is altered. However, if the duration of the interval between rhythmic groups is changed, the latter are not altered. From the point of view of perception, the interval between them is non-existent—it is just a gap.

There are temporal limits to the perception of duration. In the case of a sound, for example, the end must follow the beginning within 1.5 to 2 seconds, if we are to perceive its duration. If a sound continues longer, we are not able to organize succession and if it continues indefinitely we will perceive no change. "The noise of a stream has no more perceived duration than the light of day."[12]

It has been generally recognized that rhythm is important in our perception of succession and duration. According to Bachelard, "The phenomena of duration are constructed with rhythms; but the rhythms are by no means necessarily founded on a uniform and regular temporal basis." Fraisse interprets these words to mean that "the perception of duration is that of the duration of an organization."[13] Bergson believed that we could apprehend pure duration as the form "which succession of our conscious states assumes when our ego lets itself *live*, when it refrains from separating its present state from its former state."[14] Contrary to Bergson, Bachelard asserted that there is never at any level continuity of duration, but always an alternation of fullness and emptiness, of action and rest. Bergson, however, recognized the importance of the basic elements of consciousness. "It is possible to conceive succession without distinction, as a mutual penetration, a solidarity, an intimate organization of elements, of which one is representative of the whole and is only distinguished or isolated from it for a mind capable of abstraction."[15] In this context Bergson also refers to rhythm, as the *quality* exhibited by a quantity through organization of the whole.

In a different context Wundt believed that sensations of time were linked with rhythms, first with the rhythm of walking, to which vocal and auditory rhythms are later associated. Mach also derived the existence of a *time sense* from rhythm. He thought that a real sense of time analogous to the other five senses might exist. According to him, if we recognize the same rhythm in two different melodies, we perceive a scheme of duration independent of their base in sensation, and this can be done by perceiving these durations in themselves, through a sense of time.

The fact that for so many authors rhythm is important in the interpretation of our "perception of time" is hardly a casual matter. May it not be that the primordial rhythm of reflexivity intrinsic to temporality, to time, is emerging here at a different level, at the level of psychological interpretation and understanding? We shall come to the primordial rhythm of reflexivity in the final chapter of Part II.

Psychological tests in the late 19th century by Wundt and his pupils showed that an interval of around 0.75 seconds was the one most accurately estimated. Shorter intervals were overestimated and longer ones underestimated. Considering phenomena with the same duration, he came to the hypothesis: "Surprisingly enough, this interval is almost the same as that taken for the swing of our leg when we are walking quickly. It seems not unlikely that this psychic constant for the mean duration of reproduction and the most accurate estimation of intervals has developed under the influence of body movements, which are the movements most frequently exercised, and which have determined the tendency we have to organize and give rhythmic arrangement to large spaces of time." Guyau affirmed the same view: "Even today we still adapt the speed of our representations to the rhythm of walking and it is a natural tendency to adapt the pace of time to the pace of our thoughts and our steps."[16] Many other tests have confirmed the significance of 0.75 seconds as a psychic constant. There is presumably a neurophysiological basis for this psychic constant, which represents an optimum rhythm for successive associations in the nervous system.

It is notable that both Bergson and Husserl in their phenomenological discussion of temporal experience use examples of sound, tune, rhythm, and melody. This reflects not chance nor arbitrary choice, but rather a basic difference in the way our sense organs may perceive change. To be accurate, the temporal characteristics of our sensations must be similar to those of the corresponding stimuli: the receptors must have little or no inertia. The organs of smell and taste have a high degree of inertia; thus the beginning and end of the stimuli are uncertain, and the corresponding sensations of indeterminate durations. The retinal receptors also have considerable inertia. Sensations are slow to become established and they linger. If successive stimuli follow rapidly, they merge; if the frequency is slightly lower, it causes flicker. However, the receptors of hearing and touch have practically no inertia. In comparison with hearing, the scope of touch is limited, because it provides us information only concerning changes perceived through bodily contact. Thus hearing is the main sense modality in the perception of change and time. It is considered the "time sense" as sight is that of space. "Hearing only locates stimuli very vaguely in space, but it locates them with admirable precision in time. It is par excellence the sense which appreciates time, succession, rhythm, and tempo."[17]

It has been claimed that the physical referents of vision are objects, and the physical referents of hearing are events. An experiment varying light and noise showed that variation in auditory stimuli had an effect on reproductive time estimation. Small time intervals were first presented in conditions of quiet and subsequently in conditions of noise; they were longer in this sequence than when noise preceded quiet. Variations in light, however, had no effect on the reproductive estimates.

The role of hearing in the perception of time is certainly enhanced by vocal utterance, by speech. The psychologist Bourdon believed that for himself durations were apprehended not so much by sensations of hearing or any other kind but by "vocal imagery" which provided a scale against which to measure other durations. Whether this is a general phenomenon or not is uncertain. However, the sounds of speech do certainly enable us to order our successive sensations. We are able to accompany these sensations by a succession of sounds which we *produce*. In this way we can order the sensations and their duration even if they are not spontaneously organized. For instance, in psychological tests persons comparing two durations defined by the sequence sound-light-sound tend to synchronize with this a sequence of vocal sounds, such as "boom-boom-boom," thus creating a uniform unit of perception. Furthermore, the sounds of speech have a temporal order, and this order is essential to the meaning. There is a curious phenomenon, which is quite common, called metathesis, the exchange of the temporal position of speech sounds in words or phrases. This occurs in normal language development, but also as a clinical symptom in abnormal cases, such as childhood brain damage and adult dysphasia. The cause is not an inability to pronounce the sound, since they are correctly reproduced, but rearranged in temporal order. The temporal order of the sounds of speech is separate from the sounds themselves; it is imposed upon the sounds by the self in its effort to communicate, a complex process with lapses of many kinds doubtless derived from many causes.

Chapter 3
The Perceived Present

Through the perception of succession and the perception of duration, the existence of the present is established. In the past hundred
years, the present has been described by many different terms: the
"specious present" by Clay in 1882, the "sensible present" by William James in 1891, the "psychic present" by Stern 1897, the "mental
present" by Pieron 1923, the "actually present" by Koffka 1935, and
the "perceived present" by Fraisse 1963.

No one has expressed the nature of the present better than William
James in the following passage from his *Psychology, Briefer Course*,
1892: "The only fact of our immediate experience is what has been
called the 'specious present,' a sort of saddle-back of time with a
certain length of its own on which we sit perched and from which
we look in two directions into time. The unit of composition of our
perception of time is a *duration*, with a bow and stern as it were—a
rearward- and a forward-looking end. It is only as parts of this
duration-block that the relation of *succession* of one end to the other
is perceived. We do not feel first one and then the other after it and
from the perception of the succession infer an interval of time
between, but we seem to feel the interval of time as a whole, with its
two ends embedded in it.... The moment we pass beyond a very few
seconds our consciousness of duration ceases to be an immediate
perception and becomes a construction more or less symbolic."[18]
The image of time flowing like a stream has been used since time

99

immemorial. Pieron in 1923 used this image in connection with the present as follows: "There exists a *durable present*...in which we apprehend a succession of diverse facts in a single mental process which embraces, in the present, a certain interval of time, just as you can hold a certain amount of water in the hollow of your hand as it runs down from a spring; the water is renewed but the quantity is limited and can never increase."[19]

Pieron's picturesque imagery does point to an apparent paradox in the perception of time. There is a discreteness about time, separate limited units of the present, together with a continuous flow of time. The discreteness/continuity of time is analogous to the particle/wave phenomena of quantum physics. As we have seen in Part I, some phenomena of quantum mechanics are explicable only by interpreting the basic material elements as particles, while others are explicable only by interpreting the basic elements as waves. The two interpretations are adjudged to be complementary. Similarly, the discreteness aspect and the continuity aspect of time we may have to understand as complementary, or better *conjoint*.

If we can reproduce several elements of perception after having seen or heard them, we can do this not by eliciting them from memory but by the capability of our perceptual span which is able to grasp several simultaneous or successive elements in one unit. This *perceptual span* is sometimes called *immediate memory*, thus indicating the possibility of immediate unitary reproduction. Immediate memory is, however, basically different from memory in as much as it does not imply the existence of a past in relation to the present. In Delacroix's words, "It is certain on the one hand that the different aspects of the present are not all on the same plane, as otherwise the present would seem static, and on the other hand that the present does not contain a unique element which has the nature of the present, all the rest being pure memory."[20]

Both the duration of the perceived present and the richness of its content are primarily determined by the direction of our attention, which organizes successive elements into one unit. Bergson noted that "attention is something which can be lengthened or shortened like the distance between the two points of a pair of compasses."[21] However, the pair of compasses cannot be opened indefinitely. The field of attention reducible to a single sensation has an upper limit. The factors on which this upper limit depends have been analyzed by Fraisse under the following headings: (1) the temporal interval between stimuli; (2) the number of stimuli; (3) their organization. These three factors are interdependent.

(1) *The Interval between Stimuli.* If the interval between two stimuli is too long, the first is past when the second is present. In the case of sounds, this limit can be determined by slowing down the succession of sounds in a rhythm until the rhythm disappears and nothing remains but a succession of independent sounds. Experiments have shown that the rhythm disappears when the interval between the sounds is about two seconds. Thus, two seconds would represent a limit for any unitary organization of two successive stimuli. Within this limit there is an optimum interval of succession estimated by Wundt at between 0.3 and 0.5 seconds.

(2) *The Number of Stimuli.* Experiments have shown that our capacity to perceive succession is limited to five or six elements. Children of four to six years old who are unable to count can reproduce a series of five or six chimes of a clock without making mistakes. Adults cannot do much better. When the clock strikes midnight we all have to count. This limit of perceptual span has operated implicitly in the invention of human means of communication: no signal in the Morse code contains more than five elements; the Braille alphabet uses combinations of one to six dots.

In an experiment by the Fraisses, the average number of sounds apprehended, checked by immediate reproduction in the form of tapping, varied as shown in the following table:

Interval between Sounds	.17 sec.	.37 sec.	.63 sec.	1.2 sec.	1.8 sec.
Number of Sounds Apprehended	5.7	5.7	5.4	4.0	3.3

"The total duration of the series apprehended, counted from the first sound to the last, is 0.8 seconds for an interval of 0.17 seconds and 4.2 seconds for an interval of 1.8 seconds." Thus, "the duration of the perceived present varied more than the number of elements perceived; this shows clearly that the present does not simply correspond to a temporal field which is independent of its contents."[22]

(3) *Organization of the Stimuli.* "It is a known fact that far more elements may be perceived in space if they form a spatial configuration or a unit of significance. The same is true for time. If identical sounds are grouped, for instance in twos, threes, fours, or fives, we can perceive four or five groups of these sounds without counting...

in the most favorable case, a total of twenty to twenty-five sounds can be perceived."[23] To achieve this result, the speed of succession must facilitate the grouping. In the foregoing experiment, an interval of 0.18 seconds was used between sounds and 0.36 seconds between groups, with maximum duration thus not exceeding 6 seconds.

As might be expected, there is an increase in perceptual span as children grow older. At three years of age, a child normally can reproduce a series of three numbers; at seven, five numbers; at ten, six numbers. Apprehension is obviously improved if a unity of meaning is discerned in the organization of the elements. Thus an average adult is able to apprehend and repeat without error a sentence of twenty to twenty-five syllables. It takes about five seconds to pronounce such a sentence. And five seconds is the approximate upper limit for the duration of the present; in special cases, it may be possible to attain a longer present—twelve seconds is the maximum claimed—but most often our present consists of only two or three seconds.

The incredible sensitivity of the human organization is illustrated by the fact that the lower limit of the time span of awareness is miniscule. Tests using continuous lights have reached a figure of 0.12 seconds, with continuous sounds 0.01 to 0.05 seconds; even smaller limits are reached for the time where successive stimuli apparently fused to a whole unit for sounds, 0.02 to 0.06 seconds, for touch 0.027 seconds, for light 0.043 seconds. The latter is the interval between successive lights at which flicker ceases to be perceptible; this is called the critical flicker-fusion interval. Where the successive stimuli are to different senses, the lower limit increases.

The perceived present is a psychological unit of time. What is the physiological basis or counterpart of this psychological unit? Is there a physiological unit of time? The present state of knowledge in neurophysiology does not provide us answers to these questions.

It has long been conjectured that rhythmic processes might be the basis for human time perception. Mach in 1885 suggested that "the perception of time is closely related to processes repeating themselves in a periodic or rhythmic manner."[24] James in 1890 and Wundt in 1911 are also said to have supported the concept of periodic processes as the basis for time perception. Thus psychologists have expressed a view corresponding to Einstein's (see p. 22), namely that periodic occurrences is psychologically as well as conceptually prior to time. Recent psychological tests seem to confirm a rhythmical organization in time perception. An article by Ernst Poeppel entitled "Oscillations as Possible Basis for Time Perception" sets forth the evidence. Poeppel states his conclusion as follows: "...the temporal continuum is subjectively quantitized into discrete units, which successively follow each other. The duration of these units is indicated by the grouping effects in subjective random series and is found to be roughly between four and seven seconds. It is thus approximately equivalent to earlier estimates of the conscious present. The quantization can formally be described as an oscillation. The duration of a 'quantum-period' seems to be influenced by several physiological conditions. The dependence on time of day has been discussed here. However, the physiological mechanism underlying this oscillatory process is unknown. A psychological influence on the length of the quantum-period can be assumed since informational cues have been shown to affect the temporal constant. Individual differences can also be considerable."[25]

We recognize that the time we experience is presented in discrete units—buds of experience—but this is only one aspect of time. Time also has a continuity, though it may not have the continuity of a mathematical continuum. Nevertheless it has a continuity, which is clearly evident in the nature of the experienced present, the "saddle-back" of James, looking out in two directions. In one direction memory is a prime factor, and as Delacroix wrote, "Memories are born in the very midst of perception."[26] In the other direction anticipation is a prime factor of the continuity. Anticipation may in some sense reside in every living organism. In humans anticipation becomes the purposive look to the future; Minkowski wrote, "Our life is essentially oriented towards the future."[27] However that may be, the continuity of time rests on the sequential interrelatedness of the units of temporal existence; these units are not external to one another. In fact, the continuity is as truly experienced as is the discrete unit.

It has been suggested that there may be a physiological rhythm which underlies the units of temporal perception. If so, the continuity of time in a bare structural sense may rest on the repetition of the rhythm which creates the temporal unit. But this gives mere structure. Is it not mind which discerns meaning, and through meaning overcomes whatever paradox there is between the discreteness and continuity of time? Fraisse writes: "...one unit of perception succeeds another. Between them there is a slight lapse, a pause that we do not even notice; in speech its presence is marked by punctuation. But discontinuity in perception is disguised by the continuity afforded by the emotional quality of events and their unity of significance. Each unit perceived takes its place in a stream in which the durability of our attitude and our memory are the factors which determine continuity. The part played by meaning is obvious in the case of language, whether poetry or prose; in music the discontinuity of the rhythms is scarcely noticed, for each unit is part of a musical flow which gives unity to the whole."[28]

Chapter 4
Individual and Social Aspects of the Experience of Time

How does the individual experience time? Let us consider a few of the many aspects to this question.

Although it may seem comical to begin with boredom, nevertheless the feeling of boredom appears to represent the simplest and clearest experience of time. Lavelle wrote, "In its purest form the consciousness of time is boredom; that is, the consciousness of an interval which nothing crosses and which nothing can fill." The German word for boredom, *Langeweile*, etymologically means *a long time*. According to Bachelard, "We only find *length* in time when we find it *too long*."[29] An eloquent expression of the phenomena of boredom in the life of the World War I soldier is set down in a paragraph in Minkowski's *Lived Time*, which I am citing in full:

The monotonous life in the trenches sometimes made us forget the date and the day of the week. Under these conditions, cut off from the continuity and usual routines of life, these facts were after all of no immediate interest to us. We substituted another 'calendar' for them, more appropriate to the situation: we simply counted the days that had passed since we came to the front and those which separated us from our return to the rest camp. Sometimes we were disoriented in time in the usual sense of the word. But we would have protested if someone had told us that we were beings 'without time.' On the contrary, all our suffering, outside the devastations shown by death, came from time. We succumbed to the tedium and the monotony of

the succession of days and we fought boredom—obviously an essentially temporal phenomena—to reduce it to nothing. Didn't we say,
during the war, that it was not just the enemy we had to face, but
boredom as well?[30]

A friend observed the other day, "Our life consists more of waiting than of anything else." Not all waiting is endless, like *Waiting for
Godot*. Waiting is not easy even for adults; for a young child waiting
may be so difficult that it gives way to impatience or tantrums; only
as a child develops emotional self-control does he learn to endure
waiting. Waiting occurs most poignantly in the context of expectations or anticipation. While learning to endure waiting, we become
conscious of the interval which separates us now from the expected
event. Hence it has been observed that our consciousness of duration is most manifest in expectation. Indeed some writers have
regarded this as the original experience of time; for instance, Guyau
wrote: Time is "fundamentally nothing but the conscious interval
between a need and its fulfillment."[31] Even when we are awaiting an
unpleasant occurrence—sitting in the dentist's chair before a tooth
extraction—the time does not appear short, it seems longer to us
because our attention is focused on it and thus every moment is
expanded in its felt length. "In cases of waiting, therefore, an immediate feeling of time being too short is never found."[32]
   The normal activity of a living being works into, or tends toward,
the future. As Minkowski pointed out, in expectation the future
comes toward us and we wait for that expected future to become
present. He finds primary expectation "always connected to an
intense anguish. It is always anxious expectation."[33] This is not
surprising since expectation involves a suspension of activity, which
is so essential to life itself. Of course, there can be expectation of
happy events, but even these are tinged with the anxious uncertainty
that they may not be fulfilled. Anxiety is one of the most significant
human emotions. In a scale of emotion, it is at the center between
positive emotions, such as confidence and hope, and negative emotions, such as despondency and despair. Also it is intrinsically ambi-
valent, in as much as it involves a felt time-perspective with respect
to the future. There is an intrinsic uncertainty about the future which
is reflected in an uncertainty of the self anxiously viewing the future
with conflicting emotions, hopes and fears.
   The ambivalence of anxiety becomes clear in its effects, which
seem to be dependent on the degree of anxiety. A moderate degree
of anxiety usually is a creative force; it motivates our efforts to bring

anticipation of, and hopes for, the future to bear on present actions so that they will improve prospects for the desired outcome in the future. The scope of temporal integration of the self is expanded when under the influence of a moderate anxiety a person seeks ways to realize the envisaged future. On the other hand, an excessive anxiety which becomes intolerable can have a drastic negative effect, resulting in a dissolution of temporal integration, with images of the future losing connection with the present and hence their efficacy with respect to present action. In such cases a person may become confined to the present moment. For instance, it has been noted that the psychopathic criminal "is a man for whom the moment is a segment of time detached from all others. His actions are unplanned and guided by his whims." H. Cleckley observed that one of the most basic characteristics of the psychopathic criminal is his "relative freedom from anxiety and apprehension."[34] Psychological tests have shown that psychopaths score significantly lower on measures of manifest anxiety than other prison inmates.

There are many creatures other than psychopathic criminals who live primarily in the present. In 1925 the French psychologist Paul-han coined the word "presentism" to characterize the phenomenon of those who lived in, and experience, only the present. The "presentists" seem to lack the capability of thinking beyond the present instant. There are, of course, many types of, and many causes for, presentism. Most animals seem to live primarily in the present, as do babies and certain types of mentally deficient people who lack a temporal perspective in their existence. "They see no further than enjoyment of the present; the rest is more or less outside the bounds of their appreciation." According to Minkowski, manics have contact with present reality, "but it is only an instantaneous contact" without a temporal horizon. These people are very sensitive to the external world: "An object on which their glance falls, an inscription, an incidental noise, a word which happens to ring in their ears are embraced one after the other in their speech...they express their perceptions in words and find themselves carried along, without purpose, by the stimulus thus created."[35] They are, as it were, playthings of the immediate present which is ever changing from moment to moment.

"Presentism" also occurs in many old people in a form of non-demential senility. Many old people give little thought to the future and have great difficulty putting together recollections of the past. Courbon relates an extreme case of an eighty-year-old woman, coming to the conclusion: "Such a complete detachment from the past and the future, from people and things, combined with the preservation of the ability to adapt to the present, is perhaps only the normal end of human mentality, when the organism, spared from sickness, submits to the physiological exhaustion of age." He also noted, "This incapacity for anticipation and this imperfection in her retrospection cause her not to care. This is not indifference but serenity."[36] This serenity, he also relates to a phenomenon so well known, "the serenity before death."[37]

Dire pressure from external circumstances can also cause people to live only in the present. Concentration camp inmates in Nazi Germany, having adjusted to the agony and hopelessness of their situation, have been described as follows: "The prisoners lived, like children, only in the immediate present; they lost the feeling for the sequence of time; they became unable to plan for the future or to give up immediate pleasure satisfactions to gain greater ones in the near future."[38] The same phenomenon occurred among persons deported, or affected by racial persecution, during the war: "Driven from place to place, oppressed, threatened, terrorized, often faced with an apparently closed and hopeless future, these subjects finally got into the habit of not thinking of the future and also of stifling all memories of their past lives. *They now live only in the present* and they have destroyed the continuity of the past into the future. This fixation in the present of their entire psychological orientation has far-reaching consequences. It destroys the impression of the purpose and finality of the personality and also the concept of the very value of this personality."[39]

We are all familiar with the strange temporal disorder and illusion of dreams. In dreams, there is no chronology, or what there is, is chaotic; the temporal horizon is disordered; memories have little relation to reality, and they are interspersed with imaginative fantasies. Dreams of apparently long duration with many complex events may take place actually in a matter of a few seconds or minutes. This phenomena has been related to the accounts given by people revived after nearly drowning. During the few moments of unconsciousness they had relived long periods of their lives and, after being revived, they believed that the time of their unconsciousness was much longer than it actually was. In Freudian theory, dreams are a product of the unconscious system. The temporal disorder of dreams is related to Freud's theory of the intemporality of the unconscious: "The processes of the Unconscious system are *intemporal*, that is they are not ordered in time, they are not modified by the passing of time, in fact they bear no relation to time. Relation to time is linked to the workings of the conscious system.... The sense of reality and the sense of time are both apparent in the system of Perception-Consciousness alone. The unconscious knows nothing of them..."[40] This confirms what we have already stated several times, that time is a construction of mind, a construction of the self in its adjustment to the ambient becoming of the world in which it finds itself.

As we have stated before, Minkowski stressed that "our life is essentially oriented toward the future." In his discussion he points out that desire and hope take us out of the immediate and enlarge the perspective of the future before us. This perspective comes from the fact that desire and hope are intrinsic to the nature and being of the self. We know how to desire and to hope. Both have positive value— "Desire and hope are sweet."[41] As Bergson wrote, "What makes hope such an intense pleasure is that the future which we dispose of at will appears to us at the same time in a multitude of forms, all attractive and all possible. Even if the most desirable among them were to be realized, we would have to lose the others, and we shall have lost a great deal. The idea of the future is full of an infinite number of possibilities and is thus more fruitful than the future itself, and this is why we find more charm in hope than in possession, more in dreams than in reality."[42] Minkowski points out further that in hope the self lives becoming in the same direction as in expectation, i.e., in the direction of the future coming to the present and not in the direction of the present going to the future. However hope extends further into the future than expectation, which is usually related to the more immediate future. Moreover, "hope liberates us from anxious expectation."[43] However, there can be a negative effect to the orientation of the self to the future, if an excessive preoccupation with future anticipation were to disrupt the normal link with present activity. In his *Study of Human Time*, Poulet cites two pertinent instances. Montaigne wrote in his *Essays*: "We are never at home; we are always beyond it. Fear, desire or hope drive us towards the future and deprive us of the feeling and contemplation of what is." Alfred de Vigny said, "I do nothing, as you have guessed, but dream of a few projects for the future;... I have always been so afraid of the present and the real in my life...."[44]

Josiah Royce set forth the view that "the self is a purpose." In lectures at Yale published in 1928 under the title *The Self: Its Body and Freedom*, going beyond Royce, W.E. Hocking affirms that the self "is a system of *purposive behavior emerging from a persistent hope*. The kernel of the self is its hope. All the good one discovers in experience contributes to the color of that hope; and that hope, in turn, becomes the object of all action. *Meaning descends from this single source* upon the details of behavior."[45]

Beyond desire and hope there is a limit to the perspective in the future of the self. This limit is death, the inescapable destination of the individual self, the shadow of intrinsic finitude. According to Hocking, death demonstrates "the most complete and universal assertion of nature's power over man."[46] But is this really so? Can we conceive of man without death? Death may be as essential to man, to the self, as life. A child who experiences the death of a parent, a relative, or a friend may suffer grievously, but he does not normally as a result relate this death to his own self. A youth filled with the overpowering strength of animal vitality is as little likely to relate a death to his own self-feeling. It requires a certain maturity of experience for a human creature to relate death to himself. Some people may never achieve this maturity of experience; others will do it at very different ages. In our present society with its extended life span, this maturity of experience may not be reached until a person is in the fifties or sixties of life. In societies where the work ethic is still prevalent and the preoccupation with work all-absorbing, a man may not apprehend the significance of death until retiring from his work preoccupation.

It has been observed that death causes anxiety in us or, as an escape from this anxiety, a religious attitude. Indeed it has been affirmed that all religion has stemmed from man's consciousness of time, that awareness of time involves awareness of decay and death, of individual mortality, and that mankind has sought in religion security from this hard and certain end. This quest appears in the religions of mankind, all of which are said to be motivated by a desire to overcome the destructive process of time and to achieve individual "security in some post-mortem form."[47]

Fraisse observes that death "never becomes part of our temporal perspective, whatever our age,..."[48] At a certain psychological level of consideration, this may not be erroneous. However, there is a deeper level of understanding of the relation of death to human temporal existence. It is sketched out, in part, in Minkowski's *Lived Time*. We are all familiar with death in the form of the skeleton Father Time with his scythe. "But, on the other hand," Minkowski asks, "what but death could give life the dignity that it has? We have a need of death in order to live."[49] It is only through death that we come in contact in a primitive and intimate way with *a* life. "A life," in his sense, "begins only insofar as it will one day end. Death is a vital phenomenon, while birth is not; birth is only a biological fact...It is not in being born but in dying that one becomes a whole, a man."[50] The Greeks knew the meaning of death in relation to human life. Did not Aristotle affirm that the happiness of the individual, which is his sought-after goal, could not be adjudged until his life had been terminated by death? Minkowski finds that death "bears with it the notion of a life, a notion that reunites, in a single synthetic unity, all that has preceded that death."[51] It is for this reason, I would say, that death is a part of our temporal perspective, a goal that we can look forward to with joy and serenity. As Minkowski states, "A life is achieved not by its works—with those one is never finished—but by death."[52]

We have been considering the individual experience of time, but there is no purely individual experience of time, for man is a social animal, born as a member of a group or groups. These social aspects of human existence permeate all individual experience, and naturally, of course, the experience of time. Born of parents, usually in a family, our first memories of childhood include our parents, and in a sense, the memories of our parents, and these two sets of memories play a role in the development of our temporal perspective. In the rearing of children, the child is taught to adapt the cycle of its activities and desires to the rhythms of the adults. The parents fix the time of getting up, going to bed, meals, playtime, and work. Later school, a job, the neighborhood, the city add their influence and demands.

The importance of social environment in the content of individual memory is observed in the different chronological series of our memory corresponding to the different groups to which an individual belongs. "The time of professional life, family, religious, civil or military life is different and has different origins."[53] The social framework of an individual life affects the experience of time, as does the social environment at any given moment. There is one time in the office, another for the home, and another for the street; also one time for work and another for holidays; a time for weekdays and another for Sunday. This variation, with its alternation of tension and relaxation, is beneficial, aiding the establishment of a rhythm for the individual's life. "We all know the relief brought by a weekly rest, the holidays, those breaks in the infernal rhythm of town life."[54]

The significance of the social group in the constitution of the temporal horizon was brought out clearly by two French anthropologists, Bernot and Blancard, in their study of a small village in Normandy, inhabited by two different social groups, peasants who had been rooted for generations in the same soil and workers in a glass factory recruited from other parts of France. The peasant lives in a longer, deeper past than the factory worker; his recollections go back beyond his personal memories. "This land was bought by his grandfather, this building was constructed by his father."[55] To him every land contour, every pathway, every inhabitant recalls the past. The factory worker was an immigrant, removed from his forefathers; his own memories of his childhood and youth are not related to the new background; as a result, immersed in present circumstances he looked to the future as an unconnected image of a better life, with little awareness of the steps needed to make that image a reality. On the other hand, the peasants with their sense of continuity with the past and with the land of their family, looked to the future as a further extension of that same continuity. Just as he had been provided for by his father and grandfather before him, the peasant tended to plan ahead to provide for his children in turn. To generalize the results of this study, it is very likely that the deeper the ties of an individual with the past, the longer will be his perspective into the future.

The role of the social environment in the form and content of temporal perspectives can be seen particularly clearly in the case of social instability. For example, psychologists interviewed many families which had fled to Bogota after having been victims of the banditry and violence which for many years had taken place in the Columbian countryside. Their attitudes were compared with those of families which had not similarly suffered. The victims of the violence showed a much greater sense of insecurity and pessimism with respect to their personal future; having experienced their social world as threatening and unstable, they showed little tendency to look forward in time. Under conditions of social instability, "a mutilation or destruction of time perspective takes place." On the other hand, a stable social context will have the opposite effect, opening up to the individual the perspective of the future, and encouraging him to believe that present actions may result in fore-seeable future outcomes. Such an orientation toward the future is the "subjective counterpart of a stable social order and of stable social institutions, which not only permit but sanction an orderly progression of expectations with reference to others and to one's self."[56]

If the social aspect is so important in the human experience of time, it is natural to expect considerable cultural variation in this experience. The linear, future-oriented time of modern Western society is a specific construct of rather recent origin; as we have seen, its origin goes back to the late 17th century in Western Europe and the rise of modern science and technology. The temporal perspectives of previous cultures and of primitive societies were different. In Part III we shall be dealing with several cultures in the chapter entitled "Time, History, and Culture"; here we shall outline some variations in primitive societies. However, the process of modernization taking place throughout the world is likely to have the effect of making the linear, future-oriented time the dominant form of temporality eventually in nearly all human societies.

In recent decades ethnographers and anthropologists have given considerable attention to the temporal perspectives in primitive societies—that is, societies with an unwritten language, based on subsistence agriculture, hunting, or fishing, and living with direct experience of the rigors and rhythms of nature. In societies with no written records, the tribal memory rarely goes back more than a few generations so that the narration of past events, history, soon merges into mythology. Writing of the people of the Trobriand Islands, Dorothy Lee said, "History and mythical reality are not 'the past' to the Trobriander. They are forever present, participating in all current being, giving meaning to all his activities and all existence." A student of the 19th century myths of the Pawnee Indians observed that they regarded the past primarily as a "timeless" storehouse of tradition. "Life had a rhythm but not a progression. It was a series of cycles or repetitions."

In primitive societies time is often expressed in relation to recurrent natural events or social activities. Among the Nuer in central Africa, temporal reference is made by "I shall return at milking," or "I shall start off when the calves come home."[57] For the Bahan of Borneo, the year is divided into eight periods according to the agricultural activity: clearing of the brushwood, the felling of trees, the burning of the wood felled, the sowing, the weeding, the harvest, the conclusion of the harvest, and the celebration of the rice year. In Zambia, for the Luvale tribe, the year is divided into twelve periods by changes in the climate and vegetation. These periods are not of equal length. Instead of the week or fortnight, an eleven-day period is used as an interval, hinging on today, with names for four days counting backwards and for six days forward. Within the day, ten distinct stages are found, hinging on noon.

In most primitive societies, the rhythmic alternations of natural phenomena provide the major temporal reference points, but only in connection with significant social activities. Among the Trobriander, as among the Bahan, the "seasons" refer primarily to agricultural activities rather than climatic changes or lunar divisions of time. Periods of the day when no significant changes in collective activities occur are apt to be ignored, while fine distinctions may be made during the early morning or evening hours when different activities follow one another in rapid succession. As Sorokin and Merton observed, "Time here is not continuous—its hiatus is found whenever a specific period is lacking in social interest or importance. The social life of the group is reflected in the time expressions." In these communities, it has been noted, time is discontinuous, with temporal divisions being used to mark social events occurring in predictable succession. It has been suggested that such divisions are apt to be "thought of not as growing out of each other or as following each other progressively, in a continuum, but as standing side by side in isolation."[58] For example, the Balinese calendar system displayed a conception of time as "punctual" rather than durational. "It was a device for classifying discrete self-sufficient 'days,' which appeared and reappeared in endlessly repeated cycles, each a particular manifestation of the fixed order of things." With time apprehended in terms of recurrent events, the future as well as the past becomes a part of the fixed cycle of repetitive occurrences. According to Margaret Mead, "The intensely crowded life of any Manus generation existed between two voids: it was tacitly assumed that the past has always been like this and the future always would be."

Both the environmental and social modes of temporal experience are infused with predictability. According to Evans-Pritchard, "Seasonal and lunar changes repeat themselves year after year, so that a Neur standing at any point of time has conceptual knowledge of what lies before him and can predict and organize his life accordingly. A man's structural future is likewise already fixed and ordered into different periods, so that the total changes in status a boy will undergo in his ordained passage through the social system, if he lives long enough, can be foreseen."[59] Thus an identity exists between the known past and the expected future. Margaret Mead used the term "post-figured" to describe the future in such societies for a child who sees others go through ordered sequences of changes and activity through which he himself will later go. Such a future contrasts, of course, with the perspective in modern and modernizing societies where change is rapid, and where individuals tend to regard the future in terms of possibilities, opportunities, and personal choice.

Cultural variations are also reflected in linguistic variations. In the

Indo-European linguistic tradition, we find tenses, indicating past, present, and future as successive segments of a unitary time. Dorothy Lee comments, "Our language codifies reality in such a way as to predispose us to view events in terms of temporality." Whorf's analysis of the Hopi language found that it contains "no words, grammatical forms, constructions, or expressions that refer directly to what we call 'time,' or to past, present, or future."[60] On the contrary, there are two tenses, one used to designate events directly experienced, including all past occurrences known to the speaker as well as all present activities and their inherent future extensions; the other referring to mythological events as well as the speaker's thoughts, dreams, and emotions. In his comparison of Hopi and English, Whorf notes that in Hopi the days are not added up, e.g., ten days; they are referred in their order, e.g., the tenth day. "It is as if different days were thought of as reappearances of the same entity rather than as completely separate and distinct slices of time."[61] With time viewed in this way, "preparations" are regarded as important, for what is done at one time might have an influence on "reappearances" of the same time. To the question whether modern society would be possible if we spoke only the Hopi language, Whorf answered: "Whether such a civilization as ours would be possible with a widely different linguistic handling of time is a large question—in our civilization, our linguistic patterns and the fitting of our behavior to the temporal order are what they are and they are in accord."[62]

Chapter 5
The Subjective Experience, Self-Awareness, of Animals

Have you ever had a fight with a drake? I have, with a Muscovy drake, known to be a mean creature. The circumstances were as follows:

My wife had planted expensive grass seed on the slopes south of our new home. We had at the time three Muscovy ducks, one female and two drakes. One drake was the dominant one, accustomed aggressively to advance on, and nip at, all humans who chanced to be near him. He made no distinction between family and strangers. He could be fearsome to other animals; I have seen a big dog who attempted playfully to approach him cower with fear when the drake spread its three-foot span of wings and flew flapping at the dog's head.

As caviar for Muscovites, grass seed is a great delicacy for Muscovy ducks. My wife had tried repeatedly to drive the three ducks from the area where the grass seed had been sown, to no avail. The ducks would depart, but shortly thereafter would return. One sunny day, seeing the ducks from our breakfast nook above, I decided to try my hand at chasing them away from the seeded area. Waving a towel, I had no trouble driving the three ducks up the slope. Having gone back upstairs, I noted several minutes later that the mean drake had returned alone to the grass seed. Annoyed by this effron-

116

tery, I returned now with the *Alpenstock*, my Swiss mountain-climbing cane, which I normally carried to prevent the drake from nipping me. The drake was not inclined to respond to my gestures and shouts by departing. He stood his ground. I swung the cane in front of him and may have tapped it on his beak. The drake became visibly angry; his emotion was clearly expressed in his face. Flapping his wings, he rose in the air and flew towards me. It is a fearsome sight when a big full-grown drake with a three-foot wing span flapping flies at you, at groin level. I was frightened; my heart was pounding, my breathing short and heavy, and I was sweating. Frightened, I retreated slowly step by step. The *Alpenstock* I then used as a stick, striking the drake on the neck as he flew at me, so that he was knocked to the ground. This happened five or six times with me retreating a step or two each time. Finally, thoroughly frightened, I hit the flying drake with a strong backhand stroke. It must have been a hard blow; the drake landed on the ground in an awkward position. I stood still. The drake remained still for about fifteen seconds; the angry expression on his face had dissipated and was replaced by another expression, difficult to define, perhaps "puzzled" or "uncertain" would express it. Then the drake rose on its legs, turned its back, and waddled slowly up the slope off the seeded area.

It is well known that mammals and birds exhibit strong emotions; hence it is hardly merely anthropomorphic projection to use the descriptive terms "angry," "puzzled," "uncertain." For a few days the drake was markedly less aggressive when he saw me with the *Alpenstock* in hand. Then one day as I stood by the garage door leaning on the cane, the drake waddled past me, and as he did, he took a fierce bite at the cane with his usual mean facial expression when biting. I laughed, of course, and maybe there was no connection with the previous incident. At any rate, within a few more days the drake was as aggressive towards me as previously. Since the brain is so small, one would expect that the memory of a drake would be short and the temporal perspective very limited.

If mammals and birds exhibit strong emotions, are these animals *aware* of their emotions? Can a creature, animal or human, have *emotions* without being in some sense aware of them? If there is awareness, can there be awareness without self-awareness, in some elemental way? Even awareness in animals—must there not be for such awareness a primitive form of self-awareness? From animal to man may there not be an *evolution* of self-awareness? If so, then the level, acuity, or quality of self-awareness may be the feature distinguishing man from animal. How shall we ascertain this quality, how describe it?

Mammals and birds, as we have said, exhibit strong emotions. Mammals and birds also dream, while the reptiles, their common ancestor, do not. We are all familiar with the phenomena of a dog dreaming. Our dog Becky makes sounds while sleeping, with her whole torso heaving; these sounds are light staccato cries, perhaps a subdued barking. What is a dream but a mental image, or rather successions of mental images in a sleeping creature? Is not the fact that a dog can dream a sign that a dog has a consciousness, with a capacity for mental images? However, there are many other signs of conscious awareness in dogs. We humans communicate with dogs and they respond. We play with dogs; we teach them proper habits; they learn to follow direction, given by words or gestures. Dogs can be very sensitive to tones of human speech. We once had a dog Benjy, known in the neighborhood as a *talking* dog. Whenever we started a walk with Benjy, he would make talk-like, bark-like sounds which communicated his joy that we were starting a walk together, sometimes with an accent of scolding since so much time had elapsed since the previous walk. The sound was not a bark, at least not the bark that Benjy used to communicate with dogs. He made noises which communicated messages. If a dog has emotions, dreams, and communicates, must it not have a conscious awareness, a mental experience? And must there not always be a primordial element of self-awareness in every form and instance of awareness?

Because of the superficial abstractions current as assumptions among contemporary behavioral scientists, one has to argue nowadays that animals have emotions and mental experiences. Charles Darwin took for granted the fact that animals had mental experiences and emotions; one of his major works, published in 1872, dealt with the behavior patterns by which animals express their emotions. An exception among contemporaries, Konrad Lorenz, the great Munich biologist and ethologist, expressed his belief that animals have subjective experiences in a lecture given at the Munich Institute of Technology in 1963, entitled "Do Animals Undergo Subjective Experience?" In this lecture, he states: "My knowledge about the subjective experiences of my fellow men and my conviction that higher animals (such as a dog) also experience things are two quite closely related phenomena." He attributes to one of his teachers the demonstration that "the assumption of other human subjects with similar experience is an inescapable and compulsive train of thought. It is a genuine a priori necessity of thought and interpretation, which is just as evident as any axiom."[63] Of course, the difficulty in understanding the emotions and subjective experiences of an animal such as a dog is much, much greater than understanding the subjective experiences of fellow men, a task difficult enough, as we all know. Nevertheless, it would be a form of intellectual escapism to postulate the impossibility of interpreting the subjective experiences of the higher animals from the evidence of external signs. The philosopher Wittgenstein wrote once: "If a lion could talk we could not understand him."[64] I doubt if he is right. Certainly if a bounding lion came roaring at him, he would understand the message of roar-talk. If a lion in a quieter mood talked, it would be more difficult to interpret the message, but time and patience might well produce an understanding.

Our discussion of the psychogenetic development of the consciousness of time showed the importance of representations, of mental images. The capacity for mental images is not limited to man; studies made during the past 50 years or more have revealed this capability in non-human primates. The higher one ascends the evolutionary scale of animals the more rare becomes the domination of fixed reaction-to-stimuli patterns. In higher animals there are evidently mediating processes in the brain; that is, communication appears to go on within the brain, as well as into and out of it. Physiologists connect this with the development of "association areas" in the brain, of neural cells not devoted to receiving incoming stimuli or forwarding outgoing responses, but available instead for learning complex behaviors and for representing goals to be achieved through such behavior. As we have seen, this takes place very early in the growth of a child, as does the shift from primarily reflexive to primarily purposive behavior.

Thirty-five years ago the primatologist Yerkes demonstrated the presence of mental imagery in chimpanzees, the capacity for delayed response and for remembering the location of a reward after a single visual experience. A chimpanzee that has seen a banana put in one of several unfamiliar boxes and is then taken out of the room will go to the right box immediately on returning to the room, if the delay is not more than two minutes. If during the delay the experimenter substitutes a piece of lettuce for the banana, the chimp will usually refuse to take it. Shrieking in anger, he looks through the other containers and around the room for the lost banana. Normally lettuce is an acceptable food, but apparently not when the chimp expects to find a banana, its favorite. In another experiment Yerkes put the banana into one of two differently colored boxes, with the chimp watching. When the chimp was out of the room, he then switched the position of the boxes. When brought back, the chimp went directly to the place where it saw the food concealed and kept searching for it there, not going to the other box. Yerkes commented on this surprising limitation of the chimpanzee's capacity for mental imagery as follows:

"To us it seems almost incredible that with both boxes before it, but interchanged in position, the animal should go where the food had been concealed, in spite of the altered appearance of the box, and there search persistently for its expected reward. Under like circumstances a person would notice at once the changed appearance of the food box and look about for the original box...We finally were forced to admit that our subjects either failed to perceive the essential clue, or were unable to hold it in mind because they lacked a symbol or representative process comparable with our word 'green.' "[65]

Even without the benefit of language, however, the chimpanzees are capable of anticipatory and purposeful behavior. It has been related that captive chimpanzees, after seeing a visitor coming towards their cage, will often go over to the faucet, fill their mouths, and going back to the front of the cage, wait there quietly until the visitor is within range, at which juncture he is suddenly drenched with water. The chimp is clearly able to anticipate a goal and to plan a series of actions in order to carry it out. The time span of anticipatory behavior in animals, however, is limited; only in humans does it extend beyond minutes or hours to weeks or years or decades.

Carl Sagan begins his discussion of "The Abstractions of Beasts" by quoting John Locke's pronouncement that "beasts abstract not"—to which he adds Bishop Berkeley's rejoinder: "If the fact that brutes abstract not be made the distinguishing property of that sort of animal, I fear a great many of those that pass for men must be reckoned into their number."[66] Language is the conventional human avenue to abstractions. The pharynx and larynx of the chimp, however, are not suited to the sounds of human speech. Noting this fact, two American psychologists, Beatrice and Robert Gardner, decided to try to teach a chimpanzee American sign language, known as Ameslan, making thus use of the manual dexterity of the chimpanzee. The Gardners and others have been enormously successful in teaching Ameslan and other gestural languages to chimpanzees. There are chimpanzees with working vocabularies of up to 200 words; moreover, they have been very inventive in constructing new words and phrases. It has been shown that chimpanzees are able both to ask questions and to deny assertions put to them. Chimpanzees have no difficulty in using swear words, and even in devising new ones. One lady chimp, highly irritated, called her trainer "you green shit." Man has sometimes been described as "the laughing animal," as if laughter and humor were the characteristics differentiating him from beasts—a view going back to later Greek philosophy which "defined man as the only animal capable of laughter" and was cited by Bergson in the book *Laughter* (English translation 1921). Studies of chimpanzees have shown, however, that they too have a sense of humor: a chimp, astride her trainer's shoulders, once wet him, perhaps by chance; immediately she made the sign "funny, funny." She must have been laughing inside, and presumably it was visible on her face, since the chimpanzees as well as other higher non-human primates are able to smile and laugh.

Tests with animals, using operant conditioning techniques, indicate that animals can perceive duration, or can react to different durations as if they perceived duration. For example, rats entering a maze had to choose between two passages identical from every point of view; when they went through these passages, they were detained in a small chamber, one minute in one passage and six minutes in the other, before they could reach their food. They learned gradually to choose the chamber detaining them only one minute. Thus it was shown that a rat can distinguish between two intervals of time. Other tests have confirmed this result, and not surprisingly, marked individual differences were discovered in the capability of the rats to distinguish the length of duration. Given the continuity of nature, one must expect that humans also have a biological basis for estimating duration, which operates together with mental representations of time. This may be related to the fact that a general biological capacity seems to determine perceptual span. Fraisse has shown that children four to six years old who cannot count have a perceptual span (five or six elements) comparable to that of adults. He points out that the same span has been found in birds. Fraisse believes that the higher vertebrates perceive time under similar conditions to man, and this because of a common dependence on the general properties of the receptor centers in the brain.

Do animals have a temporal horizon? We would have to know much more than we do, or more than we can, about the awareness and self-awareness of animals, in order to answer this question with much clarity. Let us first ask what temporal horizon means with respect to mankind. We live in the present, as do animals, but intrinsic to the human present is constant reference to the past and to the future. In the most brilliant discussion of the experience of time ever written, St. Augustine in Book XI of his *Confessions* sets forth the dimensions of the present: "...the present of things past, the present of things present, and the present of things future." Human actions depend not only on the immediate situation, but also on all our past experience and our future expectations. This is the *temporal horizon* of man. Do animals have a temporal horizon? Even if animal behavior is primarily dependent on a present perception of external stimuli, the significance of the stimulus is determined by previous experience, a connection having been established between the stimulus (which has become conditioned) and the reaction. The conditioned stimulus determines anticipation behavior, such as seeking food. Fraisse states: "Animals do not, however, refer explicitly to past events in their behavior; nor do they have a purpose. Their temporal horizon is purely implicit."[67] We really do not know whether the temporal horizon of animals is "purely implicit"; we know too little about the nature of awareness and self-awareness among animals. Certainly it cannot be excluded that the higher primates have some explicit forms of temporal awareness. What Fraisse means by animals not "referring explicitly" to past events in their behavior is unclear; while they may not communicate explicitly with us, their behavior often indicates a reference to past events which may be in some sense explicit to them. Nor does it seem to me correct to say that animals have no purpose; there have been too many accounts of purposeful and anticipatory behavior on the part of chimpanzees to cast doubt on the capability of some higher animals to act purposively.

Wittgenstein in his *Philosophical Investigations* poses some pertinent questions: "We say a dog is afraid his master will beat him; but not he is afraid his master will beat him tomorrow. Why not?

"One can imagine an animal angry, frightened, unhappy, happy, startled. But hopeful? Why not?

"A dog believes his master is at the door. But can he also believe his master will come the day after tomorrow? And *what* can he not do here? Can only those hope who can talk? Only those who have mastered the use of language?"[68]

Wittgenstein is raising doubts about the time span of a dog's anticipation into the future. He may be right, but if a dog is able to anticipate events beyond today, he is not able to communicate this to us, nor are we able to ascertain it from the dog's behavior.

Animals, babies, and some types of mentally deficient people live primarily in the present because they are incapable of constructing an explicitly temporal horizon. Adult humans are not immersed completely in present experiences for any prolonged period; associated events from past and future continually intrude into consciousness and are integrated there into contemporaneous patterns of action and meaning. This "temporal integration" process causes stimuli of perceptual experience to lose their predominance. Thus representations of objects and events determine the behavior of humans as much as direct perception. The great human capacity for representations far exceeds the capacity of the brightest chimpanzees for mental representation.

The Gardners' study of chimpanzee communication has demonstrated that chimpanzees have a memory capability and also a sense of the immediate future. In reply to a question at a colloquium in Paris December 1970, Professor Gardner stated: "She [Washoe] could sign 'gimme food please' when she saw one of her human friends serving food at lunch time. She could also sign 'time food' before lunch. The fact that she could discuss her lunch when it was not present depended upon her ability to remember that lunch was usually served at the same time each day. She could also ask for things locked away in cupboards and even tell new assistants where to find things they asked for. Here again the only way she could know where the objects were kept was by remembering their customary location. Whether she asked for them verbally or attempted to pry open the cupboards for herself is a question apart. Granted that Washoe could discuss in sign language objects that were present, it should not surprise you that she could also discuss the same objects from memory."[69]

Washoe's sense for the impending future is illustrated by the following story: "It is late in the day, and getting dark outside. Washoe and a human companion are inside her house trailer, and he peers out the window and comes back to initiate the following interchange:

Person: 'Washoe, there's a big black dog outside—with big teeth. It is a dog that eats little chimps. You want to go out, now?'
Washoe: (Prolonged and emphatic) 'Noooooooo.' "[70]

The 97th sign which Washoe acquired was for "time,"[71] which referred to events in the immediate future; it was almost always combined with a sign designating action, e.g., *Time eat, Time out, Time tickle*. Thus Washoe used the sign *time* as a modifier of action signs rather than as an independent sign form; replies combining time with a single additional sign were regarded as temporal verb phrases. Further studies of chimpanzees' communication on a longer term and continuing basis may hopefully reveal more information about the extent and scope of the chimpanzee's temporal perspective.

Let us return to the question whether an animal can have "subjective experience." The Gardners have proved beyond a doubt that chimpanzees have subjective, i.e., mental, experience. If an animal talks to itself, in the chimpanzee case makes signs to itself in Ameslan, then surely this is an expression of subjective, mental experience. On the subject *Signing to Herself*, the Gardners have written: "Washoe often signed to herself in play, particularly in places that afforded her privacy, i.e., when she was high in the tree or alone in her bedroom before going to sleep. While we sat quietly in the next room waiting for Washoe to fall asleep, we frequently saw her practicing signs, just as Ruth Weir has reported for young children. Washoe would stop if she noticed that we were watching.

"Washoe also signed to herself when leafing through magazines and picture books, and she resented our attempts to join in this activity. If we did try to join her or if we watched her too closely, she often abandoned the magazine, or picked it up and moved away. Our records show that Washoe not only named pictures to herself in this situation but that she also corrected herself. On one occasion, she indicated a certain advertisement, signed *That food*, then looked at her hand closely and changed the phrase to *That drink*, which was correct.

"Washoe also signed to herself about her own ongoing or impending action. We have often seen Washoe moving stealthily to a forbidden part of the yard, signing *Quiet* to herself, or running pell-mell for the potty chair while signing *Hurry*. On one occasion, Washoe was near a ladder, scribbling on a piece of paper, while her companion was otherwise occupied. Suddenly she signed *Up hurry* to herself and rushed up the ladder. When she climbed down, she resumed her play with the pencil and paper, then once again signed to herself *More up* and did what she had told herself to do."[72]

William Ernest Hocking began his work *The Self: Its Body and Freedom* with this paragraph: "Man has been said to be the animal that laughs. The distinction is probably safe, though not wholly unassailable. But surely man is the animal that makes pictures." He goes on: "He has been at it from very early times—witness the aboriginal cave drawings, the carved handles of knives and the like.

And he is always at it. It expresses the peculiarity of his mind—disinterested thinking. Whoever makes a picture has turned a corner in evolution: he has become so far a mental being that the form of an object is worth something to him without the object. He has an 'idea' which is worth keeping: and the visible mark, however rude, aids him to steady that idea before his mind and think about it."[73]

The above paragraphs appeared in 1928. We now know that laughter as the distinction between man and animal is not "safe," since chimpanzees and other nonhuman primates are capable of laughter. The Gardners may now also have shown that man is not the only animal that makes pictures. Their chimpanzees draw pictures, and rather interesting ones. When their chimpanzee, Moja, became three years old, they started half-hour daily school sessions; drawing was one of the tasks in these sessions. A remarkable development took place six months after the beginning of these sessions. One day Moja made a drawing with just a few lines, quite different from the usual drawings, with many lines helter-skelter. "Because so few lines had been made, the research assistant put the chalk back in Moja's hand and urged her to *Try more*, but she dropped the chalk and signed *Finish*. The reply was unusual, and looking at the drawing the assistant noticed that it too was unusual in form. He then asked Moja *What's that*, and she replied *Bird*. Since that time, Moja has labeled additional drawings that she produced; she has drawn and then labeled figures as requested by the teacher...and she has replied appropriately to questions asking her to name both the artist and the subject...."[74] If "whoever makes a picture has turned a corner in evolution," then the chimpanzee Moja has also turned "a corner in evolution." We shall have to look elsewhere for the distinction between man and other animals. However, it must be noted that as yet chimpanzees have not been found to draw pictures spontaneously, but only after they have been taught to draw through training by humans.

In a recent book entitled *The Question of Animal Awareness*, Donald R. Griffin points out: "The possession of mental images could well confer an important adaptive advantage on an animal by providing a reference pattern against which stimulus patterns can be compared.... Even greater adaptive advantage results when such a mental image also includes time as one of its dimensions, that is, the relationships to past and future events. Mental images with a time dimension would be far more useful than static searching images, because they would allow the animal to adapt its behavior appropriately to the probable flow of events, rather than being limited to separate reactions as successive perceptual pictures of the animal's surroundings present themselves one at a time. Anticipation of future enjoyment of food and mating or fear of injury could certainly be adaptive...."[75] He goes on to say that mental images including both spatial and temporal dimensions approach a working definition of conscious awareness. In Griffin's view, the evolutionary kinship of animals and man indicate "that an animal which communicates about its internal images may also be aware of them on some occasion."[76] To be sure, but is this cautious language necessary? Is there any awareness, any conscious experience without in some sense a self-awareness, self-consciousness? Intrinsic to awareness is the diremption of subject and object where the subject may become its own object. Indeed, in mental experience the creature subject is always its own object concomitant with its awareness of the external other, whether that other be things or creature. In the lesser creatures on the evolutionary scale awareness may be vague and blurred and self-awareness merely implicit. In man self-consciousness may become exquisite and poignant, although for most of our lives it remains a mute and implicit concomitant of consciousness. We can only learn the level and scope of consciousness and self-consciousness in the higher animals by communicating with them, and this we have just begun to do.

The Confucian sage Mencius (4th century B.C.) wrote that the distinction between men and animals was slight and that only the "gentleman" possesses this distinction while the "small man"—i.e., the ordinary man—does not. For him men were different from animals because of their *hsin*, which may be translated either "heart" or "mind," the heart being regarded as the seat of thought in ancient China. "Mind" did not mean the power of reasoning which Aristotle said distinguished men from animals; Mencius was concerned with thinking about moral duties. The Confucian philosopher Hsun Tzu (3rd century B.C.) said that man is not man by reason of his upright posture, his ability to speak, or any other distinguishing feature, but by reason of his ability to make distinctions and to form groups for cooperative action. He also thought a moral quality distinguished men from animals, a sense of justice on the basis of which men were able to form groups and organize themselves in a social order.

Charles Darwin in his *Descent of Man* wrote, "The difference in mind between man and the higher animals, great as it is, certainly is one of degree and not of kind.... If it could be proved that certain high mental powers, such as the formation of general concepts, self-consciousness, et cetera, were absolutely peculiar to man, which seems extremely doubtful, it is not improbable that these qualities are merely the incidental results of other highly advanced intellectual faculties; and these again mainly the results of the continued use of a perfect language."[77] The British ethologist Thorpe, who has sought to formulate criteria distinguishing human language from animal communication, has written, "Human speech is unique only in the way it combines and extends attributes which in themselves are not peculiar to man but are found also in more than one group of animals.... Yet...there comes a point where 'more' creates a 'difference.'" It may be recalled that Alfred North Whitehead in his *Modes of Thought*, 1938, stated: "The distinction between man and animals is in one sense only a difference in degree. But the extent of the degree makes all the difference. The Rubicon has been crossed."[78]

Chapter 6
Biological Rhythms

Every living organism is characterized by the rhythms intrinsic to its constitution. Some periodic phenomena are endogenous, appearing to have no relationship to the external rhythms of the natural environment, e.g., heartbeat, breathing, and the electric waves of the brain. Many rhythms of organisms are exogenous, caused by the external rhythms of the natural environment. The major external rhythms are the geophysical cycles, i.e., the day (24 hours), the lunar day (24.8 hours), the month (29.5 days), or the year (365¼ days). Organisms are sensitive to changes of day and night, season, temperature, weather, and all atmospheric periodicities. Information can be conveyed to organisms by many means, including light and heat, and by magnetic, electric, and low-frequency electromagnetic fields, as well as by high-energy background radiation. The exogenous rhythms caused by the ambient environment create endogenous rhythms in the living organism. The potentiality for such responsiveness is presumably fixed in genes by natural selection and maintained by genetic transmission. There are also rhythms intrinsic to the basic elements and structures of an organism: the molecules, cells, membrane.

Biologists have demonstrated that the capacity for rhythmicity is innate, by raising animals from birth and seeds from the time of germination in noncyclic laboratory conditions. The developing

128

organism becomes rhythmic spontaneously, or else can be made to become rhythmic by a single, nonperiodic stimulus. The latter has been exhibited by tests with the fruitfly (Drosophila). In its development from egg to adult, the fruitfly passes through larval and pupal stages; at the end of the pupal stage, the new adult emerges. In natural conditions, this emergence, called eclosion, takes place normally around dawn. If batches of eggs are laid and develop in constant conditions, eclosion eventually takes place at all times of the day, the population having become a-rhythmic. After fifteen generations of a-rhythmicity in constant conditions, when the developing pupae were given one nonperiodic stimulus (a light was turned on and left on), an eclosion rhythm was established in the population. This is interpreted to signify the existence of an innate property of protoplasm to measure off periods of about twenty-four hours.

Rhythms are not necessarily the product of complexity in plant or animal organization. Rhythms have been found at the unicellular level of organization, in algae and protozoans. In fact, rhythms may persist in a single cell from which the nucleus has been removed, e.g., the diurnal photosynthetic-capacity rhythm in the single-celled alga Aectabularia. Moreover, more than one rhythm can occur in unicells at the same time. Whether each rhythm has its own clock mechanism or whether a master clock determines all the rhythms by separate coupling units is not known.

Rhythmic changes are common in the plant world. Many flowers open at specific hours of the day. Linnaeus planted "Flora's Clocks," each hour being indicated by a different flower. The leaves of leguminous plants lie in one position by day and another by night, an alternation which seems to be innate. If a bean plant is kept under a constant light, the alternation persists. However the rhythmic movement of the leaves may be reversed if artificial lighting is used at night and the plants are kept in the dark during the day. This shows that only the actual alternation is endogenous, while the synchronization with night and day is induced by the circadian rhythm itself.

The presence of rhythms in animals is very widespread and even more prominent than in plants. Seasonal or diurnal rhythms have been found in almost all animal species. Circadian rhythms in animals, it is believed, are almost always acquired, unlike plants. The alternation of periods of waking and sleeping, activity and rest, is a necessity for the life of an animal; circadian rhythms accomplish the synchronization of this alternation with the cycle of day and night.

Many experiments have shown that animals raised in laboratory-constant conditions can be adapted more readily to a twenty-four-hour rhythm than to any other. This would seem to indicate an inherited predisposition to a twenty-four-hour rhythm, which would not be surprising. In certain exceptional cases, however, animals have been trained to rhythms of a somewhat longer period, e.g., white rats have been trained to sixteen-hour alternating periods of activity and rest. Nevertheless, according to Fraisse, "No animal escapes the domination of the circadian rhythm, except perhaps deep-sea fish"[79] (which sleep much longer than twenty-four hours). Related species sharing the same habitat often have similar, but differently phased, circadian rhythms. For example, there are nocturnal and diurnal varieties of beetles—just as there are nocturnal and diurnal varieties of men.

Aside from animal responsiveness to circadian and other geophysical rhythms, animals seem to possess a physiological capability for measuring intervals of time within the larger rhythm. For instance, if food is laid out for bees at the same place and the same time for several days, they will subsequently return every day to feed at the same time and they will continue to do this for some days after the food is removed. Fish come every day at the same time to the same place in which they are fed and the activity of birds is increased just before their feeding time. These rhythms are the result of acquired experience, which adjusts an internal clock mechanism. Experiments have shown that the internal clock may act regardless of external conditions. In a famous experiment, bees were trained to come for food at a certain hour in a bee room in Paris. Between two feeding times, they were flown from Paris to New York, placed in an identical bee room, and deprived of food. On the following days they came for food at the same time as in Paris, although the time of day in New York was different. When the experiment was repeated with training in New York preceding translocation back to Paris, corresponding results were obtained.

Evidence of an internal clock has also been given by experiments showing that insects, crustaceans, and birds can move in a given compass direction, guided only by the position of the sun. To do this, the animal must be able to allow for differences in the position of the sun. For instance, bees trained to go westward for food in the afternoon, go in the same direction the next morning, even if their hive has been moved during the night and the exit turned in another direction. A starling can be trained to seek food to the east, no matter what the time of day. The presence of a physiological clock is shown by the following experiment: the cage of a starling, trained to fly east in daylight, is placed in a dark room in the center of a circular tent of white canvas which diffuses the light from an electric bulb acting as an artificial sun. At the usual time the bird will turn toward the east, its direction making the same angle with the artificial sun as it did with the real sun. A few hours later, the light being in the same position, the bird will err toward the west, allowing for a difference in the position of the sun, as if it had really changed. The bird thus makes a mistake, since the artificial sun has remained in the same position.

The internal clock may also be set wrongly. After starlings have been trained in one direction in any hour of the day, they are put under the influence of an artificial day, consisting of alternating light and darkness, reproducing the diurnal rhythms but with a discrepancy of six hours from the sun. After several days, when the starlings are given orientation tests by real light of day, at three p.m. they will fly in the correct direction for nine a.m. This error results clearly from a false setting of their internal clock, having adapted itself to the rhythm of the artificial day. By virtue of their physiological clocks, organisms can evidently adapt themselves to regular changes. Experiments have shown that an animal may be conditioned to periods unrelated to natural rhythms, so long as these periods are less than twenty-four hours. For example, bees have been trained to come for food every twenty-one hours. Efforts to train animals to follow a rhythm of more than twenty-four hours have generally failed.

The more complex an organism, the more complex and varied are the rhythms intrinsic to its constitution—and also the more scope there is for individual variation. Mankind is as subject to the light-dark diurnal rhythm as plants or other animals. Most human beings work during the day and sleep at night, thus relating the organic need to rest after activity with the diurnal rhythm. The pulse, blood pressure, and body temperature show diurnal rhythms in humans as well as in many animals. The maximum human temperature is in the late afternoon and the minimum at night, with a difference of about 1.8°F. Early in this century, a French psychologist showed that the temperature change was reversed in the case of nurses changing from day to night duty. The reversal was gradual and took thirty to forty days for completion. Aside from the temperature rhythm, the rhythms of many other physiological functions are connected with phases of activity and the day-night rhythm. In man these rhythms all seem to be acquired. While the embryos of birds show a light-darkness cycle in a movement rhythm, with man there is no evidence for any circadian periodicity in the foetus or the newborn child, either in its physiological functions or its activity. Rhythms appear to develop at different times after birth. Some rhythms e.g., sleep, waking and pulse frequency, appear later in premature children, which indicates that a certain stage of development may be required before the rhythms can appear. For a newborn child the periods of sleep are very numerous, without apparent preference for day or night. Very soon the periods of sleep become longer and less numerous; at the end of one week, nocturnal sleep is already more important than sleep during the day. The temperature rhythm only becomes clear in the course of the second year. It is believed that these rhythms result from the establishment of a periodic rhythm of activity rather than through the direct influence of light or darkness, although the periodicity of activity is influenced by the alternation of day and night.

It is of interest to note that a correlation has been discovered between body temperature and the subjective perception of the length of temporal intervals. The discovery was first made under the following circumstances: A Harvard physiologist went to a drugstore for medicine for his wife sick with influenza. When he returned fifteen minutes later, his wife scolded him for having dawdled and taken so long. Unabashed, he took her temperature and asked her to estimate intervals of sixty seconds by counting at a rate of one number per second. Being an accomplished musician, proud of her sense of timing and rhythm, she performed this chore faithfully forty times during her illness. Each time he measured the duration of her count with a stopwatch and plotted the results against her oral temperature, which varied between 97.4 and 103°F. He discovered that she unknowingly counted faster at higher temperatures than at lower ones, thus estimating that more time passed than really did. Further tests have shown that the general relationship between body temperature and time estimation is approximately a ten percent speeding up for each 1°F. rise in temperature. Thus it appears that the subjective perception of time passage is not under the direct control of a biological clock, but rather is subject to the body's temperature rhythm. Human time estimation can also be slowed by some chemicals and speeded up by others. True biological rhythms, however, are not generally influenced by temperature change or by most chemicals.

In 1851 it was discovered that the rate of division of root and stem cells in flowering plants was rhythmic. Even when the plants were maintained in constant light and temperature, the rhythms persisted. Meanwhile many other mitotic rhythms have been observed in many organisms, including algae, protozoa, and the rodent. In 1939 a lady physician in New York City demonstrated that similar rhythms occur in humans. Since circumcision is very common in New York City, she collected tiny excised foreskins during all the day. Her collection was homogenous, since all the donors were six to eleven days old and lived together in the same hospital conditions. Data gathered from fifty-seven penes showed that cell division was greatest during the afternoon and early nighttime. It is possible that cancer, a disease characterized by excessive cell division, may result from a breakdown of normal mitotic rhythms by loss of the biological clock control of cell division.

The heartbeat for a young adult is slightly over seventy beats per minute when measured during the day. However, when measurements are taken over the full twenty-four-hour span, a diurnal rhythm has been discovered, with the heart beating faster during the daytime than at night. A relation between the heart rate and body temperature has also been found, with the heart rate increasing by ten to fifteen beats per minute for every 1°F. rise in temperature. However, while the temperature change may play a role, it does not cause the heartbeat rhythm. Studies made with heart transplants indicate that the heart cells themselves contain the rhythm mechanism. Nevertheless this heartbeat rate rhythm also seems to be acquired, as are the other human rhythms. The tiny fetal heart begins to beat about four weeks after conception; during the seventh month the beating rate is a nonoscillating 133 beats per minute; throughout the ninth month, it averages 129. The heartbeat rhythm first makes its appearance four to five weeks after birth, when the nighttime rate begins to decrease.

Rhythmic oscillation seems to be a basic property of living matter, as mentioned earlier, extending down to unicellular organisms. It is not surprising then that rhythmic oscillation appears to be a characteristic of the functioning of the nervous system. It has been shown that the rhythms of the heart, of breathing, and of the electric activity of the brain are not periodic responses to periodic stimuli; the only effect of stimuli is to accelerate or slow down the oscillation of the nervous centers; thus these rhythms are spontaneous and endogenous. Nerve tissues not spontaneously rhythmic (reflex centers, the sensory fibers, and motor fibers) do, however, respond rhythmically when exposed to a constant stimulus. The centers and fibers have their own period of response and the rhythm of response only corresponds roughly to the rhythm or to the intensity of the stimulus. In the scratch reflex of the dog, a stimulus can cause a series of periodic movements which occur even if the afferent pathways of the muscles concerned have been cut. It is concluded that the rhythm of such a movement can only be explained by the repetitive activity of a nerve center.

It is interesting to note that there is a tendency of nervous rhythms to synchronize with each other. The periodicity of one nerve rhythm often acts as a pacemaker for others. The sinus node in the heart is considered to be a pacemaker for a number of other centers, each with their own periodicity. The rhythmic cerebral waves recorded by electroencephalography are the result of a widespread synchronization of the electrical activity of the nerve cells. The regularity of the pulsations of any organ or center is regarded as due to the coordination of a large number of elementary pulsations. Also, certain rhythmic activities can become synchronized with stimuli which are themselves rhythmic. For instance, the alpha rhythm of cerebral waves can be regulated to a certain extent by an intermittent light. Also, it is assumed that the nervous system has the capability "of reproducing activations in the same order as that in which they were originally aroused by the corresponding stimuli."[80] Popov gave this property the name *cyclochronism.*

Cyclochronism takes place not only at the cortical level of the brain but also in subcortical centers. Pigeons whose cerebral hemispheres have been removed still follow the acquired day-night temperature rhythm. The regulation of sleep depends on the activity of a hypothalamic center; a dog with his cortical cerebrum removed still has the normal alternation of waking and sleeping. While the hypothalamic region is generally regarded as responsible for the regulation of organic cycles, it is also believed that the temporal integrations of periodic reactions also take place in this region. This has also been confirmed by a study of Korsakov's syndrome, a psychopathologic illness characterized by temporal disorientation, and particularly memory disintegration. The memory failure applies primarily to the most recent events. "The patient may talk about past events without making mistakes, but not remember what has just been said to him or what he has just done; he asks for some object when he has it in his hand, he wants to eat when he has just left the table, to be put to bed when he is already there, etc."[81] Perception is normal in such people, and sometimes it becomes a memory, but the few fixed memories remain, in Jaspers' words, as "isolated fragments."[82]

It is now recognized that Korsakov's syndrome results from an affliction of the basal nuclei in the subcortical region of the brain. Thus it has been established that "physiologically, the reproductivity of the events of our life depends, right from the phase of its formation in the cerebral cortex, on the reenforcement of the cortical traces by a subcortical mechanism which leads from the hypothalamus to the cerebral cortex and acts on the cortex in a way which cannot at the moment be defined as to quality but which is very probably sensitizing."[83] Two hypotheses have been set forth to explain the actual mechanism of the subcortical influence on the integration of experiences: 1) the subcortical bodies emit a basic rhythm indispensable for the development of psychological activities in the cortex; 2) they act selectively on the mechanism of memory by registering a temporal sign.

Periodicities in living organisms which synchronize with periodicities in nature constitute a form of adaptation to the temporal conditions of existence. Such induced organic rhythms permit living creatures to turn reflex reactions into anticipatory actions. For example, the flat shore worm (Convoluta) burrows down into the sand as soon as the motion of the rising tide begins and before it is covered by it. Sea anemones close before the tide ebbs, thus keeping their water and avoiding dessication. A Swiss physician first discovered the time-sense of bees: honeybees came each morning at his outdoor breakfast table to feed on his marmalade; they would come each morning then even when there was no food on the table. He attributed these visits to a *Zeitgedaechtnis*, or memory for time. Bees come to a buckwheat field only in the early morning, at the time the buckwheat flowers secrete nectar; similarly bees go to other flowers at the regular time of the secretion of nectar, which differs from flower to flower. If bad weather keeps bees from leaving the hive for several days, they return *on time* to feed when clear skies appear again.

Man too has an internal biological clock, presumably based on the endogenous rhythms produced by response to periodicities in the natural environment. William James cites the case of an idiot who could not read clock time but asked for her soup every day at exactly the same hour. The fundamental organic rhythms of food and sleep, and more generally of metabolism, provide the fundaments of the human biological clock. Experiments with men shut in a sound-proof, air-conditioned room with only artificial light disclosed that the rhythm of sleep, acting as a clock, enabled a fairly normal time judgment. In another experiment, volunteer subjects were awakened between midnight and five a.m. with a query as to what time it was; the average error in time estimation was only fifty minutes.

Furthermore, numerous experiments have confirmed the existence in many, but not all humans, of an ability to wake up in the night at a time previously decided upon. Since the cues for waking were not external it is assumed that they must have been internal, indicating the existence of a physiological clock. It is well known that sleep does not usually entirely suppress the function of vigilance. It has been noted that persons who must wake up at a fixed time are more restless and do not sleep well. The worry of a possible delay disturbs them; their dreams are affected, and they may wake up as the result of a dream. The dreams show that the person continues to "keep an eye on the time" while asleep. The study of dreams has shown, moreover, that when asleep we are sensitive to imperceptible organic stimuli; for instance, premonitory dreams of illnesses sometimes occur before the symptoms appear at a conscious level.

When organisms are exposed to periodic changes, they are usually able to adapt to them. The variations in their psychological life thus come to synchronize with external changes and they learn to repeat beneficial behavior in anticipation of the periodic return of corresponding situations. This adaptation has psychological importance as well as biological. The induction of organic rhythms from geophysical rhythms results in a double system of signals coordinated with each other. The importance of the physiological clock is obscured by the preponderance of the cues provided by geophysical and man-made clocks. The physiological clock probably explains the so-called *time sense*: intuitive knowledge of the time, or temporal orientation due more to physiological signals then external cues. Thus "the ability of a man to wake himself up at a fixed time is no more mysterious than the spontaneous behavior of an animal at regular times, even in the absence of the external stimuli which originally determined this."[84]

The physical universe is basically rhythmic in nature. The dominant rhythms for life on this planet are the geophysical rhythms, mentioned earlier. It can hardly be doubted that the survival of biological species depends on their capacity to adjust to these geophysical rhythms. J.D. Palmer has related this dependence to the evolutionary process: "Rhythms that match the major geophysical periods of the earth and that persist in constant conditions are ubiquitous in their distribution throughout the living kingdom. It is thought that this clock capability arose long ago in some primitive organism, where it was found to have a significant survival value in that it could 'notify' its owner in advance of coming periodic environmental events, such as sunrise, sunset, and the flood tide. It was therefore selected for in the evolutionary process and eventually became widely established in the plant and animal phyla."[85] Palmer comments further that very little is known about the fundamental nature of the biological clock underlying these rhythms, although there has been in recent decades a great deal of speculation concerning the nature of the clock.

Chapter 7
The Self and Time

We have seen that rhythms are an intrinsic characteristic of the natural universe, of the plant and animal world, and of human life. We have learned earlier in Part I (see p. 22) that when considering the origin and empirical content of the concept of time, Einstein put the concept of periodic occurrence ahead of the concept of time. Since a periodic occurrence is a rhythm, he is testifying that rhythm is the primordial ground of time. The essence of rhythm is a *return* in some sense. Rhythmic return is a form of reflexivity. What is the meaning of *reflexivity*? The dictionary says "turn back upon itself." Reflexivity is a more primordial concept than rhythm; rhythm is derived from reflexivity, and rhythms are born of reflexivities. Is not reflexivity intrinsic to consciousness? Is not the self in a primordial sense born in reflexivity? The I=I of the self is not a simple identity; it is a rhythmic reflexivity. Is not the reflexivity of the self in self-consciousness necessary for, a prerequisite of, consciousness? In his *Encyclopedia*, Hegel wrote that self-consciousness "is the foundation of consciousness in the sense that self-consciousness is in the existence of all consciousness of another object."[86] The self can also make itself an object of its consciousness, albeit only obscurely, for the self can never apprehend itself with perfect lucidity and objectivity. There is an intrinsic and ineluctable opacity in the self's apprehension of itself. If we ask what is the source of this opacity and why it cannot be overcome, the finitude of man is the answer that comes to mind, and we cannot overcome this finitude. The intrinsic opacity of self-consciousness, derived ultimately from human finitude, may be the source of the pervasiveness of self-deception in human existence.

What is the relationship between consciousness, self-consciousness, and time, temporality? Insight into the relationship between self-consciousness and time goes back at least to Aristotle in the 4th century B.C. Aristotle is usually cited as the exponent of the view that time and motion are intrinsically related and that time is just this: "number of motion in respect of 'before' and 'after.' "[87] However, in the closing chapter of his work *On the Senses*, Aristotle specifically connects the perception of time to self-awareness, arguing that the perception of succession requires the ability "to perceive every instant of time" and that the perception of any entity in time requires consciousness of one's own existence: "...it is inconceivable that a person should, while perceiving himself or aught else in a continuous time, be at any instant unaware of his own existence."[88]

Some 500 years later, Plotinus reiterated the connection between time and the self, albeit in a very different context. He defines time "as the Life of the Soul in movement as it passes from one stage of act or experience to another."[89] Further, "the soul-act...is the essence of Time."[90] As to the origin of time, "time came into being simultaneously with this All (the totality of engendered being): the Soul begot at once the Universe and Time; in that activity of the Soul this Universe sprang into being: the activity is Time, the Universe is a content of Time."[91] Toward the close of his discussion, Plotinus asks, "Is Time, then, within ourselves as well?" And replies, "Time is in every soul,... present in like form in all;..."[92]

St. Augustine, who died about 150 years after Plotinus, was profoundly influenced by Plotinus' thought. He disregarded Plotinus' conception of the All, the world-soul, and directed his attention to the individual soul, pursuing Plotinus' view that time is somehow linked to the soul of the individual perceiver. He finally comes to the conclusion that time is somehow a protraction, or extension, of the individual human mind: "Time is nothing else but protraction...of the mind itself."[93] "It is in thee, my mind, that I measure time."[94]

An explicit assertion of the connection between self and time is set forth in several places in Hegel's works: in the *Phenomenology*, "time is the pure self in external form, apprehended in intuition, and not grasped and understood by the self, it is the concept apprehended only through intuition" (Sie [die Zeit] ist das äussere angeschaute vom Selbst nicht erfasste reine Selbst, der nur angeschaute Begriff;...");[95] again in the *Phenomenology*, we read of the spirit "intuitively apprehending outside itself its pure self as time..." ("sein reines Selbst als die Zeit ausser ihm...anschauend").[96] The same thought is contained somewhat more clearly in the *Philosophy of Nature*: "Time is the same principle as the I=I of pure self-consciousness, but the same or the simple concept, still in its complete externality and abstraction, as mere becoming intuited..." ("Die Zeit ist dasselbe Prinzip, als das Ich=Ich des reinen Selbstbewusstseins; aber daselbe oder der einfache Begriff noch in seiner gänzlichen Aeusserlichkeit und Abstraction, als das angeschaute blosse *Werden*...")[97] To my knowledge there is no philosopher in the whole of the philosophic tradition whose thought can be characterized in the same sense as Hegel's as being permeated with rhythmicity. Hegel's dialectic is a rhythm formula, an alternation of thesis and negation by antithesis followed by a synthesis which becomes a new thesis. Hegel's logic is a brilliant exfoliation of the meaning of philosophical concepts in the rhythmic structure of dialectic. He applies the same rhythmic dialectic in an effort to understand nature and history, and indeed the totality of existence. We should not be surprised then to find this assertion of the connection between the self and time in a thinker whose thought is imbued with the rhythm of being. Nor should we be surprised that Hegel's dialectic has been so severely criticized for imposing his dialectic rhythm on concepts, facts, and history where it may not apply. However profound and widespread the rhythms in being, there is an a-rhythmia in being, also widespread.

The connection between the self and time has been asserted, of course, by other thinkers, and more recently. According to Merleau-Ponty, "consciousness unfolds or constitutes time."[98] In another passage, Merleau-Ponty writes: "It [time] is born out of my relationship to things,"[99] a formulation which might better be stated this way: time is born out of the relation of the self to the universe. Discussing the nature of the temporal present, Minkowski finds that the present is not a primitive given concept. The present contains action, but all living beings act, and not all these actions constitute a present. He finds no way of deriving the present from a simple act. He goes on, "When I say, 'This is my present,' I do nothing else but give a narration of my act either to myself, or to someone else, at the same moment that I execute it. Thus the present is an account of the act that we execute while we are in the process of acting."[100] "The present" as a temporal dimension thus arises in this reflexivity. Once the present has been thus instituted, the other temporal dimensions, of past and the future, can be discerned in an unambiguous way, according to Minkowski.

If we seek to look behind these varied formulations, we will find, in my opinion, that reflexivity is the primordial ground of time, as it is of the conscious self. The intrinsic rhythm of reflexivity engenders both time and self-consciousness. It is for this reason that the self and time are mutually interdependent, reciprocally derived. Of course, they are not the same. But can they exist separately, completely separately?

PART III
TIME AND HISTORY

Chapter 1
History of Nature vs. History of Man

In Part I, we have sketched the temporal course of the natural universe from the standpoint of contemporary science. We have spoken of the "history" of the natural universe, and shown how this interpretation of nature arose, not from astronomy or physics, but from geology and biology, in the period from 1750 to 1860. The geologists learned that the earth had an ordered temporal development, a "history." Darwin extended the temporal developmental scope to living organisms. He also confirmed and clarified the directedness of the temporal development. As stated earlier, the contemporary view of the origins of life likewise reveals a clear temporal direction. The conceptual presuppositions of temporal direction, elaborated by geology and biology, have in this century influenced the contemporary views of astronomy and physics, leading to a cosmology which finds temporal direction in the totality of the physical universe. According to contemporary cosmology, the universe has been expanding for about ten to fifteen billion years, and this expansion as evidenced by the recession of the galaxies has been termed "time's arrow." If after fifty billion years, the universe were to begin a contracting phase, the arrow of time would be as evident in this contraction of the universe.

We have been using the word "history" in a loose sense. What is

145

"history"? Is history merely a sequential order of events? If it is more, we must seek to ascertain what *more* is involved.

Does not History require Man? It certainly requires an *observer*, if nature can be said to have a history. It requires a *conscious* observer who can apprehend the sequence of events and record it in utterance or in writing. The observer is a self, a subject, and we come here into the dialectic of subject-object. Perhaps quantum physics can give us a clue to understand anew this ancient theme. Quantum physics has come to a limit of its objective understanding where the subject and his instruments have an effect on the object so as to limit its possible understanding. We have noted earlier that space-time, wave-particle, are conjoint concepts in contemporary physics. Perhaps we should understand the subject-object likewise as *conjoint* conceptually. There is no subject without an object; no object without a subject. In self-consciousness the subject is object for itself, and therein may lie the uniqueness of human consciousness.

A conscious observer is self-conscious, if he *records*, if he sets down the record of events in nature or in human history. We have said earlier in Part II that there is no consciousness without self-consciousness. The self-consciousness may not be explicit, it may be immanent, as the "foundation (*Grund*) of consciousness" in Hegelian terms. Perhaps we might even regard consciousness and self-consciousness as *conjoint*, conceptually intertwined, ontologically inseparable in an ultimate sense. Then, is self-consciousness required for history, does real history begin with Man, with human history? What is the difference between the "history" of nature and the "history" of Man? Is it merely a difference in subject matter? The history of nature deals with events, with inanimate and animate entities. Man, of course, is an animate entity, and hence in a sense might be included in a history of nature. However, Man is also a spiritual being; and this, no matter how profoundly the evolutionary development from the animal kingdom may have influenced human nature.

Broadly speaking, there is a division in human knowledge between the natural sciences (*Naturwissenschaften*) and the social or humanistic sciences (*Geisteswissenschaften*). If we recognize that there is a history of nature and also a history of Man, then may we not regard history as the link between these two great branches of knowledge? And why is history the link? History is the link because of the temporal character of reality. The sciences, whether natural or humanistic, when authentic, are studying reality, and when successful, are explicating, revealing reality. History is the human understanding *sans pareil* of temporal reality. And Man is capable of history because he is a temporal being in an ultimate and essential ontological sense. History arises in the reflexivity of temporality in the human mind, which is itself characterized by reflexivity in self-consciousness. The great history in the human sphere was written by self-conscious men, conscious of history in the making. The introductory remarks of the histories by both Herodotus and Thucydides illustrate this most clearly. Herodotus wrote: "What Herodotus, the Halicarnassian, has learnt by inquiry is here set forth: in order that so the memory of the past may not be blotted out from among men by time, and that great and marvelous deeds done by Greeks and foreigners and especially the reason why they warred against each other may not lack renown."[1] Thucydides begins his work with the following words: "Thucydides, an Athenian, wrote the history of the war waged by the Peloponnesians and the Athenians against one another. He began the task at the very outset of the war, in the belief that it would be great and noteworthy above all the wars that had gone before, inferring this from the fact that both powers were then at their best in preparedness for war in every way, and seeing the rest of the Hellenic race taking sides with one state or the other, some at once, others planning to do so. For this was the greatest movement that had ever stirred the Hellenes, extending also to some of the Barbarians, one might say even to a very large part of mankind."[2] Of course, great history has also been written after the lapse of centuries by men, reliving the experience of the men of the past period with the help of documents, annals, relics, and other evidence.

In connection with history, there is an issue with respect to the nature of time which needs classification. One often reads statements such as "...actually real is only the present,"[3] or "the past, of course, does not, in any ordinary sense of the word, exist at all."[4] Both of these statements are versions, in my opinion, of the same error. As to the first, it is dubious to equate actual reality with presentness. Past and future are modes of being, different from one another and different from the present. They are not, however, less real than the present—and not less actually real than the present, unless "actually" were taken to signify "presently" which would be a meaningless tautology. As to the second statement, that the past does not exist at all, it makes the same mistake by equating *existence* to *presentness*, being present now. It is not merely the present that exists. The past exists, as does the future. The nature of past existence is, of course, quite different from present or future existence.

Existence is a concept or category which includes the fullness of temporality, all the dimensions and aspects of time, past, present, and future. *Being present now* is most difficult to define or specify; in a sense it is a superficial and evanescent concept in an ontological sense. Existence is not; it is ultimate and all-encompassing. Presentness has little meaning except in relation to past and future, to the passage from future to past. There is an ideational thread in the history of philosophy which relates presentness, the "Now," to eternity. This "Now" is neither related to, nor derived from, the experience of temporality, except perhaps as the denial of temporality. We shall return to this topic later in our discussion of Hegel. Here, suffice it to say, that the interrelationship and interpenetration of past, present, and future constitute temporality, forming thus the structure of time which gives time its historic character.

Chapter 2
Prehistory: The Temporal Span

In Part I, we cited the current view that life appeared on the Earth a billion or so years after the formation of the earth, 4.5 billion years ago. We have also set forth in Part I an outline of the temporal sequence in the evolution of living organisms from the Cambrian beginning about 600 million years ago. Although the first mammals evolved from reptiles about 180 million years ago, the reptiles were dominant from 180 to 60 million years ago, after which the mammals became dominant. All of the modern groups of mammals had appeared by thirty-five million years ago. Molar and premolar teeth of the earliest known primates (the order including monkeys, apes, and men) have been found in Montana and dated as 65 million years old. Based on fossil evidence, the most widely accepted theory of human origin is that apes and humans separated from a common ancestor about 20 or 30 million years ago.

The term *prehistory* was first used by a French scholar named Tournal in 1833 to refer to that part of human history before the time of written documents and archives. It is not certain just when the species *Homo* developed within the family of Hominids. Present archeological evidence would indicate a time bettween 5 and 3 million years ago. At any rate 99.8 or 99.9 percent of the temporal span of human existence lies in prehistoric time. After all, the earliest written records were set down in the Near East a mere 5 thousand years ago. Although writing and written records came into use later elsewhere in the world, the invention of writing some 5000 years ago is generally accepted as "the official end of prehistory."[5]

One of the earliest Hominids is a primate named *Ramapithecus*, found first in Northern India, and subsequently in Kenya. The Kenya specimen has been potassium-argon dated to about 14 or 15 million years ago. Possible specimens have also been found in China, Spain, and southern Germany. It is uncertain how close *Ramapithecus* lies to the origin of human lineage among the apes. It seems that Ramapithecines may have walked upright and used their hands more than apes do. The period from 14 to 5 million years ago was a time of great geological upheaval, and accordingly fossil deposits from this period are rare. Fossil evidence has revealed the appearance some 5 to 6 million years ago of two types of *Australopithecus* ("the southern ape of Africa"). The two species were *Australopithecus africanus*, a gracile creature about 42 to 50 inches tall, and weighing from 40 to 70 pounds; it walked upright, had a rather human skull, with an average brain size of about 450 cubic centimeters, slightly larger than the chimpanzee (400 cc), but much less than that of a modern human male (1350 cc average). *Australopithecus robustus* was a larger creature, with a low forehead, massive chewing muscles, and huge cheek teeth, unlike the reduced teeth and lighter jaw of *Australopithecus africanus*.

Australopithecus is believed to be on the direct line of ancestry of modern man. These creatures lived for at least 3½ million years in Africa, and many traces of *Australopithecus* and of a more advanced hominid have been found in northern Kenya and southern Ethiopia. The more advanced hominid had an unmistakably enlarged brain; one complete skull found in northern Kenya is dated to about 2.9 million years ago. It is believed that the Australopithecines and the more advanced hominids may have lived alongside each other for about 2 million years before the Australopithecines became extinct.

In the Olduvai Gorge in Northern Tanzania, the Leakeys found on a campsite dated to about 1.75 million years ago, alongside the skull of a robust Australopithecine, fragments of a more gracile and advanced hominid, with a larger brain than a gracile Australopithecus, and hand bones revealing an opposable thumb which permits both gripping and precise manipulation of objects as well as perhaps the ability to make complex tools. This creature is probably related to the advanced hominid found in northern Kenya. Louis Leakey regarded this creature as a new genus of *Homo* more advanced anatomically and a more skillful toolmaker than Australopithecus, and termed it *Homo habilis* ("handy person").

Remnants of the first humans have been found thus far only in Africa and Asia. The stone tools on these early campsites were very crude, only broken pebbles and flakes. However, these choppers and flakes were quite practical tools, used for skinning and butchering even large animals. This tool kit "could perform all the basic tasks of tropical, nonagricultural hunter-gatherers, whether they were predominantly hunters or foragers. It remained in widespread use without major change from at least 2 million to 500 thousand years ago."[6] The campsites were home bases, temporary but well established, where the hominids returned from hunting or foraging to live, eat, and sleep. The basic hunter-gatherer subsistence pattern had presumably been well established by the time of the Olduvai hominids.

In the words of Brian Fagan, "The earliest chapters of prehistory paint a picture of slow biological and cultural evolution, one where the first humans abandoned the individual foraging habits of their ancestors and began to share and carry food, carry tools, and return to well-established home bases. These momentous shifts in primate behavior may have contributed to the physical selection pressures that promoted an increase in the brain size of ancestral hominids. This in turn enhanced the human ability for effective communication, an essential prerequisite to the dramatic cultural evolution of later hunter-gatherers."[7]

Homo erectus was first discovered in Java, later in China, and more recently in tropical Africa and Southeast Asia. With a brain capacity of between 775 and 1300 cc, *Homo erectus* had a larger brain than earlier humans. The skull is more rounded than that of earlier hominids, has a prominent brow ridge, a sloping forehead, thick skull bones, and a massive jaw. *Homo erectus* was about five feet tall, with limbs and hips completely adjusted to an upright posture and with hands capable of precision gripping. *Homo erectus* specimens have been found in a wide geographic area, in many extremes of climate, from tropical savannah in Africa to temperate latitudes in China and Europe. The earliest *Homo erectus* thus far found is from Kenya and estimated to be 1.5 million years old. By 750 thousand years ago, *Homo erectus* had settled in southeast Asia and in China; by 500 thousand years ago, in central and western Europe.

With *Homo erectus* came improved tools, including large numbers of "hand axes" and "cleavers," both of which are general-purpose tools, with short cutting edges and rounded bases. They were probably used for many purposes, from skinning to digging up wild roots. The hand axe used by *Homo erectus* is called Acheulian (after the town of St. Acheul in France) and has been found over vast areas in Africa, India, the Near East, as well as Western Europe. Acheulian hand axes found in Olduvai are more than a million years old; similar hand axes were still being made in central Africa some 60 thousand years ago, which indicates how slow the rate of technological change has been in early prehistory. *Homo erectus* lived at Choukoutien near Peking, China about 300,000 years ago. There are hearths there, which are among the earliest evidence of the use of fire. Fire was important as man moved into colder climates; it kept him warm at night, gave him light, enabling him to work after dark, and protected him at night from predators. Also, with the availability of fire, hunter-gatherer bands could survive more readily far from their home bases, beyond the normal range of more nonhuman primates.

The one and a quarter million years of the existence of *Homo erectus* was a period of very slow cultural evolution, with only gradual changes in the Acheulian tool kit. About 200 or 250 thousand years ago *Homo sapiens* emerged, a human with a brain size as large as that of modern man. The earliest fossil remnants of *Homo sapiens* have been found in Swanscombe, England, Steinheim, Germany, and Fontechevade, France. Although the skulls found there had the larger brain capacity of *Homo sapiens*, they retained the massive chewing muscles and pronounced brow ridges of *Homo erectus*. Although these skulls were found in Europe, it is generally believed that *Homo sapiens* evolved in Africa and Asia as well.

Over 125 years ago a primitive-looking skull was found in a cave near Neanderthal, Germany. Since then large numbers of similar skulls have been found in Western Europe, and in the Near East, Africa and Asia as well. The Neanderthal people are regarded as a subspecies of *Homo sapiens*. The brain size is within the range of modern ones, but the Neanderthal skulls are lower and flatter than those of modern man; there were prominent brow ridges, no chin. The height of the Neanderthals was slightly over five feet; they had relatively short forearms, but they walked fully upright and nimbly. The Neanderthalers first appeared in an interglacial period between 120,000 to 75,000 years ago. Outside of Europe there is much variability among the Neanderthals with less extreme brow ridges and other skull features; at Mt. Carmel in Israel, the skeletal remains indicate a gradual transition to more modern forms.

The Neanderthalers were hunter-gatherers with a tool kit superior to that of earlier humans. They produced many types of composite tools—for example, a wooden spear with a stone tip. Also, they produced numerous points and scraping tools, sharpened by fine trimming, which were used in hunting, for wood-working, and for preparing skins. The Neanderthalers hunted, certainly by group cooperation, large animals such as elephants, rhinoceroses, bison, and cave bears. Evidence from a French cave indicates that the Neanderthalers in this area had a bear cult; the cave bear seems to have been an object of special attention, perhaps even of reverence, and an important component of hunting ritual. Among the Neanderthalers, we find the first signs of temporal awareness and of concern with existence after death, for it is evident that the Neanderthalers intentionally buried their dead. "Single burials are the most common, normally accompanied by stone implements, food offerings, or even cooked game meat."[8] Thus it has been observed that "in the Neanderthals the first roots of our own complicated beliefs, societies, and religious sense"[9] are found.

About 40,000 years ago, *Homo sapiens sapiens*, a larger-brained form of *Homo sapiens*, emerged in the Near East, Europe, Asia, and Africa. It is not known whether *Homo sapiens sapiens* arose first in the Near East and then migrated to the other areas, or whether there were independent centers of this development, such as France or China as well as the Near East. At any rate the archeological record from 40,000 years ago to the present appears to be the work of *Homo sapiens sapiens*, modern man. Also, all humans living today, the aborigines of Australia, the Bushmen of Africa, as well as the denizens of New York, Paris, London, and Moscow subways, are all examples of *Homo sapiens sapiens*. With the advent of *Homo sapiens sapiens*, areas of the world previously uninhabited became occupied: Australia more than 30,000 years ago, North and South America by at least 25,000 years ago, and Japan by 20,000. The *Homo sapiens sapiens* hunter-gatherers also populated areas of Africa, India, and Southeast Asia which were previously for the most part uninhabited.

While the paleontological record is by no means complete, the gaps do not break the overriding evolutionary continuity of the development of man as a biological organism. Current views on major steps in this evolutionary process are set forth in the following account. Primate hominids, the ancestors of mankind, it is believed, come to walk upright as a gradual adaptation to a life in the extensive grassland plains of the African savannah. Bipedalism or walking upright is not an inevitable consequence of coming down to earth from the trees, for some primate species like the baboons live on the ground without walking upright. Also, apes and monkeys walk upright occasionally just as men go on all fours, if necessary. Chimpanzees generally move around on the ground by knuckle-walking, i.e., the backs of the fingers are placed on the ground, serving as weight-bearing surfaces. Although chimpanzees get nearly ninety percent of their food from trees, they spend much of their time on the ground and knuckle-walk most of the time. Knuckle-walking is regarded as a possible intermediate stage between the ape's physical adaptation to life in the trees and the human bipedal posture. It is interesting to note that the assumption of an upright posture preceded the rapid increase in the size of the brain: the Australopithecines walked upright although the brain capacity was still within the same order of magnitude as that of the great apes, 470 to 585 cc. Grahame Clark states: "The most important and decisive biological change...was the adoption of a habitually upright stance, since until the hands were freed from the task of locomotion they were not so readily available for manipulating objects and ultimately making the tools and weapons by which the aims of the organism could be more effectively realized. This morphological change may well be related to the fact that, in contrast to the great apes who lived in a forest environment and continued to rely to a considerable degree on the forelimbs for getting about, the immediate ancestors of man were apparently adapted to life in the open where the need to cope with other animals placed a premium on freeing the hands."[10]

The earliest tools of human manufacture, stone chopper tools, have been found at Koobi Fora in north Kenya, dated by potassium argon methods to about 1.85 million years; as of 1979 no earlier tools have been dated with any certainty. It is believed that *Homo*, or a hominid more advanced than the Australopithecines, made the earliest stone tools. However, there may have been a slow evolution through man's hominid ancestors, in the development of the tool-making capability. Contemporary apes, chimpanzees and gorillas, studied in the wild, have been observed using objects such as sticks and branches for play and display, for self-defense against one another, or to scare off a predator. Chimpanzees also make tools to obtain termites, evidently regarded as a great delicacy. The chimpanzee takes a slender stick, breaks it off to the proper length, chews and licks the stick before probing into the termite hill at the places where the termite hill shell is thin late in the autumn. They have even been known to carry such a probe-stick a considerable distance while inspecting termite hills, then dropping the stick if the search was unsuccessful. If a chimpanzee is able to make and use tools, then it may be assumed that the hominid ancestors of man enjoyed a similar capability, and this capability developed steadily, albeit slowly, in as much as the better toolmaker groups among the hominids would have a better survival chance. It may even be, as Charles Darwin suggested, that the advantages of tools used by hands may have been a stimulating pressure towards full-bipedalism. Also it is evident that there was no clear break between man and other primates in the paleontological record, whether in respect to physical development or in the use of tools.

Another possible factor cited in the shift from part-time to full-time bipedalism is food eating and sharing. Bipedalism is a way of carrying food more efficiently for chimpanzees as well as for humans. Wild chimpanzees have been seen "loading their arms with choice wild fruits, then walking erect for several yards to a spot of shade before sitting down to eat."[11] Plant foods, however, are rarely big enough to be shared. A hunter may obtain ten or fifteen pounds of meat, even from a small animal, more than he can eat alone at the spot, and hence the remainder will be worth carrying back to a camp. Man is not the only primate who shares; wild chimpanzees have been observed sharing meat; a hunter will tear a piece of meat off a dead victim and give it to a fellow troop member who begs with outstretched hand. It may be noted here that group hunting and regular food sharing are basic features in the life of meat-eating non-primate animals who live in groups, such as wild dogs, wolves, hyenas, and lions. With respect to hominids, "hunting had major unifying as well as divisive effects. It increased cooperation among all members of the group, not only among certain males. Man became the only primate to kill regularly for his living and the only primate to share regularly on a day-to-day basis involving the entire group...Even more important,... another unique development came with the hunting—a division of labor between the sexes, with the males concentrating on obtaining animal foods and females concentrating on plant foods."[12] In the evolution of hominids towards man there seems to have been a reciprocally stimulating interrelationship between bipedalism, toolmaking, hunting, the carrying of food into a home base, food sharing, and group life in a social unit.

There is another factor which should be added to this complex of reciprocally related and reciprocally stimulating factors, namely, the growth in the size of the human brain. According to Grahame Clark, "The enlargement of the brain that helped to define the earliest men may well have been assisted by or even have resulted from the stimulus that came from the greatly increased use, and in due course the manufacture, of tools and weapons."[13] The growth of the skull from the hominids to modern man has been measured by plotting the size of the brain cavity of dated fossils against geological time. It has been shown that the brain of the Australopithecines increased very little during the lifetime of this species; the growth rate has been found to be about 1 to 2 percent for 100,000 years. "*Homo erectus* had a considerably faster rate of skull growth, 4.6 percent each 100,000 years. With *Homo neanderthalensis* the rate rose to 7.5 percent each 100,000 years."[14] Of course, size alone is not so significant; it is size in relation with internal brain differentiation and organization as well as the specific sites of internal cortical expansion. It is generally believed, however, that expansion preceded differentiation. Granit conjectures that the development of language may have played a role in the Neanderthalian increase to 7.5 percent each 100,000 years. In *The Emergence of Man*, Pfeiffer specifically relates the increase in brain size during the time span of *Homo erectus* to the rise of hunting. Similarly Pfeiffer relates to hunting the change in the brain of modern man from that of the Neanderthals, which was not so much a change in size as in internal differentiation and organization. Neanderthal hunters were members of one band (average size, twenty-five persons) and killed one animal at a time. Modern man hunted hard animals, big game, by a cooperative effort of many bands. Group hunt required and prompted improved means of communication, articulate speech, as well as concentration on common social purposes.

It has been generally observed by prehistorians that in the development of man social and cultural evolution was as important a factor as biological evolution, and that in the long range of prehistory social and cultural evolution gradually replaced biological evolution as the predominant distinguishing characteristic of humans. Man is a peculiar kind of animal, in so far as his behavior is patterned by the particular society and culture to which he may belong. Arnold Toynbee has written: "We have said that primitive societies are as old as the human race, but we should more properly have said that they are older. Social and institutional life of a kind is found among some of the higher mammals other than man, and it is clear that mankind could not have become human except in a social environment. This mutation of sub-man into man, which was accomplished...under the aegis of primitive societies, was a more profound change, a greater step in growth, than any progress which man has yet achieved under the aegis of civilization."[15] This muta-tion took time, millions of years; it was a slow process indeed. If we are to understand man, society and culture, civilization and history, we must take cognizance of the broad temporal perspective which includes the prehistoric development of mankind.

There is a rather general consensus among prehistoric archeolo-gists, physical anthropologists, and biologists that human develop-ment is to be explained on the basis of natural selection. While biological evolution proceeds on a genetic basis, cultural evolution proceeds on a social basis. Culture is transmitted by particular societies which are themselves constituted by sharing particular traditions. Natural selection, it is said, can operate on cultural varia-tions as well as on genetic mutations. As Grahame Clark points out, cultural diversity was not the only source of variability in human society, "the emergence and enrichment of human personality was another potent source of deviation on which the forces of natural selection could play."[16]

The artifacts which the prehistoric archeologist studies reveal the social and cultural stage of hominid or human existence; tools used to manipulate the environment, clothes and their fastenings to cover the body, houses to provide shelter, weapons to hunt wild animals and if necessary to fight other men, digging sticks for working the ground. Flints and stones were shaped according to socially inher-ited traditions and their biological effectiveness was determined by their fitness for the particular task. Economic competition is held to be the most important medium through which natural selection has operated. Social and cultural evolution, it is believed, was polycen-tric, developing in many separate, often interconnected areas. "The immense range of environments occupied by man would alone ensure that natural selection would result in a variety of cultural manifestations at any one moment of time." Also, "every advance in the complexity of social life opened up an increasingly large number of alternatives. The existence of distinct cultural manifestations in neighboring territories...was of extreme importance from an evolu-tionary point of view, because it offered a wide range of alternatives on which the process of selection could play."[17] Cultural contact was a significant factor in social and cultural development. As Clark stresses, "no significant human societies have ever existed perman-ently in complete isolation,"[18] and those most cut off from contacts were generally those most resistant to rapid advance.

We of the contemporary generation are very conscious of the accelerating course of change during our own lifetime—change which has affected nearly all aspects of human existence, material, technical, political, social, moral, cultural. Viewing the whole temporal scope of prehistory, it is clear that the rate of cultural advance has exhibited an increasing acceleration in the course of time. For millions of years change was so slow that it could be measured in geological time. Only some hundred thousands of years ago do we find marked local variation and more rapid change. This acceleration and this diversification occurred at the same time as evidence appears for human self-awareness and a growth in individual thought and feeling. Articulate speech was another factor in the acceleration of social and cultural evolution. The emergence of a settled way of life, based on farming and husbandry, recognized to be a necessary condition for civilization, was also another factor in the acceleration of the rate of human change. As Grahame Clark has noted: "More has happened during the last two hundred than during the previous fifty thousand years and more in the last fifty thousand than during the preceding two million years."[19]

It is startling to learn that in the long span of human development in prehistoric time, the domestication of plants and animals only took place some 9,000 to 11,000 years ago. For more than a million years man was a hunter-gatherer, picking wild plants, fruits, and nuts and hunting wild animals; for only 10,000 to 11,000 years has he primarily *produced* food, and this by way of domesticating plants and animals. Gordon Childe termed this process the "food-producing revolution," and it did have revolutionary effects. Indeed in human development it is perhaps second in importance to what Toynbee termed the "mutation of sub-man into man," and that because it was the basis of the village-farming community which in turn was the locus of the rise of civilization. As Grahame Clark has written: "No society dependent on catching or gathering has ever achieved literate civilization on its own; and, conversely, all literate civilizations can be seen to have developed from and still to depend ultimately upon the practice of farming."[20] However, food-production is a necessary, but not a sufficient, condition for civilization, for not all food-producing peoples attain civilization.

The food-producing revolution did not take place in one fast sweep, but rather gradually. In a sense man may have been an incipient cultivator and domesticator for a long time; he doubtless had learned much about the plants and animals which provided food; seeds of collected wild plants may have dropped in fertile soil at his campsite, and baby wild animals may have been brought back alive by hunting parties. Early village farming arose in the Near

East, as did the earliest civilization. Robert Braidwood estimates that the gradual transition to food production took at least several thousand years in the Near East 11 to 9 thousand years ago. Goats and sheep were domesticated in the Zagros Mountains area of the Near East by 11,000 years ago. In the same area, effective food production, as evidenced by tool kits and settlement patterns, had taken hold around 9,000 years ago, by which time barley and wheat had probably been domesticated. However, food production did not just begin in this area alone. It is known that cattle were tamed in Greece by 7,000 B.C., that in Southeast Asia root crops may have been cultivated as early as 9,000 B.C., and that in Northern Mexico some plants had been domesticated by 6,500 B.C.

Once the village-farming community level was reached, economic, social, political, and cultural development came very rapidly. By 6,000 years ago, the descendants of the first villages in the Mesopotamian valley had developed plough agriculture and wheeled chariots and were living in towns with temples. The earliest civilization in the Near East, and perhaps in the world, had arisen in Mesopotamia by 3,500 B.C., a civilization characterized by literacy, cities, political organization, monumental art and architecture, craft specialization and trade, and temples for religious worship. "Relative to the million years of food gathering which lay behind, this had been achieved with truly revolutionary suddenness."[21]

Around 3,000 B.C. the Early Dynasty period began in southern Mesopotamia, while writing appeared in this area several hundred years earlier. In Egypt the beginning of the First Dynasty may have been slightly later, but was also close to 5,000 years ago; writing probably did not appear there much earlier. The invention of writing which appeared thus 5,000 years ago, and some 5,000 years after the emergence of agriculture, is regarded, as mentioned earlier, as the end of prehistory. At any rate, we may say that history and civilization were well under way in both Mesopotamia and Egypt about 5,000 years ago. Braidwood believes that "learning to work together for the common good" in the control of the rivers (irrigation in the case of the Tigris and Euphrates and flooding in the case of the Nile) "was probably the real germ of the Egyptian and Mesopotamian civilizations."[22] Although there are certain general characteristics of the civilizations as they developed from early settled life, nevertheless they exhibit unique aspects as well. This is very evident in the scripts in which their earliest written records were set down. Henri Frankfort made the following comment about the two earliest literate civilizations of the Old World: "A comparison between Egypt and Mesopotamia discloses not only that writing, representational art, monumental architecture, and a new kind of political coherence was introduced in the two countries; it also reveals that the purpose of their writing, the contents of their representations, the functions of their monumental buildings, and the structure of their new societies differed completely. What we observe is not merely the establishment of civilized life, but the emergence, concretely, of the distinctive 'forms' of Egyptian and Mesopotamian civilization."[23] As Grahame Clark adds, by widening the range of comparison to include the Chinese, Greek, Indian, and Mayan civilizations, the same point becomes even more apparent.

In a superb book, *Aspects of Prehistory* by Grahame Clark, the last chapter is entitled "The Dawn of Self-Awareness," and includes a section on the awareness of time; this chapter is related to matters discussed in Part II in a different context. According to Clark, man is very different from other animals in his capacity for objectification. He finds, quoting Francisco Romero, this "capacity to distinguish objects, to individualize them" to be highly cognitive and distinct from the functional awareness related to vital activities, e.g., reproduction, as found among other animals. The manufacture and use of tools was a result of this capacity. In Romero's words: "The successful handling of things presupposed the capacity for objectification. To manipulate things to the degree necessary to derive knowledge from their handling presupposes the possibility of discerning them as things, of being aware of their relations, modes, and properties."[24] The capacity for objectification depended on certain biological characteristics developed in the course of evolution, such as stereoscopic vision, relatively unspecialized hands, and brains which are not only larger than those of nonhuman primates, but also enlarged particularly in the occipital lobe concerned with vision, the temporal and frontal lobes concerned with perception and memory, and the lower part of the parietal lobe concerned with speech and the use of symbols. This capacity for objectification led to articulate speech, abstract thought, use of symbols, art, concepts of persons, obligations and values, and self-awareness in a social context.

Articulate speech has been an indispensable prerequisite of the development of culture and civilization. The lack of articulate speech is generally regarded as the greatest limitation on the development of the nonhuman primates. Like other animals, the great apes communicate with one another, by sounds, gestures, facial and bodily expressions, postures, etc. These aural and visible expressions are signs which communicate meanings to others; they communicate emotions and desires, but as Wolfgang Kohler wrote, they "can only express emotions, never designate or describe objects."[25] Speech and thought are intrinsically interrelated, as the Greeks knew and expressed in their word *Logos*. As Julian Huxley wrote: "True speech involves the use of verbal signs for objects, not merely for feelings.... And to have words for objects at once implies conceptual thought;..." "Words are tools which automatically carve concepts out of experience."[26]

The Gardners have shown by teaching chimpanzees Ameslan that they can use signs for objects as well as emotions, and can develop a considerable vocabulary. This indicates an unusual, perhaps unique among the great apes, capability of chimpanzees. However, this sign language was taught to the chimpanzees by humans; the artist chimpanzee Moja received instruction in art from a human trainer. So far as we know, and wild chimpanzees have been extensively studied in recent decades, wild chimpanzees have not among themselves developed an elaborate sign language for communication nor engaged in the practice of art. The chimpanzees are termed "man's closest relatives"[27] and the Gardners' work has certainly demonstrated a profound commonality between chimpanzees and humans. Nevertheless, it still seems true that "the real dividing line between man and animals...is the possession of conceptual thought and of speech."[28]

In the several million years of prehistory, intentional and careful burial of human remains was a recent phenomenon. Some 50 to 60 thousand years ago, over a broad area from France to Palestine and Uzbekistan, Neanderthal man began to bury the dead in caves, or as at Mount Carmel on a terrace in front of an inhabited cave, or as at the Shanidar cave in Iraq in a shallow pit on a bed of flowers and covered with more blooms. At Teshik-Tash, Uzbekistan, a child is buried surrounded by a ring of goat's skulls set with horns downward—whatever the precise meaning, it certainly indicates concern for the dead. "The first overt sign that men were beginning to be aware of themselves was the formal recognition of death implied by the practice of careful burial."[29]

No ornament has been found in any Neanderthal burial site. Thirty to forty thousand years ago, with the rise of *Homo sapiens sapiens*, beads and personal ornaments have been found in burial sites indicating that the dead were probably buried fully clothed. Clark regards the adornment of the person as a further step in personal self-awareness. By painting, combing, and ornamenting themselves, humans showed that for whatever purpose in life, they were sufficiently aware of themselves to make the effort. Naturally this carried over to the treatment of the dead in burial. The dead body was covered with red ochre and a diverse supply of grave goods was placed with the dead.

The first people to ornament themselves were also the first artists. Whistles and pipes made from the bones of wild animals are the only remnants of the musical art. However, for the last 30 thousand years, the archeological record displays a fullness of graphic and representational art, engravings, paintings, reliefs, and sculptures. Graphic art first appeared in a rudimentary form in the Aurignacian culture in France between 33 and 28 thousand B.C. and flowered in the Gravettian period 26 to 20 thousand B.C. "The practice of art...implies a capacity not merely to visualize the outer world, but to conceptualize and in a sense to recreate it in the imagination. It is thus a manifestation of an advance in the power of objectification and in the capacity to symbolize the outer world."[30] The quality of this early art was superb. Indeed, Herbert Read, in a lecture on *Art and the Evolution of Man*, is cited as follows: "Some of the painters of Greek vases, some of the medieval illuminators of manuscripts, the great painters of the Renaissance, certain painters of the 19th century—all these have perhaps reached the level of aesthetic quality present in the cave paintings of Lascaux or Altamira, but they have not exceeded that original standard."[31]

It is generally agreed among primatologists that the great apes have a very limited sense of past and future time, which along with their lack of articulate speech is one of the greatest impediments to their development. Indeed, there seems to be a close link between a limited awareness of time and lack of articulate speech. The Gardners' research has cast doubt that the chimpanzees "are more or less trapped in the present." Nevertheless it is clear that the temporal horizon of the chimpanzee is quite limited in scope and that temporal awareness is most particularly focussed on imminent actions or on ending activities of the immediate past. At any rate it seems reasonably certain that only man is aware that he exists in time and that this self-awareness of his existence in time constitutes one of the most profound differences between man and the nonhuman primates as well as all other animals.

As we have seen earlier in Part II, biological clocks, perhaps activated primarily by changes in the intensity and duration of light, seem to regulate the daily and seasonal activities of all organisms. "Man is subject to the same organic regulators; but as he has become aware of time he has devised cultural means to supplement physiological time, just as in communication he has reinforced gestures by speech. In doing so, he has improved his biological effectiveness by extending the depth and range of his self-awareness."[32] Humans are subject to biological time like other animals, but unlike them they have exhibited an awareness of time by dividing time into segments related to their economic life or celestial occurrences and eventually by measuring time.

In regard to time men have not been motivated by merely practical utilitarian factors. "Exploration of the environment for instance, is as basic a drive in men as in rats."[33] The movements of the sun, the moon, and the stars certainly were observed carefully by primitive man beginning at some stage of his development and increasing thereafter. We have evidence of this from the behavior of existing primitive peoples. "The Bushmen, for instance, do not merely observe closely the phases of the moon and divide the day according to the position of the sun, but some of them foretell seasonal change from the stars; the Naron, we are told, accept the heliacal rising (i.e., the last rising before dawn) of the Pleiades as a herald of the cold season."[34] Other evidence of prehistoric man's observation and conceptualization of time have been found in incisions on ivory and bone artifacts. Incisions cut on a mammoth bone from a site at Gontzi, South Russia, dated approximately as 12 thousand years ago, seem to reveal a sort of notation in terms of four cycles in the waxing and waning of the moon, as cited by Clark from a 1964 article by Alexander Marshack. Meanwhile, Marshack has found markings, notches, and engravings on bones, stones, and other material going back about 35,000 years ago, which can possibly be interpreted as a notation for lunar phases. He develops very persuasively in *The Roots of Civilization* the role of "time-factored and time-factoring" thought in the cultural development of *Homo sapiens sapiens* for the first 30,000 years.

It is generally accepted that the massive stones of Stonehenge in England, termed "perhaps the most famous prehistoric monument in Europe,"[35] were set out in accordance with astronomical observations. It seems clear that, at each stage of its development over a thousand years or more, the monument was designed in relation to observed positions of the moon as well as of the sun. The numbers of component elements appear to correspond to such astronomical factors as the number of days in the lunar month or the number of years involved in the periodic swing of the moon. The authority—it may have been a kind of priesthood—directing the work at Stonehenge over so long a period of time had a vital interest in the movement of the heavenly bodies. The prestige and authority of this priesthood may well have been derived from its ability, "using the monument as a kind of observatory, to predict such events as eclipses."[36]

Of early settled civilized communities, the Mayas of eastern Mexico and northern Guatemala have a special interest to us because of their preoccupation with time and their amazing astronomical and mathematical achievements. The monumental ceremonial centers were designed so that the sun might be seen rising at solstices and equinoxes over key points. Special observatories were built with openings in the wall which afforded sightings from a central chamber on the north-south declinations of the moon and the setting of the sun at the spring equinox. The Mayas appeared to have been obsessed with a concern for the continuance of time. For this purpose it was of essential importance to schedule their ceremonials correctly, and this required complicated time-counts and exact measurement of astronomical events. The priests maintained two distinct counts: for religious purposes they used a sacred year made up of thirteen twenty-day units; for civil purposes, they used eighteen twenty-day counts plus five days and an occasional correction. "The Maya were well aware that the solar year was in fact rather longer than 365 days and developed a method of correcting the discrepancy between solar and calendrical years by calculating with surprising accuracy the length of the solar year: the Maya value of 365.2420 days was in fact closer to the modern astronomical value (365.2422) than was the corrected Gregorian calendar (365.2425). They also derived an accurate lunar calendar and calculated the intervals between eclipses of sun and moon."[37] The power of the priests presumably was based on their control of the calendar and their ability thereby to predict astronomical events that would otherwise have caused alarm. By combining the two time-counts, the Maya achieved the concept of what they hoped would be an endless cycle of Calendar Rounds, each equivalent to 52 civil and 73 sacred years; they also constructed a hierarchy of temporal units rising from the 360 days through multiplication by 20 to a unit of 23,040 million days. "Plainly, these hypothetical units served a psychoreligious rather than a strictly economic purpose. Above all they were designed to assuage the haunting anxiety that time might one day end."[38]

Clark comments that man's curiosity is not restricted to utilitarian matters any more than the curiosity of a dog, but unlike the dog he has the capacity to try to explain what he perceives. Self-awareness is accompanied by, and may even generate, apprehensions. Explanations are an effort to meet, to assuage, to dissipate these apprehensions. "The thirst for knowledge is a direct outcome of self-awareness. And of all the mysteries that confronted man as he emerged from the womb of instinctive life into the world of self-awareness and culture, none can have been more frightening or more poignant than the mystery of time."[39]

Chapter 3
Time, History, and Culture

We have observed earlier the marked differences between the two earliest literate civilizations, the Egyptian and the Mesopotamian. They each had a distinctive character, and this despite the fact that at the end of its prehistoric period, Egypt was stimulated by certain borrowings from Mesopotamia. These were the cylinder seal; monumental architecture, with mud brick used in decorative paneling, which appeared suddenly fully developed in Egypt at the final predynastic period; and certain artistic motifs in relief sculpture. In metallurgy, the Mesopotamians were ahead of the Egyptians, and Egypt may also have acquired better methods from there. Mesopotamia was also ahead in writing, with notation on clay tablets gradually developing over several centuries into a fuller record. Writing appeared suddenly in Egypt, and seemed to have certain features belonging to an advanced stage of writing. The first Egyptian writing may have been lost to us because it was done on perishable material, like wood. However, it is also possible that the principles of picture writing, including the rebus-principle, were borrowed from Mesopotamia, which would have been a tremendous stimulus in the Egyptian advance into literacy. In these matters the cultural leadership was certainly Mesopotamian, and no evidence has been found in the archeological record of Mesopotamian borrowing from Egypt.

Our aim is to set forth the meaning of time and history in the major early great civilizations. Despite the temporal priority of Mesopotamia and its evident influence on Egypt, for the purposes of our discussion we will deal first with Egypt, aiming to elucidate attitudes toward time and history ingredient in Egyptian civilization and culture.

Egypt

As Herodotus observed, Egypt is the gift of the Nile. There is practically no rain in Egypt, and were the Nile somehow to be cut off, Egypt would quickly become a part of the broad North African desert. A thin band of fertile black land, confined closely to the banks of the Nile, runs on a single north-south axis: to the south in Upper Egypt sharply demarcated by the desert cliffs, in the north by the red desert sands. Only in the Nile River delta of Lower Egypt is this north-south axis lost in the broad flat land spreading out in every direction. The sea to the north, the deserts to the east and west, the arid land and the cliffs to the south gave the land of Egypt a certain physical isolation from the large-scale movement of peoples into Egypt—although not from small-scale contact and commerce, as evidenced by the early Mesopotamian influence, which presumably came by coastal vessels from the Syrian or Palestinian littoral, or else by trade caravans across the Sinai Desert. In Egypt's later history, great folk movements did crash through these barriers of desert and sea. However, in the earlier historic times, the physical isolation brought a sense of security to the Egyptian, which allowed a certain individual freedom and bred a gaiety and optimism about his life in this world and the next. Under such conditions of relative isolation, naturally the Egyptians were a people centered on themselves; they had a sense of superiority, distinguishing between themselves as "people" and foreigners, a common enough attitude in ancient times (as well as modern!).

If Egypt is "the gift of the Nile," then the rhythm of the Nile is perhaps the most essential factor in the life, customs, and mind of the ancient Egyptian. Egyptian life was dominated by the periodicity of the Nile, its ebb in spring, its rise to flood in summer, its inundation of the plain with attendant revivication of the fields, and then the slow decline of the waters. The Nile never failed the Egyptians; to be sure, it might be low in some years and thus cause famine conditions, but it never ceased utterly, and eventually always came back with full strength. "In its periodicity it promoted the Egyptian's sense of confidence; in its rebirth it gave him a faith that he, too, would be victorious over death and go on into eternal life."[40]

Primitive and early peoples, living much closer to nature than modern man, were very sensitive to the many rhythms of nature, night and day, waxing and waning of the moon, equinoxes and solstices. The Egyptian god Osiris—who, among other things, brought the "fresh water" and was the life-force manifest in vegetation—was associated with the Nile flood in the main seasonal celebrations. The celebration of the New Year was meant to coincide with the rise of the Nile; the Great Procession at Abydos, a center of the Osiris cult, took place at this time. Great popular celebrations were also held at the time the waters of the Nile subsided and the fertilized fields emerged. Keenly aware as he was of the rhythms of nature, the ancient Egyptian sought to bring social and political life in harmony with nature. The coronation of a king in Egypt would be delayed until a new beginning in the natural cycle would provide a favorable starting-point for the new reign: in early summer, when the Nile began to rise, or in the autumn, when the flood had receded and the fertilized fields were ready to be sown.

The sun brought the dominant rhythm in the daily life of the Egyptian. In a sky with few or no clouds, the sun was ever present in the day; in the evening it sank into darkness, but came back clear and warm in the morning. The sun died every night and was reborn with brilliant strength every morning. The daily rhythm of the sun, like the annual rhythm of the Nile, bolstered the Egyptian's confidence that he also would conquer death. The importance of the sun to the Egyptian is attested by the fact that the sun-god Rē was believed by the Egyptians to have been the first ruler of Egypt and that the pharaoh, to the extent that he ruled properly, was regarded as an image, perhaps even emanation or incarnation, of Rē. Since the sun-god Rē had been the first ruler of Egypt, "no pharaoh could hope to achieve more than the establishment of the conditions as they were in the time of Rē, in the beginning."[41] As J.A. Wilson writes: "So this little pharaoh who sat upon the throne of Egypt was no transitory human but was the same 'good god' that he had been from the Beginning and would be for all time. So the relationship of beings was not something which had to be worked out painfully in an evolution toward even better conditions but was magnificently free from change, experiment, or evolution since it had been fully good from the Beginning and needed to be only reaffirmed in its unchanging rightness. Aspects of the divine kingship and of *maᶜat* (rightness) might be subject to temporary misfortune or challenge," but these two concepts were fundamental and immutable.

These two concepts, in Wilson's opinion, were present in Egyptian consciousness before the dynasties, i.e., before 3100 B.C. The first two dynasties, during a period of about four centuries, had the task of articulating these concepts to the new nation being constructed. Thus it was not until the Third Dynasty, 2700 B.C., that "Egypt really became Egypt" and "entered upon her characteristic career of essential sameness for 1500 years."[42]

It might be said that the ancient Egyptian looked to the past, that the past was normative for him, since the standard had been set under the reign of the sun-god Rē. However, the ancient Egyptian did not think in temporal terms. For him the gods had created a universe which has been essentially static from the beginning. He did not think in catenary or consecution terms, antecedent-consequence, cause-effect. Phenomena were explained as brought about by divine agency; thus they were not open to human questioning, there was no interest in the movement of time, and little impetus to seek out causes for effects. "To the ancient, phenomena were momentary flashes of a timeless and boundless universe, the realm of the gods, and therefore always subject to divine control or intervention. He thought in terms of a mirror image: that his experience was an illustration of the plans of the gods as revealed from the beginning."[43]

H.A. Frankfort has termed the ancient Egyptian, as well as Mesopotamian, mentality a "myth making" mentality. The ancients related their experiences to myths told about the activities and interests of the gods. By referring an observation or experience to a myth of divine agency, they did not need to seek causation in the past or take special measures for the future. If transitory phenomena can be related to the timeless and unchanging, fears can be reduced. This was done by myth making, whereby phenomena of the ancient's little world were regarded as "momentary flashes of the everlasting, rocklike order of the gods."[44]

Since the ancient Egyptian "lacked a sense of time, relativity, or impersonal causation, he was no historian."[45] Thus the two basic sources for our historical understanding of ancient Egypt—written records and records in art—show no concern with the progress of time and with the chain of cause and effect. Since in ancient Egypt the king was the state as well as the god, state efforts sought to support this dogma; thus the written records presented the divine, miraculous, and unchanging. These records have been termed "propagandistic," and distortions of truth or clear falsity have been discovered in certain cases by modern western historians. The art of ancient Egypt is as timeless and propagandistic as the written records and the literature. If the ancient data are partial, biased, and full of the myth making psychology, such data cannot speak for themselves. "...for the pre-Greek world there is no history in the strict sense, there are only historians, moderns who try to organize, understand, and interpret that which refuses to speak for itself but insists upon talking about the gods."[46] This quoted sentence, as we shall see later, is not true of China, nor of Israel.

The artistic expression of ancient Egypt from the Fourth Dynasty, 2650 B.C., until the 14th century B.C. carried the same message as the written records. The statues and relief sculpture were "designed for eternity. Each figure claimed eternal life by solidity and stolidity; by avoiding the appearance of flexibility, momentary action, or passing emotion; and by standing massive and motionless, sublimely freed from a single location in space or a single moment in time. As the Egyptian myths made momentary activities timeless and everlasting, so Egyptian art made the depicted individual a stereotype, and thus immortal."[47] Lesser beings, such as playing children, servants, peasants, and artisans might be shown in activity, "but the lord whom the arts served was shown in timeless and untiring majesty. For that purpose, the squared-off, striding profile, with its wide, unblinking eye, was beautifully adapted."[48]

This classical Egyptian art tradition was broken in the 14th century B.C. under the heretic pharaoh, Akh-en-Aton, in his new capital city Amarna. There a new naturalistic art emerged. In contrast with portraits in normal periods of Egyptian history, where the perceived was covered over with the idealized type best serving eternity, at Amarna the current exciting adventure was more important than eternity. With the purpose of art being removed from eternal and unchanging poise to a portrayal of today's aspects, there was a sudden recognition of time and space, formerly absent. Subjects were portrayed in action, lively, straining, and with an inner emotional excitement. The famous painted bust of Queen Nefertiti, which is a gracious and natural portrait with sloping lines and flowing surfaces is termed, "decidedly non-Egyptian," because it is "idealizing the current and temporary instead of the other-worldly and eternal."[49] Although the heretical doctrines of Atonism were soon wiped out by reactionary forces, Egyptian art never returned to its ancient hieratic dignity, but retained the naturalism which emerged so strongly at Amarna. From this time forward there was a very different Egypt from the ancient Egypt which has been our topic of discussion.

One topic of this difference remains to be mentioned. For 1,400 years from the Fourth Dynasty (2650 B.C.) on, tomb scenes stressed a gay and rich life which denied the validity of death. About the end of the 19th Dynasty (1222 B.C.), a drastic change took place within the time of two or three generations: the tombs discarded their devotion to this world and dedicated all their wall space to death and the next world. "The shadow of uncertain eternity had dropped over the sunny gaiety of Egypt." In the tomb scenes and texts life had been suddenly cast away and death embraced as inevitable. "The next life was now presented as a release from this life and as a reward for humble patience in this life." Thus, "the perennial joy of Egypt was gone."[50]

Mesopotamia

The geography of Mesopotamia is markedly different from that of Egypt. Egypt is physically isolated, bounded by deserts, mountains, and sea. Mesopotamia, the land between and about the two rivers, the Tigris and the Euphrates, does not have clear boundaries; hence it was attacked time and again by mountaineers from the east or nomads from the west. While the Nile fluctuates in its flooding, it never fails to rise. In contrast, the Tigris and the Euphrates are undependable, turbulent, violent, and dangerous rivers. Moreover, the rainfall in Mesopotamia is quite uncertain. The physical isolation of Egypt and the dependability of the Nile bred a sense of security, expressed in Egyptian attitudes and culture. In contrast, there was a feeling of insecurity and human frailty in almost every manifestation of Mesopotamian culture.

A remarkable feature of Mesopotamian civilization was its essential uniformity despite a great diversity of peoples. Unlike Egypt with its single dominant ethnic group, Mesopotamia included Sumerians, Babylonians, Assyrians, Chaldeans, and others. Moreover, the language of the Sumerians was quite distinct from the language of the other ethnic groups. In fact, for thousands of years, Mesopotamia had many languages—no wonder the story of the Tower of Babel is related to Mesopotamia. In the last two thousand years of its early history, Mesopotamia was bilingual for all cultural purposes, since not only Sumerian but also the Semitic Akkadian were both used in literate works. However, a common civilization transcended the ethnic, linguistic, and political boundaries, achieving a cultural unity despite the tremendous diversity. This unity is generally regarded to have been due to the Sumerians, since the dominant governing features of the culture are clearly Sumerian.

As in the case of Egypt, the practices of Mesopotamian civilization were correlated to the great rhythms of nature. The succession of the seasons was the dominant feature, and human societies stayed in harmony with nature by a recurring sequence of religious festivals. The mourning of the death in the heat of summer of a god known best as Tammuz was the most popular celebration, but the chief state function was the New Year's festival, with the celebration of the god's resurrection, his victory over the powers of evil, and his marriage to the mother-goddess. The seasonal changes represented cosmic crises; by these celebrations, the human society participated actively in these crises. In Mesopotamia, "the festivals were never free from anxiety and those which we know best show a change from deep gloom to exultation as the aim and the result of the solemnities."[51]

There is a remarkable consonance between the political and religious pattern of Mesopotamian civilization and culture. This pattern was essentially Sumerian. It may be approached either from the political or from the religious side. We choose to start with the political around 3500 B.C., when the Mesopotamian civilization and culture took shape. The political pattern of the new civilization is termed by Thorkild Jacobsen as "Primitive Democracy." In the new city-states of Mesopotamia, "ultimate political power rested with a general assembly of all adult freemen."[52] A council of elders attended to public affairs in normal times. However, if war threatened, an assembly could make one of its members a king with absolute powers. This kingship was held for a limited term; when the crisis was past, the assembly could revoke it. While in Egypt the king was a god, in Mesopotamia the king was a "great man," *Lugal* in Sumerian. The authority of a Mesopotamian king was circumscribed in two ways: 1) his authority derived from the gods to whom he was responsible; 2) his power was limited by the principle of government by assembly. No major undertaking could be launched without the prior approval of the proper assembly or assemblies. Before Gilgamesh, lord of Uruk, hero of a Sumerian epic, can start on a dangerous venture against the ruler of Kish, he must receive the approval of two assemblies, first the assembly of the elders, and next, the assembly of the warriors. Although Gilgamesh is the hero of a poetic cycle of legends, nevertheless it is believed that he may have been an historical figure, in fact that his victory over Kish may represent the emergence of the Sumerians as the political masters of Sumer and Akkad, major portions of Mesopotamia.

The religion of Mesopotamia was essentially Sumerian. Two features of this religion are most prominent: the identification of the gods with the powers of nature and the cosmos, and the human characteristics of these gods. No one god was the sole source of power and authority; all the gods had themselves been created. Ultimate authority in the cosmos resided in the general assembly of the gods. The leader of the assembly was the god of heaven, *Anu*. His son *Enlil*, the god of the storm, had the executive task of carrying out the decisions of the assembly. Mesopotamian literature portrays the functioning of the assembly in very human terms: one god usually raised the matters to be considered; the gods discussed these; through discussion the issues were clarified and the consensus would emerge. The voices of a small group of the most prominent gods, the seven gods who determined destinies, were most important in leading to a decision. When all the gods had finally agreed, the decision was announced by Anu and Enlil. The great decisions regarding the course of all things and the fates of all beings were thus formulated and confirmed by the members of the divine assembly.

However, there was an intrinsic uncertainty about the actions of the gods, the divine powers of nature in the cosmos meeting in assembly. Each god had a will of his own, and the strength of his will was related to the natural power personified. Thus the gods and their decisions were unpredictable. Accordingly the Mesopotamians had a violent and dramatic conception; nothing was permanent and settled. As a result, an anxiety and insecurity permeated humans, who must constantly seek by ritual and sacrifices to propitiate the gods in order to obtain favorable decisions on matters of importance to the individual or to the human community. Only by this effort could the human entertain hope.

The cosmic state which constitutes the universe and is governed by the assembly of the gods ruled the territory of Mesopotamia. Man was created for the benefit of the gods and his purpose is not primarily to seek the welfare of humans, but the welfare of the gods by serving them. The gods owned the land, the big estates, in this way: the temple of the city god was usually the biggest landowner in a city-state; other temples of other deities related to or associated with the chief city god also owned land. It has been estimated that around 2500 B.C. most of the lands of a Mesopotamian city-state were temple lands. As expressed in the Mesopotamian myths "man was created to relieve the gods of toil, to work on the gods' estates."[53] In the life of the city-state, the city god originated by divine direct command all significant efforts: war, peace, new laws and customs, the building of a temple, etc. These direct commands were communicated by omens, dreams, or interpretation of sacrifices, to the *Ensi*, who was the highest human servant of the gods, the manager of the god's estate and of his city-state.

There was an important distinction between the city-state and the national state in Mesopotamia. While the city-state was oriented to a great god in his capacity as a private citizen of the cosmic state, the national state was oriented to a great god in his capacity as an official of the cosmic state, thus becoming an extension of a governmental organ of the only truly sovereign state, the divine cosmic state.

If the affairs on earth were directed from heaven, history was necessarily "theocratic history," but not in the sense of the Old Testament, which we shall deal with later. For the supreme god of Mesopotamia was not an omnipotent being; his authority was not only affected by the divine assembly but also by extraneous circumstances, e.g., the theft of the Tablets of Destinies. It has been observed that "in Mesopotamia history ruled the gods more than the gods ruled history."[54] After all, for the Mesopotamian theocratic government was at a different level than human government, but not remote from, indeed like unto, human government. Since for the Mesopotamian the gods of the city-states were bound together in the assembly of the gods which made and executed decisions, historical events were interpreted in this framework. Any conqueror, if successful, was recognized as the agent of the storm god *Enlil*, who with force and violence executes the decisions of the assembly of gods. The classical example is the "historical" account of the fall of the city of Ur which had long ruled over Babylonia, when it was destroyed by barbarian Elamitic hordes coming down from the eastern mountains. In our view, the city was destroyed by the barbaric hordes which attacked it. In the Mesopotamian's view, the enemy hordes were but an outward form through which the wild destructive storm essence of *Enlil* manifested itself in the attack. *Enlil* was executing a verdict passed on Ur and its people by the assembly of the gods.

With respect to the long succession of dynasties, in the Mesopotamian theocratic view, each succeeding dynasty was usually regarded as the instrument whereby the gods had displaced the previous incumbent. Sometimes the gods might send a strange new people as a scourge, which was the case when the Umman Manda broke the rule of the Sargonids. Naturally, there was a theocratic reason for such change. A ruler would offend the gods in some way, perhaps by transgressing his oath of office or by overstepping the bounds set for him by his god. "This motif of theological offense as grounds for historic change confronts us throughout Mesopotamian history."[55] For example, in the chronicle account of the Sargon dynasty, Sargon is described as faithful and punctilious in matters of cult and ritual, and hence he was prosperous and successful in his ventures. His son, Naram-Sin, was not, as a result of which divine retribution was accorded him through the means of barbarian warriors. This narrow temple interpretation of history was not the prevailing view, but only a special case within the general conception of theological offense as explanation for historic change.

As mentioned before, a ruler not only needed the approval of the assembly, but also a divine sanction for major undertakings. This sanction was obtained by oracular guidance provided by omens. Sometimes these came in dreams; more often, examination of the organs of sacrificed animals by a seer provided the signs interpreted by a diviner. The priest had detailed, elaborate manuals; the recording of omens for future reference was an established practice by the end of the third millennium B.C. Divination was a vital factor in Mesopotamian civilization as in Greek; not in Egypt, however, since "a god incarnate does not take his cue from the liver of a sheep."[56] The importance of the omens in Mesopotamia showed the dependence of the ruler in all matters on the will of the gods. The ruler, of course, sought to please the gods; if necessary, in adverse circumstances to appease the gods. Since no individual god was really omnipotent, the purposes of the cosmic society were unclear, uncertain, and difficult to ascertain. The gods were distant, but distance in the literate society can be overcome by writing letters. Although the Babylonians never had letters to the gods nor formal annals, the Assyrian kings did petition their gods by letters, just as their subjects petitioned them.

E.A. Speiser points out that the history of the dynasty of Akkad beginning with Sargon was "a vivid example of ebb and flow in the fortunes of an empire. It brought into sharper relief the rise and decline of other dynasties. There was an almost rhythmic regularity to this unvarying alternation. Regularity was suggestive of cosmic laws. In short, here was a ready basis on which to found a system for the interpretation of history."[57] He cites in this connection the views of the German historian of the Ancient Near East H.G. Güterbock, and following him believes that by 2000 B.C. a Mesopotamian thinker saw the past in terms of recurring cycles, with alternating periods of bliss and disaster. However, H.A. Frankfort rejects Güterbock's thesis, stating that he "has not proved, to my mind that the Mesopotamians at any time regarded their history as an alternation of times of blessedness with times of misfortune. Individual cities suffered decline; individual kings were sometimes punished with defeat for their transgressions—that is all that we may conclude from the material."[58] Despite Frankfort's rejection, it seems to me reasonably persuasive, as Dr. Güterbock stated to me in a telephone conversation, that some few Mesopotamians did comprehend their past history in the terms of such alternation.

China

Ancient China was very remote geographically from the other ancient civilizations. Chinese civilization, like Egyptian, developed in relative isolation; indeed it was probably more isolated than the Egyptian, since we know of Egyptian borrowings from the Mesopotamians at a crucial stage of its development. Unlike Greek civilization, which was urban and subject to many outside influences, China was agricultural and isolated. Unlike Egypt with its symmetrical landscape along the sides of the one great river, Chinese topography was expansive and variegated, with river plains, hills, lakes, and craggy mountains. As primitive as other ancient peoples, the Chinese lived close to nature, and their experience of nature is reflected profoundly in the ancient Chinese world-view.

For many years it had been believed that early features of ancient Chinese civilization, particularly bronze technology, writing, and chariot warfare, were the result of diffusion from Western Asia. Recent archeological evidence from the Shang period (ca. 1760-1111 B.C.) has tended to confirm that these were all indigenous products of the developing East Asian civilization. In general, links have been established between the Shang civilization in which writing first appears and the earlier neolithic cultures of the Shang region which had already been explored by archeologists. Also, a recent study by a Chinese historian has shown that the very distinctive features of early Chinese agriculture make it exceedingly unlikely that early Chinese civilization arose through a cultural diffusion from other early civilizations. Thus "it increasingly becomes clear that the nuclear area of Shang was the central point from which bronze metallurgy, agricultural advances, and perhaps a complex of spiritual and social elements were diffused not just throughout the Chinese culture area, but also to all of East and Southeast Asia."[59]

It is true that Sumer possessed writing about 2,000 years before China. The earliest Chinese writing has been found on "oracle bones" with divination texts from the Shang-Yin period (ca. 1500-1100 B.C.); these reveal a Chinese script which is already highly developed, and hence it has been estimated that 1,000 or more years may have been required for the development of this writing system. Nevertheless, the Chinese attached great value and importance to their written records and they were industrious and prolific writers. As Professor Mote states, no earlier civilization has left a body of literary materials from 1000 to 500 B.C. so broad in range and so great in quantity as those of pre-imperial China.

Like the Egyptians and the Mesopotamians, the Chinese were profoundly conscious of the basic rhythms of nature. In an agricultural society, the rhythm of the four seasons made, of course, the greatest impression. Also the Chinese apprehended nature in the terms of fundamental dualisms, such as night and day, the heavens above and the earth below. From this apprehension came the conception of the *Yang* and the *Yin* as the two complementary principles of nature which found expression in pairs of opposites: light and dark, sun and moon, male and female, positive and negative. These dualistic conceptions were seen to apply also to the world of man with the contrasts between ruler and subject, superior and inferior, gentleman and "small man." Also the Chinese "naturally thought of the world in terms of a dualism between inner and outer, between private life and public life, and between family and state."[60]

The early Chinese are unique in having no creation myth. Also there was no tendency in their thought toward monotheism. The universe including nature and man was spontaneously self-generated and self-generating, without a creator, god, or cause otherwise outside of itself. The Chinese universe was characterized by movement and change, not random change, but rhythmic organic change, like the processes of an organism. "...all of the parts of the entire cosmos belong to one organic whole and...they all interact as participants in one spontaneously self-generating life process."[61] Comparing the Greeks and the Chinese, Joseph Needham has written: "For the Greeks what mattered was an ideal world of static form which remained when the world of crude reality was dissolved away. For the Chinese the real world was dynamic and ultimate, an organism made of an infinity of organisms, a rhythm harmonizing an infinity of lesser rhythms."[62]

This organic Chinese world view becomes apparent in one of the earliest Chinese books, the *I Ching* (*Book of Changes*). It is a remarkable work, a book of divination, as well as a book of wisdom and rational thought expressed in poetic images. The divination texts probably go back to twelfth century B.C. oral traditions, which may not have been set down in written form until the seventh century B.C. These texts have been elaborated by commentaries by Chinese thinkers down through the centuries from the sixth century B.C., the time of Confucius. A clear expression of the "organismic" quality of Chinese thought may be found in the interpretive commentary to Hexagram 32, Duration, as follows: "Duration is rather the self-contained and therefore self-renewing movement of an organized, firmly integrated whole, taking place in accordance with immutable laws and beginning anew at every ending."[63] The next sentence which notes that the end is reached by contraction and this inward movement turns into a new beginning, with movement directed outward in expansion, could find an example in the current conception of the "oscillating universe"!

In the introduction to his translation of the *Book of Changes*, R. Wilhelm notes that the underlying idea of the whole book is the idea of change, and that if the meaning of change is perceived, then attention focuses not on transitory individual things but on the immutable eternal law at work in all change; and that change is conceived partly as the continuous transformation of one force into the other, and partly as a cycle of complexes of phenomena in themselves connected, such as day and night. One feature to be noted specially is that the Hexagrams and their interpretation deal simultaneously with the world of nature and the world of man. Two examples are as follows. In the interpretation of Hexagram 22, "By contemplating the forms existing in the heavens we come to understand time and its changing demands. Through contemplation of the forms existing in human society it becomes possible to shape the world."[64] In the interpretation of Hexagram 49, "Times change and with them their demands. Thus the seasons change in the course of the year. In the world cycle also there are Spring and Autumn in the life of people and nations, and these call for social transformations."[65]

For the early Chinese, "spiritual" beings existed, spiritual in the sense of existing apart from normal human life, but material in representing different states of matter; for example, "spirits of deceased persons continued to linger about, the lighter and heavier parts of their noncorporeal selves having separated from the corpse at the moment breath left it, and these then separately go their more terrestrial or more ethereal ways for a time (on the basis of affinity between their substance and earth or air), until they at last return indistinguishably again into the flux of universal matter. By that time, if not sooner, they have lost all traces of the individual's identity."[66] This is, of course, a naturalistic conception, with "spirit" having the same qualities and undergoing the same processes as natural beings. Furthermore, the Chinese venerated spirits and lesser gods, but these tended to merge with other aspects of nature and had less significance than their analogues in other cultures.

The first Hexagram of the *Book of Changes* deals with the concept of *Ch'ien*, which may be translated as "heaven," "nature," or "the creative." By 600 B.C. this concept, which 1,000 years earlier was an anthropomorphic conception of a deified ancestor, had become an abstract conception of cosmic process. This has been interpreted as a rise of rationalism during this period of Chinese culture, and well it may be, in the sense that rationalism and abstraction are correlated concepts. However, in contrast with Western thought Chinese abstractions always seem to have a reference or applicability to the world of nature and man: they are not logical abstractions of Western type; in Hegelian terms, they have a concreteness. The early Chinese apprehended a cosmic dynamism, explicable in terms of its internal harmony and the balance among the parts of a naturalistically observed and conceptually known world organism.

A major principle of Confucian doctrine is that man must establish a harmonious relationship with the universe in order to secure social harmony and individual happiness; in other words, the social order must be adjusted to the cosmic order. Man is seen as in close relationship with Heaven and Earth. "The norms of Heaven and Earth are what men take as their pattern striving to imitate the brilliance of Heaven and according with the natural diversities of Earth." The ancient Chinese even discerned a trinitarian relation between man and Heaven and Earth, "each performing its appropriate function in the cosmic order." The Confucian sage of the third-century B.C., Hsün Tzu, stated: "Heaven has its seasons; Earth has its resources; Man has his government. This means that Man is capable of forming a Trinity with the other two." For such a role Man must have qualities of heroic, cosmic dimension. Thus only a sage can achieve the proper harmony between the human and natural worlds, and the moral virtues which enable man to carry out such a relation to Heaven and Earth perforce become cosmic principles. It is evident that the Chinese believed that "...human moral behavior interacted with the processes of Heaven and Earth."[67] For example, if the weather was bad, this might be due to the ruler's improper conduct; if the ruler ordered executions in Spring, it could have a damaging effect on the crops.

Viewing the relationship between the social order and the cosmic order in the terms of the French sinologist Granet, who regarded the concept of *Order* as the basis of the Chinese world-view, Joseph Needham states: "The uncreated universal organism, whose every part, by a compulsion internal to itself and arising out of its own nature, willingly performed its functions in the cyclical recurrences of the whole, was mirrored in human society by a universal ideal of mutual good understanding, a supple regime of interdependence and solidarities which could never be based on unconditional ordinances, in other words, laws." In a note to this passage, Needham adds: "It may, of course, be said that the converse would be a truer statement, namely, that the Chinese conceptions of the world mirrored the characteristics of their society. To this I subscribe..."[68] We may note here the same pattern which we found in Mesopotamian thought, namely, that the cosmic order, in the Mesopotamian case the assembly of the gods, may be regarded as mirroring the social and political order.

Given the trinitarian relation between Man and Heaven and Earth, it is not surprising that we find Chinese rulers called the Sons of Heaven. The concept of the Son of Heaven goes back to the days of the Shang kings, in the second millennium B.C. Chinese kings and emperors ruled over vast territories and large populations, but they were not merely concerned with worldly affairs. As Sons of Heaven, they must also seek by their own proper conduct to maintain the proper working of the natural order, for natural disasters affecting the human social order would result if they deviated from proper conduct. According to Confucius, just as there are not two suns in the sky, so there are not two Sons of Heaven on Earth. This amounted to a kind of cosmic justification that the emperor was not just the ruler of China, but the sovereign of all-under-Heaven; from this was derived the expectation of tribute from the barbarian neighbors and distant peoples.

The Chinese ruler became the Son of Heaven through the Mandate of Heaven, which could be withdrawn if he proved to be unworthy. Natural disasters or popular rebellion could indicate the withdrawal of the Mandate. The rulers who lost the Mandate and were replaced by new dynasties were bad rulers, while emperors of new dynasties usually exhibited by their worthy acts possession of the Mandate of Heaven.

By ritual observances and personal conduct, the Son of Heaven carried out his important role in maintaining cosmic order as well as social order. Thus there developed a tradition that "the emperor's cosmo-magical role meant that practical matters should be left to his officials,"[69] appointed because they were men of ability and wisdom. The great Chinese administrative bureaucracy, which goes back more than 2,500 years, was developed on this doctrinal basis. Despite the title of Son of Heaven, the Chinese emperors, however, were not considered to be divine, as were the Pharoahs of Egypt.

Raymond Dawson believes that the doctrine of the Mandate of Heaven may have been set forth by the founders of the Chou Dynasty (1122-249 B.C.). According to this view, the Mandate has been held first by the Hsia Dynasty (2205-1766 B.C.) and then by the Shang Dynasty (1751-1122 B.C.) and "each had forfeited it by abandoning the virtuous ways of its founders which had caused Heaven to confer upon them the Mandate to rule over mankind, and thus it had come into the hands of the latest exponents of supreme virtue, the Chou conquerors. The theory not only explained the past, but carried implications for the future; for it constituted a pledge that the Chou rulers would continue to govern with piety and wisdom or else run the risk of losing the Mandate in their turn. When they were in the course of time overthrown, this confirmed in the minds of the Chinese a way of looking at history which persisted right through to the twentieth century. The very success of the Han founder, Liu Pang, in conquering Ch'in and uniting the empire, although his peasant qualities did not mark him out as an obvious recipient of Heaven's trust, was firm proof that he had the Mandate, and sound justification for approaching him with the awe and veneration which became the standard treatment for emperors."[70]

As the Egyptians, the Greeks, and so many other ancient peoples, the Chinese looked to the past for ideal government. Reform in Chinese society down the centuries has often been seen as a renewed effort to return to the true harmony and unity of the *Tao*, the Way. The word *Tao*, which literally means "a roadway," had the extended metaphoric meaning of "the way." In Confucian thought, *Tao* meant the Way of the ancient sage kings, i.e., the state of harmony in which good government prevails. In the Taoist school of philosophic thought, *Tao* means the Way of nature and the cosmos. In Taoist thought, man is seen as ideally living in harmony with nature and, if necessary, isolated from other men; nature, not man, is the crux of Taoist values. In Confucian thought, man should live in harmony with nature and with men, with man being the measure of Confucian values.

In the fourth century B.C. the Confucian philosopher Mencius described the Way of a true king as follows: to exercise natural benevolence and to promote agricultural production and social welfare to the end that the needs of all the people were met and everyone "had the leisure to cultivate the virtues necessary to the harmonious ordering of society." The reward of proper kingly conduct is popular support: in Mencius' words, "the one who gets the Way will have many supporters, but the one who loses the Way will have few supporters."[71] If a king did not properly take care of the people's welfare, according to Mencius, he was not entitled to retain his rule. And if he seeks to rule by force, arbitrary violence, and repression, the people have the right to rebel against him, even to kill him, for tyrannicide is not regicide. He also related the Mandate of Heaven to the people's consent and well-being by saying, "Heaven hears as the people hear; Heaven sees as the people see."[72] Thus the people in the ancient Chinese tradition became the standard for judging rulers and government. Mencius wrote: "There is a way to win all-under-Heaven; if you win the people, then you will win all-under-Heaven. There is a way to win the people; if you win their hearts [regarded as the seat of mind in ancient China], then you will win the people."[73]

As we have seen, the earliest Chinese philosophic thought was concerned with the problem of change, and this concern covered the process of change both in the natural and in the human world. This prepossession lead the Chinese to be industrious recorders of change in human affairs, tireless readers and writers of history. China possesses "the greatest of all ancient historical traditions...the Chinese were the most historically minded of all ancient peoples."[74] The importance of history in Chinese thought is attested by the fact that proof by historical examples prevailed very early in Chinese culture over proof by logical argument. The former was suited to feudal bureaucratic states with absolute rulers; the latter to democratic city states with assemblies, where every member was an equal citizen and could talk back. The Chinese method was analogical: "like causes bring like effects, as it was then so it is now and so it will be forever."[75]

History has been termed the queen of the sciences in Chinese culture. In fact, the quality of Chinese historical writing is superior to that of any other ancient civilization except the Greek. Indeed it is comparable to the Greek, as has been demonstrated by Professor S.Y. Teng in his article entitled "Herodotus and Ssu-ma Ch'ien: Two Fathers of History."[76] Professor Teng points out that both developed distinctive methods of *learning by inquiry* about the past, which was the original Greek meaning of the word *history*; in her introduction to the *Shu ching, Book of History*, Clae Waltham also states that for the Chinese "history exists in its original concept: inquiry into the past."[77]

As evidence of the Chinese concern with history, we find that the oldest complete ancient Chinese classic is the *Shu ching, Book of History*, although parts of the *I Ching, Book of Changes* have older sections. The documents commence with the reign of Yao in the 24th century B.C., and, with gaps, come down 1,700 years to King Hsiang (Chou Dynasty, 651-618 B.C.). The authenticity of these documents has been the subject of controversy, partly because most chronical and historical materials of this early period were lost in wars and uprisings during the unification of China by the Ch'in Dynasty or were destroyed in Ch'in's notorious "burning of the books." These ancient documents contain themes which we have noted earlier as prevalent in Chinese thought and culture: the interaction between man and nature, natural calamities being caused by the degenerate and licentious conduct of rulers; the sage king acts in reverent accord with the ways of Heaven, taking the all-intelligent and observing Heaven as his pattern, and the people as a result will be well governed; the highly moral tone, as exemplified by the pronouncements about drunkenness and luxurious ease; the passage of the Mandate of Heaven from the degenerate ruler of one dynasty to the virtuous ruler of a new dynasty; and the rewarding of virtue. "Great Heaven has no partial affections; it helps only the virtuous."[78]

The first appointment of a court historian in China goes back into the shadow of legend, being attributed to Huang Ti, the Yellow Emperor, who is supposed to have lived in the 27th century B.C. Recent archeological finds have disclosed that the court diviners of the Shang kings (1766-1122 B.C.) maintained records of their divinations, inscribed on bone and shell. Thus there was an early relation between magico-religious operations and record-keeping which persisted in China for millennia. It is believed that Chinese rulers employed court historians beginning with the early part of the Chou period (1122-250 B.C.). From the eighth century B.C., with the gradual emergence of semi-independent states, historical records were maintained in several courts. It is known that members of the Ssu-ma family had served for centuries as archivists to the Chou kings before the birth of the Grand Historian, Ssu-ma Ch'ien, in 145 B.C. Ssu-ma Ch'ien inherited the post of Grand Historian on the death of his father in 110 B.C. He was responsible not only for historic records, but also for astronomical studies and the calendar as well as the custody of old books and the supervision of government dispatches. Joseph Needham points out that the title *Thai Shih* could be translated at that time as Astronomer-Royal, Astrologer-Royal, and Historiographer-Royal. This office clearly had both an earthly and a heavenly function, and combined the two in its astrologic function. One hundred and fifty years later, the Bureau of Astronomy and the Bureau of History had become two entirely separate branches of the court bureaucracy.

Ssu-ma Ch'ien's *Shih chi, Records of the Historian*, is a history of the Chinese and foreign peoples from earliest times down to the years of Ssu-ma Ch'ien's life. His history dealt not just with China, but the world as known to him. Most of it deals with China, of course, the center of the world in his eyes and the highest point of human culture; he also deals, however, with Korea, Southeast Asia and other lands bordering on China; he had no knowledge of lands and peoples farther away. Moreover, it is a history of the entire knowable past. He is silent on the origin, size, and shape of the world and on the origin of mankind. Unlike Hebrew and Christian historians, there is in his work no datable beginning to the world nor to human history; also there is no single point in time to which all other events are temporally related. The dates of human history are recorded in terms of the years of rulers. He begins with an account of the five legendary ancient rulers, the paragons of Chinese political virtue. Then he deals with the history of the first dynasty, Hsia, the second, Shang, and on to the Chou and Ch'in dynasties, and finally the Han dynasty of his lifetime. The chapters concerning events close to or contemporary with his own life-time are the major portion of his history and, as with Herodotus and Thucydides, are naturally the best.

Ssu-ma Ch'ien stated as his aim: to "examine the deeds and events of the past and investigate the principles behind their success and failure, their rise and decay." His work is didactic, in the Confucian tradition, intended "to censure evil and encourage good."[79] Likewise following Confucian tradition, his work exemplifies the duty of the historian to judge the events and acts of the past objectively and fearlessly, even though he is an official of government.

While it may be disputable, as we have seen, that the Mesopotamians viewed their history as a rhythmic rise and fall of dynasties, in China there is no doubt that this view of the dynasties prevailed. For the Chinese, history proceeded by discrete dynasties, lasting as long as the descendants of a ruler inherited his throne. They were thought of "as a kind of organism, which passed through periods of growth, maturity, and decay like any other life cycle."[80] This pattern in history is an inevitable natural exemplification of a basic general pattern of all life. "When things flourish they shall then decay." As a part of life, human history "must follow this law of growth and decay, of waxing and waning, which characterizes the life of all heaven and earth."[81] This concept of life-cycles in history appears in the earliest Chinese literature.

The rise and fall of dynasties had a pattern prevalent in Chinese historical thinking as follows: each dynasty begins with a sage king of great wisdom and virtue, and closes with an evil, degenerate monarch after a gradual decline. This pattern of rise and decay is generally varied in the middle period of the dynasty by worthy rulers who restore for a time the original excellence of the dynasty. The cycle begins anew when a new hero-sage, founder of a new dynasty, overthrows the evil despot at the end of the former dynasty. As Burton Watson remarks, the Grand Historian Ssu-ma Ch'ien regarded it as his task to set forth the accounts of the early dynasties and feudal states so as to make clear this pattern of growth and decay. Describing Ssu-ma Ch'ien's history, Burton Watson writes: "The 2,000 years which it records move with a ceaseless rhythm of rising and falling political fortunes, a rhythm which to the Chinese is a natural and inevitable reflection in the human realm of the larger rhythm of the seasons and the stars."[82]

The early Chinese thought in terms of patterns and cycles. Joseph Needham has pointed out that their thinking has a kinship with Whiteheadian "process," a patterned interweaving of events, which contrasts with the Newtonian view of a series of discrete events in a causal chain. This kinship derives from the deeper kinship of the Chinese conception of the internally differentiated, self-generating, and self-integrating cosmos with the thought of Leibniz and Hegel as well as Whitehead's philosophy of organism, a kinship also set forth by Needham. In this Chinese world-view the conception of time is based on the cycles of natural change through the seasons, and on the regular motions of the heavenly bodies. The movements of the planets and the stars embody and disclose a series of cycles which extend indefinitely into the past and the future; since the Cosmos was not created, designed, nor externally controlled, there is no limit to its past or future. Not having a creation myth, the Chinese also "never had any belief in the fixity of species;"[83] living things could turn into each other, given sufficient time, and the possibility of slow evolutionary modifications was recognized.

Aside from the cyclic cosmic time, in Chinese thought there was also the linear advancing time of human history. There were two views of what happened to human society in time. The first, characteristic of ancient Taoist philosophers who opposed the feudal society, that there had once been a Golden Age of sage-kings after which a steady decline took place. Second, characteristic of Confucianism, with its emphasis on development and social evolution, that culture-heroes arose from time to time, first to stimulate human development out of primitive savagery, and thereafter to advance further the civilization and culture of human society. Confucian thinking usually didn't go beyond a new and better dynasty, but more visionary thinkers occasionally reversed the time direction of the regressive conception to make it a progressive one, for example Ho Hsin in the second century A.D., by which time religious Taoism was already looking towards a Golden Age in the future as well as the past. Although cyclic time with eternal recurrence was an element in Chinese thought, in Joseph Needham's opinion the concept of linear progressive time was dominant in China.

In an article published in 1946, Derk Bodde writes: "Connected with their intense preoccupation with human affairs is the Chinese feeling for time—the feeling that human affairs should be fitted into a temporal framework. The result has been the accumulation of a tremendous and unbroken body of historical literature extending over more than 3,000 years. This history has served a distinctly moral purpose, since by studying the past one might learn how to conduct oneself in the present and future."[84] Reiterating the theme that "the Chinese historical experience is by far the most fully documented one in all human history," Fredrick Mote explains that this comes about "largely because the Confucian mainstream of later Chinese intellectual life took the lesson of history so seriously; history functioned as revelation did in other civilizations."[85] Recalling Hegel's pronouncement *Die Weltgeschichte ist das Weltgericht* (World History is the Last Judgment), we find here another analogue between Chinese thought and the deepest stream of European philosophy.

The Hebrews

Between the sunny valley of the Nile and the flood plains of Mesopotamia lies the rugged terrain of northwest Arabia, with many mountain peaks, volcanoes, large expanses of desert, and uncertain rainfall. In this terrain, Syria and Palestine (Canaan) together have been regarded as the largest and richest oasis, hence the "fertile crescent." Between Egypt and Mesopotamia, Canaan occupied a geographically central position across the line of communications and transportation for merchants and armies. In a sense, it was a buffer area, or better, a frontier area, but one which managed to preserve its own character and individuality. Since they were situated between two great political powers, the history of the Hebrews in Canaan was related to, and subject to, these great powers. Were it not for a power vacuum in this frontier area for several centuries at the beginning of the first millennium, due to internal weakness in both Egypt and Mesopotamia, the Kingdom of David and Solomon might not have come into existence and certainly would not have attained its maximum expanse. The main highway between Egypt and Mesopotamia passed through the northern part of the Kingdom of Israel (established after Solomon's death in 922). The Kingdom of Judah was comparatively isolated in mountainous terrain to the south and economically poorer; hence Judah was able to survive another century and a half after the Assyrians took Samaria and Israel in 722 B.C.

Historically the Hebrews appeared late upon the scene in the ancient Near East towards the end of the second millennium B.C., and they settled in a country subject to cultural, as well as political, influences from the two older adjacent cultures, Egypt and Mesopotamia. Egyptian and Mesopotamian beliefs are reflected in many passages of the Old Testament, but the overall impression is not one of derivation, but of originality. In the essentials, Hebrew religion and thought is *sui generis*, different and unique.

Most nations have deep ethnic, linguistic, and territorial roots in a remote and obscure past; their nationality has chthonic sources. With the Hebrews it was different. The origins of the Hebrew nation are in an historic experience, that of Exodus and Sinai. Moses lead out of Egypt a mixed group, certainly not all descendants of Jacob. There was, as the Bible says, a "mixed multitude," a "rabble," with the Hebrews. These were presumably also fugitive slaves, perhaps Egyptian, perhaps Khapiru (a term denoting a stratum in society, a class of people of diverse races without citizenship, and without a fixed position in the social structure). Moses' father-in-law was a Midianite, and his clan is said to have joined Israel on the march in the wilderness. Also, Caleb and Othniel are called Kenizzite—i.e., of an Edomite clan. Thus, even in the wilderness the Hebrews were joined by groups of diverse origins, some of whom doubtless had been neither in Egypt nor at Sinai.

The Hebrew nation and Hebrew history proper begin with the

Exodus. Although there is no extra-Biblical evidence of the exodus, we have no reason to doubt that the exodus was an historical event; *qua* event, it was probably a small marginal affair, certainly not "headline material." Egyptian inscriptions and records show no evidence of the Hebrews' presence in Egypt nor of the exodus. According to the Bible, the escaping Hebrews were caught between the sea and the Egyptian army and were saved when a wind drove the waters back, allowing them to pass over to the other side; the pursuing Egyptians were drowned in the returning flood. The records of the Pharaohs do not normally mention reverses; moreover, an event involving a party of runaway slaves would not have been of significance to them. It has been estimated that only a very few thousand participated in the exodus; all of later Israel was certainly not descended from this small number.

The historic experience of the Exodus which created the Hebrew nation was also at the core of Hebrew religious faith. Indeed it was because Exodus was at the core of faith that it created a people and has sustained it by cultic memory to this day. As witness, consider a credo in Deuteronomy believed to go back to the earliest period: "A wandering Aramean was my father; and he went down into Egypt and sojourned there, few in number; and there he became a nation, great, mighty, and populous. And the Egyptians treated us harshly, and afflicted us, and laid upon us hard bondage. Then we cried to the Lord, the God of our Fathers, and the Lord heard our voice, and saw our affliction, our toil, and our oppression; and the Lord brought us out of Egypt with a mighty hand and an outstretched arm, with great terror, with signs and wonders; and He brought us into this place and gave us this land, a land flowing with milk and honey. And behold, now I bring the first of the fruit of the ground, which Thou, O Lord, hast given me" (Deut. 26:5-10).

After the exodus from Egypt came the years of wandering in the wilderness of the Sinai peninsula. During this period the Hebrews acquired their distinctive faith, and that primarily at Mt. Sinai. At Mt. Sinai the Hebrews received from the hand of Moses the covenant with the "new" god, Yahweh, which was, and has remained, at the heart of Hebrew religious faith and the Hebrew interpretation of their own history. Before the time that the Hebrews came into Canaan as worshippers of Yahweh, there is no evidence indicating the presence of Yahwism either in Canaan or anywhere else; the name "Yahweh" has not been found in any text of an earlier period. In some of the very early poems, Yahweh is referred to as "the one of Sinai." Exodus, the Sinai events, and Yahwism were evidently linked from the beginning. The prime element in this linkage is the covenant made by the Hebrews at Mt. Sinai with Yahweh.

It is estimated that the exodus from Egypt took place around 1280 B.C. and that the conquest of Canaan began around 1250 B.C. In between these dates the covenant event took place at Mt. Sinai. For the Hebrews at the time, and forever thereafter, their covenant with Yahweh was an actual event which took place at a particular historical time and a particular place, Mt. Sinai. Their god revealed himself; the people heard his voice, though they did not see his being. It was a unique event, no other people has experienced anything similar. There and then the Hebrews received the Ten Commandments from Yahweh and the ordinances of the covenant which were publicly read. The Ten Commandments and the covenant ordinances were accepted by the people, who said "we will be obedient." The bond with God was sealed with the sacrificial blood thrown upon the people, "the blood of the covenant which Yahweh hath made with you" (Exod. 24:8). This covenant is often called the Mosaic covenant, but it is unlike the covenants with Abraham and David, which were personal covenants; the Mosaic covenant is not a covenant with Moses directly, but a covenant with the Hebrew nation through Moses.

The Hebrew nation thus was based not in blood but in historical experience and a free act of accepting moral and religious obligation. This historical experience and obligation has been accepted as their own by all subsequent believers in the Hebrew faith. Indeed all subsequent historical events have been interpreted in terms of the covenant relationship with Yahweh, history being presented in the Old Testament primarily as a drama concerning Hebrew faithfulness to Yahweh. The Hebrews had a special relation with Yahweh, not only through the covenant, but also through their consciousness of being the "chosen people" of Yahweh. This consciousness arose from their interpretation of the Exodus. The Hebrews were an oppressed, enslaved people who had been rescued from Egyptian bondage by the miraculous powers of Yahweh. Their rescue was a result of no particular merit on their part; Yahweh had seen their need, heard their call, and out of his grace and goodness had come to bring them out of Egypt and into the promised land flowing with milk and honey. Yahweh had revealed thereby that He had *chosen* them to be His people. This conviction of the Hebrews that they were a chosen people has been a permanent and significant feature in their entire history. Henri Frankfort writes: "The tenacity of the Hebrew struggle for existence in the sordid turmoil of the Levant was rooted in the consciousness of their election. This animated the leaders of the people, whether they were kings like David and Hezekiah, or prophets opposing kings in whom belief in the unique destiny of Israel had been compromised. But this intimate relationship between the Hebrew people and their god ignored the existence of an earthly ruler altogether. Hebrew tradition, vigorously defended by the great prophets and the post-Exilic leaders, recognized as the formative phase of Hebrew culture the sojourn in the desert when Moses, the man of God, led the people and gave them the Law. Kingship never achieved a standing equal to that of institutions which were claimed—rightly or wrongly—to have originated during the exodus and the desert wandering."[86]

In the development of the Hebrew religion, the Covenant and the Election came first, not the formulation of Yahweh's cosmic attributes. Originally the Hebrews were tribal nomads, living between the desert and fertile land; or more precisely, they were semi-nomadic stock breeders, ass nomads, since the camel was not generally domesticated at that time. The experience of the desert, which appears as a complete negation of life, was very important for the Hebrews and affected their thought and spiritual life. Yahweh, who revealed himself to the Hebrews in the Sinai desert, was, as has frequently been observed, a desert god. The desert god does not tolerate graven images; He is not to be seen in image representations. Unlike other contemporary ancient religions of the Near East, which were all religions oriented to nature in its aspects of rhythmic fertility and rhythmic celestial order, the Hebrew religion was not oriented to nature but to human society and its history. Nature played a subordinate role, except as used by Yahweh in his historical work in human affairs. Beaucamp comments: "...taken as a whole, the Bible makes scant reference to natural order in the cosmos."[87] Inevitably thus there was a conflict between Yahweh and the fertility gods of agriculture, which emerged persistently in the history of the Hebrews after their transition from nomadic herding to agriculture in Canaan. "And actually the whole history of Israel has only one theme: the struggle between the lonely desert god...and the *baalim*, the gods and goddesses of the earth"[88]—there were other themes, but it might well be argued that this was the major theme.

The proper dwelling of the desert god Yahweh was a tent (II Sam. 7:6f); the portable tent-shrine and the portable throne of the God-King (Ark) were evidence of faith in the desert god. Yahweh, who did not tolerate graven images, had no physical form and was not so worshipped, except perhaps in the earliest days of the nation's life in

Canaan; Yahweh's presence was invisible. A piquant tale illustrates this: "When Pompey in 63 B.C. stormed Jerusalem, he forced his way into the Holy of Holies, much to the horror of the Jews, in order to see for himself what was the inmost secret of this unusual religion. And there he found—...nothing but an empty room!"[89]

A dominant tenet of Hebrew thought from the beginning was the absolute transcendence of God. Yahweh is not immanent in nature; natural phenomena, earth, sun, and heaven are creations of God, reflections of his greatness. The God of the Hebrews is a transcendent creator, the ground of all existence; He is pure being, unqualified, *sui generis*. The monotheism of the Hebrews derives from their conception of the transcendent, unconditioned nature of God. The attributes of God—righteousness, justice, love, grace, jealousy, and anger—are not directly discernible, but are disclosed in the process of human life, in the historic course of human society. Yahweh is a personal God who addresses the Hebrews at Sinai as "Thou." The desert god who has no physical form cannot be perceived nor can He be contemplated. "Man confronting God will not contemplate him but will hear his voice and command, as Moses did, and the prophets, and Mohammed."[90]

By the burning bush in the wilderness at Horeb, Yahweh told Moses of his task to deliver the Hebrews from Egyptian bondage. Then Moses said to God, "If I come to the people of Israel and say to them, the God of your fathers has sent me to you, and they ask me, what is his name? What shall I say to them?" God said to Moses, "I AM WHO I AM" (Ex. 3:14). It seems to me that there is a simple interpretation of this seemingly enigmatic name: God is *existence*, but not simple existence and not simply conscious existence; God is reflexive self-identity, self-conscious existence. That is why man, self-conscious man, is in the image of God. This is the unique connection between God, the Creator, and man, his creature. There is more than mere self-consciousness in man, there is also the correlated consciousness of individual responsibility, a phenomenon unique in man. Eichrodt cites this consciousness of responsibility among the Hebrews, saying "...in no other people of the ancient East is the sense of the responsibility of each member of the people so living and the personal attitude so dominant."[91]

There is another aspect of the Hebrew God which we must mention here namely the Will of God. More than pure existence and transcendence, Yahweh was a personal God with a decided will. The will of God towards the Hebrews was expressed to them in the covenant at Sinai with its commandments and ordinances; the

Hebrew problem henceforth was to conduct themselves in obedience to the will of God. Henri Frankfort cites the tendency to
overrate the similarities between Mesopotamian and the Judeo-
Christian views. The Mesopotamians, he finds, lived under a divine
imperative and recognized that they failed to fulfill what was asked
of them but they did not have the specific commandments and
ordinances. "The will of God had not been revealed to them once
and for all, nor were they sustained by the consciousness of being a
'chosen people.' They were not singled out by divine love, and the
divine wrath lacked the resentment caused by ingratitude. The
Mesopotamians, while they knew themselves to be subject to the
decrees of the gods, had no reason to believe that these decrees were
necessarily just.... The Mesopotamian recognized guilt by its consequences: when he suffered, he assumed that he had transgressed a
divine decree."[92] Often he did not know the offense against the
gods. At Sinai the Hebrews had heard the word of God, his commandments and promises, and had learned of God's will towards
them; in the covenant they had accepted the moral burden of
obedience. According to Hebrew thought, man was a servant of
God, with the task of effecting the realization of God's will. Thus
God and man are correlated in a historic course which unfolds in
time.

Having been created as a nation by the historic experience of
Yahweh's activity in the Exodus and at Sinai, the Hebrews regarded
history as the locus of God's activity. Neither the national nor the
religious literature of other peoples contemporary with the Hebrews
exhibit a similar interest in history. The ancient polytheist religions
were oriented to nature; they had no sense of history. The polytheist
worshipped the forces of nature as gods, who had somehow established a divine harmony in nature. The polytheist sought to participate in this harmony by adapting himself to the cosmic rhythms of
nature; thus his life took place in a cycle corresponding to the cycle
of nature. The Hebrew God, Yahweh, was not primarily associated
with recurrent events of nature, but with the unique, unrepeatable
historical events in which he acted purposively. This was evident in
the Exodus and at Sinai, and continued to be manifest to the
Hebrews in all the subsequent events and stages of their history.

The origin of the Hebrew preoccupation with history has been set
forth by Walter Eichrodt in the following terms: "The roots of this
peculiar viewpoint, by which Israel clearly is to be differentiated
from all other Near Eastern peoples, doubtless lie in those happenings of the early time, which gave the impulse to the genesis of the

Israelite people, in the events of the time of Moses. The deliverance from Egypt and the uniting of kin and families of wandering cattle-breeders in a sacral tribal covenant during the wilderness period were those events which have impressed the national Israelite consciousness as the basis in determining acts for all time of the Divine self-disclosure. If one observes the completely unique importance which these events have gained in the total religious praxis and tradition, in the cultic hymns no less than in the prophetic admonitions, in the liturgy and cultic instruction of the priests as well as in the parental teaching of the children, in the explanation of the pastoral and agricultural festivals no less than in the establishment of all law-giving at the time of Moses, then no doubt can exist that this first experience of a Divine encounter was decisive for the fundamental conception of the Divine revelation in Israel. Here one learned to understand the being of God from history and to exhibit his works in the forms of history."[93] The Hebrew conception and knowledge of God was thus not derived from natural observation or speculative thought, but from an inferential explanation of what actually had happened in Hebrew history.

Wright points out that "the very anthropomorphism of the Biblical vocabulary concerning God is witness to his primary relation to history and human society."[94] In the polytheist religions the main metaphors for depicting the gods were taken for the most part from the natural world. In the Bible, the language of nature is clearly secondary; God is known primarily in terms relating Him to society and to history. A major reason why no other gods are to be worshipped is historical, namely because no other god was with Yahweh when he accomplished His great redemptive acts. He alone is directing the course of history. No graven images are to be made of Him because those who heard the voice of God at Horeb "saw no manner of form" on that day (Deut. 4:15). Thus the only possible image of God is the mental image of a person; hence anthropomorphism indicates God's personal relation to history.

It has been observed that the greatest annual feasts in the Hebrew cult were much older than the Hebrew nation itself, and were of agricultural origin, except for the Passover. The Hebrews, however, gave these ancient feasts new meaning; they ceased to be mere nature festivals by acquiring a historical content, namely, as occasions for celebrating the historic acts of Yahweh. Passover was "historicised" as the flight from Egypt; the feast of Tabernacles, as the wanderings in the desert; Pentecost, as the promulgation of the law on Sinai.

Though more than prophet, Moses was the first Hebrew prophet. As all the later prophets, Moses was a spokesman of Yahweh, an intermediary between Him and His chosen people. What Moses and the later prophets spoke out was not their own words, but the words of Yahweh given to them to transmit to His people. Commenting on the succession of Moses, Elijah, Amos, Hosea, Isaiah, Jeremiah, Ezekiel, and Second Isaiah, Christopher North has written: "What nation so small as Israel has given birth in so short a time to a more astonishing succession of geniuses of any kind, let alone religious geniuses?"[95] It has been observed that the idea of divine acts in history may be found in much the same form in the Hebrews and in neighboring peoples. However, "...the idea of historical events as divine manifestations has marked the Israelite cult in a way that lacks real parallel among Israel's neighbors."[96] As we have already seen, Yahweh's saving deeds in history have the central position in the Hebrew cult dominating Passover and the other ancient feasts; there is nothing comparable in the other religions of the ancient Near East.

Moreover, the meaning of the historical events is not necessarily immediately apparent from the events themselves; to the events of history are added the *word* of revelation about the historical events. It is the prophets who transmit the word of revelation, just as the Election of the Hebrews and their Covenant with Yahweh were announced to the Hebrews by Moses through Yahweh's own words. Thus Yahweh's purposes in historical events are disclosed in the words which Yahweh speaks out through his messengers, the prophets. "Israel's knowledge of God's purposes in history is not obtained through history but through the divine word about history."[97] The concept of the Divine Word, it may be noted, from which the Christian *Logos* is derived, is of very ancient Semitic, not Hellenic, origin.

Also, and this is most significant with respect to the emergence of an understanding of history based on linear temporality, in the Old Testament God speaks to man *before* his historical deeds, communicating His purposes and intentions, as God did to Moses before the Exodus at the burning bush. "Far from the incident at the burning bush being an interpretation of the divine acts, it is a direct communication from God to Moses of his purposes and intentions. This conversation, instead of being represented as an interpretation of the divine act, is a precondition of it. If God had not told Moses what he did, the Israelites would have not demanded their escape from Egypt, and the deliverance at the Sea of Reeds would not have taken place."[98] To a large extent the prophets speak out what God intends to do in the future; the historical event and Yahweh's purpose in the event are proclaimed by the prophet before the event. "Indeed, no prophet ever interpreted an event as an act of Yahweh *after the fact*."[99] Furthermore, in the ancient Near East it was generally believed that a god may speak to man, and prophets claiming to reveal divine messages, it is said, are known also among other peoples than the Hebrews. However the content of the Hebrew prophetic revelation "is in several respects unique. It is here that we learn about Yahweh's purposes and intentions, his true nature and the innermost thoughts of his heart, his gifts and his claims, which make him different from all the other gods of the ancient Near East."[100]

The prophets were not passive transmitters of messages; at times they played an active role seeking to affect the course of historic events. The prophet Elijah urged Jeroboam to revolt; Elisha instigated Jehu's usurpation of the throne; Isaiah tried unsuccessfully to dissuade Ahaz from seeking the protection of Assyria and later his help was sought at the time of Sennacherib's invasion; Jeremiah urged Zedekiah to surrender, and when the king refused, he advised the soldiers defending Jerusalem to desert to the Chaldeans. More usual and significant than the active participation in historic events was the prophets' role in pronouncing judgment upon the Hebrews for their failure to keep the obligations of the moral and religious covenant with Yahweh. The settlement itself of the promised land Canaan brought a decline from the covenant ideals and the simple moral and religious practice of the wilderness days. The Mosaic religion was a faith of a minority in the very mixed population of Canaan, and most of the minority were probably not spiritually enlightened enough to distinguish properly the religious principles of Yahweh over those of the gods indigenous to Canaan. During the centuries of political independence after the settlement in Canaan, the Hebrews repeatedly turned from Yahweh to the *Baals* and *Astartes* of their neighbors. The wilderness herdsmen had become farmers in an agrarian society with ancient religious traditions rooted in the land and based primarily on fertility cults. It was the task of the prophets to seek to maintain Mosaic principles in this situation, and this the prophets did by pronouncing judgment on the Hebrews for their moral and religious apostasy, and with a vision of Yahweh's inevitable punishment for their faithlessness. We have noted earlier that the Chinese have regarded natural calamities as a sign of delinquent conduct of the Son of Heaven. Similarly the prophet Amos regarded such natural calamities as famine, drought, mildew, locusts, and pestilence as related to the divine judgment. For the most part, however, the prophetic judgment on the Hebrews for their sins involved historic events, wars, and disastrous military defeats. The prophetic visions of Yahweh's punishment from Elijah to Jeremiah were confirmed and justified by the political and military disasters of subsequent historical events. In this way the historical events acquired religious significance by appearing as expressions of Yahweh's will. "Thus, for the first time, the prophets placed a value on history, succeeded in transcending the traditional vision of the cycle,... and discovered a one-way time." Further, according to Eliade, we find thus affirmed "the idea that historical events have a value in themselves, in so far as they are determined by the will of God." This God is a person who constantly intervenes in history, revealing His will through events. Historical facts, involving the relation of man to God, thus "acquire a religious value.... It may, then, be said with truth that the Hebrews were the first to discover the meaning of history as the epiphany of God...."[101]

The gods of other religions, e.g., the Mesopotamian and the Greek gods, also on occasion intervene in human history. What distinguished Yahweh in this regard from the gods of other religions is the continuity of Yahweh's acts in relation to his chosen people, the Hebrews. For the Hebrews, Yahweh could intervene in historic events at any time and at any place. Moreover, Yahweh's presence was indwelling in the total course of historical events. Furthermore, Yahweh's powers were not restricted to the Hebrews; He used other nations, even the greatest of the time, as His instruments of judgment. Isaiah saw mighty Assyria as Yahweh's tool, His chastising rod who, having served the purpose of divine chastisement for Hebrew sins, would in turn be cut down because of her godless pride. Similarly some hundred years later, the prophet Habakkuk viewed the Babylonians as the instruments of Yahweh's punishment who, having served that purpose, would themselves in turn be judged. Some fifty years later, Second Isaiah found Cyrus to be the tool of Yahweh's purpose who Yahweh had brought up to execute judgment on Babylon and to use for the reestablishment of Yahweh's faith at Jerusalem, the return of the Hebrews from the Babylonian exile and the rebuilding of the Temple.

The great powers and the other peoples in general were much more in Old Testament thought than mere tools and instruments of Yahweh in His relations to the Hebrews. Alongside the exclusivist view of the Hebrews as Yahweh's chosen people, and in tension with it through the centuries, there is also a universalist aspect in Old Testament thought, which regards all peoples as members of one great family, as creatures of the one God. This concept of humanity is quite different from the views generally held among the peoples of the ancient Near East. The list of all the peoples, including the Hebrews, in Genesis 10 is unique in ancient Near Eastern literature. When Yahweh spoke to Abraham, He said in Gen. 12:3, "In you all the families of the earth will be blessed." Thus at the beginning of Hebrew records mankind appears as a single entity, a view later to be affirmed and elaborated by the prophets. Amos asserts in clear language the common human bond among diverse peoples:

> "Are you not like the Ethiopians to me,
> O people of Israel," says the Lord;
> Did I not bring up Israel
> from the land of Egypt;
> and the Philistines from Caphtor,
> and the Syrians from Kir? (Amos 9:7.)

Imbued with a sense of common humanity, Amos does not hesitate to announce God's coming punishment of the Hebrews' neighbors for moral reasons: Damascus and Ammon for excessive cruelty in war, Tyre and Gaza for selling whole peoples into slavery, etc. Later in the Servant Songs and the Book of Malachi, we find the view that the Lord's name was revered among the Gentiles and that Gentile peoples were coming to Jerusalem for worship, affirming thus a common human acceptance of the same moral and religious principles as the Hebrews.

If Yahweh, who alone is God, is the Lord of history, then He must be the Lord of all human history. Emmanuel Mounier writes: "In the whole of antiquity, during that era of world religions which marks the first thousand years before the coming of Christ,... one religion alone [the Hebrew religion] held with force and earnestness the belief that the world has a single universal history."[102] The prophet Second Isaiah, who wrote immediately before and during the conquest of Babylon by Cyrus, expressed this view most clearly and emphatically. For him Yahweh, the God of incomparable power, alone Creator of all natural forces and beings, was in complete control of history. Creator of the universe, in which human history takes place, He is the sovereign Lord of all historical events, for they are fulfilling His purposes. The Babylonian exile, he understood like other prophets as Yahweh's judgment on the Hebrews for their faithlessness and sins, but it was His purpose, not to disclaim the Hebrews, rather to punish them and thereby redeem them for the return and restoration of Jerusalem. Then, according to the prophet, Yahweh's rule was to be universal, including the Gentiles as well as the Hebrews, and He looked forward to the time when all nations would recognize Yahweh as their God. He even expected Cyrus, recognizing Yahweh's role in his conquests, to acknowledge Him as the true God. Also Second Isaiah set forth the obligation of the Hebrew nation in a worldwide perspective. By their very existence, the Hebrews were a witness to Yahweh's purpose and history and to His status as the one true God. The Hebrew nation had a duty and a mission to serve as the instrument of Yahweh's purposes. This mission of the Hebrews set forth so poignantly by Second Isaiah in the second half of the sixth century B.C. was not a new element in Hebrew thought. G. Ernest Wright finds that this consciousness of the Hebrew mission goes back at least as early as the tenth century; he states, "God's dealings with Israel were of profound significance for universal history because his revelation to Israel was the light which must some day through Israel illumine all nations...."[103]

The prophets' vision of the impending doom of the Hebrew nation under the might of Assyria and Babylonia did not usually foresee the utter extinction of the Hebrews, rather a small remnant would be saved, and though scattered in exile, would ultimately be returned to restore Zion, Yahweh's city of Jerusalem. Even if the Hebrews had sinned by their faithlessness, their failure to fulfill the obligations of their covenant, and were therefore punished, Yahweh remained loyal to the covenant bond with His chosen people. Hence a remnant would be redeemed in order to restore the covenant faith. Here we can see, in capsule as it were, the importance of the Hebrews for the development of a consciousness of history: looking to the covenant of the past, the prophets foresaw the oncoming disaster implicit in the present situation, and beyond this disaster an opening to the future with the restoration of a remnant. When past, present, and future are grasped together in one temporal perspective, we have the necessary condition for a consciousness of history.

We have cited the Biblical evidence of Yahweh as the God of history, as well as the universalism in Hebrew thought. After all, however, history permeates the Old Testament: "history told from a determined point of view and with a set purpose, but, nonetheless, great history."[104] The story of the Hebrew nation is told in a world setting, thus in a limited sense becoming a world history. The first ten chapters of Genesis attempt to give an account of the creation of the universe and of human life in its early ages, ending in a survey of the peoples of the whole known world at the time. Thereafter the story narrows to that of the Hebrews, yet the consciousness of other nations and their affairs remains throughout. Egypt appears repeatedly in the story; Canaan and the small neighboring countries have an important place; then Assyria becomes the dominating theme, thereafter Babylonia, Persia, and the Macedonian kingdoms. The Old Testament is a history of the Hebrew nation in the world of its time, dealing with the other nations as they impinge upon Hebrew history, and thus in this particular and limited sense being a world history.

The Egyptians, as we have noted, did not think in temporal or historical terms because for them the gods had created a timeless universe essentially static from the beginning. For the Mesopotamians, as we have seen, no one god was supreme as the ultimate source of power; all the gods had been created. The ultimate authority in the universe resided in the general assembly of the gods. Each god had a will of his own, and thus the decisions of the gods in assembly were unpredictable. The gods might intervene in human history, but there was no continuous purposive intervention, no goal. How different the Hebrew view with the one almighty God Jehovah fulfilling His historic purposes in the temporal course of events! Despite, or perhaps because of, Hebrew material and military inferiority to Egypt and Mesopotamia, the Hebrews became one of the great creative intellectual peoples of world history. While the ancient contemporary civilizations are a faded memory, Hebrew influence lives on to this day, not only in Judaism, but even more importantly through Christianity and Islam.

From a modern historiographic standpoint, the peak of excellence in the Old Testament is obtained by the court history of King David (2 Samuel 9-20), written evidently by a contemporary. It has been termed "one of the finest examples of historical narrative in any ancient literature,"[105] and "a brilliant piece of historical writing, five centuries older than Herodotus."[106] This account accords admirably with Ranke's tenet of factual and ideational objectivity: telling a story *wie es eigentlich gewesen ist*. The historian author may well have had in mind, as did Herodotus and Thucydides, a desire to preserve important events in human memory for all time. In general, moreover, literary genius, not only in historical writing, but also in poetry, psalms, prophetic utterances, and legal formulations, has been a factor in the importance and influence of the Hebrews through these many centuries. Of course, this literary

genius was animated by, and an expression of, Hebrew devoutness-
and to this devoutness we owe the preservation of the record, the
Bible.

It remains for us to set down here a few comments on temporality
in Hebrew thought. Joseph Needham, who, as we have noted earlier, finds that the early Chinese had a linear conception of time,
states that the Hebrews were the first Westerners to give a value to
time. For the Hebrews with their prophetic tradition, which as we
have pointed out interprets the present in relation to the past and the
future, time was real and the medium of real change. As cited
earlier, the prophets discovered "a one-way time."[107] "...only the
Bible shows how the movement which animates the cosmos is a
linear, irreversible movement."[108] Where previously in ancient Near
Eastern religions, the universe was seen as caught in a rhythm of
eternal cyclical recurrence, the Old Testament finds a beginning in
the creation of the universe, the temporal course of human history as
a manifestation of God, and an end of this universe and of history in
the fulfillment of God's purpose as seen in the eschatological and
apocalyptic visions.

According to Hans Walter Wolff, the Hebrew sees the past as the
reality *before* him, while we regard the past as *behind* us. The future
for the Hebrew lies not *before* him but "at his back" (*'ahr*). "Ah^{a}rit
means the future as that which is behind and which follows me....
man proceeds through time like a rower who moves into the future
backwards: he reaches his goal by taking his bearings from what is
visibly in front of him; it is in this revealed history that for him the
Lord of the future is attested."[109] If this be so, why? We moderns
have abstracted *time* from concrete reality, apprehended it as a
form with the aid of Hellenic thought; thus we have hypostatized
time. Hence time is laid out before us as a continuum stretching
infinitely backward from the present to the past and forward from
the present to the future, while we, the present, are moving forward
in time towards the future. The Hebrews had no such abstract
conception of time. They were living concretely, as Hegel would
say, in temporal existence; their time was filled; time had not been
separated out from the events; in J. Pedersen's words, for the
Hebrew "time is not merely a form or a frame. Time is charged with
substance or, rather, it is identical with its substance; time is the
development of the very events."[110] The Hebrews saw the substantive past ahead, i.e., that which had been apprehended and comprehended, while behind them came that which had not been apprehended, the substantive future.

Commenting on the frequently stated view that the Greeks had a cyclic conception of time in contrast to the Hebrew linear conception, James Barr states, "...(a) the Greeks did not always in fact hold a cyclic view of time; (b) the Hebrews in certain cases and in certain respects did entertain a cyclic view of time;..."[111] Barr mentions that in connection with the heavenly bodies, the Hebrew understanding of time was cyclic, just as the Greek. He also points out, as do others, that in Ecclesiastes a view of time appears which is in some sense a cyclic view. However, he does find that in Hebrew thought the sequence of historical events is a purposive movement towards a goal, certainly not cyclic in the sense of something recurrent, rather non-recurrent, non-reversible, and unique. We shall be considering the Greek views in the next section.

The Greeks

For one who has seen and experienced the Greek landscape—if some fifty years ago—there are no words to describe adequately its uniqueness and peculiar beauty. Greece is a land of craggy gray-rock mountains with many peaks, and thin strands of valley breaking the mountain ranges and themselves separated by the impassable heights. It is also a land of islands, themselves mountains, with roots beneath the sea. From the mountains, aside from the remote uplands, one can usually see water, the sea, a gulf, or a bay. It is a land of contrasts, not of extremes. Even in winter there is plenty of sunshine, in summer there is intense, dry heat; most Greek rivers are torrential streams in winter, and dry, stony gullies in summer; interspersed along the irregular rocky shores there are occasional safe harbors or sandy stretches. The air is dry and clear, endowed with a remarkable luminosity. The quality of the light is unique and unforgettable. Such a landscape and such light must have helped produce the great sculptors, painters, and architects of Greece. Doubtless it also influenced the clarity of their philosophic thought, characterized by its lucidity and clear definition in formulation of interconnected abstract ideas.

The sea was also a potent influence on Greek civilization and culture. The sea had a special attraction for the Greeks; Aeschylus speaks of "the multitudinous laughter of the sea-waves."[112] The Aegean is a sea with great charm in its rippling waves or its calm, but it is very changeable with sudden winds, high short waves, and tempests, bringing forth the dangers of hidden rock and reef. The

Greeks were sailors from their earliest history; thus they were not captive to the limited horizon of small mainland city-states. Sea travel was important for commerce as well as for excitement, and it was a chief means by which the Greeks acquired knowledge of other lands and people.

"Poverty is native to Greece," as Herodotus wrote. The land is hard and poor, with not much fertile soil, incapable of feeding flocks or herds on a larger scale, and able to provide for only a small population. The hard, poor land made physical demands. Labor in the fields fostered physical strength and endurance. The male statues of the ancient Greeks reveal sturdy muscular frames and limbs, slim waists, and competent hands. The poor land required hard work, toughness, skill in artisanry, enterprise, and intelligence. The handling of ships required quickness of eye and hand, agile mobility, vigilance, and rapidity of decision. "Geographical circumstances formed the Greek character by forcing it to make the most of its natural aptitudes in a hard struggle with the earth and the elements."[113]

The Greek peninsula is a relatively enclosed space with natural frontiers, mountains to the north and surrounded by the sea on all other sides. It is not easy to enter Greece overland from the Balkans; the mountain passes are very difficult to traverse. It is easier to invade Greece from the sea, and it is believed that around 1200 B.C. the Dorian Greeks came from the northwest by sea. If not attacked from the sea, protected by the mountains in the north, the Greeks lived in a relatively isolated situation. Bowra terms Greece physically "a blind alley"—how different the situation of the Hebrews set between the great powers, Egypt and Mesopotamia, and on the land route connecting them!

The configuration and character of the mountainous landscape shaped the pattern of Greek political life. In the 13th century B.C. the Greeks were probably united in a loose confederacy under the Mycenaean kings; they were not really united again until conquered and unified under the Macedonian kings in the 4th century B.C. In between the Greek polity was divided into numerous small city-states, each with its own customs and local character and its own independent government. The city-states were separate and relatively complete unto themselves; the mountain barriers tended to prevent one state from being controlled by, or merged into, another. Even when city-states fell under the rule of powerful neighbors or were forced into a merger, they still maintained their own institutions and some aspects of political independence. If the city-states were surrounded by fertile land, the farmers living in villages were participants. If close to the sea, the sailors and fishermen, who lived in the ports where the ships were built, were also participants. There were also artisans, and many citizens combined two or three of these occupations. Living in close proximity, there was a strong sense of unity and kinship among the city-state members; nevertheless, this did not prevent bitter rivalry for local political leadership, revolutions, or class warfare, described so trenchantly by Thucydides.

A Man-Oriented Culture

Compared to the Near Eastern and the Chinese cultures, there is a remarkable brevity of the historic greatness of Greece. Commenting on this fact, was it not Hegel who said that the beautiful die young? Greek history begins really with the Homeric poems in the last part of the 8th century. Then there were some 300 years of rapid advance and maturation, the classical age of the poets, artists, and natural philosophers. When after many decades of conflict Sparta conquered Athens in 404 B.C., something essential in the Greek spirit was broken. Nevertheless, the 4th century B.C. had its high achievements, particularly in philosophy, mathematics, and science. The Macedonian conquest in the second half of the 4th century B.C., however, destroyed the spiritual unity of Greece and signaled the end of its greatness.

The spiritual depth, strength, and endurance of Christianity, as is well known, are a result of the Christian fusion of the Hebrew and Hellenic cultural traditions. Perhaps there are many reasons for these attributes of Christianity. However, one essential feature, in my opinion, may be the core of an understanding of Christian power. The Hebrews represent a God-oriented people and God-oriented culture, doubtless the fullest and richest development of a God-oriented culture in the ancient world. In contrast, the Greeks represent a man-oriented people and a man-oriented culture, indeed, the most diversified, beautiful, profound, and spirited development of a man-oriented culture in the ancient world, and perhaps for all times. Thus Christianity is the complete fusion of the most excellent God-oriented and man-oriented cultures of the ancient world, and this may be the essential feature which from the viewpoint of cultural history accounts for the power of Christianity.

In Greece there were no divine monarchs, like the Davidic kings, no privileged priests as a separate caste, like the Levites. Greek civilization and culture reveals a belief in the intrinsic and unique value of man. The chorus in Sophocles' *Antigone* sings,

"There are many strange wonders, but nothing
More wonderful than man."

Not the gods, but man, Sophocles praises in the lines: "Wise utterance and wind-swift thought, and city-molding mind," "Full of resource, without device he meets no coming time," "Inventive beyond wildest hope, endowed with boundless skill," and most important for our theme, specifically looking to the future, "With plans for all things, planless in nothing, he awaits the future." Man as the center of their thought and culture is expressed in the anthropomorphic gods, in sculpture and painting, in their poetry, their city-states which shaped men, and their philosophy which moved from the Presocratic study of the natural universe to the problem of man with Socrates ("know thyself"), Plato, and Aristotle. The Sophists are much maligned in contemporary philosophic education and the word "sophist" has acquired in English a very derogatory significance. However, when the great sophist Protagoras stated, "Man is the measure of all things," he was setting forth the quintessential Greek view. When Plato, late in life, countered in *The Laws*, "The measure of all things is God," Greek culture was in its decline.

The Homeric epics set forth the heroic ideal of the aristocratic world of early Greece which stressed the conjoint and harmonious development of the human body and soul. Competing athletes wore no clothes, displaying themselves thus as nature or the gods had made them. In Greek sports, a cult of the body naturally developed; not by chance were the major athletic games held in connection with religious festivals. The Greeks admired the body beautiful, with its harmony of proportions, its strength, and dynamic power. In this harmony of body and soul, physical strength in athletics and war were combined with mental vigor and spiritual quality. According to the conception of the hero, "a man should live for honor and renown."[114] Honor is pursued through action, but not through action alone. When Phoenix, the old teacher of Achilles, urges Achilles to rejoin the Greek force at Troy, he reminds Achilles of the heroic ideal: "to be both a speaker of words and a doer of deeds." Honor is an incentive to vigorous action of body and mind in all aspects of human life. In ancient Greece a supreme value was placed on the individual and his achievements in this life; human existence called for great and noble deeds which were honored for their own sake.

While the dead became mere soul-shadows in Hades, remembrance of the dead had a reality for the Greeks, particularly in the form of renown for brave and sacrificial deeds. Pericles in his funeral oration for the Athenian dead expresses this poignantly: "For famous men have the whole earth as their memorial; it is not only the inscriptions on their graves in their own country that mark them out; no, in foreign lands also, not in any visible form, but in people's hearts, their memory abides and grows."

Poets as Spiritual Leaders

In the account of the Hebrews in the previous section, I did not mention the significant role of music and poetry in their culture. According to the Bible, David was both musician and poet-psalmist. The Bible is replete with songs and poems; the oldest song is the powerful cultic Song of Deborah; much later is the Song of Solomon, a veritable love song. Whatever else they may be, the Psalms and Proverbs are all poetry, and then also the utterances of the prophets are full of poetry. Music and poetry were certainly as important to the Greeks as to the Hebrews, in some senses perhaps even more important. Music was regarded by the Greeks as the most important of their arts; it was indissolubly connected with poetry; unfortunately, aside from some fifteen fragmentary scores, it is entirely lost. Happily a considerable amount of poetry in epic, lyric, and dramatic form has survived. However, it is clear from fragmentary remains that a tremendous amount of Greek poetry has been lost, even of the work of the 5th century Athenian dramatists. If more of Hebrew poetry proportionately has survived, as seems likely, is it not because the Hebrew poetry was contained, enshrined as it were, in the Holy Book of the Hebrew faith, and as such preserved through the centuries?

While the poetry in the Bible is more an utterance of God than of man, with the Greeks it was different; Greek poetry was an expression of their man-centered culture. The Greek poets professed a belief that their inspiration came from the Muses, divine powers, who enter their being and guide their poetic activity. Although the Muse is supposed to be a divine power, its divinity is hardly well grounded; it is really a personification of a certain fact that poets in their creative work are carried along by inspirational forces which seem, beyond self, to control and direct their creativity. In contrast, the Greeks also held the view that poetry is a form of craft, that it required technical skill with words, and that it had its own rules in prosody, meter, and diction. By these rules intellectual process was admitted into the inspired realm of poetry, and the results were rich and marvelous. With inspiration and technical skill combined, poetry became a realm of the probing and penetrating mind; as a result it came to cover the whole realm of human existence and experience.

From Homer on, the poets were the teachers and spiritual guides among the Greeks. Poetry was at the center of their cultural advance until the middle of the 5th century B.C. Not the priests nor the scientists, but primarily the poets explained and elucidated human experience to the Greek people. The Hebrews had a canonical religious doctrine, a professional priesthood spread throughout the nation, and prophets speaking the Word of God; in their absence the Greeks had the poets. Even the Delphic oracle issues its prognostications in verse. While the Greeks regarded Homer as a teacher, Hesiod was the first Greek poet, as Werner Jaeger points out, to speak to the men of his own time in his own person about contemporary problems; he clearly believed "that his poetic mission was to be a teacher and a prophet among the Greeks."[115] It is the beginning of the spiritual leadership of the poet which is a distinguishing mark of the Greek world. In his elegies the Spartan poet Tyrtaeus (c. 650 B.C.) summoned the Spartans to self-sacrifice and patriotism at a critical period of the Messenian War; in an elegy entitled *Eunomia*, Tyrtaeus sets forth the fundamental principles and the divine origin of the Spartan constitution. In the 6th century B.C., Solon, the lawgiver of Athens, who was also a poet, is regarded as the first embodiment of the truly Attic spirit and the greatest of its creators. For Pindar, the aristocratic Theban, the poet's art brought forth *sophia*, wisdom. This view is confirmed by the work of the 5th century Attic poets. The word which best describes the essence of the poetry of the great 5th century Athenian dramatists is the word "wisdom," profound and immortal.

Not only the poets wrote in verse, most of the cosmologists and early philosophers from Thales of Miletus (640-546 B.C.) on did so as well. Anaximander of Miletus is believed to be the first to set down his views in prose (c. 550 B.C.), probably in the first person, and to publish them in this fashion. Toward the end of the 6th century, Hecataeus of Miletus, regarded as the most influential of the Ionian prose writers, set forth his historical *Inquiries* and his *Geography*, which had a significant influence on Herodotus. It has been conjectured that the beginning of Greek literary prose towards the middle of the 6th century may have been the result of the influence on the Ionians of Asia Minor of the literary works of the Near East. In the complex world of the mid-5th century, prose came to succeed poetry as the major vehicle of thought. The 5th century Sophists who sought to provide political education, training leaders to serve the city-state, became the heirs of the educational tradition of the poet. The subject of *rhetoric*, taught by the Sophists, embracing as it did ethics and politics, facilitated this transition by conscious emphasis on theory.

Greek poetry is based on a metric system, which gives it potentialities beyond nearly all other languages. Unlike the English metric which is accentual, the Greek metric is quantitative, that is, the rhythm is based on units in which the balance of syllables derives from quantity, or the time taken to speak it. With accentual languages one never quite knows what the rhythm is, because the accent is dubious and uncertain; in Greek, the rhythm is clear and emphatic from the beginning. The metric was of utmost importance to the Greeks because they believed that rhythm and harmony expressed in sounds and words were the genuine forces molding the human spirit. The sophist Protagoras in the Platonic dialogue of that name states that "harmony and the rhythm of poetry and music must be impressed on the soul to make it rhythmical and harmonious."[116] Werner Jaeger points out that when the Greeks discovered rhythm in music and dancing, it was not the rhythm of flux or flow, but *pause*, the reiterated limitation of movement. For the Greeks rhythm imposes bonds on movement and constrains the flux of things; it is the pattern of movement.

Solon's poem, dividing human life in seven-year periods, each with its own special function, "is filled with a truly Greek feeling for the rhythm of life; for one age cannot change places with another— each has its own meaning, and each is in accord with another, so that the whole rises and falls with the rhythm of universal nature."[117] Greek poetry and thought acknowledge the general conception of rhythm pervading nature and all human life. The Ionian natural philosophers and historians were conscious of it, as was the Ionian poet Archilochus, who speaks of "the rhythm which holds mankind in its bonds."[118] The Ionian philosopher Pythagoras discovered the relation between music and mathematics, that numerical laws govern musical sound. He propounded the view that number is the basic principle of all existence, natural and human. In the mathematical conception of proportion, which could be visually presented by geometric figures, Pythagoras discerned *harmony* as the structural aspect of the cosmos under firm laws. Harmony and rhythm are at the center of Greek understanding of the natural universe and the proper order of individual as well as social life. It has been observed that in Greek poetry tragedy was the first type "to apply to mythical tradition a regular structural principle—the conception of the inevitable rise and fall of human destiny, with its sudden reversals and its final catastrophe."[119] In the closing scene of the *Oresteia* Aeschylus depicts the cosmos as harmonious social order in the state, reconciling all differences and opposing forces, and itself based on the eternal natural cosmos.

Painting and sculpture were as wonderfully developed in ancient Greece as poetry. The Greeks recognized an inner relation between painting and sculpture, and poetry. The Ionian lyric poet Simonides (c. 556-468 B.C.) expressed the relation poignantly in the words: "Painting is silent poetry; poetry is painting that speaks."[120] Because the desert god Yahweh prohibited graven images, there was no painting or sculpture among the Hebrews. The difference between the Hebrew and Greek cultures, it has been said, is based on the primacy of the "ear" in one, and the "eye" in the other. The words of the invisible presence of Yahweh are heard, as are the pronouncements and predictions of the prophets. The Greeks, in their incomparable light, had a sense for visual beauty, not only with respect to natural configurations—why else build temples at such magnificent locations as Delphi, the Acropolis, and Sunium—but also with respect to the human arts of painting and sculpture. Moreover the Greek gods were so anthropomorphic in a physical sense, that they could be pictorially represented; also, the mythical figures and ancient heroes were often of partial divine origin and thus the visual arts could set forth their semi-divine nature. Inanimate nature plays little part in the Greek arts of painting and sculpture; landscape-painting did not emerge until the Hellenistic age. Greek painting and sculpture were concerned with living creatures, and with the effort to present these in their essential nature, a most important element of which was often their inner dynamic power. Who seeing the bronze statue at Delphi of the charioteer, *'o kratistos*, has not experienced the tremendous inner vitality expressed in the form and posture?

While painting and sculpture differ from poetry in the lack of a connection with music or dancing, nevertheless rhythm also entered into the visual arts. There are rhythmical elements in their fundamental pattern; Bowra finds this rhythm in "a geometrical foundation in design." As might be expected in the people who associated music with mathematics, "Greek sculptors, painters, and architects seem often to have been dominated by a sense of geometrical pattern and order." [121] However, there is another aspect; seeking to present the essential nature of its subjects, Greek art seeks beyond the superficial appearance the timeless essence of its individual figures. Thus art becomes a means of defeating time, of keeping memories alive, of maintaining glory and renown after death. The poetic task for the Greek is the same: "to give permanence to the fleeting moment...to defy mortality by creating something which time cannot harm."[122]

Religion among the Greeks

Man-oriented as the Greeks were, they had a sense of the divine, of gods with powers beyond the limitations of man. However in accord with their man-orientation, the Greek gods were extremely anthropomorphic in character, and this was often startling in its detail—for instance, when in Homer's *Iliad* Hera chucks her husband Zeus under the chin. Greek religion was an anthropomorphic polytheism, with a multiplicity of gods that could have been produced only by a people of such fertile imagination as the Greeks. Greek religion was unusual in its lack of system or of organization: there was no one eminent prophet or lawgiver, no sacred books with final authority on doctrine or moral values, no central priestly hierarchy, no revealed cosmology, no insistence on orthodoxy, no program of redemption. Thus the Greeks enjoyed great freedom in their religious experience, and a tolerance towards religious diversity. This multiplicity and diversity of religious experience contrasts sharply with Hebrew religion. Throughout Hebrew history the prophets were fighting against the encroachments of religious diversity in order to bring the Hebrew people back to the exclusive worship of the one God Yahweh and to full obedience of His commandments and ordinances. The predominant Greek divinities were the Olympians, the gods and goddesses living on Mt. Olympus with Zeus, the all-powerful hurler of thunder and lightning at their head. There were also cults which played a special role: Dionysus, the god of wine and frenetic ecstasy was worshipped as far back as Mycenaean times; the cult of the Eleusinian Mysteries, which was associated with the autumn season of plowing and sowing, was believed to gain for its initiates the favor of the underworld deities and thus ensure a better fate after death; unlike the Eleusinian, the Orphic Mysteries produced cult communities which worshipped Orpheus, son of the Muse, who made music on the lyre which did not excite in an orgiastic way as did Dionysian music, but calmed and healed.

The Greeks believed that the gods rule the world of nature and are active in the fortunes of men. Thunder and lightning, earthquakes, growth of crops, etc., were explained by divine agency, as Amos did for the Hebrews, and the Chinese thinkers did for their people. Similarly, human passions, pangs of conscience, poetry, art and inspiring thoughts were related by the Greeks to the gods. In Homer the gods moved among men, taking an active part, some on one side, and some on the other, in the Greek struggle against the Trojans. In Homer's *Iliad*, by their very human ways the gods often provide a comic relief breaking the tension or tedium of the human narrative, strangely enough very much like the clowns in Shakespearian drama.

The gods, however, were very different from men, and the Greeks were keenly aware of this difference. The gods were immortal; they suffered neither from old age nor death. Moreover, they were possessed of superhuman and inexhaustible power; in the *Iliad*, the gods were not limited by spatial and temporal parameters, particularly noticeable when intervening in human affairs. The gods seemed little concerned with good or evil in themselves or in men. "The Greek sense of the holy was based much less on a feeling of the goodness of the gods than on a devout respect for their incorruptible beauty and unfailing strength."[123] However, from the 6th to 4th century B.C., as Greek society became more conscious of civic obligations, there developed a growing belief that the gods watching over human affairs in the end punished the wicked. Powerful as the gods might be, there were some great poets and thinkers who discerned something more powerful even than the gods. Simonides called it Necessity, saying that even the gods do not fight against it. Herodotus called it Fate, which a god as well as men cannot escape. Aeschylus has Prometheus say that Zeus cannot alter what is ordained, which is itself the work of the Fates and the Furies in obedience to Necessity. Earlier, the Ionian poet Archilochus had stressed the role of Fate (*Moira*) and Fortune (*Tyche*) in the affairs of men. With these concepts the probing Greek minds were seeking to discern the laws, principles, and powers which determined the course of existence.

In prayer the Greeks sought the help of the gods. To understand in advance divine purposes, the Greeks had diverse ways of probing and predicting the future. Self-appointed sibyls and prophets might be heeded, but they were often distrusted. The flight of birds was studied attentively, particularly before battles, but sound military opinion was expressed by Socrates, saying, "The augur should be under the authority of the general, and not the general under the authority of the augur."[124] Dreams were said to have come from Zeus and hence were taken seriously, but Homer expressed uncertainty as to which dreams could be trusted and which not. The most important vehicles for predicting the future were the oracular utterances of gods pronounced by their priests and priestesses, especially those from Apollo's temple at Delphi. The prestige of the Delphic Oracle was a tribute to its wisdom, based on good general information of public affairs and on its understanding of human nature. To be sure, the oracular utterances were usually ambiguous and enigmatic; they had to be interpreted correctly by those to whom addressed. If the Oracle turned out wrong, it was usual to explain this fact by human misinterpretation. Belief in oracles remained prevalent even in the increasingly rationalist 5th century, and both Herodotus and Sophocles sought to demonstrate that the apparent failure of oracular utterances was due to misinterpretation.

From earliest times, conscious of their own specific culture, the Greeks had an exclusivist view of themselves as different from all other peoples, the barbarians. However, there were strands of a universalist view also in Greek culture, the earliest trace of which is found in the Orphic cult, which goes back at least to the 6th century. The Orphic movement produced cult communities transcending the traditional kinship social groups which were breaking up in the 6th century with the rise to dominance of the city-state. In Orphism appears the seed of the doctrine that all men are brothers. *Philia*, which meant the kinship bond of solidarity, begins to mean love, a new sense of solidarity which includes all mankind, even all living beings. In the 5th century universalism appeared in the thought of some of the Sophists. In the Platonic dialogue *Protagoras*, the universalist Hippias of Elis states: "Gentlemen, I consider you all kinsmen and friends and fellow countrymen, not of course by law but by nature. For by nature like is akin to like...."[125] The Athenian sophist Antiphon was also a universalist, who wrote: "In every respect we have all the same nature, Greeks and Barbarians alike. This can be seen from the natural needs of all men. They can all satisfy themselves in the same way, and in these matters there is no distinction between Barbarians and Greeks. We all breathe the same air through mouth and nose and all eat with our hands."[126] These strands of universalism were never strong nor widespread in the Greek cultural tradition unlike the universalism in Old Testament thought. "It was not till their civilization began to collapse that the Greeks formed their first glimmerings of the brotherhood of men, and even then it was more an abstract ideal than a purposeful conviction."[127]

As the old polytheist religion declined in the 5th century B.C., a tendency toward monotheism arose, which was rational and philosophic, unlike the personal national God of the Hebrews. The Ionian poet-philosopher Xenophanes of Colophon was the impassioned leader in the attack on the Olympian gods. His attack was two-pronged, first against the anthropomorphic conception: "...if oxen and horses and lions had hands and could paint with their hands, and produce works of art, as men do, horses would paint the forms of the gods like horses, and oxen like oxen...."[128] Negroes, he wrote, believed in flat-nosed, black-faced gods, and the Thracians in gods with blue eyes and red hair. The second attack was on moral grounds: according to Xenophanes, "Homer and Hesiod have ascribed to the gods all things that are a shame and a disgrace among men, thefts and adulteries and deceptions of one another."[129] Xenophanes sets forth his own conception of god in the following words: "One god, the greatest among gods and men, like unto mortals neither in the form nor in thought."[130] His God rules the universe by pure thought, not like Yahweh who rules primarily by will and purpose.

Philosophy and History

However many the great thinkers of other cultures, the Greek philosophers were different in depth and all-encompassing breadth, because their philosophy, their love and pursuit of wisdom, was based on pure reason, human reason. The first Greek philosophers, the Ionian natural philosophers, were cosmologists who were studying the natural universe, not for practical purposes, but for the sake of the knowledge itself. They took over the knowledge of heavenly and earthly phenomena acquired by the older Near Eastern cultures, in particular Egypt and Mesopotamia. On this basis they sought to understand the origin and nature of the universe by theoretical and causal inquiry and thus to comprehend the structure and order of the universe, the principles and generalities exemplified in particular phenomena, the reality behind appearance. The basic concepts in Greek science and natural philosophy arose from an extrapolation, or application to nature, of fundamental ideas in their conception of human society. For instance, the Greek word *cosmos* originally meant the *right order* in a state or other community. Also the idea of cause (*aitia*), which was a most important idea in the Ionian natural philosophy, originally meant the same as the idea of retribution; like the related words, cosmos and *dike* (justice), it was transferred from the human sphere to nature. When Pythagoras found harmony as the governing principle in the order and structure of the natural universe, he was likewise transferring a concept from the human sphere to nature. The transference of concepts from the human sphere to nature was, of course, not a one-way process in the development of Greek thought and culture. Once these concepts had been deepened and enriched by their application to natural philosophy, there was a return process in which these concepts brought about a more developed and profound understanding of the human sphere. Indeed, in the development of Greek thought, as in Chinese thought, there was a process of conceptual reciprocity between the understanding of human society and the natural universe; this process was fruitful and is doubtless one of the major intellectual reasons for the maturity, depth, and splendor of the Greek spirit in all of its manifestations.

The Ionian philosophers believed in coherent and consistent theoretical arguments. Later the poet and philosopher Parmenides of Elea in the 5th century B.C. formalized this belief by the introduction of logic, a rigorous formal structure in thought. According to Parmenides, "thinking is the same as Being,"[131] and thus through reason alone the totality and unity of Being can be apprehended. These early forms of theoretic and logical thought reached their fruition in the 4th century B.C. with the dialogue exchanges of Plato and the more prosaic work of Aristotle, both of whom comprehended in their thought the natural universe as well as human existence and social and political life. Conscious of the 4th century B.C. as the beginning of the decline of Hellenic culture, Hegel said: "The owl of Minerva takes its flight in the evening twilight."

Greek mathematics and Greek natural science have been built upon for some twenty-three hundred years; they have been built upon, improved, and surpassed by modern Western mathematics and natural science. Has modern Western philosophy surpassed ancient Greek philosophy? Perhaps in some senses, but certainly not completely. The depth and grandeur of Greek philosophy derives from its uniqueness as a product of the most mature and developed man-centered culture in the world. All of the other great cultures, except the Chinese, have been god-oriented. In a man-oriented culture, human thought is entirely free to proceed in any and all directions; in a god-oriented culture God, in my opinion, works as a limitation on this freedom. If this be true, the profound meaning of Greek philosophy may never be fully absorbed or surpassed by the philosophy of a God-oriented culture. If this be true, the question arises: is this limitation tyranny over the mind of man, in Jefferson's sense? Not quite. It would be, if the essence of man were not freedom, which from the Christian standpoint is God's gift.

The pre-Socratic natural philosophers called their activity *historie*, which means inquiry or learning by inquiry—Jaeger translates the word as "empirical investigation."[132] The Ionian thinkers by their philosophy of nature prepared the way for the study of man as a social and historic being, the same spirit of inquiry being applied to man. Our word "history" derives from the original Greek word for "inquiry." Bowra believes that the start was with medicine, with the Greek recognition of the dependence of health on physical conditions, and that the Greeks went on to other studies which are the beginnings of anthropology, geography, and history. From these scientific beginnings developed rapidly the great art of history writing by Herodotus and Thucydides—authentic history was originally, and still is, an art as well as a science.

Cicero named Herodotus "The Father of History." Despite modern criticism of his alleged credulity, garrulousness, and discursiveness, Herodotus has by and large retained this honorary title, certainly so far as Western history is concerned. There are many reasons for this, the first of which is the extraordinary breadth of Herodotus' conception of what is relevant to historical understanding. Herodotus treats the whole known world of his time, its countries, its customs, and its gods. Very widely traveled, he could survey this world from the vantage point of direct experience, as well as from the encyclopedic knowledge acquired from the study of earlier writings and information given to him orally. Geography, meteorology, ethnology, sociology, comparative religion, cultural history—rudimentary forms of all these are to be found in his history. Compared to Herodotus, the mental horizon of Thucydides, the incomparable exponent of political history, seems limited. Herodotus also displays a remarkable, and typically Greek, open-mindedness and tolerance. He listened well, reciting what he believed to be probably true, and even including tales or accounts with respect to which he states his disbelief. Another reason for Herodotus' preeminence is the artistry of his work; although he often proceeds on lengthy digressions, he is never tedious; Herodotus and Sophocles were friends, and he who learned from the scientists and sophists must have learned also from the Greek epics and the Attic tragedians a sense for artistry. While Herodotus in a very biographical way sees the individual will with its interests and passions deciding courses of action, nevertheless, like Aeschylus and Sophocles, he discerns a moral and divine force working itself out, correcting excessive pride, or punishing wrongdoing.

Perhaps another reason justifying Herodotus' designation as the "Father of History" is his unique sense of time. Bound by no dogma about the date of creation, he compared the alluvial deposits of the Nile in the Egyptian Delta with the other cases in the Aegean and suggested that, if the Nile were to reverse its course and flow into the Red Sea, ten or twenty thousand years would be required to fill it with sedimentary deposits. Herodotus indeed paid specific tribute to temporality when he wrote: "Everything could happen in the length of time."[133] In justification of Herodotus, Chester Starr states: "Herodotus had a more complicated view of time than any historian has ever exhibited since—sometimes Herodotean tales move down to the present; elsewhere they stretch from the present into the past; and at times they diverge into side chains of chronologically parallel events. Some modern critics, confused by this rich diversity or intolerant of his variation from our insistence on strict temporal progression, accuse Herodotus of lacking a sense of time, a view which has no justification."[134]

Herodotus was born around 480 B.C.; the battle of Marathon occurred in 491 B.C., and the naval encounter at Salamis in 480 B.C.; thus Herodotus' History of the War between the Greeks and the Persians does not deal with contemporary, but with past, events. One great difference between Herodotus and Thucydides is the fact that Thucydides was a contemporary and active Athenian participant in the war between Athens and the Peloponnesians. Regarding the Peloponnesian war as most important for posterity, Thucydides "began the task at the very outset of the war." As an Athenian participant, Thucydides could not regard historical events with the simple narrative interest or theological idealism of Herodotus, who was after all an Ionian without a feeling of responsibility for the events of the Persian war. Thus Herodotus deals more with the factual surface of narrative than with the causes and consequential relations of events, which concerned Thucydides most. Thucydides' sensitivity to political and social causation was a result of the direct experience in his youth of the politics of Periclean Athens and of the teachings of the Sophists, who were very prominent in Athens at this time. Although an Athenian participant, Thucydides' history shows no partiality. This may be, in part, a result of his twenty years exile after his failure as an Athenian general at Amphipolis in 424 B.C., during which time he had the opportunity for contact with the Spartan as well as the Athenian side. Speaking of the twenty-seven years of war from 431 to 404, Thucydides writes: "I lived through it in its entirety at a time of life when my observation was mature and with a fixed purpose of gathering accurate information."[135] Of the twenty-seven years, twenty were spent in exile; thus the isolation of exile may have been a factor in the lucidity and abstract objectivity of his presentation of the basic forces operating in his time. Thucydides' history lacks the variety and fullness of detail of Herodotus; in contrast, he rigorously selects those matters most relevant to the war. In Thucydides' endeavor to present the truth with impartial objectivity, he was imbued with the same scientific attitude as the Presocratic natural philosophers.

Taking over the concept of cause from medicine, which had made the first distinction between symptoms and real causes, Thucydides identifies the real cause of the war as different from the minor issues of disputes. Political activity thus becomes, as an independent field of natural causality, a sphere for rational understanding. In Thucydides' thought we find manifest the very Greek talent of expressing general, universal aspects without slighting the unique and without abandoning experience for abstraction. While political events are always set for Herodotus within the framework of his theological conception of history, in Thucydides nothing is left of this theological framework. Thucydides is a thoroughgoing rationalist with an exclusively rationalistic view of historical causation. Although Thucydides deals with a religious factor when it has a significant role, for him history sets forth an account of the world of men, the actions of political communities, based on economic, psychological, and political factors. He seeks to analyze, judge, disclose the inner dialectic and rationale of the events which comprise history.

The Sophists in 5th century B.C. formulated for the first time the idea of *human nature*. For them it meant the whole man, body and soul together, and in particular, man's spiritual nature. Thucydides used the concept of human nature to connote more specifically man's social and political nature. The Sophists set forth the view that human life like the natural universe, follows observable laws, and that the laws of nature govern human society more effectively than the laws of society itself. Their thought was based on an almost mechanistic view that political behavior is simply a result of natural causes and stresses operating on classes and groups. Thus to understand *human nature* means to have insight into the real causes of human action as over against superficial factors. The Sophists, and with them Thucydides, came to assume a stable human nature, so constituted that men responded uniformly to given circumstances. These uniform responses were the basis for the recurrent social forces in history. Thucydides believed that these social forces would operate similarly in comparable situations in the future and for that reason he claimed the usefulness of his work for future political leaders. Of his own history he writes: "But if it be found useful by those who wish to know the exact nature of events that once took place and, by reason of human nature, will take place again in similar or analogous form, that is enough." Thucydides' reasoning was analogic, as was the Chinese, with respect to history: like causes bring like effects.

Of supreme importance for Thucydides was correct foreknowledge, prognosis of the future based on analysis of the present and past. In praise of the untutored Themistocles, Thucydides writes: "He was a supreme judge of present policies and supremely able to conjecture what would ensue even in the distant future."[136] If political events follow a pattern and the pattern can be understood, then such an understanding can be the basis of action which will affect events, guide if not fundamentally alter the elemental forces of the pattern. Associated with recurrent social forces is naturally an element of historical compulsion, inevitability, as if the forces working themselves out were beyond the control of any human agent. Whatever the element of historical compulsion in Thucydides, it is not absolute, not completely beyond the control or guidance of man. Thucydides himself states that the loss of the war was the result of the mistakes of Athenian leadership after Pericles' death. To be sure, this poor leadership in his opinion was the result of the effect of the war, the plague, the siege, etc., on the Athenian democracy. It has been stated that for Thucydides "individuals and social forces exert an almost equal power."[137] However, it seems to me that for Thucydides the social forces are predominant, and that the individuals have decidedly less power; nevertheless the power of the individuals is certainly vigorously present, it is not as in Hegel nullified by the *Weltgeist* nor reduced as in Marx to "nudging along" the predetermined historical course.

Since a stable human nature is assumed so that men respond uniformly to given circumstances, it is possible to understand and foresee human behavior. The statesman, like the physician, requires this power of prediction. Unlike the Hebrew prophet, who received this power of prediction from God, the Greek statesman acquires this capability from the powers of reason, rational understanding of the general principles, patterns, and forces involved. While the gods may intervene in the Homeric epics and may appear in the dramas of Aeschylus and Sophocles as forces leading to justice, in Thucydides' rational understanding of human history the gods are conspicuous by their absence; neither do the gods intervene nor are the pathetic human appeals to the gods ever answered. History is based on man, and man alone; it is not "God who acts" in history, as it was for the Hebrews, but rather for the Greeks, Man who acts.

Greek View of Time

One of the most remarkable features of intellectual history is the persistence of errors. For a century and a half since the time of Auguste Comte, and persistently up to very recent times, the view has been expressed that the Greeks conceived of time as a cycle. This has been particularly prevalent in theological writings where the alleged Greek view of time as cycle has been compared to the view of the Hebrews and early Christians for whom time was conceived as a progression, finite or infinite. Indeed, this is supposed to be the most important feature distinguishing the Greek from the Hebrew attitude towards history. There is little foundation for this contrast, since the Greeks did not have simply a cyclic conception of time. The imaginative Greek mind had many diverse views of time. To be sure, the Pythagoreans had a conception of temporal cycles; in the 4th century B.C., Eudemus put forth the idea of exact repetition in the cycles; Plato in his cosmology wrote of the great concentric cycles of time and Aristotle found cycles, particularly in the natural change of the organic world, but neither for Plato nor Aristotle was a cyclic time the single predominant conception. The error has arisen by taking a partial aspect of the Greek view of time as the single conclusive view.

Chronos (Time) is not significantly present in Homer. As creator, judge, discoverer of truth, *Chronos* appears first in Solon, Pindar, and Aeschylus. For Solon the power of Justice appears in the temporal process through which all inequalities are inevitably compensated. Pindar calls time "the only witness for authentic truth."[138] In his second *Olympian* Pindar says: "Even time, father of all things, could not make these deeds undone and not realized,"[139] thus emphasizing the irreversible character of time. If time is irreversible, it is linear. According to Athenaeus, Aeschylus "dedicated his work to time,"[140] he trusted time, stressing in his tragedies that it always brings forth justice. It has been observed that Hesiod's poems know unlimited time, deal with different ages, and have a sense of chronological succession according to generations. Since Hesiod's father had emigrated from Asia Minor, a Hittite and Hebrew influence has been surmised. Herodotus saw forces operating in history—forces usually connected with the intervention of gods—which revealed themselves only at the end of a long chain of events. Herodotus chose to be the historian of the war between the Greeks and the Persians, believing it to have a unique significance, primarily as a conflict between men and slaves. When Thucydides regards his work as valuable to future generations because history repeats itself, he is not adopting a cyclical view of history in contrast to a linear temporal view. What repeats itself is the pattern, the general characteristics inherent in a cause-effect process; the pattern can occur again in a linear advancing time. If a Thucydides had written a history of the Kings of Judah and of Israel would he not have found cause-effect patterns in their historical course? Both Herodotus and Thucydides regard their work as efforts to save significant historical events from oblivion by communicating them to future generations. This may well have been their deepest motivation. Writing history for the Greeks was an action against time, against the all-destructive powers of time, in order to preserve the memory of significant events for posterity.

Associated with the erroneous view that the Greeks regarded time merely as cyclic is the likewise erroneous view that the Greeks did not acknowledge human progress, and that they looked longingly back to a Golden Age from which over the centuries there has been a decline in human society. To be sure, as so many other ancient peoples, the Greeks had a myth of a Golden Age, but this was merely one strand of mythic thought, and by no means a predominant one in their thinking and their spirit. The authoritative work of Robert Nisbet, *History of the Idea of Progress* (1980), demonstrates that the Greeks did have an idea of progress, contrary to the views of Comte and many other 19th and 20th century thinkers.

In a God-oriented culture it would not be strange for the view to prevail that man, a creature of God, has fallen from an early semi-divine condition, like Adam and Even, and that his existence is a continuing decline from an early state of bliss. In contrast, it would be very strange for a man-oriented culture to fail to have a conception of progress and to regard human existence as in constant decline from its remote beginnings. The Golden Age in Greek thought was merely a remnant of mythic thinking among the Greeks, which characterized the mentality of so many primitive and ancient peoples. It was overwhelmed among the Greeks by the rise and predominance of rational thinking. Even in Homer's *Odyssey*, there is a sense of the progress of mankind in the portrayal of the savage Cyclops as devoid of all culture, even agriculture, thus being an example of a primitive state of existence, to which the Greeks had once belonged. However, Hesiod (late 8th or 7th century B.C.), through his works *The Theogony* and *Works and Days*, is termed "the real source of the Greek belief in progress, through history and reform."[141] *The Theogony* is a cosmic history, which shows a sense of passage of long periods of time and the progressive amelioration of the conditions of the universe into which man came into existence. The *Works and Days* pertain to myths important for our theme: the myth of the successive metallic ages and the myth of Prometheus.

The myth of the successive metallic ages presents in succession the golden, silver, bronze, and iron ages (with an age of heroes between bronze and iron); mention of these ages may be also found in the much older Egyptian and Mesopotamian literature. The previous conventional interpretation had viewed this cycle as one of degeneration, beginning with the golden age and ending in the iron. However, Hesiod's sequence is now interpreted as not one of the progressively worsening of human conditions; the iron race of Hesiod's time is not completely evil; if the men of the iron age act justly, their life will be vastly improved. The myth of Prometheus is about the Titan who out of pity for the wretched original condition of mankind stole fire from Mt. Olympus to give it to mankind, initiating thereby the human advance to civilized existence, for which deed he was punished dreadfully by Zeus—as depicted so poignantly by Aeschylus. "It is a myth, clearly, in the direction of progress, man's progress from want to plenty."[142] Hesiod's myth of Prometheus was one of the important components of the Greek idea of progress; in the 5th century B.C. it was used by Aeschylus, Protagoras, and many others.

The epitaph written on Aeschylus' grave stated merely that he was "a Marathon Warrior." However, his life covered the formation of the Athenian *Polis* just before the great 5th century B.C., the wars between the Greeks and the Persians, and the subsequent tremendous advance in economic wealth, political power, and cultural genius in art, drama, history, and philosophy which made Athens for the whole 5th century the leading city in antiquity. No wonder, then, we find a keen sense of the meaning of progress in 5th century Athenians—Aeschylus, Sophocles, Pericles, Thucydides, and Protagoras—inasmuch as a belief in human progress is usually associated with an actual experience of progress.

The thought of Protagoras, the first and greatest of the Sophists, as presented in Plato's dialogue *Protagoras* acknowledges the progress of the arts and sciences from past human conditions and a belief in further improvement in the future by the use of intelligence and reason. During the discussion Protagoras asks permission to tell a story, which "story" turns out to be an account of the development of mankind from a very primitive state to civilization and culture. He relates too how Prometheus found man "naked, unshod, unbedded, and unarmed," for which reason he stole from Hephaestus and Athens fire and skills and arts. Then a detailed account is given of progress in civilization, in the arts and sciences. Soon men "invented houses and clothes and shoes and bedding and got food from the earth." Language came early, "articulate speech and names..." Then Zeus sent Hermes "to impart to men the qualities of respect for others and a sense of justice so as to bring order into our cities and create a bond of friendship and union."[143] Thus in a few brief paragraphs Protagoras sets forth the key elements of human progressive development, elements which Plato used later in *The Statesman* and particularly in his last great work, *The Laws*.

The idea of progress in Thucydides is set forth in his account of the past, the so-called Archaeology which at the beginning of his history deals briefly with the past out of which the Hellenes and their civilization had risen. In the Archaeology we find that in very early times no settled life existed. The level of culture was very low. "For as there was no traffic, and they did not mix with one another without fear, either by sea or by land; and they each so used what they had as but barely to live on, without having any superfluity of riches...they were not strong either in greatness of cities or other resources."[144] There is nothing mythic in Thucydides' presentation; using the comparative method to buttress his argument, he finds, "that the ancient Greeks lived in a manner similar to the barbarians of the present age."[145] Subsequently, as stages of progress he deals with Minos of Crete and Mycenae. After the Trojan war a troubled period of invasions occurred, and only gradually were the conditions of settled and civilized life restored. The emergence of the superior Athenian culture was for Thucydides clearly a progressive development from the past.

According to Chester Starr, Greek historical writing was linear:

"...from archaic Greece onward time was conceived as a line; before us is the future behind us is the past."[146] This is in direct contrast to the views of the Hebrew, for whom the past is *before* him, and the future *behind* him. A spatial conception of time was, of course, natural for the Greeks, the people who first really developed geometry. In this passage of time from the past to the future, for the Greeks real change takes place both in the physical world and in human society. When Thucydides comes to the major part and purpose of his work, the war between the Peloponnesians and Athens, his history is strictly chronologically ordered by succession of summers and winters. As Nisbet points out, the structure of Thucydides' presentation of historical data which became, and has remained, the conventional practice of historians, "is narrative, unilinear, and chronological,"[147] a presentation of past and present looking into the horizon of the future. The fact that Thucydides believed patterns of social forces might recur again in similar circumstances in the future does not alter his essentially unilinear conception of temporal advance, nor does it mean that he has adopted a cyclical view of history. In fact, whether societies rise and fall in cyclic rhythm as natural organisms as the Chinese thought, or whether they rise and fall cyclically as they come close to or depart from the norms of just government as expressed by Plato in the *Republic*, is by no means incompatible or contrary to the conception of time as linear progression. To be sure, time in history has its rhythms, associated with the rhythms of historical events—perhaps the temporal progression in history is sinusoidal, an irregular sinusoidal curve, irregular in period and amplitude.

Time in Greek Drama

The art form closest to human experience is drama. Since human experience moves in the time dimension at whatever the pace, the great dramatist is acutely aware of time and his imagination focuses on it. The word "time" appears at least 500 times in Shakespeare's dramas. The Greek word for time, *chronos*, occurs more than 400 times in the extant works of the three great 5th century Athenian tragedians. The Greeks originally did not speak much of time; in Homer the word is never the subject of a verb, and thus was not personified. The personification of time arose first in the 6th century among poets and philosophers, Thales, Solon, Simonides, and Heraclitus. However, time was not an important idea in Greek literature before the 5th century, when it appears in Pindar and, very prominently, in Greek tragedy.

The enhanced consciousness of time in the 5th century B.C. may be one underlying reason why both tragedy and history emerged during the same period of Greek development. As a symbol of this relation, it may be recalled that Herodotus and Sophocles were friends. The number of times in which the word "time" is used by the Attic tragedians indicates a continuing reflection about the nature of time, about the interrelations among a temporal series of events, and further, the relation of this series with past and future. The tragedians discerned causes and responsibilities in the past, and these cast shadows forward into the future.

For Aeschylus time is the means through which justice is meted out by the gods, and in proper time the divine punishment takes place. Through regret and fear and through the events revealing divine justice, man becomes wise—with time. In *Prometheus*, we learn that time as it grows old teaches everything. At the end of the *Eumenides* Athena wishes the Athenians that they may live happy "growing wise with time."[148]

The material and cultural development of 5th century Athens was remarkably rapid. Only one generation separated Aeschylus and Sophocles—Aeschylus at age forty-five fought at Salamis; Sophocles at age fifteen was one of the boys who danced at the victory celebration. The idea of time expressed by Sophocles differed from that of Aeschylus according to the intellectual atmosphere of the changing times. Athens' power was great and firm when Sophocles wrote his first tragedy. Sophocles focuses primarily on man. Time is no longer a sequence slowly achieving the aims of a divine justice as for Aeschylus, but a series of abrupt changes affecting individual attitudes and fortunes. In the *Ajax*, Athena says: "A day can humble all human things, and a day can lift them up."[149] Nevertheless, Sophocles had a keen sense of an orderly world which expresses itself in his frequent use of regular alternation in nature, days and nights in rhythmic succession, the movements of the stars, where the verb *kyklein* (to go in circles) is used. "This *kyklos* of nature, this perpetual sharing and succession in the universe does not in the least mean what we now call (speaking of the Greeks!) 'cyclic time': it means a continuous movement of all things, which may be controlled by regular laws, and yet illustrate the perpetual modification of the world we live in."[150] For Sophocles the movements and changes in nature, whether orderly or disorderly, join to increase the frailty of human existence and the challenge to human powers and endurance. This frailty and this responsive human power seem to be rooted in the nature of things as part of man's condition. Indeed, "they are the features of time,"[151] as evidenced by passages in Sophocles dealing with time. In *Antigone*, we read, "There is no state of mortal life that I would ever praise or blame as settled: fortune raises and fortune humbles the lucky or unlucky from day to day."[152]

There is another aspect of time of great importance in Sophocles. Time brings forth truth; the real nature of things and people finally comes to light in time. This idea of time appeared in Greece as early as the 6th century. Thales spoke about time "finding out"[153] everything. Solon relies on time to reveal what is right. Theognis, speaking of liars, states: "Time brings to full light the true nature of each." Pindar speaks about time "who alone establishes the correct truth."[154] Aeschylus also occasionally uses the idea, and Euripides quite often. In Sophocles, however, it has a special importance. It appears in numerous Sophoclean fragments such as: "No lie abides with time," or "Time uncovers all things and brings them to light," or "Time, seeing all and hearing all, unfolds all things." Also it is a main element in the structure of Sophocles' famous *Oedipus Rex*. Creon advises Oedipus not to form any hasty judgments, reminding him, "You will learn these things with sureness in time." Finding out the truth of who killed Laius is the subject of the whole tragedy, which begins in ignorance and error. This finding out in the course of time develops progressively as the past bit by bit is "brought to light," "unfolded," "uncovered." In the end the answer is found that Oedipus killed his own father Laius, thus leaving him destroyed by his own discovery. When all is known finally the chorus of Theban elders asserts: "Time, the all-seeing, has found you out in your despite."[155] To be sure, the anguish was corrected in time, when Sophocles presented in a later play the death and ultimate glory of his hero Oedipus.

Euripides was about ten years younger than Sophocles; hence most of Sophocles' plays were performed at the same time as Euripides'. The ten-year difference in age seems very slight, but in a time of very rapid changes in Athenian society and politics, ten years made an important difference. Since Sophocles regards time from the viewpoint of man, admitting quick changes of circumstances which affect human fortunes and feelings, the length of time is also considered from the same standpoint. Length of time is often determined by the consciousness of waiting, as we have seen in Part II. Sophocles' characters live in anxious waiting, but not for generations as did Aeschylus' characters. Rather they are concerned with their own happiness or misery. Temporal process therefore becomes an internal and psychological experience. With Euripides, the most subjective of the three tragedians, time settles into the human soul.

While Sophocles spoke of the short time sufficient for great changes, Euripides reiterates in play after play that "one single day" can bring about the greatest upheavals in individual fortune. In *Alcestis* we hear that many unforeseen happenings take place and that nothing occurs as expected. These sudden changes occur by chance, and always with a destructive effect. Time, for Euripides, thus becomes the realm of *Tyche*, chance. Also, time is considered in Euripides from the standpoint of human suffering, emotion, and sensibility. In many respects then time becomes what humans make it to be in their experience, in desires and fears. In *Heracles*, Megara says: "Time, in the interval [of waiting], hurts me and bites me."[156] The passage of time has no fixed real quality; it is long or short, as experienced according to particular human emotions. Euripides often transfers the quality of human feelings to the person or event causing them; hence emotions are pervasive and become the means and standards to depict reality. Thus by and large Euripides has a psychological view of time, focused on emotion, and the personal life of the dramatist's characters, with its fears and relief, hopes and regrets, is displayed as permeated with affective temporality.

The changing views of time of the three 5th century Attic tragedians has been well related to the rapid course of the history of Athens in that century as follows: "Aeschylus' theological faith in justice coincided with the city's dramatic recovery from an invasion that violated both piety and justice; Sophocles' moral refusal of change came from a man who formed his ideas when Athens was boldly facing the Greek world and believing in her own achievements; Euripides' interest in man's miseries and his drifting fortunes coincided with the excess of democratic individualism, with the evils of war, with the impending threat against the power of Athens."[157]

In the foregoing discussion of ancient civilizations under the title of "Time, History, and Culture" we have not attempted an exhaustive survey. We have dealt with those examples, a study of which might be particularly enlightening with respect to the general topic of "Time and History." For example, we have not discussed India because India is generally regarded as the least historically minded of the great civilizations, and that probably because of the depreciation of temporality in the ancient Indian world-view. Hajime

Nakamura comments that the Indians "have not exerted themselves to grasp the concept of time quantitatively, and have never written historical books with accurate dates."[158] Aside from the Chinese, who have been termed the most historically minded of all ancient peoples, we have dealt only with the great civilizations of the ancient Near East, among which the Greeks may be included because of the Ionians.

As we have noted in our previous discussion, some Mesopotamians viewed their history in the terms of the rise and decline of dynasties and accorded a regularity to this unvarying alternation. Likewise the Chinese regarded history as proceeding by discrete dynasties whose duration extended as long as the descendants of a ruler inherited his throne. The dynasties were thought of as natural organisms with a life-cycle containing successive periods of growth, maturity, and decay. The concept of life-cycles in history appears in the earliest Chinese historical literature going back some four thousand years ago and persists in modern times up to the twentieth century. With the Hebrews, it was different. History is for the Hebrew, as we have noted, the locus of God's activity; the transcendent God does not necessarily have rhythmic, cyclic modes of expression, like a natural organism. If history is the work of God, then it is perceived as the fulfillment of God's purposes; within such a framework, there is little room for, or little attention is given to, the ups and downs, the rise and fall of kings and peoples. Herodotus mentions the rise and fall of individual and, by implication, state fortunes. The Greek tragedians, particularly Sophocles and Euripides, express repeatedly their keen awareness of the sudden rise or fall of human fortunes, which may occur in a brief time, or even in one day. Nevertheless, neither Herodotus nor Thucydides set forth their histories systematically within the cyclic framework of rise and decline.

We wish to consider now diverse rhythms in history. Most important is the rhythm of the rise and fall of civilizations and cultures. To present different views of this rhythm, and the role of temporality in these views, let us turn to three thinkers and historians of the nineteenth and twentieth centuries: Hegel, Spengler, and Toynbee.

Chapter 4
Rhythms in History:
Hegel, Spengler, and Toynbee

Hegel

Beginning the section on Hegel in the 1980 book previously cited, Robert Nisbet states: "Apart only from Plato, Aristotle, and St. Augustine, Hegel may well be the single most influential philosopher in Western history. He was without question the preeminent philosopher of the nineteenth century."[159] There are three major reasons for this appraisal, in my opinion: 1) Hegel represents the culmination of the great mainstream of European rationalist thought, beginning with Descartes, and continuing with Spinoza, Leibniz, and Kant. 2) Hegel dealt with the entire range of human experience and human thought; he attempted an encyclopedic system covering this range. Whatever the defects of the system, Hegel sets forth his views with incomparable pregnancy and subtlety, illuminating in so many diverse spheres and particular instances. 3) No other nineteenth century thinker has had a direct comparable influence on the twentieth century. Both Marx and Kierkegaard, while disagreeing strongly with Hegel's view as they set forth their own thoughts, showed a great respect and esteem for their teacher Hegel and his work. Marx has lived on through Socialism and Communism as a mighty social, political, and intellectual influence in this century. Kierkegaard lives on in Continental existentialism, perhaps the most important twentieth century philosophical stream.

Hegel first lectured on the Philosophy of History in the winter semester 1822-23, when he was fifty-two years old and at the height of his maturity. He had already published the *Phenomenology, Logic, Encyclopedia, Philosophy of Right*, and had already lectured on the History of Philosophy, Aesthetics, and Philosophy of Religion. Although it is quite true that Hegel was preoccupied with historic problems, and sought an understanding of historic processes in the historic actuality long before he attempted to elaborate a logic and a philosophic system, nevertheless it is equally true that, on the presupposition of his entire systematic endeavors, his final Philosophy of History may be considered as the culmination point of his achievement. It was so considered even in his lifetime, or shortly thereafter, for Schopenhauer testified contemptuously that the Hegelians consider the Philosophy of History as the main purpose of all philosophy. The French historian Michelet did not hesitate to assert that the Philosophy of History is the crown of all Hegel's works. And the Scotch philosopher Seth has well expressed the view of many Hegelian commentators, writing: "It may be said with truth that it was Hegel's interpretation of history that made the success of his system and gave it its wonderful hold over a full generation. It is here...that we have to seek his actual achievement."[160]

The significance of history in Hegel's thought is not adequately expressed by the place assigned it in Hegel's final system, namely, under the State at the end of "Objective Spirit," making the transition to "Absolute Spirit." It is necessary to consider the earlier formulations of Hegel's philosophy in order to appreciate the import of history. In both the *Jenenser Realphilosophie* (1805-06) and the *Phenomenology* (1807), history appears as final and highest in his system, indeed as the Absolute itself. In the closing sentences of the *Jenenser Realphilosophie*, Hegel says directly, *"er (der Geist) ist die Weltgeschicht,"* i.e., the Spirit is world history. Similarly in the final sentence of the *Phenomenology*, the Absolute Spirit appears in history on one hand, and as phenomenology on the other, both together, *die begriffene Geschichte*, i.e., history comprehended, forming the recollection and the Golgotha of Absolute Spirit, the reality, truth, and certainty of its throne. In the Nuremberg *Encyclopedia*, around 1813, history for the first time, however, loses its place at the end of the system being replaced by the spirit *in seiner reinen Darstellung*, i.e., in its pure form, which is in the Heidelberg

Encyclopedia 1817 given its final designation as the "Absolute Spirit." Despite this shift, history nevertheless does not lose its crucial import, for the objective spirit is the domicile of the Absolute Spirit, i.e., the pure spirit-realms of the Absolute Spirit, art, religion, philosophy, are included as moments of the objective spirit-principles of the historic peoples and have their development in and through the general historic development of these principles. The creative historic energy resides with the *Weltgeist*, the World Spirit, which realizes itself in the different historic *Volksgeister*, national spirits, in their political constitutions, mores, technology, deeds, and destiny, as well as in their arts, religion, and philosophy. Thus art, religion, and philosophy each have their "history," intrinsically related to the *Volksgeist* in which their particular expressions arise. Accordingly, although in the development of Hegel's thought, the "Absolute Spirit" came to replace history as the final element in his system, the function and import of history was not thereby diminished in any essential way. In his lectures on the Philosophy of History, Hegel states specifically that "the spirit is in the theater of world history in its concretest actuality."[161]

Weltgeist (World Spirit)

The course of world history is a necessary and rational sequence because it has been the course of the World Spirit, the one spirit whose nature is ever one and the same and who exfoliates this his one nature in the existential mode of the world (*Weltdasein*). The realization of the World Spirit takes place in a spirit-mode, namely, in the articulate representation of itself through which it comes to the knowledge of what it essentially is. The separate representations constitute the particular moments of its historic existence; they are each as a determinate concrete principle, the *Volksgeist*, the Spirit of a People. The particularity of the *Volksgeist* consists in the kind of conscious representation which it makes to itself of the Spirit, and the *Volksgeister* differentiate themselves in accordance with the superficiality or depth with which they have grasped what the Spirit is. The spirit of a people contains, and towards it are oriented, all the purposes and interests of the particular people; it constitutes the law, customs, religion, political institutions, its technical skill and economic ways, its science and art. This is what gives to a people its peculiar character, not any physical characteristics. Moreover, this spirit of the people expresses itself as well in occurrences, deeds and destiny. For it is the spirit which is first, not the vital energy of the people, not the passion and animal will, but the spirit which drives forth the events and determines the historic course in accordance with its own necessity. For the modern reader who may find the Hegelian views strange and un-American, it should be recalled that Ralph Waldo Emerson wrote in an essay on history as follows: "...this universal mind...is the only and sovereign agent. Of the works of this mind history is the record."[162]

The spirit of a people is actively generating in the production of its configuration and order and in the course of its historic rise and fall. It exists first in the shape of an obscure drive imbedded in the people which is its carrier, then it clarifies and objectifies itself in their deeds and accomplishments. In its first activity this spirit is motivated only by the definite purpose presented to it by the actuality, but it has an urge to comprehend itself, to apprehend consciously its own self-representation, and fulfills this urge in science, art, political thinking, philosophy, etc. Thus each *Volksgeist* represents a particular stage of self-knowledge. The passage of these stages represents the divine absolute process of spirit, whereby the spirit actualizes itself and reaches its true being, namely, self-consciousness, self-conscious knowledge of itself. This passage is a necessary sequence of stages, where one stage in its own process of development prepares for the next and in turn, purified and clarified, is taken up into the next stage. Thus nothing is lost, and the historic process is a cumulative growth in which each stage plays a part in the development of the whole and remains thus alive in the reality of the whole. In the gigantic process of world history, one Whole comes into being, namely, the universal Spirit. Thus the Spirit setting forth its own intrinsic nature in the necessary sequence of historic epochs attains therein its own totality, and "the principles of the particular national spirits in a necessary succession are themselves only moments of the one universal Spirit which raises itself through them in history to a self-comprehending totality and concludes itself therein."[163]

Rise and Decline of a Volksgeist

We have to examine in some detail Hegel's representation of the procedure of the self-formation and decay and decline of a *Volksgeist*, as well as the passage (*Uebergang*) from one *Volksgeist* to another. For in all its cultural manifestations and historic deeds, a people is bringing forth that which is the inner determination of its own spirit and in the end sets forth what is implicit as its world. In the period of self-formation a people appears moral, virtuous, and strong because acting in accordance with the purpose of its spirit. The individuals, immersed in this activity, have not yet separated themselves out from the whole; they have the urge to defend their fatherland, to uphold the aims of their people. This is the youth of a people; though this work a people satisfies its inner urge. After the period of self-formation comes the period of enjoyment; in this its created world the spirit enjoys itself. There is no longer any opposition between the inner core and the actuality; for the particular principle has been brought to complete realization. With self-enjoyment comes fixed habitude; this habitude is no longer vital, lacking the fullness and depth of a purpose. The people can still do much in war and peace, internally and externally; they can vegetate on for a long time, but whatever busyness may be seen is animated by the particular interests of individuals, no longer by the interests of the people itself. Thus with habitude a people goes toward its natural death. In picturesque language, reminiscent of the Chinese view of the dynasty as a natural organism, Hegel states: "The *Volksgeist* is a natural individual; as such it develops, becomes strong, declines, and dies."[164]

A people reaches its highest culture point when it grasps the presuppositions of its own life, the science of its laws and moral institutions. Here the spirit knows its basic principles, the universal elements of its actual world. Sophocles, Aristophanes, Thucydides, and Plato, in these individuals the Greek spirit appropriated itself in image and thought—"In them has become historical what Greek life itself has been."[165] At the same time that this work of thought is the deepest fulfillment of the spirit, it posits the inner separation fatal to the culture. For this thinking which has attained the universal is ideal and different in form from the real actuality, the creative life through which the culture came into being. Through this general knowledge of the essence of the actuality, the spirit becomes conscious of the limitations of its established determinations, its faith, customs, laws, etc., and thus acquires grounds for renouncing established ways. Thus in the typical Hegelian way, out of that which first constitutes the highest unity of the subjective spirit with the universal and objective, namely, thinking self-knowledge, arises a separation of the subjective spirit from the universal. For the subjective spirit no longer respects the immediacy which it has come to recognize as a particular principle. The individuals withdraw out of the public world in order to live in themselves, in accordance with their own will, pursuing their own private purposes. At the same time with this withdrawal of the individual spirit in itself, thinking comes to be a special actuality, and the sciences arise; thus the sciences and the corruption, the decline of a people, are always connected with one another. This natural death of a culture is a kind of self-destruction. For the decay breaks out from within, individual desires and separate interests arising to claim the energies formerly devoted to the whole. Usually an external power appears which takes away the leadership from the people, but no force can work destructively against the *Volksgeist* if it has not itself become lifeless.

The decay and death of one national spirit effects the passage over into another principle, another national spirit. To comprehend this passage is, according to Hegel, the most important factor in the philosophic understanding of history. Its understanding resides simply in the twofold power of thought which while dissolvent is as well productive. At the same time that the thinking apprehension of the existing actuality is the effective factor in the dissolution of the national spirit, it is "the source and birthplace of the next higher form."[166] While the thinking spirit is breaking up the existential form which it has, it is attaining at the same time through its thought the universal essence of that which it was. Thus when the thought of a people, e.g., the Athenians, develops itself so far that the particularity of this people is transcended and its particular principles are no longer essential, then this people cannot exist any longer. The dissolution through thought is necessarily the arising of a new principle, and world history proceeds on in another people.

"The definite effecting cause of this passage is that that which exists is thought and therefore becomes elevated to universality."[167] The previous principle is hence preserved only not in its original form, but as transcended and transfigured through the articulation of its own universality. Insofar as the transfigured previous principle in its inner universality represents the basis for the next principle, we have here the "mechanics" of the spirit's cumulative growth. For on the basis of the universality of the previous principle, the spirit can then progress in a different configuration of itself which it next creates. "The death of a *Volksgeist* is a passing over (*Uebergang*) into life,"[168] and not as in nature where the death of the one elicits the existence of another just like it, but the world spirit strides from lower to higher principles, to more developed representation of itself.

From the foregoing exposition the efficacy of self-consciousness emerges clearly as the impelling force in the historic course of the Spirit. Self-consciousness as the essential way of the spirit's process plays the central role as the effective agency, furnishing the drive to the formation of the culture, the dissolvent to the decline, the transcendent carrier to the transition. Although the comprehension of the historic process in terms of self-consciousness may not suffice for an adequate understanding of history, nevertheless the importance of this factor can not be doubted. Its efficacy is especially clear in the destruction of a culture. For although many other elements are involved—certain natural conditions such as an intrinsic energy curve, empiric conditions such as the influence of other peoples, and formal ones such as the arrival with fruition at the constraint of inherent limitations—articulate self-conscious reflection represents perhaps the most central general factor in the self-destruction of a culture. The self-conscious comprehension through rational thinking of the character of the public actuality, the understanding of its generality together with its limitations, and the consequent juxtaposition of ideality and actuality can serve only as a solvent on the actuality. We can readily see too how impelled by the reflexivity of thought a correlated heightened internality would lead the individual self to a separation from the state. This is an eventuality whose source lies in the activity of men, and the process takes place in a causally connected order of events.

The Dubious Transition (Uebergang)

The Hegelian account of the passage from one culture to another, however, introduces a different situation, for the passage is not necessarily rooted in factual causation, but rather is effected through the one world spirit which realizes itself in the necessary sequence of culture worlds. This becomes clear in the transition from China to India and from India to Persia—in all the other transitions, since there are certain factual relations between the cultures, and hence a factual causation corresponding to the efficacy of the world spirit, this absolute power of the world spirit is obscure. In the Hegelian account of the historic course, the first culture world, the Oriental, has three major manifestations, China, India, and Persia—under Persia, or related to Persia, are considered the cultures of Asia Minor and Egypt. Leaving aside the inner dialectic connexity of these three manifestations of the Oriental world, let us note that they represent "a necessary succession."[169] When we inquire, however, as to the modus of transition in this succession, we find that there is no empiric connection bringing about the transition. "Neither China nor India continue forth in another culture."[170] "China is something first, which, however, does not constitute a beginning for anything further, nor does it proceed beyond itself." "The Indian principle is the second factor in the concept...in the world historic nexus it is the other principle, but it neither stands in relation backwards with the first principle or forwards with the next."[171] There is only such a connection between them as flowers and animals have with one another, namely, that each arises independently out of the earth, and their connection exists not for themselves but only for the thinking spirit. For Hegel the inner connection is real, grounded in the one Spirit, and the thinking human spirit merely discovers it. For Hegel, given China, because of the dialectic relation between the principle of China and India, the Indian principle must follow the Chinese, and thus through the dialectic of the Spirit the cultural actuality of India is brought about. Since the determination is set entirely through the inner conceptual movement, the absence of an external connection does not disturb the Hegelian scheme.

We have arrived here at one of those critical places where the Hegelian thinking is driven forward to take up an extreme standpoint which reveals a fundamental defectiveness of the general Hegelian view. Surely there is a radical difference between the energy of the spirit through man displayed in a causally connected order of events, and the private energy of the universal spirit which has no corresponding factual causation. For Hegel this difference is minor. The universal world spirit is primary, the effective cause and final purpose of world history; on account of this primacy it is irrelevant whether a particular passage happens to have a corresponding factual causation or not. If it be true that the Spirit can thus make its transition without factual connection, then all the factual connections which Hegel has elsewhere in his description of the transitions so brilliantly shown to be the carrier of ideational changes are put in a very questionable light.

Geography and History

A similar defect appears in Hegel's discussion of the geographic foundation of history, the consideration of the various natural conditions and elements of earth life, topographic, climactic, etc., on the basis of which human history has taken place. Hegel's detailed remarks on geography, despite the excessive use of triadic order, show his wonderful astuteness and habitual insight in matters of concrete relatedness. Insofar as history represents the unfolding of the universal world spirit in a necessary sequence of particular spirit-principles, and the spirit of a particular historic people is hence determined by its place in this succession, the natural environment of the people is, abstractly considered, "something external." And yet it is not absolutely indifferent and unrelated, for clearly it is in nature and natural environment that the spirit has, so to speak, its footing (*Boden*), and thus the geographic foundation of history is "essential and necessary."[172] This basis, moreover, is not uniform, for different geographic localities have different natural characters, or types. And a geographic type seems to be directly associated with the type and character of the people, native to the particular locality. When we ask, however, what is the precise nature of this close association between the geographic and human type, we discover the remarkable fact that the relation according to Hegel is one of *correspondence*. "The natural character of a people *corresponds* to what the spiritual principle is in the sequence of spiritual configuration." Hegel denies that there is any "relation of dependence of such a kind that the character of the peoples is formed through the natural character of the land."[173] Thus there is no *causal* connection which brings about the correspondence, for such a relation would imply a dependent spiritual being, since the world-historic peoples are essentially spiritual configurations. Occasionally Hegel makes remarks which seem to indicate a causal relation, such as, "The character of the Greek spirit, e.g., proceeds from the land, a coastal strip, which brings about the individual isolation."[174] However, later in his explicit treatment of the geographic elements of the Greek world, he writes, "The geographic dividedness and manifoldness correspond perfectly to the manifold nature of the Greek tribes and the mobility of the Greek spirit." And he continues, "From this character of the natural environment one must not seek to explain the spiritual; but one must note that it corresponds to the spiritual."[175]

It may be noted that "correspondence" is in general a very un-Hegelian concept, especially when the correspondence is merely stated, and not mediated through thought. Moreover, such a correspondence would require a kind of preestablished harmony between the spirit of a people and the native geographic locality—in his discussion of Leibniz, Hegel censures the relation of preestablished harmony sharply on the grounds of its externality and as a *begriflose Beziehung* (a relation without a conceptual basis). Unready to accept the causal efficacy of nature in the historic course of the spirit, by *force majeure* Hegel thus overcomes the givenness of geographic configuration and brings the sternest existential facts of our human habitat to harmonize directly in the value-fabric of the historic spirit. W.E. Hocking has written: "...Hegel has not given a satisfactory account of the *resistances* to the development of the spirit nor of the *materials* which are taken up into its development."[176]

Self-determination vs. Self-consciousness

In several places Hegel formulated the Spirit's nature in terms of self-determination. For example, "The appearance of the Spirit is its self-determination (*sein Sichbestimmen*) and this is the element of its concrete nature.... The appearance of the Spirit is its self-determination, and this appearance we have to consider in the form of states and individuals."[177] Hegel's usage of self-determination is not incompatible with the actualization through self-consciousness of the essentially predetermined historic reality, for this self-determination has the character of eternal logical necessity. Self-determination is perhaps a poor word, much abused nowadays, but if we understand it, not in Hegel's special eternal logical sense, but rather in the sense of actual creative self-determination in time, it represents an alternative to self-consciousness for the characterization of the way of historic process. The crux of all process, whether it be process of nature or spirit, may be expressed as the self-determination of actual creatures, in creative self-articulation and self-formation effecting real determinations. Although self-consciousness or self-awareness in some form or other seems to be connected with all mental process, nevertheless Hegel's view that self-consciousness is the crux of human activity and as such the animator of the historic course is to be questioned. For history is the product of actual decisions, and the spirit in self-consciousness does not decide what it is, but merely becomes conscious of itself as it is. Admitting that self-consciousness is always in one form or another associated with the historic process of creative determination, contributing necessary elements and impetus, this process itself appears rather as the spirit's self-determination of cultural being, with more or less explicit attendant self-knowledge, than as the spirit's more or less self-knowing determining being.

In his criticism of Hegel, Ranke writes that the development of history "depends not upon the universal principles (*Begriffe*) which may have dominated over this or that epoch but on entirely different things."[178] Further he writes: "We have to turn our attention, not to the principles but to the peoples themselves which have been active in history; to their influence on one another, their strife with one another, their development."[179] If the creative determination of peoples constitutes the sheer process of history, Hegel's conception of the *Volksgeist* is relevant still as the formal principle, the spiritual determinateness of a people. For every culture has a determinate complex spiritual form, and as such a unity, the unity of a complex, whether expressible in one explicit formula or not. This principle rather than being *a priori* determinate as a definite moment of the universal spirit, appears, we would say, initially in an irresolute shape, with formal determinations restricting an infinite range of indeterminacies. Unlike the Hegelian "*dunkler Trieb*,"[180] which is merely the absolute potency of a determinate spirit-principle, and hence not really dark, there is too the dark urge of a people seeking spiritual being—a potentiality with initial limitations derived from natural conditions, intrinsic racial character, the cultural inheritance. The historic course involves a mutual interplay between the principle with its various indeterminateness and the creatively self-determining people with its unclear potentiality, and actual determination is the result of the mutual efficacy of these two dark factors upon one another. The initial twofold irresolution finds a single resolution in the one actual historic course, resulting in a mutual definition of the principle and of the people.

This actual definition is not final, for a culture people functions beyond itself, efficient as content, standard, and lure in subsequent historic activity; and this functioning does bring new import and significances cast back on to that which was defined. Elements and ideas peripheral in one culture would become central features in a subsequent one. The "definition" is as it were re-scanned and re-criticized by the men of a new epoch seeking to determine their own way, and thus it is illuminated, added to, perhaps completed. However direct and profound the influence of a dying or dead culture world on a nascent one, there is a wide range of possibilities for the forward movement of the spirit and a fundamental indetermination concerning transmitted elements—an indetermination, contingent partly on the various accidentality along the course of empiric connection, and partly upon the self-determining creativity of the new people.

Beyond empiric connection and empiric creativity, the various actual cultures are related to one another as interconnected meanings, interwoven as spiritual expressions of mankind, and gathered together into the one history which the human race is making for itself. Whatever unity may be discerned is never sufficient, however, to determine the historic moments; whatever connection of an ideational nature, never sufficient explanation for empiric fact. The ideational correlation of cultural principles as meanings cannot exhibit these as expressions of a compelling totality, for the unity of meaning, when the subject matter is growing in time, is never compelling, never absolute—it is always being freshly determined and freshly attained.

Freedom

Just as Hegel comprehends world history as one totality in formal senses, as the exfoliation of the one world spirit, as the totality of the successive *Volksgeist* principles, and as the process whereby the spirit comes to know itself, similarly Hegel finds himself able to express the entire content and final purpose of world history in terms of one idea, namely, freedom, human freedom. It is through this content that the universal spirit is integral with man. Freedom is itself "the substance of the spirit."[181] In the historic process, in the element of human freedom, the spirit's aim is the freedom of the individual subject, that the individual attain conscience and morality, that it adopt universal purposes, that the subject have infinite value and become conscious of its own value. "This substantial purpose of the world spirit is achieved through the freedom of each and every man."[182]

Freedom is not a simple, immediate property. In line with the Kantian tradition and the general Hegelian emphasis on self-consciousness, freedom only exists and is obtained through the consciousness of freedom. Thus the world historic process is represented as one whereby the human race attains a greater freedom through the increasing consciousness of its own intrinsic freedom and the attainment in and through this consciousness of the actual objective freedom. This latter attainment for Hegel takes place in the long, hard process through which the enhanced consciousness penetrates and transforms the worldly conditions in accordance with itself. World history is then essentially the successive deepening in the human consciousness of freedom. "World history is the progress in the consciousness of freedom...a progress whose necessity we have to recognize."[183]

In accordance with Hegel's view of world history as progress in the consciousness of freedom, history is divided into three parts: the Oriental world where it is known that one is free; the Greco-Roman world, where it is known that some are free; the Germanic world, where it is known that all are free, man as man is free. According to Hegel, the Orientals do not know that the spirit or man as such is intrinsically free; because they do not know it, they are not free. They only know that one is free, setting thus an arbitrary will over them. This one is therefore only a despot, not a free man. Among the Greeks the consciousness of freedom emerged, but they, as the Romans, knew only that some are free, not man as such, for slavery was an accepted institution in the antique world. But the Germanic nations have in Christianity come to the consciousness that man as man is free and that the freedom of the spirit constitutes his unique nature. This consciousness arose first in religion, in this innermost region of the spirit, but with the acceptance of the Christian religion, slavery did not cease at once nor was the worldly regime based upon the principle of freedom. To build this principle into the world has required a long, arduous process, and this has been the historic task of Europe.

It may be of interest to compare here Hegel's remarks on the gradual abolition of slavery on the way from the natural condition of lack of freedom to the rational state with Alfred North Whitehead's account. Hegel sees Greco-Roman slavery and feudal serfdom as moments in the progress, though unrighteous as slavery, nevertheless, participating in the higher social customs and culture. Man must become ripe for freedom; hence gradual abolition of slavery is more fitting than sudden. Before the fully rational state, in which there is no slavery, the true idea of the state is in this connection present only as a *sollen* (an ought), and hence slavery is still necessary. This "ought" does not function, however; it expresses something subjective, and as such is not historical. Whitehead sees the "growth of the idea of the essential rights of human beings...its formation and its effective diffusion...as a triumph of the later phase of civilization."[184] The idea arises in the minds of a small group, is given a persuasive expression dependent on accidents of genius, receives limited application in humanizing the institutionalized Greco-Roman slavery, but the classic society which could not have withstood its full application had a necessary resistance to it. In Europe the gradual recession of slavery takes place, from slavery to serfdom, from serfdom to feudalism, from feudalism to aristocracy, etc., until the final abolition in the nineteenth century. The changing conditions have made possible the fulfillment of the initial idea; the idea has functioned as a hidden driving force, haunting humanity, as a driving force effecting transitions from social state to social state; ideas are at once gadflies irritating, beacons luring—thus functioning as efficacious ought-compulsions in a sense excluded by Hegel. It is interesting to note here that Whitehead's account of transition is bipolar, differing from Hegel's, where the transition is effected essentially through the spirit alone: "The great transitions are due to a coincidence of forces derived from both sides of the world, its physical and its spiritual natures."[185]

Freedom is for Hegel the substance of the spirit. All properties of the spirit exist only through freedom, all are only means for freedom, all only seek and produce this. His conception of freedom, further, is directly connected with the dominance of the noetic function. "Freedom...is the same one root (*Wurzel*) as thinking. Just as not the animal but only man thinks, so only man has freedom, and this because he thinks."[186] In further comments on freedom correlating it with self-conscious thinking, Hegel presents an intellectualist image for the procedure of freedom, which seems to be hardly in accord with the actual way of freedom. Hegel explicitly rejects the view in accordance with which freedom is the power of choice between opposed determinations ("*Es ist die Ansicht der Freiheit voellig zu verwerfen, nach welcher sie ein Wahl sein soll zwischen entgegengesetzten Bestimmtheiten...*").[187] However, in our opinion, choice represents an essential element in actual human freedom; if "choice" suggests perhaps a too explicit conscious apprehension, one might better say that freedom involves the resolution of indetermination. It is the capacity for absolute decision with regard to actualization, i.e., a deciding over relevant alternative possibilities with respect to their ingredience in the actuality, a deciding which is limited in scope, of course, but absolute because it issues in a definite irrevocable determination. This is "...a freedom which makes differences in the physical plane, a freedom of alternative possibility *within the field of fact*..."[188] The import of decisions varies from sheer negligibility to world-historical significance, and the efficacy of the decided doing in the world of brute fact is always questionable, for the subjective aim finds its factual realization with varying degrees of success depending on diverse conditions of external situation and internal drive. But the essence of human freedom resides in the actual self-determining decisiveness of a human being.

Men as Means

While the final purpose of world history, the spirit's consciousness of its own freedom, is attained through the advance in human freedom, nevertheless man in history is treated by Hegel merely as the means for this attainment. The immeasurable mass of human passions, interests, and activities are the means through which the world spirit accomplishes its purpose. Directed by his interests, animated by his passions, man is intent upon the accomplishment of his particular purposes. Although his immediate purposes are not those of the spirit, yet in fulfilling his particular ends he is realizing a larger purpose of which he is not conscious. At the same time that men accomplish their purposes, something else is brought about that was innerly involved, but neither in their consciousness nor intention. In fact, the individual, "the subjective side, caught in the advancing course of history, is not capable of knowing what the spirit's ultimate purpose is."[189] Even the great world-historic individuals, the heroes, who adopt and actualize "a purpose which is in accordance with the higher concept of the spirit,"[190] do not know or aim at the universal purpose which is ripe at their time. Thus although the world-historic individuals rise above the masses of individuals to lead them forward, they do not essentially enjoy a relation to the spirit different from that of the ordinary individual. Those who accomplish the great world-historic movements are as well means as those who are merely drawn along. These *Geschaeftsfuehrer* (executives) of the world spirit fulfill in each case a unique function and yet the uniqueness of their individuality is not thereby validated. In fact, when mentioning that the heroes have condemned the traditional respected ways and only therefore have been able to accomplish their novel tasks, Hegel does not hesitate to say that if they had not condemned the present order, "someone else would have accomplished what the Spirit wanted."[191]

Hegel goes even further when he says that the universal spirit forms for itself the individuals which it needs for its purposes. And the individuals do not hinder: "What must happen, happens."[192] The general indifference of the spirit to the uniqueness of the individual man could hardly be stated more crassly. The same indifference appears further in the ruthlessness of the advancing world spirit, or rather in the ready acceptance of this ruthlessness. If injustice happens to the individual, that does not concern world history, which uses the individuals as means in this advance. In the name of the world spirit the hero justifiably treats sacred rights and noble institutions with a ruthlessness. "A great figure in his forward march tramples upon many innocent flowers, must on its way destroy many things."[193] How easy to accept a ruthlessness towards individuals if "the individualities vanish for us and are valid to us only as that which brings to actuality what the spirit wants."[194]

Ultimately it is the universal which is hard and cruel. The individuals are crushed and sacrificed in fierce struggles through which the universal is realized. But the universal does not suffer; it does not endanger itself, nor enter into the opposition and combat; "it remains untouched in the background, sending forth the particularity of human individuals and human passions to wear themselves out in the struggle."[195] This is called *Die List der Vernunft* (the cunning of reason), namely, that reason employs the passions whereby not reason but these passions, these individuals, through which reason sets itself in existence, suffer and pay the forfeit. The degradation of man as means could reach no more complete expression. Ranke wrote indignantly: "The doctrine according to which the *Weltgeist* brings about things, as it were, by deception and makes use of human passions in order to accomplish its purposes is based on a highly unworthy representation of God and of mankind...." However, it is difficult to see any substantiation in Ranke's further statement that this can only lead to pantheism because "mankind is then the developing God, who creates and develops himself through a spiritual process which lies in his own nature,"[196] since in the *List der Vernunft* precisely the absolute transcendence of the universal spirit is exhibited. Croce criticizes Hegel's view just on that account, namely, that "dualism and the reciprocal transcendency of God and the world would persist."[197]

In the Hegelian view what becomes increasingly free in world history is the universal spirit, and man only derivatively. The final purpose of history is the spirit's consciousness of its own freedom, realized through men, and their consciousness of their freedom. Thus men participate in the purpose of the spirit, namely, freedom, but their freedom is subordinate to the spirit's freedom, and hence even their freedom is a means. It would not do justice to the Hegelian view to say that in world history the universal spirit is becoming more and more free while men are not. And yet there is a sense, in view of the vast distance between human individuals and the universal spirit, in which this is true. The universal spirit becomes increasingly free; the social institutions, i.e, the objective spirit, embody this increase in their structure and practice, but the human individual, the subjective spirit, although it may enjoy the superior objective freedom in the improved institutions of the higher spiritual configuration, does not become freer in itself, insofar as it always remains mean. If the individuals really knew the larger historical purposes, and through their knowledge, however complete it be, participated in these purposes, then they might attain thereby as individuals an actual freedom. Even if only the great individuals acted in accordance with such knowledge, although the masses of mankind did not, we would be justified in asserting that mankind achieved its greater actual freedom through these few. But Hegel admits knowledge of the larger historic meanings neither to the ordinary people nor to the great historic individuals.

It can hardly be denied that a thoroughgoing, unresolved contradiction makes itself apparent here, namely, a contradiction between the fact that men know one is free, some are free, all are free, and through this knowledge effect the progress in the consciousness of freedom which is the essence of history, and, on the other hand, the view that men as unconscious instruments and means are ignorant of the spirit's purposes. Is not freedom the spirit's purpose? And do they not then know the spirit's purpose in the self-knowledge which creates this freedom? It is through knowing and wanting such universal substantial objects as law and right that men create the state; the totality of cultural and historic life within the state is construed as a manifold *self-knowledge* of the particular spiritual principle at the basis of the historic existence; knowing produces the culture world and destroys it—the entire process of the historic activity is apprehended in terms of knowing—and yet we are told that men are unconscious means.

The reason why men are instruments is because of the *distance* between the transcendent infinite Spirit and man. Despite the fact that the spirit is the substantial whole of which the men are the individuations, that the universal Spirit is "essentially present" (*wesentlich vorhanden*)[198] as human consciousness, despite the presence of reason in man as his intrinsic substantial being and, albeit at first obscure and hidden, ground, despite the spirit-functioning of man in knowing, the transcendency is obdurate and the distance unbridged. There is a certain arbitrariness here. The spirit is in some senses immanent, in others transcendent—as it were, at will; and when transcendent, it is given the full transcendence of God, as if its immanence had not been previously rationally established and justified. Contradictions and paradoxes which one may be obliged to accept concerning God are not similarly tolerable with regard to an *ens rationis* such as the spirit.

In Hegel's thought there is an overweight of the universal which lies in the fact that the individual attains his own true individuality only in the animation and fulfillment of the universal, while the process of the development of the universal spirit along the course of its own universal determinations is necessarily determined, regardless of the particular output of individual strivings. Every effort to reestablish the value of the individual through his unification with the universal must break on the crucial import of this necessity. Attempting to overcome the "dualism and transcendency" of Hegel's *List der Vernunft*, where "individuals and reason would not make one but two; and the individual would be inferior and the idea superior,"[199] Croce asserts "the claim of the idealistic conception...that the individual and Idea make one and not two—that is to say, perfectly coincide and are identified."[200] Does not his identification, however, tip over in favor of the Idea through the usage and validation of universal non-temporal thought? It is a question whether this identification must not always on account of the nature of the Idea favor the Idea. At any rate, the value of Whitehead's asymmetrical relation between eternal objects and actual entities appears in this connection as a possible alternative whereby the undiminished reality of eternal ideas can be maintained together with the full, free creativity of the actual creatures involved, in this case, the human individuals.

It is certainly true that there are larger historical and spiritual ends which men unconsciously bring to pass in satisfying their particular aims. These larger ends come to pass, supervening upon a particular content and catching it up in a significance relating it beyond itself. Their realization occurs only through the activity and energy of man. They do not themselves have a self-realizing energy, directly contributing or conferring a generative power. Functioning as a lure in Whitehead's sense, however, they may elicit human energy through an obscure relevance and interconnection with those ends which are grasped. For the most part, they reside in the aura of a particular aim, that aura which renders to an aim a "kind of necessity," by the evocation of a fierce unclarified drive in the hearts of men. This aura may be ambiguous, full of various, often conflicting ideas. Only a historical span resolves it into a definiteness selecting out of it elements for a partial or complete actualization, removing others from any great relevance to the historic situation. If the transcendent idea functions, not immanently determining, but persuasively as lure, then one would arrive near to Whitehead's "the ideal in the background is promoting the gradual growth of the requisite communal customs, adequate to sustain the load of its exemplification."[201]

Hegel quite rightly saw the uniqueness of the world-historic individuals, but ultimately he attributed this uniqueness to the universality of their unique function. The function has this uniqueness, but the men as well, a uniqueness derivative from their individuality. And ultimately, with the great historic figures, the unique historic function and the unique individual have coalesced into an irreplaceable reality. The course of the American revolution without Washington is unthinkable—not unthinkable merely because the course has been, and as such is, irrevocable, but because of the peculiar historical efficacy of his unique individuality. If the mass of individuals constitute merely the plastic corpus of historic phenomena, those individuals who achieve for themselves through distinguished activity a unique historical place actively effect through their unique individuality determinations in the historic actuality. Unique potentialities among individuals do not always, however, have historic efficacy, for the historic function is necessary to actual attainment. There is a certain mutual reciprocity, however: historic needs stimulate the development of great individuals, and great individuals discern the important historic work in the welter of indiscriminate existence. Despite this, as Burckhardt wrote, "*Nicht jede Zeit findet ihren grossen Mann, und nicht jede grosse Faehigkeit findet ihre Zeit.*" (Not every period is accorded its great man, and not every great capacity comes at the right time.)[202]

Necessity and Possibility in History

In commenting on a passage where Hegel says, "It is the transience of history which can be so disturbing to us,"[203] Karl Jaspers once remarked that what is really moving in history is not the transience, but the particularity of historic configurations, the manifold unrealized possibilities, and that which, though at a particular time relevant and really possible, failed to happen. An appreciation of this aspect of history is entirely lacking in Hegel's treatment, not as a result of chance neglect, but because of fundamental tenets in his view. For Hegel the content of history is determined by an absolute necessity, which is expressed throughout his discussion. The view of necessity attains an extreme expression in the statement that "just as the seed bears in itself the entire nature of the tree, the taste and form of the fruit, so the first traces of the spirit also contain already *virtualiter* the entire history."[204] The doctrine of the absoluteness of the spirit, its immanence in the world, and accordingly its sway over history reaches here the most unqualified standpoint of predetermination and necessity with regard to the actual detail of history. W.E. Hocking has written: "The chief objection to Hegel's law [the law of history as an increase of freedom], however, is in the conception of the unfolding germ which, present in the beginning, acts as with a temporal desire for what is beyond it in point of time;..."[205]

Although Hegel often uses the word "possibility," in each instance one hardly finds possibility in any real sense involved. For example, in his discussion of the world-historic individuals, Hegel remarks that with their appearance occur "the great collisions between the extant social order and between opposed possibilities."[206] The use of the word "possibilities" here does not, however, signify any alternatives for the historic course inasmuch as the world-historic individuals represent precisely the higher universal necessary for the further development of the spirit. If the category of possibility is to have any meaning other than the obscure and illusory primal stage of necessary actualization, it must involve a real indeterminacy with respect to actualization. Since for Hegel the content of the spirit is definitely determinate, and both unicursal and univalent in its process of actualization, there is no place whatsoever in his system for possibilities, relevant to the historic actuality. Of course, Hegel would admit an unlimited diversity of possibilities among the negligible empirical particulars committed to the realm of accidentality, but these do not have any relevance to the historic course which moves securely on above the immeasurable confusion of detail and the vast turmoil of accidentality.

In our opinion, possibilities are real in the historic course of peoples, as in the life-way of the individual, real both in the presentation of alternatives and in the sheer significance of meaningful relation. Of course, it is difficult to discern with any certainty the factual presentation of real possibilities, or to estimate the approximation to actualization which any relevant possibility attained. The more remote the situation, the more its issue appears under the guise of necessity, the temporal distance functioning as a medium which fuses the actual historic welter with its aura of relevant possibilities into simple necessity. Moreover, since the actual issue of a particular situation transmits itself dominantly in the further historic course, with passage of time the influence of those unrealized possibilities relevant to a past situation—whatever their intrinsic, enduring meaning—becomes less and less unto vanishing.

If the actual historic course is to be understood in any deeper fashion than as a mere concatenation of factual occurrences, this can

can only be achieved through appreciating the relative significance of alternative possibilities to this course. Whenever the historian seeks to ground his representation of *"Wie es eigentlich gewesen ist,"* this always involves, we would say, a more or less explicit reference to other possibilities. Whether the representation explicitly goes into problems of cause and effect or not, insofar as it delivers a connected representation it grounds a particular historic eventuality in its interconnections. It must seek to show how this particular eventuality rather than some other arose at this juncture out of and continuous with these interconnections; furthermore, these interconnected eventualities were such as to elicit this eventuality, for, had they been different, some other eventuality would have taken the place of the former. The representation of the precise course is built upon two shifty elements, the eventuality and the ground of interconnections, both of which appear as they really are only with respect to what they might have been. And the nature of history is such that with very slight shifts of factual constraint at critical junctures, the course might have been different. If the sudden death of Pericles had not snatched the benefit of his sober guidance from Athenian policy, would not the course of Greek history have been quite different? Or if the genius of Alcibiades had not been contaminated by so dissolute a nature, could not he, who was so responsive in his individual life to the diversity of the Greek world, have been the enlightened unifier of Greece? In the relevance of important alternatives, the significance and pathos, the greatness and tragedy of historic events and attainments are revealed.

Since for Hegel the internal content of world history is a possibility which must necessarily be realized in its content-character, there is an unstrained passage from possibility to actuality via necessity. The passage from possibility to actuality, however, is not genuine unless it involves the resolution of indetermination by an ontologically ultimate entity. Man is such an ultimate entity. For Hegel there is a macroscopic necessity and a microscopic indeterminateness, or rather indifference to microscopic determination—for example, men as means—indifference towards particular individuals while the spirit makes its own. The truth, in our opinion, is the inverted case: the essential determinateness is microscopic rooted in men's decisiveness. Not that men create all the conditions nor determine the various possibilities nor grasp all the implications of their decisions, but the actual course of history is nevertheless determined by human decisions, by the decisions of individuals. The individual cannot effect historically whatever he will; he is limited by manifold general conditions and by the special conditions of specific historic situations—indeed also by certain general laws implicit in the structure of a cultural situation, e.g., with the best will of individuals, cultural decline where the decline has rooted structural causes cannot be held back long—for instance, the thwarted efforts of Agis and Cleomenes in declining Sparta.

We may consider individuals and their free decisiveness perhaps as points of force casting forth at each juncture their component of energy into the general wave, conditioned by the larger wave, conflicting and mingling with each other, but always active as a force component. The mass of individuals contribute each a very minor, almost negligible quantum, and yet welded together they do make out the great corpus of social force affected by and responsive to the catalytic and directive touch of those individuals who contribute the great creative force. No philosophy of history which fails to acknowledge the centrality of human decisiveness as the agency for actualization in the historic course can be adequate. This centrality is not altered by the fact that human purposes do not well agree with human effects, that the best individual self-consciousness falls very short of adequate understanding, that an existent, if not inevitable, dialectic rewards an aim with a contrary result. Neither is this centrality altered by the inescapable givenness of natural environment which limits all human creativity, nor by the obscure efficacy of transcendent lure which defies all limits. Human cultures are neither deducible as the wondrous vegetable products of chthonic powers nor as the ordered sequence of spirit-principles fulfilling a predetermined divine plan. For the historic Whole is dark and uncertain, not accidental, but irresolute, and history may be *recorded*, but not deduced.

Hegel's View of Time

The nature of time receives nowhere extensive discussion in Hegel's system. It is possible nevertheless to gain a rather clear report of the main lines of his conception of time and the role assigned it in his system. This role is essentially connected with the role of history, so that the nature of history for Hegel presupposes his conception of time, and the nature of time for Hegel alone makes possible his conception of history.

"It is in accordance with the concept of the spirit," Hegel says, "that the development of history falls in time."[207] We learn in the *Vernunft in der Geschichte* that time has two conceptual correspondences with the spirit, namely, its negative and positive characteristics. Certain passages in Hegel's *Philosophy of Nature* express the negative character of time. Time is not a receptacle in which everything is placed, as in a stream, from which it is carried along and finally engulfed. Time itself is really only the abstraction of this wasting. Thus, "because things are finite, therefore they are in time: they do not pass away because they are in time; rather the things themselves are temporal."[208] The process of actual things accordingly institutes time (*macht die Zeit*). In other words, the finite things are all temporal, because they are subject to change. Their change, the general process of their change brings with it temporality. "If everything stood still, even our mental images: then we would endure, but there would be no time."[209] We may question whether under such circumstances there would really be any duration, especially since Hegel defines duration with respect to time, distinguishing it thus from eternity, but the absence of time seems indubitable. For Hegel then, "...everything does not arise and pass away in time, rather time itself is the becoming, the arising, and passing away,... *Chronos* which gives birth to everything and destroys its own creations."[210] Time is thus not only the negative corrosive factor, but the positive becoming, the all-creating *Chronos*.

Hegel never tires of repeating throughout his system that whereas change in nature is repetition of the similar, a preservation of the species, a monotone circular process without any intrinsic advance, change in the realm of the Spirit is essentially progress. It is true that natural forms represent a succession of stages from lower to higher forms, each subsequent stage arising from the dialectic transformation of the previous one. But this is not a natural process of generation taking place in time, for there is no empiric connectedness to the forms in nature, and the transitions appear only to the thinking spirit. In the realm of the spirit, however, the higher configuration in contrast has produced itself through an actual reworking of the previous lower one, through which the latter has ceased to exist, or at any rate, pushed off to the side, has ceased to be the carrier of the world-historic spirit, while the former, taking up the latter into itself, represents its transfiguration. That one cultural configuration is a clarification, transfiguration (*Verklaerung*), of the previous one is the reason why the appearance of the spiritual configuration falls in time: "World history is accordingly in general the exfoliation (*Auslegung*) of the spirit in time..."[211] Hence time is a medium for the connected efficacy of the spirit which brings about its historic exfoliation. This connected efficacy takes place through the reworking and transfiguration of one culture principle by the next higher one, in which the higher form preserves the other as *aufgehoben* (maintained) within itself. Thus emerge three elements in Hegel's thought: namely, the relation between time and effective spirit-causation, the patience of time for the upward, onswelling movement of spirit, and the support of time for retentive, cumulative, content-growth.

Martin Heidegger has written that the Hegelian view of the relation between spirit and time was evoked by a wrestling with the problem of the concretion of the spirit. There is no doubt that the problem of the concretion of the spirit is involved in its most critical form with respect to time. A passage from the final chapter of Hegel's *Phenomenology* states: "Time appears therefore as the destiny and necessity of the spirit, which is not complete within itself; the necessity, to enrich the share which self-consciousness has in consciousness, to set in motion the immediacy of the inherent nature, the form in which the substance is present in consciousness; or conversely, taking this inherent nature, as that which is inward, to realize and make manifest that which is at first only inward—i.e., to claim it in the spirit's certainty of self."[212] The essentiality of time to the concretion of the spirit is thus clearly stated, for the necessity of the spirit to complete itself, to attain its full concretion is said to be time itself. Accordingly, through temporality alone is the spirit able to show itself to be spirit, for only in and through its concretion does the spirit emerge as spirit. We find here then affirmed in the strongest terms the ultimate ontological import of time for the concretion of the spirit, and for the being of spirit itself. Hence we are in a position to understand why history is the concretest actuality, for the concrete process of the spirit's becoming in time is history. "The process of carrying forward this form of knowledge of itself is the task which spirit accomplishes as *actual history*."[213] Again, "the other aspect, however, in which spirit comes into being, *history*, is the process of becoming in terms of knowledge, a conscious self-mediating process—spirit externalized and emptied into time."[214]

We must inquire just what the necessity of time for the concretion of the spirit involves. Time is not involved in the content of the spirit, for this content is the body of culture principles and configurations through which the spirit representing itself in objective world-form comes to know itself. Reason ruling world history is the spirit's sway in the self-realization of itself through the necessary exfoliation of these successive culture stages in a predetermined course. There is not only formal determination, lawfulness in the rise and fall, the self-formation and self-destruction of the culture worlds, there is as well predetermination of the particular culture principles and their successive appearance in world history. Although history may take place in time, the history itself, its content and course, is not essentially determined in and through the temporal process. One might be tempted to think—time being so inextricably interwoven with succession—that the fact of the succession of the stages was connected with the ingredience of the temporality, but Hegel makes it quite clear that the differentiation of the stages is rather derived directly from the dialectic nature of the spirit. One is tempted further to seek the ingredience of temporality, if not in differentiation and in succession, at least in the sheer advance, but Hegel says with regard to the process of a national spirit: "The abstract form of the *Volksgeist* is the entirely sensuous advance of time, a first activity, the more concrete movement is the spiritual activity."[215] Time is thus a minor and subordinate sensuous way of apprehending this advance; and no suggestion is made here of any important connection—though of course there must be a connection—between the abstract advance of time and the "more concrete" movement.

Content-determination, differentiation, succession, essential passage seem to be set entirely within the spirit. Thus we see how unqualified it is for Hegel that the spirit has only to do with itself. This being so, what does it mean that time is necessary for the concretion of the spirit? What does time contribute to the concretion if necessary to it? The temporal process is certainly not the locus for essential determination for Hegel, since the activity and seemingly "historic" decisions of men do not determine the historic content. If temporality does not introduce the relevance of possibilities, if the historic realization of the spirit takes place according to itself regardless of any characteristics of time, why is time necessary to the concretion? If time is necessary to concreteness, it must contribute to the spirit's process so the concreteness is comprehensible through this contribution. What is this contribution?

A clue to the answer of the foregoing question is suggested at the very end of the *Phenomenology*: "The conservation [of the culture-worlds] looked at from the side of their free existence appearing in the form of accidentality is history."[216] It is clearly indicated here that historic existence appears in the form of accidentality. Throughout Hegel's introductions to his Philosophy of History diverse remarks make it clear that the historic realization of the spirit is suspended in, or as it were, swathed in, accidentality. We shall not inquire here concerning the exact ontological status of accidentality in the Hegelian system; the problem of accidentality, or chance, is one of the most obscure and questionable issues in Hegel's thought. Inquiring concerning time's contribution to concretion, we are lead to discern accidentality as the distinctive feature of the temporal realm. Is accidentality then this contribution and is realization in, through, and despite the realm of accidentality the criterion for concreteness? The temporal process of realization involves the togetherness of the spirit-essential and the accidental. Accidentality is a distinctive characteristic of temporal process. Thus if the accidental were removed leaving merely the spirit's essential content, time also would be thereby removed. Time then, which Hegel regards as necessary to the spirit's concretion, seems in Hegel's thought to bring no other contribution to concreteness than accidentality. Accordingly, concreteness which should be made comprehensible by the contribution of time is not at all clarified but rather cast into a shadow by this contribution of accidentality. For, however we are to characterize concreteness, certainly accidentality is not the most distinctive feature of its meaning. Thus we are led to a very inadequate position. If temporal process is merely the abstract medium for the spirit's realization, this thin function may suffice to mediate the bare necessity of time for concretion, but it does not illuminate its contribution to concreteness. As equivalent to accidentality, temporality is not accorded sufficient weight to play its systematic role as necessary for the realization of the spirit.

Absolute System vs. Individual Time-Conditionedness

A philosophical fragment of Hoelderlin's "Hermocrates and Cephalus," begins as follows: "You really believe then that the ideal of knowledge could appear at some definite time embodied in some one system? You believe even, this ideal has now already become actual, and that Olympic Jupiter lacks nothing other than the pedestal?"[217] In view of the intimate friendship between Hoelderlin and Hegel in Frankfort at the time of the composition of this fragment (1798-1800), it seems certain that the poet is expressing here in beautifully clear and poignant terms the intellectual conviction of his philosopher friend. It was at the close of his stay at Frankfort, the period of his most intimate association with Hoelderlin, that Hegel wrote Schelling the oft-quoted lines that the ideal of youth had necessarily been transformed into a *Reflexionsform* and consequently into a system. The system attained, too, was not *a* system, a systematic togetherness of ideas explicatory of the universe, but *the* system, the absolute system.

On the other hand, opposed to the conviction of the absolute validity of his own system, Hegel never tires of repeating the time-conditionedness of every individual in all respects, including the intellectual. For example, "every individual is the son of his people and at the same time insofar as his state is in a process of development, the son of his time; no one remains behind his own time, still less overleaps it."²¹⁸ This applies also to philosophy, for in the famous *Introduction to the Philosophy of Right* we read: "Philosophy is its own time formulated in thoughts; it is as foolish to imagine that a philosophy can go beyond its present world as that an individual can overleap his own time."²¹⁹ Hegel thus apparently states on the one hand a thoroughgoing relativity, at the same time that he makes absolute claims with regard to his own philosophy.

This contradiction, however, is only apparent. At the beginning of the *Introduction to the Philosophy of History*, with regard to the plan of Providence in world history, Hegel asks, has the time come to comprehend it? And in view of Christianity, he finds that this time has come. For in Christianity God revealed Himself giving men knowledge of what He is, so that He is no longer something closed and secret; the development of the thinking spirit which has proceeded out of this source, namely, out of the Revelation of the Divine Being, must finally arrive at the point where it can comprehend with thought the divine plan. Whether the time has come to know this plan depends on whether the final purpose of the world has entered the actuality finally in a generally valid, conscious fashion. Hegel answers that "the time has finally come"²²⁰ to comprehend this rich production of creative reason, namely, world history. Impelled by the spirit, the temporal historic actuality grows, ripening at each stage in turn to receive and bear the destined "output" of the spirit's self-realizing activity. The cumulative character of history brings it about that the present world includes in itself as a spiritual configuration all the stages appearing earlier in history. The moments, then, which the spirit seems to have behind itself, it also has in its present depth. As the Spirit has run through these moments in history, so it has to run through them in the present—in its own conceptual insight. Accordingly, when Hegel says that philosophy has to do with the present, the actual, it is at once implied that philosophy has to do thereby with the totality of the Spirit as ingredient in that actuality, and hence in accordance with this ingredience open to the individual of a particular time. Hegel was a son of his time, subject to his time and the encompassing world-actuality, but this time, this historic actuality, was in his conviction ripe—ripe for absolute knowledge and the conceptual realization in a philosophic system of the spirit's absolute self-consciousness. When Hegel sets up therefore the doctrine that every individual is the son of his national spirit and of his time, etc., he is not contradicting himself, not invalidating his own claim for absolute validity; for his time, in his view, as the result of the entire historic development was ripe for his absolute system with its absolute claim. Nor is it proper to emphasize "his system"—Hegel was not animated by personal self-glorification—for the philosophic, as well as the other, heroes vanish as individuals in the service of the World Spirit whose "cabinet-orders they are forced to write down."[221]

Although maintaining Hegel's view here is not self-contradictory, we do not presume to defend the position Hegel adopts. Indeed, it may even suffer from an ill much worse than that of mere contradiction. Asking what is the basic defect in his thinking which forces him, or rather enables him to adopt such a position, we find that the inadequacy of his view of time lies at the root of the matter. The time becomes ripe, not in a material preparation of a situation demanding creative decision over relevant historic possibilities, but ripe for the necessary appointed manifestation of the spirit. Insofar as the temporal historic actuality is not in itself free, independent, content-forming—it is only free to produce accidentalities and inessential particularities—it does not determine its own ripeness. The eternal Spirit is *die Macht der Zeit* (the power over time) and the temporal actuality in its ripeness as well as in all other essential phases is determined by eternity, revealing itself in and through time. Hegel states repeatedly that the Spirit is eternal, not past nor to come but simply absolutely present, "now" in the sense of absolute presence. And further, "what the Spirit is now it always was."[222] Thus the various world-forms of the Spirit have temporally developed themselves independently one after another, but this temporal development merely mirrors and represents the inner differentiation of the Spirit. This inner differentiation is the eternal logical development of the Spirit's content, and if the temporal development is one with the eternal development—as it is for Hegel—it is so only on the basis of determination through the eternal. The Hegelian attempt to unify these two kinds of development under the primacy of the eternal is based on a prior unificatory relation between time and eternity under the primacy of eternity, and the breakdown of the attempt to unify temporal and eternal development is based on the prior inadequacy of the Hegelian conception of time. Before considering further the relation for Hegel between eternity and time, let us turn to the uncertain status of the future in Hegel's thought.

The Future

Hegel's remarks suggesting a future are sparse and unsubstantial. In excluding America and Russia from his world history, Hegel several times mentions them in reference to the future. Of the Slavs he says that, although they have been involved in the political history of Europe, their influence on the advance of the spirit has not been important and this great mass of peoples has not yet appeared "as an independent moment in the sequence of the configurations of reason in the world."[223] Whether it shall do so in the future he refuses to consider on the grounds that history is concerned with the past. Hegel terms America "the land of the future," "the world of the future."[224] This world of the future is in a process of becoming, has not yet—at Hegel's time—taken possession of its own land, not yet felt the need to turn inward, not yet set up a fast socio-political order. "America has to separate itself off from the basis on which world history up unto the present had proceeded."[225] As with Russia, however, Hegel declares that America as a land of the future does not concern him. For history has to do with the past and the present, while philosophy with the eternal, with reason. And "the philosopher has nothing to do with prophesying"[225]—as if the only relation of the present thinker to the future were that of prophecy! In contrast to Hegel's views let me cite a sentence from Whitehead's *Adventures of Ideas*: "Also for our purpose in this book the notion of History includes the present and the future together with the past, affording a mutual elucidation and wrapped in common interest."[226] A fundamental limitation both of Hegel's time-feel and his concept of history appears at once in this simple contrast.

The question arose very early among the Hegelians whether there is or can be any real future. Haym has recorded how in 1830, the year before Hegel's death, "the Hegelians...in deep, bitter earnest discussed the question what indeed could be the further content of world history, after the World Spirit in the Hegelian philosophy has arrived at its goal, the knowledge of itself."[227] Hegel's definition of history as "the progress in consciousness of freedom" taken in conjunction with his periodization does put in question the continuation of history in the future. For, if the goal of history be the full consciousness of freedom, and if in the third period, the Germanic nations know that all men are free, that man as man is free, then there can be no further *period* for the progressive continuation of history. Despite Hegel's mention of Russia and America in relation to the future, Hegel states in several places that "Europe is simply the end of world history."[228]

Hegel has often in a superficial way been accused of a more or less intentional glorification of the Prussian state; there is no justification for this. The main tenets of the constitutional monarchy advocated by Hegel are as well French and English as Prussian. From the biographical side, rather than being derived from a relation to the Prussian immediacy, the "end of history" in the Germanic world is grounded in a change concerning Hegel's view of Christianity. Hegel's earliest outlines of a philosophy of history contained the triad: Paganism, Christendom, and Future. Hegel seems to have had the view that the present historic moment meant the beginning of an epoch of final fulfillment. Accordingly, Christianity was placed in the past as merely an element in the building of the future. After the fall of Napoleon, the view began to prevail in his mind that the absolute epoch of religion, beginning with Christianity, was also the absolute epoch of history in general, and the division of world history into Oriental, Greco-Roman, and Christian-Germanic worlds became final from then on. Christianity, as the absolute religion, ceased to be past, becoming instead the present historic actuality, embodied in its world form, the Germanic world. The future then, as early envisaged, was as it were absorbed into the eternal present of the Christian actuality.

No modern Hegelian with best will has been able in a convincing way to explain away this "end of history." On account of the formal necessities of the dialectic structure of history, clearly no further period is conceivable, and hence all the attempts to open up a future have done so through extending indefinitely this last period of the Germanic world. To base a continuation of history on an undialectic infinite process, a form of the "bad infinite" so reprehensible in general in Hegelian thought, is quite unwarranted, however, because the specific moving spring of the whole Hegelian morphology of historic process—namely, the transition—is thereby set aside. It is not necessarily true that history stops abruptly with Hegel's time or that there is immediately after his time a diminution of spiritual substance. But insofar as the essential content of the world spirit has been realized in the historic process up to and including his time, what remains to be done can only be of a more or less trivial, detailed, empiric character, perhaps adornments to completion, but no essential work of the spirit.

The content-end of history is not a logical inconsequence in Hegel but rather a logical consequence, albeit an unfortunate one. The closure of system brings the closure of history. Ranke writes that "history can never have the unity of a philosophical system," and hence it would follow that history can never be included in a closed system. When he continues, "but it is not without inner connectedness,"[229] however, he leaves open the possibility for the philosophic grounding of this inner connectedness in a system which does not attempt definitive closure. As we have seen, Hegel conceives world history as a fully comprehended totality. A totality of time, comprehended in its totality, must have its end in time. There is hardly any compelling necessity why the end should be at this time now. However, as Burckhardt writes, "everyone regards his time as the fulfillment of all time and not merely as one of the many passing waves."[230] As a result of his intense rationalism, Hegel seems to have had a kind of aversion to the "future"—the future which is perhaps the darkest of the dark realities in human existence. Only thus can be understood the vehemence with which he repeatedly casts aside each mention of the future, as "no concern of his," "prophesying," "dreams." Moreover, if, as for Hegel, history unrolls the past and the present, and philosophy opens up the eternal present, then it is very natural for these two to find the culmination point of their contact in the actual present—the actual present in the depth of whose presentness is contained the past and in the immediacy of whose presentness is found the outlet for eternity.

There are several ways to seek to understand this lack of a future in Hegel. As we have seen, his earliest outlines of a philosophy of history contain the triad: Paganism, Christendom, and Future. The change to the Christian-Germanic world as the final epoch of history came in his intellectual development. Rosenzweig refers to a change concerning Hegel's view of Christianity, related to a reevaluation stimulated by the fall of Napoleon. However, there seems to me perhaps a more important factor in his intellectual development, namely, the growing force of the ideal of system. It is the ideal of system which, as it were, "overcame" the temporal reality, or perhaps better expressed, reduced the temporal reality to an aspect of the eternal spirit. The metaphysical ground for the depreciation of the future lies certainly in a relation between the eternal spirit and time: insofar as time is merely one side of the spirit's eternal process, and time itself is conceived in terms of a time-now correlate with the eternity-now—which we will be discussing in the next section—the eternity-content of history can appear and attain its self-closed totality in the temporal process. If time itself were an ultimate reality, not merely one subordinate side of the eternal process, then it would be impossible to arrive at such a result. If temporal process is contained within the eternal spirit as one side of its process, then the "non-existent" future can have no ultimate significance. The past is validated because through the cumulative process of the spirit, it lives on in the present, and the present is validated as concrete existent actuality, animated through the presence of the eternal present. The future must always be slighted if time is considered under the behest of the eternal present, for beyond the living past and the actual present is not the future, but eternity, the eternal present.

Time and Eternity

We come now to consider more closely the nature of time, the nature of eternity, and the interrelation between time and eternity. In the *Encyclopedia* § 258, time is characterized as "the being which insofar as it is, is not, and insofar as it is not, is—it is Becoming intuited." This thought is repeated in various places in the *Philosophy of Nature* and elsewhere, in which it is clear that Hegel conceives time in the same dialectic terms in which he sets forth the logical category of becoming, with the addition that time is in the realm of externality, sensuous objectivity, and, as such, is intuited. In Kantian terms, Hegel also calls time a pure form of intuition, rejecting of course emphatically that time is only a subjective form. In accordance with the relation of time to the logical category of becoming, the dimensions of time, past, present, future, are characterized in terms of being and not-being as follows: for the past, being is the basis from what it is started, but posited under the determination of supervenient not-being; for the future, inversely, not-being is the first determination, being the second; the present is the indifferent unity of both, so that neither the one nor the other constitute the determining factor; in other words, the present is indiscriminately the vanishing of its being in nothingness and of nothingness in its being.

As might be expected from this account, the three dimensions of time do not stand on an equal footing. This is given various expressions. In one passage Hegel writes that the finite present is the *Now* fixated as being, differentiated from the negative abstract moments of past and future, as the concrete unity, hence the affirmative. Thus the present as Now is affirmative while the past and future are negative. He goes on further: "Moreover, in nature where time is now, the dimensions of past and future do not achieve the status of *existing* differences; they are necessary only in subjective representation, in memory, and in fear or hope."[231] Hence Hegel can state, "In the positive sense of time one can therefore say: Only the present is, the before and after are not;..."[232] Similarly, while discussing Heraclitus' views of time, "the past and the future are not in time, only the now;..."[233] Thus we see that the priority of the present is rooted in the understanding of time in terms of the Now, as was noted by Heidegger who writes, for Hegel, "*Das Sein der Zeit ist das Jetzt.*" (The being of time is the now.)[234] Thus we may say, in time, the passage from being to not-being and from not-being to being is caught up in the single Now, which insofar as it is, gives way to another, and the "unceasing" Now constitutes time.

Let us inquire then how Hegel conceives eternity. Hegel says that "the concept of eternity must not be taken negatively, as abstraction from time, so that eternity exists as it were outside of time; nor taken in the sense that eternity comes after time, for then eternity is made into the future, which is a moment of time."[235] Although not outside of time, eternity is without natural time (*ohne die natuerliche Zeit*). Eternity differs from duration, which is relative, because eternity is infinite; as infinite time, as a totality, time itself is transcended. "The true transcendence of time is timeless presence, that is, eternity."[236] As timeless present, eternity neither was, nor shall be, but is. Eternity is not before nor after time, not before the creation of the world nor after its destruction, rather eternity is the absolute present, "the now without before and after."[237] Similarly in his *Introduction to the Philosophy of History* Hegel uses the archaic German word for "now," "itzt"—a word used by the German mystics of the Middle Ages—to designate the absolute presentness of the eternal spirit. Thus we find that Hegel conceives eternity as well as time in terms of the "now."

The eternity-now is the now without before and after, the *nunc stans* which neither arises nor passes away but is absolutely present; as such, it just simply is, and Hegel says again and again of eternity that it simply *is*. The eternal now then, we may say, signifies non-temporal is-ness; this accords with the statement that eternity is without natural time. If eternity is, furthermore, not outside of time, the eternal now must be in time—and this presumably through or via the temporal now. As we saw, Hegel says that only the present now *is*, the before and after, the past and future are not. In its unstable existence, passing from being to nothingness and from nothingness to being, the temporal now nevertheless is; and this is-ness which the temporal now thus attains may be considered, I think, the token of the presence of the eternity-now in it. In R. Kroner's words, "...the present is the meeting point (*Schnittpunkt*) of time and eternity, the point in which time itself arises...."[238] On the basis of such a relation between the eternal and temporal *now* the superiority which Hegel gives the present now over the past and future would then be comprehensible.

It seems evident that Hegel's view suffers from a confusion of the non-temporal *is* and the temporal *is*. Consider the following passage: "The present *is* only through the act that the past is not..."[239] It is true that the present is present only insofar as the past is not present, but it is not true that the present *is* because the past is not. Indeed, even when not present, the past is and the present both is and is present only insofar as the past is. Also, as Whitehead has said about the future: "It is evident that the future certainly is something for the present...cut away the future and the present collapses, emptied of its proper content."[240] The temporal "was," "is," and "shall be" in a non-temporal sense equally *are*. From the standpoint of the non-temporal is, the three dimensions of time are on equal footing. And even from the temporal standpoint the claims of the "specious" present for special preference have little validity in face of the mutual determination of past, present, and future; in fact, the reality of the temporal dimensions is intrinsic to time itself. Hegel himself, in one place in the large *Logic*, says parenthetically, "For every point of time is in itself the relation of past and future,"[241] but he nowhere else follows up this thought. His more usual view, with its confusion of the non-temporal and the temporal is, appears crassly in the translation in his *History of Philosophy* of Plato's *Timaeus* 38, where Hegel terms the Platonic eternal-being "the absolute essence of time," "the true time," quite inexactly, saying further, "It is the present," thereby muddling Plato's clear distinction between eternity and time. In accordance with his own view, he furthermore makes Plato state, "Time does not have the future and past as its parts,"[242] which seems to be in direct opposition with Plato's real statement.

The priority of the present seems to be rooted in the relation between the temporal and eternal *now*. In contrast with the macroscopic connection between time and eternity pointed out earlier, where time is considered one side of the eternal spirit's process, there seems to be a microscopic relation, mediated through the *now*. Earlier we pointed out the displacement of History from its role as the last and highest in the *Jenenser Realphilosophie* and the *Phenomenology* to Hegel's final view; also in the discussion of the Future, the displacement from the early triad—Paganism, Christendom, Future—to the final triad—Oriental, Greco-Roman, Christian-Germanic periods—with a consequent emphasis on the present was noted. In line with these changes, it should be noted that in the *Jenenser Realphilosophie*, Hegel stated, "The present is neither more nor less than the future and past..."[243]—in direct contrast with the primacy of the present in his final comprehension of time. Also, in the Heidelberg *Encyclopedia* (1817) there is a passage in which eternity is distinguished from the finite present because it contains the moments of past and future in its concrete unity, which hence is not the "now."[244] In the final edition (1830), edited by Hegel himself, this passage was changed. Thus we find in the development of Hegel's thought a close correlation between Hegel's comprehension of history and this element in his comprehension of time and a common displacement, equally unfortunate, in our opinion, with regard to the evaluation of history, the depreciation of the future, and the superiority of the present as a temporal dimension.

Depreciation of Time

In our opinion, time can not be taken up in, contained in, an Hegelian-type concrete synthesis. For time, the actual temporality of the universe, is intrinsically something unfinished, and even a conceptual insight into its structure cannot reduce it to something finished. As Whitehead has written: "The temporal world is not a definite actual creature. For the temporal world is an essential incompleteness."[245] In the case of actual time with its content, time, as it were, grows; it is cumulative, gathering its past into itself and increasing with it. To be sure, there is an abstract eternally necessary categorical structure presupposed by the time process, what Hegel has called "the eternal life of God in Himself, as it were, before the creation of the world, the logical interconnectedness (*Zusammenhang*),"[246] but this does not predetermine the content of the time process. Any understanding of the structure of time doubtless is developed on the basis of the eternal logical categories, but the contents of the temporal actuality are not categorically determined in eternity. Hegel has expanded the necessity for an eternal categorical structure presupposed by the time process to an eternal logical necessity predetermining as well the actual essential contents of this process. This latter is untenable for, although time and history may be talked of *in abstracto* as wholes, neither time nor its historic content can be comprehended as concrete totalities.

C.S. Peirce has written that the "Secret of Hegel" is nothing else than that "the universe is everywhere permeated with continuous growth."[247] Certainly passage, continuous growth, is an, if not the, essential insight of Hegel. The dialectic method of negation and synthesis may then be considered merely the particular method of growth which Hegel considered to be universal. Because Hegel comprehended the realm of logical categories in terms of passage and growth and was so successful in elaborating their interrelations, he was led to apply the dialectic movement to characterize as well passage in empiric process. Thus the conception of dialectic passage, the necessary passage from one idea to another, underlies his exposition of the necessary passage from one culture principle to another in the self-fulfillment of the spirit's complete self-consciousness.

If real growth, however, is construed in terms of logical growth, in the necessary making explicit that which is *ab initio* implicit, and if what appears in time exists really in an eternal present, the growth cannot be ultimately real. History, however, teaches us the reality of growth. In Hocking's words, "What grows through history is reality itself."[248] The same radical conception of real growth as rooted ultimately in the universe is expressed in different words and with an expanded conception of history by Whitehead: "There is the one all-embracing fact, which is the advancing history of the one universe."[249]

Not only with regard to growth, but in general, it is the absolute reality of the eternal present and the consequent surbordination of temporality under eternity which brings about ultimate ambiguity in Hegel's thought. In our opinion two separate motifs may be discerned in Hegel: one, an eternalism derived in its fundamental presuppositions from the traditional European rationalism, and the other, the unique sense for history and the consequent acknowledgement of temporality and temporal development; but the first has outweighed the second, preventing the full fruition of the latter either in the proper metaphysical validation of temporality or in adequate understanding of historic process.

The attempt to make world history a totality or a concrete unity in which the principles of the separate National Spirits in a necessary succession are only moments of the one universal Spirit breaks down on account of the nature of time. If time, temporal process, is essentially unfinished and cannot be taken up in a conclusive synthesis, then the historic process which is a temporal process similarly cannot be taken up in a concrete synthesis which comprehends it as a totality. Hegel could make this attempt at total synthesis both of time and history because he refused to accord ultimate reality to time. If time and natural existence are insufficiently real, then the universal Spirit can determine directly out of itself the correspondence between the particular national spirits and their geographic habitat, and can refuse to admit any important influence of the geographic conditions on the associated spiritual configuration. If time is insufficiently real, then the Spirit does not always require temporal causal connection in the successive stages of its cumulative growth, and the transitions from China to India and from India to Persia can be made through the efficacy of the internality of the Spirit itself without empiric causal connection between these cultural stages. If time is unsufficiently real, then history can be the necessary unicursal explication of an implicit content essentially there at the beginning; possibility thus ceases to have any meaning, and the sway of an infinite necessity—albeit a rational, not a blind necessity—holds over the historic course. If time is insufficiently real, then the energizing principle in history can be seen to be, not the creative temporal deed of human decisiveness, but the power of a cumulative self-consciousness. If time is insufficiently real and possibility has no actual significance, then human freedom conceived over-abstractly as formal self-togetherness, and over-objectively as contentual unification with the public state substance, fails to root freedom in self-creative individual activity. Although the final purpose of history is taken to be the progress in the consciousness of freedom and therewith the progress in actual freedom, one is forced to question whether merely the universal spirit, not man, becomes freer, insofar as men remain always the unconscious means and instrument of the Spirit's self-realization.

In our previous discussion we have made some suggestions pertinent to an alternative view, each of which presupposes rendering time, and the temporality of historic process, an ultimate metaphysical reality. With regard to the geographic foundation of world history, as we have seen in our discussion of five ancient cultures, there is a direct, empiric, causal influence of geographic configuration upon spiritual configuration. Nature is not a colorful backdrop on the historic stage, painted with foresight in accordance with the dramatist's plan. Nature may be mute and monotonous, but it is not passive; rather the land, actively molding the race of men which make their habitat there, offers a range of possibilities for spiritual self-formation. Perhaps the land as a geographic type qualifies the cultural type; doubtless particular geographic details evoke detailed effects in the culture. At any rate nature is an active force, generating with a temporal efficacy in human culture; in the words of an eminent geographer, "History does not so much occur on the earth as from the earth."[250]

Furthermore, whatever the ultimate significance of meaning or ideal connexity between separate cultures may be, there is no efficacious transition from one to the other without empiric causal connection, and no transcendent necessity determining the factual course of transition and hence the cultural issue of the subsequent stage. There is a "darkness in the economy of world history,"[251] which appears in diverse ways, e.g., in the given conditions of external nature and in the given conditions of internal human nature. This darkness is nowhere more apparent than in the empiric course of transition from one culture-world to another: what stones of the old shall be taken along, how shall they be used in the new; there is the weight of giant forces and the play of accidentality, there is continuity and novelty. Perhaps an obscure human destiny, groundless unless faith be a grounding, is slowly speaking out in history a deep truth, but assuredly there is no transcendent predetermined totality forcing the empiric movements. Let us be grateful, however, to Hegel, for, had he not cast history so completely in the bright light of rationality, we could not now see so clearly the darkness.

Furthermore, with the ultimate reality of time, the temporal process becomes the locus of the essential creative determination of the historic content. Thus history can no longer be the necessary explication of an implicit content already there at the beginning inasmuch as the historic content is being decided in the temporal striving. Self-conscious individual self-clarification may be the surest guide to worthy historic aims, but self-consciousness is not the energizing principle in history, for the temporal agency of human creativity animates the historic course with decision passing over into deed. In the temporal efficacy of creative decision, freedom is manifested, not merely in formal self-togetherness, but in self-creative activity. This intrinsic functional freedom, though it may become enhanced, was never acquired and cannot be lost, for it is man's essential being. Notwithstanding that it cannot be lost, as merely subjective it can be thwarted and constrained; it requires objective fulfillment in a free life amidst social institutions giving it valid purposes. Progress in history is the progress of this objective freedom, whether or not an increased self-consciousness of freedom always promotes it or is produced by it. Beyond the purpose of human freedom in history may well be a divine Purpose, not however one which transcendently immanent uses and yet is indifferent to human individuals and their striving, but rather one which immanently transcendent is attained through the unqualified human freedom and its issue. No universal purpose, however, is unendangered, for with all the lawfulness of the structure of the universe, in the temporal process of free, creative becoming there is a total danger. Human history, rather than being through its spiritual essence superior to and free from the specific strains and uncertainty of temporal process, represents the highest and most concrete form of the same, finding its attainment precisely through such strains and hazards, and—as the ancient Greeks knew—"overcoming" time in the value attained despite the intrinsic temporality of becoming.

Spengler

Shortly before his death in September 1918, Georg Simmel, a protagonist of *Lebensphilosophie* (Philosophy of Life), wrote in a review of Oswald Spengler's *The Decline of the West* that Spengler's work was the "most important philosophy of history since Hegel."[252] It is recorded that Spengler took great pride in this comment. Nevertheless, Spengler deals very little with Hegel in his lengthy two-volume work. Of course, he must have had some familiarity with Hegel, but he mentions his name only occasionally, and often as a name with other philosophers indicating a trend. In contrast, he deals with Kant at length and in great detail on specific issues. Kant is the great *Systematiker* (systematic thinker), the exponent of critical reason, the culmination of the European rationalist tradition, and the fulfillment of rational understanding of Nature. Spengler continually sets forth his views of the proper mode of understanding History in contrast to Kant's method of understanding Nature. It seems likely that Spengler deliberately avoided an intellectual confrontation with Hegel, and for good reason. Kant dealt relatively little with history; he wrote some fascinating political essays, but never attempted a systematic treatment of human history; in fact, his greatest contribution to history was in the field of natural history, with his essay "Universal Natural History and Theory of the Heavens." However, Hegel was a systematic thinker who included History as a most important element of his thought. Spengler lists Hegel with the Romantics, but he was also a rationalist. In the *Introduction to the Philosophy of History*, Hegel states that reason rules the world, and that accordingly there has been a rational course to world history. However, for Spengler reason is a limited form of understanding and it neither comprehends nor rules the historic world.

In his preface to the 1922 revised edition of the *Decline*, Spengler states that he owes practically everything to Goethe and Nietzsche. "Goethe gave me method, Nietzsche the questioning faculty."[253] Spengler goes on to say that Goethe was, without knowing it, a follower of Leibniz in his whole mode of thought. Like Leibniz, Goethe maintained that everything in nature is in some sense animate. The universe consists of an infinite number of unique beings, each alive and harmonious with all the others, as were the Leibnizian monads. The essential character of these individual beings is activity and creativity. This is Goethe's "Living Nature," referred to so often by Spengler. Goethe's method is to intuit, sense (*erfühlen*), the essential character of an object rather than to dissect and analyze it. For Spengler as for Goethe, a primal or root phenomenon (*Urphänomen*) is one in which the idea of becoming simply reveals itself (*die Idee des Werdens rein vor Augen liegt*). Goethe believed that intuition and imagination, as distinct from the Kantian faculties of reason, understanding, and sensibility, were pathways to knowledge which might penetrate the very heart of nature. Through intellectual intuitions men could discover the primal phenomena of nature. In the organic realm there are primal modes of development which nature repeatedly uses; the same organ is transformed manifoldly through metamorphosis. Goethe sought to disclose the principles according to which nature operates by a morphological study of the process of development. Spengler writes, "Culture is the *primal phenomenon* of all past and future world history."[254] As he specifically states, he aims to apply to history the ideas and methods of Goethe which Goethe discovered in his "Living Nature" and made the basis of his morphological researches. From Goethe too, Spengler took the figure of Faust to represent the *Urphänomen* of

Western culture, namely the unlimited urge to strive onwards and upwards, a striving involving his total being and his creativity, permeating every action and experience. Faustian culture is expressed in the spires of Gothic cathedrals soaring skyward, in the distant perspectives of Western painting, the extensive form of the fugue, and the expansive nation state as well as many other phenomena.

Spengler states specifically that he owes his philosophy to Goethe, "and also (but in a far less degree) to that of Nietzsche."[255] The difference between Spengler's relation to the two men is indicated by the fact that in Volume I of the *Decline* there is not one uncomplimentary comment about Goethe, while half of the forty-six references to Nietzsche in the same volume are critical. However, Spengler did acquire much from Nietzsche, both in substantive content and particularly in style. Like Nietzsche, his style of thought was expressed in aphorisms and oracular pronouncements. He composed his ideas originally in the form of aphorisms and this becomes clear in his otherwise repetitious, turgid style in the *Decline*, when suddenly there appears a bright and striking, brief, aphoristic sentence. The aphorisms were kept in a portable trunk which he left with friends whenever he took a trip. Many of his books seem to have started simply as collections of aphorisms. He learned from Nietzsche his view of the Greek spirit as Apollonian, a term originally used by Nietzsche; he also learned the integral view of cultures, a sense of "individuals and classes born to rule";[256] hostility to the Darwinian theory of progress, and a non-biological concept of race and "style." Furthermore, the distinction between "culture" and "civilization," so important in Spengler's thought, was originally devised by Nietzsche.

Like Nietzsche, Spengler regarded the idea of a *Volk* (folk) as an empty invention of German Romanticism. For him race was a product of geographical influences and of common feelings developed in a common history; race revealed itself in the qualities of form and tradition expressed by rare individuals. This attitude toward race definitely separated Spengler from National Socialism. For this and other reasons, though repeatedly approached by Gregor Strasser, an early Nazi leader, he refused to associate himself with the Nazi movement. Later his book *Die Jahre der Entscheidung* (The Hour of Decision), published in 1933, disclosed so subtly his repudiation of Hitlerism that the Nazi leadership became aware of its thrust only after 100,000 copies had been circulated. Further circulation was then prohibited and German newspapers were forbidden to mention the name of Spengler. How different from the "profound" Freiburg existentialist philosopher, Martin Heidegger, who became Rector of the University of Freiburg in the spring of 1933 and gave rabble-rousing Nazi harangues—one of which I heard that spring in the courtyard of Heidelberg University, with Heidegger standing on a barrel surrounded by brown-shirted student Storm Troopers holding torchlights!

In an address on the eightieth anniversary of Nietzsche's birth, Spengler stated that Nietzsche was the first to recognize that history was not just a series of events but that all cultures and races have a soul development like individual human beings, which he asserted was a great step forward in historical understanding. He claims that he sought to widen Nietzsche's prophetic vision, his outlook (*Ausblick*), into a total view (*Überblick*) of history and the destiny of Western man. He criticized Nietzsche on the grounds that while he knew what to deny he did not know what to affirm. Nietzsche's "historical horizon" was too limited: "His conception of decadence, militarism, the transvaluation of all values, the will to power, lie deep in the essence of Western civilization and are for the analysis of that civilization of decisive importance. But what, do we find, was the foundation on which he built up his creation? Romans and Greeks, Renaissance and European present, with a fleeting and uncomprehending side-glance at Indian philosophy—in short, 'ancient, mediaeval, and modern' history. Strictly speaking, he never once moved outside the scheme...."[257] Also, while Nietzsche was the first to have an inkling that there are as many ethical systems as there are Cultures, he came to no objective morphology of ethics. "And so here, as in all his crucial penetrations, he got as far as the door—and stood outside."[258] While Nietzsche was clear in negation, he could discuss only in "nebulous generalities" the Whither, the Aim. With all his criticism, however, Spengler was profoundly aware of his debt to Nietzsche. When he died in 1936 his family placed in his coffin a copy of Nietzsche's *Also Sprach Zarathustra* alongside a copy of Goethe's *Faust*.

Intellectual humility is not a characteristic of German thinkers. Hence it is not surprising to find echoes of, or similarities between, Hegel's view of his own philosophy and Spengler's view of his thought. As we have seen, Hegel regarded his philosophy as the final absolute system and claimed absolute validity for his own system; at the same time he believed that every individual, even the philosopher, is the son of his own time and that philosophy is its own time formulated in thoughts. Hegel believed that as a result of the whole cumulative historic development, his time was ripe for an understanding of world history and for his absolute system. Similarly, Spengler wrote in the preface to the first edition (1917) of the *Decline* that his work was not one of several possible philosophies but "*the* philosophy of our time," an idea "that does not occur within an epoch but itself makes that epoch."[259] In the preface to the revised edition (1922), he writes, "A thinker is a person whose role it is to represent symbolically the times through his own perception and understanding."[260] And well he may represent his times, for reading Spengler one has the *unheimlich* (uncanny) experience that this man, in his style and limitations, is a piquant example of that civilization phase in the decline of a culture which he describes so poignantly.

For Spengler, Cultures are the fundamental data of all history. They are the *Urphänomen* (primal phenomenon) of all past and future world-history. "Cultures are organisms, and world-history is their collective biography."[261] Instead of one linear history leading up to the present, Spengler finds eight great Cultures, none of which has a privileged position or is more important than any of the others. These eight Cultures are: Babylonian, Indian, Chinese, Egyptian, Apollonian or Classical (Greco-Roman), the Magian or Arabian (Iranian, Hebrew, early Christianity, Byzantium, and Islam), Mexican (Mayan-Aztec), and Faustian (West European). "I see, in place of that empty figment of *one* linear history,... a *number* of mighty Cultures, each springing with primitive strength from the soil of a mother-region to which it remains firmly bound throughout its whole life-cycle; each stamping its material, its mankind, in *its own* image; each having *its own* idea, *its own* passions, *its own* life, will and feeling, *its own* death.... Each Culture has its own new possibilities of self-expression which arise, ripen, decay, and never return. There is not *one* sculpture, *one* painting, *one* mathematics, *one* physics, but many, each in its deepest essence different from the others, each limited in duration and self-contained.... I see world history as a picture of endless formations and transformations, of the marvelous waxing and waning of organic forms. The professional historian, on the contrary, sees it as a sort of tapeworm industriously adding on to itself one epoch after another."[262]

How a Culture originates is never clearly set forth by Spengler. There are, however, rather obscure formulations such as "a Culture is born in the moment when a great soul awakens out of the proto-spirituality (*dem urseelenhaften Zustande*) of ever-childish humanity, and detaches itself, a form from the formless, a bounded and mortal thing from the boundless and enduring. It blooms on the soil of an exactly definable landscape, to which plant-wise it remains bound. It dies when this soul has actualized the full sum of its possibilities in the shape of peoples, languages, dogmas, arts, states, sciences,..."[263] Once the entire content of inner possibilities have been actualized, the Culture hardens, loses its force, declines, and becomes Civilization. According to Spengler, every Culture passes through the age-phases of the individual human being—childhood, youth, maturity, and old age. The Cultures are organisms, with an intrinsic order or inner necessity, with a rigorous structure and articulation. As we have seen, Hegel likewise speaks of the *Volksgeist* as an individual natural organism which develops, becomes strong, declines, and dies. However, with Hegel it is quite clear that he is speaking in metaphoric terms. While Spengler is very conscious of, and discusses, the opposition between Nature and History, nevertheless when he deals with "the secret of world history," the cultures, "the story of higher mankind as an organism of regular structure,"[264] the concept of organism seems less a metaphor than a transference into history of a concept of nature. After all, these cultures "belong, like the plants and the animals, to the living Nature of Goethe, and not the dead Nature of Newton."[265] Likewise, "these Cultures, living beings of the highest order, grow with a sublime aimlessness, as do the flowers of the field."[266]

That Spengler is not using the phases of growth merely in a metaphoric sense is explicitly confirmed by the statement about the world of human Cultures: "Let the words youth, growth, maturity, decay...be taken at last as objective descriptions of organic states."[267] Our Western development he finds differing from the Classical world "in every detail of the surface but entirely similar as regards the inward power driving the great organism toward its end."[268] At the end of every Culture comes the phase of Civilization, "the organic-logical sequel, fulfillment and finale of a Culture."[269] Every Culture has in a necessary organic succession *its own* Civilization. Civilization is the inevitable *destiny* of a culture, an irrevocable end, which is by inward necessity reached again and again. Greek *soul*—Roman *intellect* is an antithesis which reveals the differentiation between Culture and Civilization. The transition from Culture to Civilization in the Classical world took place in the 4th century B.C.; in the Western world it has taken place in the 19th century. The nature of Civilization Spengler vividly describes: megalopolitanism, giant cities dominating the countryside, rise of the masses in the great cities, materialism in practice and together with scepticism dominant in thought, scientific irreligion, imperialism, and Caesarism. Thus the title *The Decline of the West* means simply that the Western world (Western Europe and America) are at present in the phase of Civilization. The intellectual impact of Spengler's work at the time of its publication and thereafter has largely been a result of this "pessimistic" diagnosis of contemporary times.

There is a series of stages traversed in an ordered and obligatory sequence in life, in living organisms, and in the historical organisms, Cultures. Through comprehension of this necessary sequence we are able to arrive at "*a morphology of world history.*"[270] The "morphological relationship" inwardly binds together the expression forms of *all* branches of a Culture. By Analogy, a method of understanding living forms and the "polarity and periodicity in the world,"[271] we come to understand that these morphological relationships within the separate Cultures are strictly symmetrical in structure. The inner structure of one Culture corresponds precisely with that of all the others; a counterpart of every phenomenon of deep importance in one culture can be found in every other; this counterpart is to be found in a characteristic form and in a perfectly definite chronological position. It is on the basis of this fundamental conception that Spengler has made the many striking analogies between the phenomena of the separate cultures which are so fascinating to his readers. In his view, the great problem of the 20th century is to explore carefully the inner structure of the Cultures, the organic units through and in which world history fulfills itself, "to separate the morphologically necessary from the accidental,"[272] and thus to comprehend the real meaning of the events.

As we have mentioned, for Spengler every major element of a separate Culture has a definite chronological position. Further, "every culture, every adolescence and maturing and decay of a Culture, every one of its intrinsically necessary stages and periods, has a definite duration, always the same, always recurring with the emphasis of a symbol."[273] He makes this more explicit in the form of a series of questions, quite unusual for a thinker who generally speaks out in aphoristic dogmas: "What is the meaning of that striking fifty-year period, the rhythm of the political, intellectual, and artistic 'becoming' of all Cultures? Of the 300-year period of the Baroque, of the Ionic, of the great mathematics, of Attic sculpture, of mosaic painting, of counterpoint, of Galileian mechanics? What does the *ideal* life of one millennium for each Culture mean in comparison with the individual man's 'three-score years and ten'"?[274] It is clear that the duration of these periods is meant to be suggestive and approximate. Nevertheless, Spengler also appends to his introduction three chronological charts showing the parallel course of spiritual, artistic, and political epochs in four different cultures. In these chronological tables, the regular duration of the time-spans becomes more rigidified; as a result, gaps and ambiguities in his comparisons show up in such a way as to expose these morphological comparisons to the enjoyment of hostile critics. When the Cultures become Civilizations, the precise durations no longer apply; for Civilizations can endure for hundreds or even thousands of years, as evident in China, India, and the Islamic world.

In contrast to Hegel, for whom there was no real future, Spengler has a real sense for the future. In fact, he terms his thought "*the* Philosophy of the Future...the only philosophy which is within the *possibilities* of the West European mind in its next stages."[275] By an analogic grasp of the present stage of Western Culture in comparison with the development of the other Cultures, we come to recognize the true nature of the present. In this way we arrive at the key to understand our own future. The 19th and 20th centuries are not "the highest point of an ascending straight line of world history," but a stage of life observed in every culture that has ripened to its limit. "The future of the West is not a limitless tending upwards and onwards for all time toward our present ideals, but a single phenomenon of history, strictly limited and defined as to form and duration, which covers a few centuries and can be,... in essentials, calculated from available precedents."[276] This decline, namely in the transition to Civilization, which has occurred with respect to all previous Cultures, is now taking place in the West and "will occupy the first centuries of the coming millennium."[277] And beyond the Faustian culture and its civilization, in the last paragraph of Vol. I of the *Decline*, he speaks of new Cultures arising in the future.

The recognition of the present civilization stage of the Western world, Spengler believes, will enable us, already accustomed to regard world-historical evolution as an organic unit seen backwards from the present, to look into the future comprehending the broad lines of its course. This will mean recognizing the limitations on the possibilities relevant to the present: for instance, there can no longer be great painting, great music, great architecture, for these possibilities have already been exhausted in Western culture. He hopes that men may be moved by his book to occupy themselves now with "technics instead of lyrics, the sea instead of the paintbrush, and politics instead of epistemology."[278]

From now on we must learn what *can* happen and therefore "what with the unalterable necessity of destiny and irrespective of personal ideas, hopes or desires, *will* happen." By "freedom," we mean "freedom to do, not this or that, but the necessary or nothing."[279] In the previous section we have discussed the ambiguity and evanescence of real human freedom in Hegel's thought. Similarly in Spengler we find the determinate structure of the development of the Cultures overriding human freedom in the essentials of the actual historic course. There is a minimum of freedom in the course of historic events; "Every situation has its elastic limit,"[280] and the statesmen must estimate it precisely. Within the predetermined course, there is some room for individual initiative; the precise fashion in which predetermined developments will take place depends on individuals. "Within every epoch there is an unlimited abundance of surprising and unforeseeable possibilities of self-actualizing in factual details, but the epoch itself is necessary, for the organic unity is present in it. Its inner form constitutes its specific determination. Accidentalities can shape...its development, but they cannot change it."[281]

As a living organism, "every great culture is nothing but the actualization and structure of a unique soul."[282] The concept of soul in Spengler is difficult to comprehend; as with so many basic concepts, he gives diverse formulations, each suggestive but not necessarily connected. Of the distinction between *soul* and *world*, Spengler states that these two elements can be distinguished only verbally, artificially, for they are always associated, intertwined, and present themselves as a unity, a totality. Further, *soul* is the possible, *world* is the actual, and *life* is the *Gestalt* (structure or form) "in which the actualization of the possible is accomplished." Also, "*soul* is the still-to-be-accomplished, *world* the accomplished, *life*, the accomplishing."[283] In a more general formulation, "Everything whatsoever that has *become* is a symbol, and the expression of a soul."[284] A more extensive discussion relates the development of the individual soul to the soul of the Culture. At a certain stage the Destiny-idea, which is an essential element of the soul of a culture, "manifests itself in every aspect of a life. With it alone do we become members of a particular Culture, whose members are connected by a common world-feeling and common world-form derived from it. A deep identity unites the awakening of the *soul*, its birth into clear existence in the name of a Culture, with the sudden realization of distance and time, the *birth of its outer world* through the symbol of extension;..."[285] which is the *basic symbol* of that life. This basic form of a culture is *innate*, an original possession of the soul of that Culture, and every individual soul of that Culture reenacts for itself that creative act and unfolds in every childhood the symbol of depth to which its existence is predestined, as the emerging butterfly unfolds its wings. Spengler's views here, as elsewhere in his thought, are suggestive, not ordered nor organized; hence it would be futile, and indeed improper from his standpoint, to attempt here to explain his thought on this obscure subject.

The unqualified separateness of the Cultures is correlated with an extreme relativism in Spengler's thought. Each great Culture has its own language of world feeling, a language only fully comprehensible by someone whose soul belongs to that culture. Hence, "...every thought lives in a historical world.... There are no eternal truths."[286] The Western thinker fails to recognize "the *historically relative* character of his data, which are expressions of one *specific existence* [i.e., Culture] *and one only*...his 'unshakable' truths and 'eternal' views are simply true for him and eternal for his world-view."[287] He does not hesitate to apply this drastic relativism to his own thought, stating that it expresses *only* the Western soul, "and that soul *only* in its present civilized phase."[288]

Even mathematics is included in Spengler's concept of cultural separateness as well as in the morphological principle of cultural parallelism. As the most abstract of intellectual activities, mathematics is generally regarded as seeking abstract verities, somewhat disassociated from the cultural world, and hence to have its own historical development. Not so for Spengler: "*There is not and cannot be, number as such.* There are several number-worlds as there are several cultures."[289] *Our own*, Western mathematics is not the culmination of 2000 years' evolution, but "a perfectly new mathematic."[290] Like arts, religion, or politics, mathematics expresses man's conception of himself; like these other elements in a culture it exemplifies "the way in which a soul seeks to actualize itself in the picture of its outer world."[291] For this reason, after the Introduction, the *Decline* begins with the chapter entitled "Meaning of Numbers," a very remarkable synoptic view of the diverse concepts of number.

Spengler carries out lengthy and oft-reiterated discussions of epistemology, not in the conventional sense of the use of that word in philosophical circles, but nevertheless quite illuminating as to the intellectual methods of his thought. He uses the word "Morphology" to comprise all modes of comprehension. Morphology is divided in two spheres thus: "The Morphology of the mechanical and extended, a science which discovers and orders nature-laws and causal relations, is called Systematic. The Morphology of the organic, of history and life, of everything which bears within itself direction and destiny, is called Physiognomic." In our Western culture the Systematic mode reached and passed its culmination in the 19th century; the great days of Physiognomic lie in the future. "In a hundred years all sciences...will be parts of a single vast Physiognomic of all things human"[292]—an unlikely prediction, with the first sixty years having given no sign of its fulfillment. At any rate, this is what, he states, the "Morphology of World History" means.

A discussion of the difference between Nature and History makes clearer the distinction between Systematic and Physiognomic. "The cognized and 'Nature' are one and the same,"[293] or better, the completed issue of that act of experience termed cognition is "Nature." Everything cognized is the same as the world of things brought under law. "Nature is the totality of that which is necessary by law." In contrast to cognition (*Erkennen*) is Goethe's concept of *Anschauen* (insight, intellectual insight, which seems to me better than Atkinson's translation "contemplation or vision"). "*Anschauen*...is that act of experience which, as it takes place, is itself history. That which is experienced thus is a happening, is history (*Erlebtes ist Geschehenes, ist Geschichte*)."[294] Spengler goes on to say that every happening takes place only once and is never repeated; it is characterized by direction, i.e., by "time," by *irreversibility*. On the contrary, everything cognized is *timeless*, neither past nor future, but simply present (*vorhanden*) and accordingly of enduring validity, as are the laws of nature. However, pure becoming, life, cannot be measured or dissected; it is beyond the domain of cause and effect, law and measure. And Spengler makes here a dubious pronouncement: "No deep and genuine historical research seeks causal laws; if it does so it has not comprehended its own essence"[295]—as if Thucydides had never lived! Insight into history when grasped as "nearly pure becoming" is an experience which can be only expressed in forms of art. "Nature is to be handled scientifically, History poetically." Yet there are no exact boundaries between the two forms of knowledge. "However great the contrast between becoming and that which has become, the fact remains that they are jointly present in every kind of understanding."[296]

In a lecture on Hegel's Philosophy of History in 1932, Karl Jaspers once commented that given the sparse historical data at the time, it was amazing how penetrating and accurate were Hegel's descriptions of the diverse ancient cultures, that contemporary specialists were generally impressed by this fact and had a positive view of Hegel's presentation. With respect to Spengler's account of the separate cultures, it has been quite different. As an undergraduate at

Princeton in the late 1920s, I learned that a study group of academic experts had been established to examine together Spengler's *Decline of the West* and that each specialist had found Spengler quite wrong in his description of the particular culture of the specialist, but otherwise seemed fascinating and quite acceptable for all the others; the general consensus became then that Spengler was faulty throughout. Perhaps the difference lies between the power of Reason (Hegel) in contrast to Physiognomic, which can hardly avoid becoming idiosyncratic. Moreover, in the physiognomic approach the temptation to twist and torture facts so as to make them fit into the physiognomic vision must be quite overwhelming.

It is a pity that Spengler never traveled to Greece. He traveled extensively in Germany, made many visits to Italy, one to Spain, and one to the Baltic countries. Had he ever visited Greece, experienced the Greek landscape, and seen original statues in their natural setting or in the museums nearby, he might have acquired a very different view of the Greek phase of the Classical world. Reading Spengler on the Greeks gives one the sad impression that he must have been too much influenced by the Hellenistic copies of Greek statues, or the plaster casts of these, so abundant in European museums. According to him, for the Greeks "all experience, not merely the personal but the common past, was immediately transmuted into a timeless, immobile, mythically fashioned background for the particular momentary present."[297] Greek culture was "ahistoric"; it possessed no memory, no organ of history; past and future are absent, and the "pure present" fills classical life. This pure Present represents "the *negation of time* (of direction)."[298] Classical history-writing invariably "sets forth matters within the political present of the writer"[299]— not true for Herodotus, born around 480 B.C., the same year as the naval battle at Salamis, as mentioned in our section on the Greeks. Thucydides makes "alive and self-explanatory the events of the *present*"[300] but he lacks "perspective, the power of surveying the history of centuries"[301]—not true for Thucydides, who gives an account of the past at the beginning of his history and gives clear evidence of a belief in the progress of the Greeks from a primitive past as well as the progress of Athenians during the 5th century, as discussed earlier. In the light of our previous discussion on the Greek views of time and progress, Spengler's view of Greek culture as based on the "pure present" and the "negation of time" seems quite untenable. He finds that the Greeks have "a symbol of the pure present in every one of their statues," a static quiet present with the rhythm of the body "based upon a simultaneous relation of the parts."[302] One is led to the conclusion that Spengler simply failed to grasp the dynamism of Greek life and culture. Had he seen the bronze statue of the charioteer, *o kratistos*, at Delphi, he would have experienced this dynamism. There is abundant evidence of this dynamism in Herodotus and Thucydides as well as the Greek dramatists. To my mind it was precisely the violence of human passion and the intense dynamism which led the Greek spirit to seek something stable behind the apparent changing world and therefore to discover the pre-Socratic material substances, the Platonic ideas, harmony, the Golden Mean between fluctuations and extremes.

The difference between classical tragedy as situation-tragedy and western Faustian tragedy as character-tragedy is discussed at length by Spengler. He states, "What happened to Oedipus—unlike the fate of Lear—might just as well have happened to anyone else."[303] And again, "Consider Oedipus once more: that which happened to him was wholly extrinsic, was neither brought about nor conditioned by anything subjective to himself,..."[304] In this interpretation Spengler is missing an essential feature of *Oedipus Rex*, namely that Oedipus throughout was striving to find out the truth about his birth. Oedipus says, "Then once more I must bring what is dark to light."[305] Charged by a drunken man of not being the son of Polybos of Corinth, disturbed and restless he went secretly to the Delphic oracle to seek the truth about his parentage. When Iocaste urges him not to summon the shepherd who might be able to enlighten him, Oedipus replies, "I will not listen; the truth must be made known."[306] Interrogating the shepherd, Oedipus drew from him what he did not wish to utter. When the shepherd said, "For God's love, my King, do not ask me any more!" Oedipus answered, "You are a dead man if I have to ask you again."[307] When the second messenger says, "The greatest griefs are those we cause ourselves,"[308] he is talking about the striving for the truth by which Oedipus brought about his own self-destruction. Was not that which happened to Oedipus brought about by something "subjective to himself?" Perhaps this striving for the truth of Oedipus was not perfectly Faustian, not unlimited, it had a limit in the truth, but it was a genuine striving.

Of particular interest for us is Spengler's statement that "the separate cultures are differentiated by their intuited sense of the meaning of time" (*dem gefühlten Sinn der Zeit*).[309] As we have seen, Spengler regarded the Classical culture as lacking a sense of time, indeed as negating time. Likewise Indian culture is ahistoric, without a sense of time, with no clocks, no sort of time-reckoning, and therefore no life memories, no history—a view of Indian culture generally accepted. However, not generally accepted is Spengler's view of Egyptian culture as possessing a keen sense of time and being "conspicuously historical"[310] (see our previous section on Egypt). Generally accepted, I believe, is also Spengler's view that Chinese culture, as well as our own Western, has a keen sense of time and history, although it seems doubtful to me that "the untranslatable 'Tao,' the basic principle of Chinese existence, derives all its meaning from a deep historical feeling."[311]

The cultures are also differentiated by the diverse concepts of space which are characteristic of the separate cultures. In a quotation set down above, Spengler states that the symbol of extension is the basic symbol of a culture, "imparting to it its specific style and the historical form in which it progressively actualizes its inward possibilities."[312] As an example, "The Egyptian soul saw itself as moving down a narrow and inexorably prescribed life-path to come at the end before the judges of the dead."[313] Hence the typical constructions of Egyptian architecture "are not 'buildings' but a path enclosed by mighty masonry."[314] The Egyptian, according to Spengler, is "in resolute march down the path once entered."[315] For the Chinese life is a "way" (*Tao*). However, the Chinese man does not tread a prescribed path like the Egyptian, but he "*wanders through this world*," conducted to his god or ancestral tomb "by friendly nature herself. Nowhere else has the *landscape* become so genuinely the material of the architecture.... This Culture is the only one in which the art of gardening is a grand religious art." As a stroll through a garden by "devious ways through doors, over bridges, round hills and walls,"[316] the Chinese regards his life's way. The space concept of the Classical world was "the near, strictly limited, self-contained body," expressed by the free-standing nude statue and the temple enclosed by a colonnade. For the Arabian Culture the basic experience of space is "the world as a Cavern." For the Western Culture the basic experience and symbol of extension is the "infinitely wide and infinitely profound three-dimensional Space."[317]

"...every Culture is aware (each in its own special way) of an opposition of time and space, of direction and extension, the former underlying the latter as becoming precedes that which has become."[318] The precedence of time is repeated also in the following statement: "It is of the essence of the extended that it overcomes directedness, and of Space that it contradicts Time, *and yet the latter, as the more fundamental precedes and underlies the former.*"[319] However, a few pages later, we find that Space seems to have the precedence when Spengler states: "Time is a *Gegenbegriff* (concept opposed) to Space, arising out of Space...."[320] And later in the same paragraph, we learn that "the understanding...created 'time' out of space as its opposite."[321] There is a seeming contradiction here. To be sure, it is obscure; however, is it really a contradiction? According to Spengler, everything living is indivisible, irreversible, unique, and not repeatable; Time has these organic essential characteristics, while Space does not. Space is a concept, while "Time is a *word* to indicate something inconceivable." It is impossible to bring Time with Space under one Critique, as Kant tried to do. It is a sign of Kant's failure to grasp the nature of Time that there is not a word in his Critique about Time's directedness. Space exists in and with our sense-world as an extension of self (*sichausdehnen*). "'Time,' on the contrary, is a *discovery*, which is only made by thinking. We create it as an ideal or notion and do not begin until much later to suspect that *we ourselves are Time*, inasmuch as we live."[322] In a note Spengler points out that only sensuous *experience* and intellectual *experience* are of spatial nature; the sensuous life and the intellectual life are time. Thus, we may say that for Spengler in the existential reality of life, of living organisms, time has precedence over space, but in the development of our conceptual understanding, space comes first because we come to sense the meaning of time as a concept opposed to, and arising out of, Space. In this way the seeming contradiction of precedence may perhaps be resolved. But, how to reconcile that time is something inconceivable (*etwas Unbegreifliches*) and also a *Gegenbegriff* to Space, I leave to the reader with the suggestion that perhaps the concept of time does not disclose the full reality of time, which is something beyond conceptual understanding.

The difference between space and time is related by Spengler to the difference between Causality and Destiny. Early in his Introduction to the *Decline*, he points out that there is, besides a necessity of cause and effect which he calls the *logic of space*, "another necessity, an organic necessity in life, that of Destiny—the *logic of time*—...a fact which suffuses the whole of mythological religions and artistic thought and constitutes the essence and kernel of all history [in contradistinction to nature]..."[323] He further states: "Mathematics and the principle of Causality lead to a naturalistic Chronology and the idea of Destiny to a historical ordering of the phenomenal world. Both orderings, each on its own account, cover the whole world."[324] The distinction between Causality and Destiny thus corresponds to, and is related to, the distinction between Nature and History, which we discussed earlier.

Like the historian Stuart Hughes who "confesses that he is far from fully grasping the 'ultimate meaning' of Spengler's word 'Destiny,' "[325] I would not pretend a complete understanding of this essential concept in Spengler's thought. Spengler himself states that although destiny "is of inward necessity," it is not to be explained by any reasons; the thought which Augustine expressed about Time, he also finds valid of destiny, namely, "if no one questions me, I know: if I would explain to a questioner, I know not."[326] The destiny-problem, which is the problem of time, is for him the true problem of history and should be treated with a scientifically regulated *physignomic* in order to grasp the "strangely constituted necessity" in its operation "so completely alien to the causal." In this context, the time of the occurrence of a phenomenon "is *never* irrelevant."[327] The destiny-idea requires life-experience, not scientific experience, the power of seeing not calculating, depth not intellect. There is an *organic logic* opposed to the *logic of the inorganic*, a logic of direction as against a logic of extension. Thus "Destiny and Causality are related as Time and Space."[328] Causality is the reasonable, the law-bound, the describable; Destiny is an inner certainty that is not describable. The former distinguishes, dissects, destroys; the latter is creative. Thus Destiny is related to life, Causality to death. "Real history is heavy with destiny but free of laws."[329] When history is thus comprehended, Time ceases to be "a riddle, a concept, a 'form' or 'dimension,' but becomes an inner certainty, destiny itself; and in its directedness, its *irreversibility*, its vitality (*Lebendigkeit*) is disclosed the meaning of the historical world-picture."[330] Destiny cannot be "cognized" or defined, and can only be felt and inwardly lived. In this way Destiny can be apprehended as "the true *existence-mode of the primal phenomenon*, that in which the living idea of becoming unfolds itself immediately to the intuitive vision."[331] Hence the destiny idea dominates the world picture of history, while causality dominates understanding of the world of nature. Just as the separate cultures are differentiated from one another by the meaning they intuitively attach to Time and to Space, "each culture must necessarily possess its own destiny-idea."[332]

The word Time to Spengler summons up something highly personal which he calls *das Eigne* (one's own)—which with an inner certainty we oppose to something *Fremd* (alien, something outside the personal realm), of which we become aware through the impressions of sense-life. In this context he makes the enigmatic statement: "*Das Eigne, das Schicksal, die Zeit sind Wechselworte.*" (One's own, destiny and time are interchangeable words.)"[333] The thought is not further developed, it is obscure, and yet it shimmers with meaning, as often poetry does. Perhaps the core of Spengler's thought might be described as aphoristic intellectual poetry.

Toynbee

The phenomenon of two men independently around the same time arriving at the same discovery in science is well known, e.g. Newton and Leibniz with calculus, Darwin and Wallace with natural selection and evolutionary theory. In the study of human history it is quite uncommon. Indeed I know of no case similar to the almost simultaneous adoption by the British historian Toynbee and the German thinker Spengler of cultures as the primary intelligible unit for the study of human history. Spengler's vision came to him in 1911, Toynbee's around 1914. Of course, as we have seen, Hegel interpreted history from the standpoint of the great cultures and civilizations, but for him the cultures were expressions and embodiments of the *Geist* (Spirit); as such they were parts of his philosophical system; the cultures were not *per se* the focus of his study of history. With Spengler and Toynbee, the cultures, or the civilizations in Toynbee's usage, were themselves the ultimate proper units of historical study. Why did this simultaneity take place? A question easy to ask, but perhaps unanswerable. Hegel would say that it was "*an der Zeit,*" that circumstances in Europe were ripe for such an interpretation of history, that the temporal human reality evoked it. On the threshold of World Wars I and II, when internecine fratricidal warfare among the European nations was to lead to the destruction of Europe as the center of political and economic power in the world, the vision of cultures and civilizations transcending national states emerged in Spengler and Toynbee. Was it premonition on a giant scale? Or was it merely the irony of history? Perhaps it was both.

Arnold Toynbee was a classical scholar in the Oxford tradition, so well grounded in the Greco-Roman culture that it was as easy for him to write poetry in Latin as in English. In 1914 he was expounding Thucydides to Oxford students; the outbreak of war suddenly made him realize that his experience in his world was the same as Thucydides' experience in the world of his time; thus Thucydides' world and his world were revealed as "philosophically contemporary," and beyond these two civilizations arose a vision of the philosophical contemporaneity of all civilizations. He was led then to consider the problem of the rise of civilizations from primitive human life in which man had lived for hundreds of thousands of years. The differentiation in cultural level between extant human societies, brought to his attention by the works of Professor Teggart of the University of California, had all taken place within a brief six thousand or so years. "Here was a promising point to probe in investigating, *sub specie temporis*, the mystery of the universe."[334]

While still considering the question of what had roused the relatively few societies to develop civilizations, Spengler's *Decline of the West* in 1920 came to his attention. He relates: "As I read those pages teeming with firefly flashes of historical insight, I wondered if first whether my whole inquiry had been disposed of by Spengler before even the questions, not to speak of the answers, had fully taken shape in my own mind. One of my own cardinal points was that the smallest intelligible fields of historical study were whole societies and not arbitrarily insulated fragments of them like the nation-states of the modern West or the city-states of the Greco-Roman world. Another of my points was that the histories of all societies of the species called civilizations were in some sense parallel and contemporary; and both these points were also cardinal in Spengler's system." However, Spengler had no answer to his question about the origin of civilizations. He found that for Spengler civilizations arose, developed, and declined in conformity with a fixed timetable according to an unexplained law of nature. This seemed to Toynbee too dogmatic and deterministic. Since the German *a priori* method had provided no answer to his problem, Toynbee decided to see if English empiricism might do better. He would seek, he said, to "test alternative possible explanations in the light of the facts..."[335] Critics have assailed Toynbee's claim to have adopted an empirical method for his study of history, alleging that he used unstated assumptions and preconceptions, that he selects and sometimes even distorts the facts, and that he shapes the presentation of the facts to fit conceptual patterns not empirically derived. Whatever the shortcomings of his English empirical approach, it is quite different from Hegel's rationalism and Spengler's intuition, both of which approaches likewise have shortcomings, as we have seen.

For Spengler the word "Civilization" had a specific meaning as the end-phase of a culture. Toynbee does not make this distinction between culture and civilization. For Toynbee the word "Civilization" has the same meaning as Culture for Spengler. Civilization is a species of human society which has arisen from, and differentiated itself from, the age-old primitive human society. Whereas Spengler discerned eight cultures: Babylonian, Indian, Chinese, Egyptian, Greco-Roman, Magian (including Iranian, Hebrew, Early Christianity, Byzantium, and Islam), Mexican, and Western European or Faustian, Toynbee finds twenty-one or more civilizations. Added to his original list were the abortive civilizations and the arrested civilizations, both of which categories are quite dubious; in fact, Toynbee dropped entirely from his list the so-called arrested civilizations toward the end of his final volume entitled *Reconsiderations*. During the many years of his study minor changes in Toynbee's list of civilizations were made which need not concern us here. The original list is as follows: Western Christendom, Orthodox Christendom (which is divided into an Orthodox-Byzantine and an Orthodox-Russian society), the Iranic and the Arabic (now united in the Islamic civilization), the Hindu, the Far Eastern (which is divided into a Chinese and a Korean-Japanese Society), the Hellenic, the Syriac, the Indic, the Sinic, the Minoan, the Sumeric, the Hittite, the Babylonic, the Egyptiac, the Andean, the Mexic, the Yucatec, and the Mayan.

While there is a fundamental similarity in the structure of Spengler's and Toynbee's approaches to history, Toynbee does not accept Spengler's view that civilizations are natural organisms with predetermined stages of development, rise, growth, maturation, and decline; he finds it foolish to declare that every culture has a predestined time-span. Toynbee's civilizations are not completely separate as are Spengler's cultures. The civilizations have diverse relations, apparentation, and affiliation, direct encounters affecting their development, and indirect encounters through renaissances whereby one civilization appropriates from an earlier one. Also Toynbee rejects Spengler's determinism and his dogma of inevitability, which he finds unproven. For Toynbee, "Empirically observed matters of fact are not necessarily the outcomes of inexorable fate."[336] Like Spengler, Toynbee rejects the linear succession of ancient, medieval, and modern, as " 'History,' writ large,"[337] which he finds an egocentric illusion of Western civilization. In his early volumes he assumed like Spengler that all civilizations are philosophically contemporaneous and on a par with one another. Subsequently he found them unequal in value, due to their relation to the history of Religion. For Hegel, as we have seen, a factual connection between civilizations was not necessary because they were essentially embodiments of a spiritual process; likewise there was no influence of geographic and environmental factors on the spirit of a people, rather merely a *correspondence*. For Toynbee environmental and climactic factors have a direct and real influence on historic developments. Also Toynbee sets forth in great detail the empirical connections between civilizations and the factual role of religions in the transitions from one civilization to another. Unlike Spengler, whose eight cultures are entirely separate, Hegel expounds a cumulative growth in the totality of history with the progressive fulfillment of the nature and purposes of the Spirit. Toynbee displays a suggestive sense for progress, with cumulative growth in one civilization itself—"a cumulative progress in one direction"[338] which reaches its goal and end—but not in the historic whole, for in his thought history is no totality. He states: "If human history repeats itself, it does so in accordance with the general rhythm of the universe; but the significance of this pattern of repetition lies in the scope that it gives for the work of creation to go forward."[339] This creative work is envisaged as following "the guideline of History in a progressive increase in the provision of spiritual opportunities for human souls..."[340]

Toynbee found, as mentioned, that Spengler had no explanation for the origins of civilizations. He quotes the passage from Spengler about a culture being born when a great soul awakens out of the proto-spirituality of ever-childish humanity (see p. 269) and naturally finds this quite inadequate. Of the twenty-one civilizations listed by Toynbee, fifteen are affiliated to predecessor civilizations. Six civilizations in his view have emerged direct from primitive human society: the Egyptiac, the Sumeric, the Minoan, the Sinic, the Mayan, and the Andean. The mutation of primitive societies into civilizations, Toynbee finds, lies in a transition from a static condition to a dynamic activity. This transition likewise takes place when a new civilization arises from a previous civilization which in its disintegration has come to a static condition. He comments: "This alternating rhythm of static and dynamic, of movement and pause and movement, has been regarded by many observers in many different ages as something fundamental in the nature of the Universe."[341]

Granted a dynamic quality in the process of civilization-building, this does not give us the positive factor providing the impetus for the dynamic movement. Toynbee examines briefly race and environment and finds that neither, taken by itself, can be the positive factor. This factor he discovers in the psychological formula of "Challenge-and-Response." The challenge of dessication in Afrasia after the close of the Ice Age brought the response of civilization in Egypt and Sumer. In response to the changing climate, these two peoples changed their way of life from food-gathering and hunting by taking to agriculture and by domesticating animals. The challenge which brought about the origin of the Sinic civilization in the lower valley of the Yellow River came from the natural and environmental conditions in that area, which were so much harder than, for instance, in the valley of the Yangtse. "The challenge to which the Mayan Civilization was a response was the luxuriance of the tropical forest."[342] There were two challenges for the Andean Civilization: one, the bleak climate and barren soil on the Andean plateau; two, on the Pacific Coast the heat and drought of an almost rainless equatorial desert at sea level. The response to the challenge of the sea brought about the Minoan Civilization. In the cases of the affiliated civilizations, while some element of environmental challenge may have been present, "the principal and essential challenge was a human challenge arising out of their relation to the society to which they were affiliated."[343]

This bare thumbnail sketch of "Challenge-and-Response" does not, of course, do justice to the virtuosity of Toynbee's presentation of his conception throughout his work. It is central to his thought. Critics have pilloried Toynbee for his Challenge-and-Response formula as too simple in character, insufficiently broad to encompass the multiplicity of historic factors, too pat, leading to stock answers, overworked, and overused; an anonymous reviewer in the *Times Literary Supplement* claims it is derived "from the ethics of the playing field, itself, of course, a schoolboy version of late Victorian muscular Christianity."[344] The critics rather uniformly fail to recognize an important element in this conception which Toynbee suggests occasionally, but does not develop insistently. As a young man Toynbee was very much influenced by the French philosopher Henri Bergson. Why does one society respond effectively to a challenge, when others similarly do not? It is the *élan vital* of a particular society underlying the effective response to a challenge. This effective response comes from the creative minority in a society, those creative geniuses who, grappling with a challenge, envisage an effective response and bring the more passive majority of the society forward by a strength of leadership which causes the majority to follow them. Seen in this light Toynbee's conception of challenge and response is not as superficial as his many critics make out. In general, when critics become snide and funny, they usually become more superficial than the object criticized.

The conception of "Challenge-and-Response" was not derived from a careful, inductive study of the separate civilizations, leading to this generalization. Toynbee does not claim that it is so derived. Indeed, Toynbee himself gives two sources for his conception of challenge and response, one Goethe's *Faust* and the other Robert Browning. Armed thus with the conception, he states: "Let us review the origins of our twenty-one civilizations in order to ascertain, by an empirical test, whether the conception of 'Challenge-and-Response' answers to the factor of which we are in search...."[345] Toynbee's efforts in this empirical test have been severely criticized by academic specialists. For example, the Australian geographer O.H.K. Spate states that Toynbee's attempt to reconstruct the primitive environment of the Lower Nile shows a "lack of a sense of scale and the neglect of all the factors of environment except terrain (in the most limited sense) and vegetation...."[346] He points out the peculiar advantage of the Etesian winds blowing upstream, facilitating the role of the river as a highway, unmentioned by Toynbee, and also its value for irrigation in the development of Egyptian civilization. Toynbee also omits mention of the abundant and excellent tool- and building-stone in the Lower Nile, as well as, at a later stage, the readily accessible copper and other minerals of Sinai. "Without these things it seems unlikely that there would have been an Egyptiac civilization."[347] Given the scope of Toynbee's work, such criticisms do not seem too important. Wayne Altree similarly rejects Toynbee's finding that the Sinic Civilization arose in the Yellow River basin because of the challenge of rigorous terrain and climate. He alleges that Toynbee's description of the Yellow River basin is false; it was not a hard region nor a place of adversity. North China in ancient times was largely open grassland, with little forestation, the soil being loessal and rich in quality. The region had sufficient rain, and the Yellow River with its silt content was an important fertility factor. The climate was warmer than now. He quotes a Chinese scholar writing in 1936: "The swampy jungle-covered Yangtze Valley of ancient China must have offered infinitely greater obstacles to early settlers than the Northern steppes and Yellow River...."[348] Perhaps Toynbee was in error using earlier sources of information. However, when Altree goes on to argue that Chinese society was not autonomous and self-determined, but rather derivative in important respects from outside sources, he is in 1955 presenting a thesis which more recently has been discarded by contemporary scholars, who have found in recent archeological exploration evidence that the early Chinese civilization was autonomous, a continuous development from an earlier Chinese Neolithic culture. Perhaps Toynbee would have done better to avoid the nomenclature and theory of empirical tests. We have seen earlier that the natural sciences are intrinsically unstable, how much more so all the human "sciences." The value of Toynbee's effort may be diminished by its factual limitations and argumentative shortcomings, but it is thereby far from being nullified.

The origin of the affiliated civilizations, with the principal challenge being a human challenge arising from their relationship to the parent society, is elaborated by Toynbee as follows: when a civilization begins to lose its creative power, the creative minority becomes a dominant minority, no longer leading but ruling with increasing oppressiveness, causing an internal and external proletariat to arise. The repression of the dominant minority causes the proletariats to secede. The conflict continues while the declining civilization moves towards its final destruction. In this conflict between the proletariats and the dominant minority, Toynbee discerns "one of those dramatic spiritual encounters which renew the work of creation..."[349] The word "proletariat" in Toynbee's usage refers to any social group "which in some way is *in* but not *of* any given society at any period of that society's history."[350] In the Hellenic or Greco-Roman model on which Toynbee's thought is primarily based, the internal proletariat are the common people among whom Christianity spread and finally became dominant; the external proletariat are the warlike bands on the frontiers.

The conception of Challenge-and-Response is not only used to elucidate the origin of civilizations, but also the process of their growth. The optimum challenge is one which stimulates the challenged party not only to achieve a successful response, but also to acquire a momentum that leads to a new challenge. If origin is to be followed by growth, there must be a repetitive, recurrent rhythm through which the growth is accomplished. On this rhythm of growth, Walt Whitman is quoted: "It is provided in the essence of things that from any fruition of success, no matter what, shall come forth something to make a greater struggle necessary."[351] In this connection, Toynbee specifically cites Bergson's *élan vital*, stating, "Civilizations...grow through an *élan* which carries them from challenge through response to further challenge..."[351] As growth in a civilization proceeds, challenges come less from the outside but rise from within, "and victorious responses do not take the form of surmounting external obstacles or overcoming an external adversary, but manifest themselves in an inward self-articulation or self-determination."[352] In this growth the civilization tends to become its own environment, its own challenger, and its own field of action, as a result of which the sign of growth is progressive self-articulation. Thus by a so-called empirical method, we arrive at a criterion for the growth of a civilization rather similar to Hegel's spiritual process of self-realization.

The conclusive difference between Toynbee and Hegel, however, lies in the role of the human individual. For Hegel the generative force in the growth of civilizations and in the historic course, in general, is the *Geist* (Spirit). As we have seen, men are merely means for the self-realization of the Spirit; they do not even know the purposes of the spirit which they are accomplishing; while men accomplish their envisaged purposes, through the "cunning of Reason" they are also accomplishing the purposes of the World-Spirit (*Weltgeist*), which are different from their purposes. Toynbee approaches the role of the individual from a discussion of the relation between society and the individual. A human society, he states, is a system of relationships between human beings who are not only individuals but also social creatures, since their existence as human beings presupposes their relation to one another. A society is a product of the relations between individuals and these relations arise from the coincidence of their individual fields of action. This coincidence creates a common ground, and this we term a society. There is an obvious element of circularity in this argument, but no matter. The important point follows as a corollary: "Society is a field of action but the *source* of all action is in the individuals composing it." Bergson is cited in confirmation of this view: " 'The great subterranean currents of thought,'... only flow in consequence of the fact that masses of men have been carried away by one or more of their own number...It is useless to maintain that [social progress] takes place of itself, bit by bit, in virtue of the spiritual condition of the society at a certain period of its history. It is really a leap forward...the society must have allowed itself to be convinced, or at any rate allowed itself to be shaken; and the shake is always given by *somebody*."[353] The specific character of these rare historical individuals Toynbee terms personality. "It is through the inward development of personality that individual human beings are able to perform those creative acts in the outward field of action that cause the growths of human societies."[354] How different from Hegel's overriding spiritual process in history and Spengler's overriding organic structure!

If all the creative effort in the growth of a civilization is the work of individuals or of small minorities, how shall the great majority of the members of the society be brought to participate? Toynbee believes that in every growing civilization the great majority of human beings are in the same stagnant condition as the members of a static primitive society. In the growth of a civilization the superior personalities are able to lead the majority to follow them, some by direct inspiration, but the rank-and-file by what Toynbee calls mimesis, imitation, by the practical method of social drill (*dressage* in Bergson's terminology). Social drill, which is a general feature of the life of primitive mankind, is thus made to serve social progress when creative leaders are followed.

Toynbee's conception of the "breakdown" of a civilization caused so much criticism from academic readers that the editor of the Abridgement felt obliged to clarify it in a note. Breakdown does not mean disintegration. While it is followed eventually by petrification or disintegration and complete destruction, "breakdown" means simply "the termination of the period of growth."[355] A living organism has its life-span determined by its physical nature; growth terminates comparatively early in the life of a living organism. However, there are no limits to the possible life-span of a society and the termination of its growth-period is not a predetermined natural event as in the event of a living organism, but is rather due to human miscalculation, error, or failure. Toynbee sums up the nature of the breakdowns of civilization in three points: a failure of creative energy in the minority, as a response a withdrawal on the part of the majority, and a consequent loss of social unity in the society as a whole. Although cast in different terms, the loss of social unity as a sign of breakdown was also set forth by Hegel, as we have seen. "The individuals withdraw out of the public world in order to live in themselves, in accordance with their own will, pursuing their own private purposes." (see p. 231) For Toynbee it is the individuals of the majority who withdraw to constitute the internal proletariat. The loss of social unity expresses itself in a corresponding loss of self-determination, termed by Toynbee "the ultimate criterion of breakdown," the inverse of the fact that "progress towards self-determination is the criterion of growth."[356]

The nature of breakdown is also characterized by Toynbee in terms of Challenge-and-Response, but in this case the response fails to meet successfully the challenge. While in the growth of a civilization a series of challenges each different in character are successfully met, in breakdown and the ensuing disintegration of a civilization the same challenge is repeatedly presented and each time the response fails to meet the challenge adequately. For example, Hellenic Society was confronted in the 5th century B.C. with the task of establishing a political world order; the Athenian attempt to solve the problem by means of the Delian League failed, as became clear during the Peloponnesian War; likewise Phillip of Macedon's attempt by means of the Corinthian League failed, as did Augustus's attempt by means of the *Pax Romana* upheld by an Emperor. "When the outcome of each successive encounter is not victory but defeat, the unanswered challenge can never be disposed of and is bound to present itself again and again until it either receives some tardy and imperfect answer or else brings about the destruction of the society which has shown itself inveterately incapable of responding to it effectively."[357]

There is an important corollary to this discussion of the breakdown of civilization, which Toynbee makes explicitly and insistently, namely, that it is a process of self-destruction. The phenomenon of self-destruction is pervasive in human existence. We are all familiar with it in the life-course of many individuals. It is easily recognizable in the history of many states: in Athens after the death of Pericles, under the pressure of the Peloponnesian War, by the choice of its leaders, by submission to their demagoguery and imprudent plans, by their brutality and their hubris. Hence it is not surprising to learn that civilizations also destroy themselves. Normally a violent attack of any external enemy on a society or civilization has a stimulating effect leading to positive achievements; the best an alien enemy can do is give the *coup de grâce* to an expiring suicide. As we have seen, Hegel also discerns the death of a culture to be a kind of self-destruction since no force can overcome a *Volksgeist* if it has not itself become lifeless.

Toynbee abhors war. To my knowledge, no great writer on historical matters has so consistently and repeatedly stressed the destructive force of war. It is a motif which appears throughout his entire work. From a personal side perhaps it was derived from his experience of World War I. If so, his study of the entire range of historic civilizations confirmed this view. Militarism, he states, is a perversion of the human spirit into channels of mutual destruction. The commonest cause of the breakdowns of civilization is militarism. It "breaks a civilization down by causing the local states into which the society is articulated to collide with one another in destructive fratricidal conflicts."[358] In this suicidal process the entire social fabric goes up in flames. In another place, he states, "Fratricidal warfare of ever-increasing violence had been by far the commonest cause of mortality among civilizations of all three generations."[359] Discussing the development of militarism in Prussia and in

Germany, he compares "the mad-dog militarism of a National Socialist Germany with the furor *Assyriacus*" at the time of Tiglath-Pileser III in the 8th century B.C.; meditating, he doubts whether the utter destruction of the National Socialist war machine has "destroyed the will to militarism in all parts of a Westernizing world."[360] Very different from Toynbee's thoroughgoing condemnation of war in human life and the historic course are the views of Hegel and Spengler. Hegel discerns a positive ethical function in war; war makes individuals "feel the power of their lord and master, death," thereby preventing them from separating themselves from the social community, and thus "guards the ethical order from sinking into merely natural existence,..."[361] An enduring peace would bring about stagnation and corruption; just as the winds preserve the sea from stagnation and putrescence, war preserves the ethical vitality of the nation. War is even more for Spengler: "War is the creator of all great things. All that is meaningful in the stream of life has emerged through victory and defeat."[362] It would be silly to interpret this comparison as a clear expression of the British spirit against the German; many Anglo-Saxons share Hegel's and Spengler's view, many Germans share Toynbee's and yet—do not the great minds of a people often articulate the dominant views?

While in the process of growth, the civilizations become increasingly differentiated from one another; in the process of the disintegration of civilizations there is a tendency to standardization, in Toynbee's view. The standard pattern of disintegration is a schism of the society into three groups: the dominant minority, the internal proletariat, and the external proletariat, each of which is the source of an institution—universal state, universal church, and barbarian war-bands, respectively. The standard pattern does not include a definite time-span, for one reason because a civilization can survive for thousands of years by becoming petrified—Egypt is cited as the classic example. While the breakdown of a civilization is due, not to external factors, but to an inward loss of self-determination, a civilization which has broken down is subject to external factors and activities on its way through disintegration to dissolution. A prime example is the Judaic source of Christianity, the universal church which emerged in the disintegration of the Greco-Roman civilization.

No recent author on historical matters, to my knowledge, has been more sensitive to, and perceptive of, the manifold rhythms which permeate the course of human history. We will cite some specific rhythms in history subsequently, but here we wish to set forth the first discussion of a major rhythm which appears at the close of Volume VI in a chapter entitled "The Rhythm of Disintegration." Of course, the formula of Challenge-and-Response itself has a rhythmic content. When Toynbee speaks of "the rhythm of growth," he is referring to this, a succession of challenges met by successful responses. The failure of a civilization to respond successfully to a challenge means a cessation of growth, a breakdown. Then the rhythm of disintegration sets in: the challenge continues to present itself, a second effort to meet it may have partial and temporary success; after its eventual failure, comes a further relapse, perhaps followed by another partial and temporary success. This process continues until the dissolution of the society. Toynbee expresses the rhythm as rout-rally-rout-rally. This rout-rally formula has been ridiculed by many critics—it was certainly not a happy formulation— and particularly because Toynbee claims to have found that three-and-a-half beats represent "the pattern which fits the histories of a number of disintegrating societies."[363] As examples, Toynbee gives an account of the disintegration of the Hellenic Society which was undoubtedly the model in this connection as well as elsewhere in his thought, followed by accounts of the disintegration of the Sinic Society, Sumeric Society, and of Orthodox Christendom. Fortunately, Toynbee recognizes that there is "no special virtue" nor necessity in the number three and a half; the general rhythm of disintegration could take place with more or fewer beats. In general, Toynbee avoids definite time-spans for the various phases of the historic course of a civilization. However, with respect to disintegration he does adopt more or less uniform time spans: 400 years from the initial breakdown to the universal state, and approximately the same time-span from the universal state to complete disintegration. Since the breakdown of the Hellenic Society is dated at 431 B.C. and the establishment of its universal state by Augustus at 31 B.C., and the Roman Empire went to pieces in the western provinces in A.D. 378, the model of the Hellenic Society may have been overwhelming in this regard. While there is no uniformity in the number of challenges and responses in the growth of civilizations, Toynbee finds a uniformity in the disintegration process. He claims moreover that this lies in an intrinsic difference between the growth-process and the disintegration-process, but this intrinsic difference is nowhere set forth in a convincing way in my opinion.

In a discussion of the relation between higher religions or universal churches and civilization, with the Hellenic model in mind, Toynbee points out that the Christian religion which arose in the disintegration of the Hellenic civilization served as a chrysalis for the development of Western civilization. Surveying the broad historic range of civilizations, he finds no higher religion at all between primitive societies and civilizations of the first generation (Egyptiac, Minoan, Sinic, Sumeric, etc.), nor between civilizations of the first and those of the second generation (Hellenic, Syriac, Indic, etc.). Only between civilizations of the second and those of the third generation (Western Christendom, Orthodox Christendom, Islam, the Hindu, and the Far Eastern civilizations) do we find the higher religions intervening to serve as a chrysalis for the development of the later generation of civilization. "...*all* the known universal churches were developed within the disintegrating body social of civilizations of the second generation..."[364] All the existing civilizations, the third generation, had universal churches as chrysalises: the Western and Orthodox Christian civilizations, the Christian church; the Far Eastern civilization, Mahayana Buddhism; the Hindu civilization, Hinduism; the Islamic civilization, Islam.

In the later volumes of his Study, Toynbee discusses the relation between the universal churches and civilizations in quite different terms. The universal churches of the higher religions represent now a higher species of society. They are no longer subordinate to civilizations, in the dual role of furthering the disintegration of one civilization in order to serve as the chrysalises of another civilization. It is rather the civilizations which serve to bring forth the higher religions and achieve therein their fulfillment and purpose. Toynbee has been pilloried for this later view by historian critics who seem to believe that he has thereby nullified his whole previous discussion. Of course, Toynbee is a Christian thinker, animated by a real and profound faith. This is naturally offensive to secular-minded historians. Were we to leave aside for the moment the question of the relative value of churches and civilizations—and are they not so inextricably interwoven that a separation for value-determination is dubious?—we might well acknowledge that civilization and religion are two fundamental elements mutually and reciprocally acting upon one another in the historic course. For Toynbee, however, the value-judgment is clear and consistent: the higher religions and their universal churches are of a higher order than the civilizations, and the final interpretation of civilizations does not reside so much in terms of their own destinies, but rather of their effect on the history of Religion.

The primary civilizations achieved only the rudiments of higher religion, but they brought forth the second generation of civilizations out of which the higher religions did eventually arise, and the rudimentary religious elements of the first civilizations made their contribution to higher religions produced by the second generation. In Toynbee's opinion, "the successive rises and falls of the primary and the secondary civilizations are examples of a rhythm"[365] which brings about advances in the spiritual development of the higher religions. From Abraham of Ur in disintegrating Sumer, through Moses in the breakup of the "New Empire" of Egypt, and Hebrew history in the breakdown of the Babylonic and the Syriac civilization, to the breakdown of the Hellenic civilization, "...Christianity could be seen to be the climax of a spiritual progress which had not merely survived successive secular catastrophes but had drawn from them its cumulative inspiration." In general, Toynbee finds the history of religion "to be unitary and progressive by contrast with the multiplicity and repetitiveness of the histories of civilizations..."[366] Likewise Toynbee notes that Christianity and the other three currently extant higher religions (Islam, Hinduism, and Mahayana Buddhism) have a closer affinity among themselves than their civilizations. The universal churches of the higher religions are for Toynbee diverse approximations on Earth to one and the same Commonwealth of God; this Commonwealth of God is the single representative of a spiritually higher order of Society than that represented by civilizations.

Unlike Hegel and Spengler, Toynbee does not discuss directly the problem of time. In a section on "Universal States" in Volume VII, he deals briefly with the measurement of time and notes there "a traditional association between the measurement of time by human intellects and the hold of religion over human souls."[367] The word "time" is often used by him in phrases or passing references and in poetic or prophetic utterances. For example, conscious of historical relativity, as a historian he is aware of himself as "a piece of sentient flotsam on the eddying surface of the stream of time."[368] Nevertheless, Toynbee's treatment of history presupposes the ultimate reality of time in a profound sense, quite foreign to the thought of Hegel and Spengler. Both Hegel and Spengler in different ways sought to nullify or "overcome" the reality of time, Hegel through the *Weltgeist* and Spengler through the organically determined structure of the Cultures. As we have already cited from an autobiographical statement, Toynbee's effort was to investigate the mystery of the universe under the aspect of temporality (*sub specie temporis*). Both Hegel and Spengler were regarding the universe under the aspect of eternity (*sub specie aeternitatis*), and hence there was really not that much mystery, for conceptual understanding does not tolerate mystery which it aims to dissipate and overcome.

The ultimate reality of time in Toynbee's thought is revealed by his conception of the role of the individual in history, of human decisions as the ultimate source of determination of the historic course, and of the significance of human choice. It is also revealed by the reality of the future, and by a grasp of the supervenient progress taking place along with the myriad rhythms and cycles of the historic course. As we have already mentioned (see p. 240), Hegel completely rejected the view that choice, the power to make decisions, was an essential component of human freedom. It follows for him then that individuals are merely means for higher purposes and that even the great world-historic individuals neither know nor aim at the universal purposes which they actualize; the universal spirit makes for itself the individuals it needs for its purposes, nor can individuals impede these, for "what must happen, happens." For Spengler, the matter is not much different; for him freedom is to do that which is necessary, or to do nothing. However, he at least allows a minimum of freedom in the course of historic events, the "elastic limit." The predetermined course will take place, but individual initiative can shape the way in which the predetermined developments occur. For Toynbee the ultimate significance and reality of choice in human affairs is grounded in the nature of consciousness: "The distinctive power conferred in the gift of consciousness is a freedom to make choices...."[369] Also, with respect to alternative developments of our Western civilization, Toynbee states: "As human beings, we are endowed with this freedom of choice, and we cannot shuffle off our responsibilities upon the shoulders of God or nature."[370] We have already set forth Toynbee's view that the individuals composing a society are the source of all action in the historic course of that society.

The depth of Toynbee's comprehension of temporality is demonstrated by his view of the future. The future does not really exist in Hegel's Philosophy of History, as we have seen. To superficial critics it has seemed that history ended in Hegel's own time, as philosophy in him. However, it was Hegel's claimed conceptual grasp of the totality of reality which necessitated the closure of history in his system. In other terms, his system comprehended reality *sub specie aeternitatis*, and if time is conceived in subordination to the eternal present, then the future can have scant reality. (see p. 258) In contrast, as we have shown, Spengler had a sense for the reality of the future. However, it is a future severely limited and constrained by the organic structuralism of his concept of culture. All the separate cultures have a predetermined organic course of development and decline. In his time Western culture, he finds, has reached the end-phase of a culture, the civilization phase, and will run its final course in a matter of centuries. His passing phrase about "cultures yet to be"[371] in the last paragraph of Volume I of the *Decline*, however, shows some sense of a future beyond Western culture.

Toynbee's recognition of the reality of the future has no Spenglerian limitations and constraints; it is open-ended. It is expressed clearly in relation to his conception of Challenge-and-Response in the growth of a civilization: "*Pace* Spengler, there seems to be no reason why a succession of stimulating challenges should not be met by a succession of victorious responses *ad infinitum*."[372] Likewise, in another context, "...indeed we have failed to find any reason *a priori* why a civilization should not go on growing indefinitely once it has entered on this stage."[373] If the creative force of individuals in a society is the source of historic advance, it would naturally follow, as it does for Toynbee, that we cannot know the future of any society or civilization nor does the study of past history help us in this respect. "Our *post mortem* examination of dead civilization does not enable us to cast the horoscope of our own civilization or of any other that is still alive."[374] Nevertheless, no recent historian has spent so much time and effort throughout his whole life to peer into the future, as we shall see subsequently.

The mention and discussion of cyclic and rhythmic phenomena throughout Toynbee's study display his intense feel for temporality. In Volume IV he discusses the cyclic theory of history. While "an obvious element of recurrence" appears in history "there is manifestly a developing design" (in the tapestry woven on "the loom of Time") and "not simply an endless repetition of the same pattern."[375] He frequently invokes the example of the wheel's movement, repetitive in relation to its own axle, but at the same time moving a vehicle forward. The harmony of two diverse movements, a major irreversible movement borne by a minor repetitive movement, is, he suggests, the essence of rhythm. In this connection he gives many examples of this play of forces in the organic rhythms of life. The detection of periodic repetitive movements in the process of civilization, he concludes, does not imply that "the process itself is of the same cyclic order as they are," but rather that "the major movement which they bear along is not recurrent but progressive."[376] An address given at Harvard in 1947 entitled "Does History repeat itself?" introduced further enlightenment into this view in the following: "If human history repeats itself, it does so in accordance with the general rhythm of the universe; but the significance of this pattern of repetition lies in the scope that it gives for the work of creation to go forward. In this light, the repetitive element in history reveals itself as an instrument for freedom of creative action, and not as an indication that God and man are the slaves of fate."[377]

In his later volumes, as we have noted, Toynbee stresses the view that the successive rises and falls of civilizations may be subsidiary to the growth of religion. However, this view appears as early as 1940 in a lecture given that year in Oxford under the title "Christianity and Civilization." He states there specifically that while the movement of civilizations may be cyclic and recurrent, "the movement of religion may be on a single continuous upward line,"[378] this upward movement being effected by the movement of civilizations round the cycle of birth, death, birth. The secular historian critics of Toynbee have been probably more irritated and indignant about the religious character of his thought than even by the concept of civilizations as the only intelligible unit of history. How appalling to be told that the historical function of civilizations is to serve by their downfall "as stepping-stones to a progressive process of the revelation of always deeper religious insight..."![379]

Unlike Hegel and Spengler, who deal primarily with the major rhythm of the rise and fall of cultures, Toynbee has also a keen sense for the multiplicity and complexity of the minor rhythms displayed in the historic existence of civilized man. In a section entitled "Law and Freedom in History" in Volume IX, he deals relatively briefly with many of these cycles. He mentions business cycles in an industrial Western society, first described in 1837 by Lord Overstone. He quotes at length from the 1927 book of an American economist, W.C. Mitchell, for example the following: "The conception of business cycles obtained from a survey of contemporary reports starts with the fundamental fact of rhythmical fluctuations in activity, and adds that these fluctuations are peculiar to countries organized on a business basis, that they appear in all such countries, that they tend to develop the same phase at nearly the same time in different countries, that they follow each other without intermissions, that they are affected by all sorts of non-business factors, that they represent predominant rather than universal changes in trend, and that, while they vary in intensity and duration, the variations are not so wide as to prevent our identifying different cases as belonging to a single class of phenomena."[380] Toynbee also cites an early work of W.W. Rostow on the economic history of Great Britain 1790-1914, from which he quotes the following: "...one is impressed with the solid reality of the cyclical pattern which steadily recurs, in Britain and then—gradually widening—throughout the World, from the end of the American Revolution to the outbreak of the First World War. No two cycles, of course, are quite the same; and one can trace, as well, certain long-period changes in the character of cycles. But it is evident that the whole evolution of Modern Society in the West occurred in a rhythmic pattern which had consequences for social and political, as well as for economic, events."[381] The diversity of the wave-length of cycles discovered by economists is quite impressive; Mitchell found a wave-length of three and a half years in the United States as a variant of similar short-wave cycles in Western Europe in the range of three to six years; other economists have discerned a nine-year cycle, going back to the French economist Juglar in the late nineteenth century; Dutch economists and the Russian economist N.D. Kondratieff have described a long-wave economic cycle of about fifty years. Toynbee comments that the believers in the three-and-a-half-year cycle and those in the nine-year cycle were each sceptical about the others' views, and that both schools alike were even more sceptical about the reality of the fifty-year Kondratieff cycle. Economic cycle theory is evidently not an exact science, and presumably will never be.

From economic cycles Toynbee proceeds to war-and-peace cycles, discussing with particular emphasis the wars of the national states of the Modern Western world. The Modern period of Western history is taken to have begun towards the end of the 15th century, with thus a four-century time-span to consider. Viewing the matter from the British standpoint, he notes that on four occasions, separated from one another by slightly over one hundred years, the British helped to destroy in war a continental power seeking to establish for Western Christendom a universal state or, in the traditional terms, "upset the balance of power." First came Spain, and the defeat of the Spanish Armada, 1588; second, the France of Louis XIV, Blenheim, 1704; third, the France of the Revolution and Napoleon, Waterloo, 1815; fourth, the Germany of Wilhelm II, November 1918—and revived under Hitler—May 1945. He discerns here "an unmistakable cyclical pattern viewed from an insular angle,"[382] each of these wars being separated by about a century. Examining the three inter-war centuries he notes a midway or supplementary group of wars in each case fought for the supremacy over Germany rather than over Western Europe as a whole. Also he claims to find occasionally premonitory wars before the general war. All this is set down in a table, and similar tables for the war-and-peace cycles in post-Alexandrine Hellenic history and in post-Confucian Sinic history are produced to show patterns similar in structure and in time-spans to those of Western History.

Few elements of Toynbee's thought have been more severely criticized than his war-and-peace cycle. Concerning the cycle of premonitory wars, a general war, a breathing space, supplementary wars, and general peace with five cycles for the period 1494-1945, the Harvard sociologist Sorokin states that when "his data are checked by the number and duration of the wars, the size of the armies, the magnitude of war casualty for each of his cycles, several of his periods of 'general peace' turn out to be as belligerent as his periods of 'general war' and visa versa."[383] Referring to the same cycle presentation, the Dutch historian Geyl states: "It looks beautifully 'simple'...I have rarely seen a more arbitrary juggling with the known facts of history."[384] The British historian Trevor-Roper states: "Why, for instance, are Philip II's operations in the Netherlands and the accompanying desultory sea-war described as 'general war,' while the Thirty Years' War which involves all Europe, and Hitler's War, which involves the world, are only 'supplementary wars'? The answer seems to be, to fit the theory. And why, if the Balkan campaigns in 1913 and the Italian occupation of Tripoli in 1911 are worth mentioning, do we see no mention of the Balkan campaign of 1878 and the French occupation of Tunis in 1881? The answer seems to be that the first set of campaigns is needed to illustrate a period of 'premonitory wars,' the second, since they fall in the period earmarked for 'general peace,' must be suppressed...."[385] Toynbee was very sensitive to the views of his critics and quite willing to make changes, as is evident by his final volume, Volume 12, *Reconsiderations*, with over a thousand pages in small print of afterthoughts and detailed consideration of criticism, and including a four-page bibliography of all reviews of his work. Volume IX was published in 1954, with the tables on war-and-peace cycles. Trevor-Roper's review containing the mention of Hitler's War appeared in October 1954. Somervell's abridgement of volumes VII-X was concluded at the end of 1955, though first published in 1957. In the table on page 272 of this abridgement volume, Hitler's War is no longer tabulated as a supplementary war, but included in the general war whose dates now extend, not from 1914-18, but from 1914-45; unfortunately this change in the table is not recorded for the reader.

Toynbee does not seem to have been aware of Quincy Wright's great work entitled *A Study of War* published in 1942. Wright deals at length with periodicity in warfare. First he notes that a day has been the normal period of a battle; warfare at night has not been common until the 20th century, when, as a result of changes in military technique, land battle in World Wars I and II often continued during the night and nocturnal air raids were frequent. The second period, that of the campaign, has been seasonal. Thucydides' chronology is based on the beginning of campaigns in the spring. "Wars in the North Temperate Zone have ordinarily begun and been fought most intensely in the Spring or Summer. The campaign has lasted until Winter and then the armies have hibernated." However, in World War I the men remained in the trenches all winter, and the war on the Western Front was a continuous campaign, with the campaign nearly a continuous battle. Wright notes that the Japanese have not shared the antipathy of the Europeans both to night fighting and to winter fighting. "Japan has often started battles in the middle of the night. It started the Russian War of 1904 and the Jehol operations of 1933 in the middle of winter. Its operations begun in China in 1937 did not diminish in vigor during the winters."[386] The momentous attack on Pearl Harbor took place on December 7, 1941. However, most wars have been started in the spring or summer. For example, "The United States began the Revolution, the Civil War, and the wars against Spain and Germany in April, the Mexican War in May, the War of 1812 in June, and the naval hostilities against France in July 1798."[387] March was Hitler's month: for his rearmament (1935) and the Rhineland remilitarization (1936), for the seizure of Austria (1938) and Czechoslovakia (1939); however, the invasion of Poland (1939) was delayed until September, probably in part because of the timing of the Ribbentrop-Molotov negotiations and partly because of waiting for the weather conditions to produce the dried terrain required for the maximum effectiveness of rapid-moving tank columns.

Another periodicity which Wright notes is that of the duration of a war, a period of four or five years. Although many wars have been shorter because of a defeat, in modern times from 1450 to 1930 the average length of the 278 wars was 4.4 years. Where the belligerents are nearly equal in strength, a war is apt to carry on for four or five years, as did the American Civil War and World War I. "Perhaps four or five years of the strain of war is as much as people can stand without resting."[388]

In addition to these three foregoing periods, Wright has also detected a longer period of approximately fifty years for concentrations of warfare in Europe during the last three centuries. He notes a similar periodicity in the United States between major wars. After the American Revolution, a major war, there was an attempt to maintain neutrality, which broke down in a minor war against France in 1798, followed by a second major war with England in 1812. After a period of quiescence military interests revived in the

1830's, which led to the minor war against Mexico in 1846. This was followed by a major war, the Civil War (1861-65) which brought about an exhaustion of the military spirit for several decades. It began to revive with naval building in the late 1880's and a minor war took place against Spain in 1898. After this, military and naval preparations came rapidly and the U.S. entered World War I in 1917. In Wright's opinion a similar fifty-year periodicity between major wars appears likewise in British history.

Spengler also noted a fifty-year periodicity of war, citing the three Punic Wars, "and the series—likewise comprehensible only as rhythmic—Spanish Succession War, Silesian wars, Napoleonic Wars, Bismarck's wars, and the World War."[389] He connects this with the spiritual relation between grandfather and grandson, implying presumably that the grandfather not wishing to fight again himself prejudices his son against war, but the grandsons in reaction come to think of war with positive enthusiasm. Spengler also refers to a book by R. Mewes, *Die Kriegs-und-Geistesperioden im Voelkerleben und Verkuendigung des naechsten Weltkrieges* (1896), in which these war-periods are related to weather-periods, sun-spot cycles, and certain positions of the planets, from which Mewes foretold a war for the period 1910-20.

The fifty-year war periodicity, according to Quincy Wright, is not regular enough to permit prediction. However, he suggests that "biological, psychological, economic, and political conditions may at times have tended to stabilize the fluctuations of war and peace about such a period."[390] In this connection he refers to the long economic cycle of about fifty years, which we have previously mentioned; also he mentions the view that a political party in England and the United States has tended to dominate for about fifty years.

While Spengler makes passing mention of the generation cycle in connection with the fifty-year war, Toynbee discusses more generally "the human generation cycle of birth, growth, procreation, senescence, and death"[391] in connection with social changes. He relates how it took three generations to transform an Italian family into an American family. Also, in class-conscious England, it has usually taken three generations to make "gentlefolk" out of a working-class or lower-middle-class family. In the field of religion he also cites examples to show three generations as a standard, e.g. from the ex-pagan convert Constantine I to the devout Christian-born emperor Theodosius; from the ex-Calvinist Henry IV to his grandson, the intolerantly devout Catholic-born Louis XIV. Giving examples from the histories of Petrine Russia, British India, and the Ottoman Empire, Toynbee notes four generations, or an average length of about 137 years, as the time-interval between the creation of an intelligentsia and its revolt against its creators. However, this four-generation effect is not explained in any way and hence seems to be more numerology than anything else. Toynbee also believes that a series of four generations may also "determine the wavelength of a war-and-peace cycle,"[392] this being based on his view of about one hundred years separating the general wars.

The Spanish philosopher Ortega Y. Gasset regards the generation as "the fundamental concept of history."[393] His concept of generation is quite different in time-span from that of Toynbee, Spengler, and most other authors. Gasset distinguishes five ages of about fifteen years in a man's life: childhood, youth, creation or initiation (in the sense of taking the initiative), dominance, and old age. The historic reality, he claims, is carried forward by men in two stages of life: thirty to forty-five, the period of creation and conflict; forty-five to sixty, the period of dominance and command. These are the two historical generations; they don't just follow each other, they overlap or are spliced together. "Always there are two generations active at the same time, in the full surge of activity, working on the same themes and concerned with the same things—but with a different index of age and therefore with a different meaning."[394] The truly historic stage in human life lies thus in the two mature periods, that of initiating and that of dominance. Hence Gasset claims that "a generation lasts fifteen years,"[395] and "the tone of history changes every fifteen years."[396] While appearing quite different from the usual concept of generation with a time-span of twenty-five to thirty years, in the final analysis Gasset's view seems to me rather a fine-tuning of the usual concept setting forth an internal differentiation based on a fifteen-year span.

Before proceeding to a discussion of Toynbee's view of the prospects of Western civilization, let me mention some other rhythms and cycles in historic existence. There are doubtless a myriad of such rhythms, and it would be far beyond the scope of this work to attempt to deal with them thoroughly. In fact what has been done in this field, and most of it in this century, is probably only the beginnings of a study of very complex and interrelated phenomena. Frank Klingberg, a student of Quincy Wright, published in *World Politics*, January 1952, an article which has received considerable attention, but perhaps not the attention it deserved. It was entitled "The Historical Alternation of Moods in American Foreign Policy."

Klingberg presents cogent evidence to indicate that the moods of introversion and extroversion have alternated throughout American history at fairly regular intervals. Three full cycles, in his opinion, have been completed since 1776, each with an introvert phase averaging twenty-one years, followed by an extrovert phase averaging twenty-seven years. "A fourth cycle appears to have begun about 1919, and its second or extrovert phase was entered upon around 1940."[397] According to his thesis, the waning of the Vietnam War in the late 1960's presumably has resulted in an introvert phase, and certainly there has been much evidence in the intervening years though 1980 to confirm this. Whether the Reagan administration represents a real break in this phase or merely a superficial theatric performance unrelated to the basic popular mood, it is too early in 1982 to tell.

In a chapter entitled "The Tides of National Politics" in his book *Paths to the Present* (1949), Arthur M. Schlesinger discerns an alternation between liberal and conservative periods in American history going back to 1765. The average length of the eleven periods up to 1947 he finds to be 16.55 years, with the actual duration seldom varying much from this norm. A major deviation occurred in two instances: the eight-year liberal period from 1861 to 1869 and the following thirty-two-year period of conservatism. Leaving aside these two atypical periods, conservative regimes average around fifteen years, liberal ones about sixteen years each. It is interesting to note that there seems to be no direct correlation between Schlesinger's alternation of liberal and conservative periods and Klingberg's introvert and extrovert foreign policy phases. This would seem to indicate the independence of these two rhythms in American sociohistoric life. To what extent the manifold rhythms of national life may be independent, may influence one another, or may be directly correlated, could only be resolved by a study of these rhythms much more extensive and profound than has been hitherto undertaken. Schlesinger points out that the liberal-conservative alternation does not seem to have been correlated with economic cycles. He also notes that no correlation between foreign wars and the liberal-conservative alternation was found; neither the progressive enlargement of the electorate, nor the physical growth of this country, nor the improvements of transportation and communication, nor the extension of popular education, have affected, in Schlesinger's opinion, the duration of the liberal-conservative periods. Even the liberal-conservative phases within the development of the separate states does not seem to have conformed to the alternating periods of national policy. Seeking an explanation, he finally comes to a possible psychological explanation, namely, "the fact that human beings in the mass, unlike inanimate Nature, respond to psychological impulses."[398] Noting analogous alternations in theology between orthodoxy and heterodoxy, in literature between classicism and revolt, and in the fine arts between stylistic rigidity and variety, he argues: "It is reasonable to believe that American politics has undergone a similar interplay of subjective influences—influences springing from something basic in human nature."[399]

Toynbee was also led to a psychological explanation of regularities in social change through the vehicle of three or more generations. He extends his psychological explanation to a larger span of historic change by reference to Jung's theory of the Subconscious. Between the Primordial Subconscious, common to all human beings and reflecting the common experiences of mankind, and the top level of the individual's subconscious, the Personal Subconscious, reflecting a person's individual experiences, there are "intermediate layers deposited neither by racial experience nor by personal experience, but by corporate experience of a supra-personal but infra-racial range." Thus there are layers of experience common to a family, common to a community, or common to a society. If there are psychic images expressing the particular character of a society, then the impress of these on the individual Psyche "might account for the length of the periods which certain social processes seem to require in order to work themselves out."[400] However, when Toynbee extends this psychological explanation to suggest that 400 years are required to cast out the idol of the parochial sovereign state and 800 or 1,000 years for individuals to disassociate themselves from a civilization and be prepared to accept the impress of another civilization or of a higher religion, then he does seem to be spinning out gossamer threads unable to carry any weight, much less over such time-spans.

The examples of rhythms of social change we have been thus far discussing have all been taken from the capitalist world. Are there cycles in Communist societies analogous to those in the democracies? Alternating phases or cycles are identifiable, different in content because of the nature of Communist regimes. For example, in the Soviet Union they are discernible in the methods of governance, i.e., from repression to relative relaxation and back again to repression: massive terror was used in the Civil War (1918-21), followed by a relaxation under the NEP (Lenin's New Economic Policy) and thereafter severe repression and terror, murder of the Kulaks in the collectivization of agriculture (1929-34), and the execution by Stalin of all possible elements of opposition to him in the Great Purge (1936-39). Leninist intolerance towards the internal opposition has been a permanent feature of Soviet rule, with the selective arrest of real or potential dissidents: Stalin's regime was most "conservative" in this respect, Khrushchev's was the most "liberalizing," while Brezhnev's has been somewhere in the middle in this regard. Alternating phases with respect to political leadership are also to be noted in the Soviet Union: the death or ouster of the top leader is followed by the emergence of a duumvirate or triumvirate; after Lenin's death came Stalin, Zinoviev, and Kamenev; after Stalin's death came Beria and Malenkov, Khrushchev and Malenkov, Khrushchev and Bulganin; after Khrushchev's ouster came Brezhnev and Kosygin. After about five years, autocratic one-man rule emerges again, either in unlimited form as with Stalin or limited as with Khruschev and Brezhnev. With respect to food production and the control of the peasantry under Soviet rule, there has been an alternation in the Soviet regime's practice, usually related to the magnitude of the harvest: after poor grain harvests more scope has been allowed for the peasants' personal initiative (size of private household plots, numbers of livestock, etc.); later, when the general food production has improved, controls of the peasantry have been tightened again. An alternation in Soviet foreign policy, somewhat analogous to Klingberg's introversion-extroversion in American foreign policy, is also detectable: introverted, anti-League of Nations (1921-34); extroverted, after Hitler seized power in Germany, under the theme of collective security, the Popular Front, and the Grand Alliance (1934-45); introverted, as suggested by the Cominform, the Cold War, anti-U.S. militancy arising from the U-2 incident (1947-63); extroverted, partial nuclear test-ban treaty, and other nuclear treaties (ocean, space, Salt I & II), the general mix of detente and third-world probing, and support of "national liberation revolutions" (1963-present).

In the brief history of Communist China there is already remarkably clear evidence of an alternation in foreign policy between introversion and extroversion. From 1949 to 1958 Communist China was in an extroverted "revolutionary" mood: entry into the Korean War, support of the Vietminh, participation in the 1955 Bandung Conference of twenty-nine Asian and African nations, trade-and-aid programs around the world in accordance with the "Bandung Spirit," development of ties with Communist parties and sympathetic splinter groups throughout the world in implicit competition with the U.S.S.R. From 1958 to 1971, the Chinese Communists were relatively withdrawn from the world scene, introverted, preoccupied with domestic problems and Sino-Soviet relations. In 1958 they initiated the economic Great Leap forward; they fell on their face, and it took until 1963 to return to the production level before the Great Leap. The years 1963-1965 saw the highpoint of the Chinese-Soviet ideologic polemics and the open conflict for leadership of the world Communist movement. The Great Cultural Revolution took place 1965-1969, producing internal anarchy, which had finally to be suppressed by the Chinese army. The Soviet occupation of Czechoslovakia in 1968 was a shock to the Chinese Communists, who came to fear that the Soviets might try to apply the Brezhnev doctrine to China. In March 1969 Soviet-Chinese fighting broke out on the Ussuri River border in northern Manchuria; while previous border skirmishes had gone unreported, in this case bellicose propaganda appeared on both sides; the Soviets threatened to use nuclear air strikes to destroy the Chinese nuclear capability, to which the Chinese answered that nuclear attack would be met with "revolutionary" war. This led to the next phase of extroversion, 1971 to the present. It was initiated by the famous Chinese ping-pong diplomacy in the spring of 1971. An international ping-pong meet had taken place in Japan; the American team along with the British, Canadians, Colombians, and the Nigerians were invited to play thereafter in Peking. At a reception in Peking, Chou-en-lai remarked on the historic friendship between the Chinese and American peoples, stating "a new page in the relations of the Chinese and the American people has opened." A few months later Kissinger made his secret visit to Peking, at which President Nixon's February 1972 visit to China was arranged, culminating in the Shanghai Communique looking to normalization of Chinese and U.S. relations. Communist China's entry into the U.N. and general participation in world affairs then ensued.

Frank Klingberg suggests that great world political cycles may have taken place, analogous to the introvert and extrovert phases. He cites periods of intense diplomatic pressures and wars among the Great Powers, as some of them sought expansion: 1798-1823, 1846-1871, 1893-1919, and from 1939 on. "The 'causes' of these cycles are perhaps largely inherent in the national and international political processes involved (including the 'balance of power' principle), and perhaps have occurred simultaneously for many nations as a result of 'contagion' as well as interaction."[401] He does not regard these world political cycles as the basic cause of the American alternation, but thinks it more likely that some larger factor or inherent tendency was operating in both. He believes that another tendency which may have intensified the American pattern is the principle called by Toynbee "withdrawal and return," the process by which the "creative minority" prepares new successful responses to new challenges.

We come now finally to deal with Toynbee's views concerning the prospects of our Western Civilization. As mentioned earlier, no recent historian has been more concerned with the future, and specifically the future of Western Society. From his earliest considerations at the outbreak of World War I in 1914, a motivating element in his thinking seems to be a profound concern for the future of Western civilization and concomitantly for the future of mankind. Despite his concern, he has recognized the terrible limitation imposed by the essential nature of temporality on the human capacity to look into the future with confident predictions. At the outset of his early work in the 1930's, he states, concerning Western civilization, that "we are at once confronted with the fact that we can not know its future."[402] Although this recognition is reiterated frequently throughout his whole work, nevertheless it has not constrained him, animated by genuine concern (akin to what Kierkegaard and the later existentialist philosophers call *Sorge*) to seek to penetrate by thought and by faith the darkness of the future.

Consistency is *not* what is to be found in Toynbee's thought on the future. We should not be disturbed by this hobgoblin of academic philosophy with respect to this. Consistency is a fine norm for abstract thinking, but when we are discussing the vital issues of human existence, the norms of abstract thinking are not particularly relevant. Toynbee's thought on the future changed and developed from his early work in the 1930's to the later works after World War II. Thus they changed with time and concrete circumstance. Also he often seems to be carried way by the specific subject-matter he is discussing to make particular comments about the future arising from the specific subject-matter.

Let us consider first Toynbee's comments on the future of Western civilization in the early volumes. Discussing the growth of civilizations, he notes that geographic expansion is sometimes associated with growth, but more often with decline and deterioration in quality. The worldwide expansion of Western civilization in recent centuries poses the question of association with growth or decline. "In our generation," he states, "a prudent man will offer no confident answer."[403] Discussing the breakdowns of civilizations, Toynbee notes that, aside from Western civilization, all the other living civilizations have already broken down and are in the process of disintegration. What of Western civilization? Judging by subjective feelings, "the best judges would probably declare that our 'time of troubles' had undoubtedly descended upon us"[404]—however, it should be recalled that the "time of troubles" is normally the first sign and stage of breakdown. Further along in his discussion of breakdown, he states that the major movement of the process of civilization is not recurrent but progressive. Although all the other previous and contemporary civilizations are either dead or dying, our Western civilization is not doomed by a necessary natural course or by fate. "The divine spark of creative power is still alive in us, and, if we have the grace to kindle it into flame, then the stars in their courses cannot defeat our efforts to attain the goals of human endeavor."[405] How tentative and uncertain Toynbee's thinking on this subject is emerges some pages later when he states that our own civilization "may also have passed its zenith for all that we as yet know."[406]

We have already mentioned that Toynbee regards war and militarism as the commonest cause of the breakdown of civilization. Unless Western civilization is able to abolish war through a cooperative system of world government, the cycle of wars will end in the forcible establishment of a universal state by a single surviving power—thus moving on to the next stage of disintegration. "Whether we in our world will succeed in achieving what no other civilization has ever yet achieved is a question that lies on the knees of the Gods."[407] This problem cannot be resolved if national sovereignty remains an object of idolatrous worship. Perhaps the British Commonwealth, the Soviet Union, or some international organization like the League of Nations will lead the way. Discussing the nature of disintegration, after noting that the Orthodox Christian civilization broke down in A.D. 977, Toynbee states that the Western civilization certainly grew for several centuries longer "and—for all we yet know—may not have broken down even yet."[408] Farther along in his discussion of the disintegration of civilizations, Toynbee remarks that "if our Western Civilization has indeed broken down, its disintegration cannot yet be very far advanced."[409] However, in his chapter entitled "The Rhythm of Disintegration" at the close of his early work, Toynbee states that "we are already far advanced in our time of troubles,"[410] with the main trouble being nationalistic internecine warfare reinforced by the forces of democracy and industrialism.

At the close of Volume IX published in 1954, the concluding

chapter is entitled "The Prospects of Western Civilization." Two novel elements enter into this discussion written after World War II. The first is the atomic bomb and the awe-full capability of nuclear warfare to destroy most if not all of mankind and most if not all of life on this planet. The second is the reconception of the relation between civilizations and higher religions, mentioned earlier, whereby the essential role of civilizations is to develop the higher religions rather than the religions developing civilizations. One is led to wonder whether there is not a subtle interrelation between these two novel elements which is obscured by the detailed discussion of civilizations and higher religions and their relation to each other. Faced with the awesome consequences of nuclear warfare, can men have hope in reason, rational analysis of the past, and reasonable prediction of the future? Given human nature, given the role of warfare in past and present civilizations, would not rational foresight lead to recognition of a very high probability of all-destructive, all-encompassing nuclear warfare? Under such circumstances hope must be grounded in faith, religious faith. Perhaps Toynbee in his thought is expressing the paramount question of our times for all mankind and reaching hopefully for an ultimate support.

Toynbee begins his discussion of the prospects of Western civilization with three "facts": 1) in the second quarter of the 20th century, all the extant civilizations, except the Western, were indisputedly in disintegration; Western society alone was "possibly still in its growth phase"; 2) through Western transportation and communication the whole world has been unified physically and Western civilization is exerting a powerful force on the other civilizations as well as primitive societies, so that all mankind is embraced "within a world-encompassing Westernizing ambit";[411] 3) for the first time in history, all mankind is threatened by annihilation in the event of a Third World War fought with nuclear, chemical, or bacteriological weapons. Since the inception of civilizations, in Toynbee's view, war and slavery had been the "twin cancers of civilization." Slavery had been overcome by the force of the Christian ideal; perhaps warfare could also similarly be overcome. Thus, writing in 1955, he finds "the crucial questions confronting Western man were all religious."[412]

In previous cases of the breakdown of civilizations, fratricidal warfare has been overcome only by elimination of all but one of the warring states. However, according to Toynbee, this fact is no very strong presumption against the possibility that in response to the challenge of establishing a unified social order, another civilization might make a spiritual advance leading to other means than a universal state to curb fratricidal war. Earlier civilizations, Toynbee points out, have caught sight of an alternative solution, e.g., in the Hellenic world the vision of an Homonoia or Concord had been set forth by certain Hellenic thinkers; in Sinic history, both Confucius and Lao-Tse had expressed ideals of spiritual harmony to be embodied in social institutions. In this century the League of Nations and the United Nations Organizations have likewise been derived from similar spiritual sources. Under the conditions of nuclear war, it is hardly possible that a general peace, a *Pax Romana*, can be achieved by one power through warfare eliminating all the others. The most likely consequence of nuclear warfare would be the total ruin of mankind, with at best a small remnant surviving to seek the tortuous climb again towards civilization. The forces of reconciliation, Toynbee notes, are stronger now than "any corresponding forces at work in the Hellenic society at a corresponding stage in its history."[413] The difference, in his opinion, is due to the continuing operation of a spirit of Christianity, which still had a hold over the hearts of Western men and women, even though their minds may have rejected the creed.

War cannot be abolished, in Toynbee's view, unless the control of atomic energy be held by one political authority, a World Government. Given the post-World War II bi-polar situation, there must be a transition from a world partitioned into an American and a Russian sphere to a World united under a single political authority. He poses the questions for the future, whether this transition is to be pacific or catastrophic; if catastrophic, whether partial or complete; if partial, whether the remnants would ever be able to achieve a recovery. He hopes that the governments and peoples of the United States and the Soviet Union will have patience in pursuing a policy of "live and let live." The United Nations, he regards as "evidently incapable of becoming the embryo of a world government."[414] It is more likely, he believes, that "an eventually inevitable world government" would develop either from the government of the United States or the government of the Soviet Union. The virtues of the United States he finds in its reluctance to play a world-governing role, its generosity as evidenced by the post-World War II treatment of Germany and Japan and by the Marshall Plan, and also by its commitment to the federal principle. The constitutional problems of a unified world order, he opines, could only be solved by some form of federal union.

Toynbee's thought in social and political terms on the need for a

unified political world order and on the prospects of Western civilization are not so different from the views of many recent and
contemporary thinkers. What distinguishes Toynbee most is the
religious aspect of his thought. He is an authentic Christian thinker,
and his thinking in this regard has been much more consistent
throughout all his life and works than other aspects. In a passage
written in the 1930's, Toynbee suggests that Western history may not
follow the course of Hellenic history by having some new church
arise amidst the internal proletariat of a disintegrated civilization,
but rather that Western civilization may be saved, in spite of itself,
by the Christian church. "...an apostate Western Christendom may
be given grace to be born again as a *Respublica Christiana*, which
was its own earlier and better ideal of what it should strive to be."
The modern Western secular civilization arose out of medieval
Western Christendom as a result of the renaissance of the Hellenic
institution of an absolute state, in which religion was subordinated to
politics. As to the future prospects, in general, of the several religions
throughout the world, Toynbee states: "Either the various churches
and religions will snarl each other out of existence...or else a unified
human race will find salvation in a religious unity." He clarifies this
latter alternative by stating: "Either a single religion might prove
victorious or the competing religions might reconcile themselves to
living side by side...."[416] By unifying the human world in a physical
and material sense, modern Western civilization is performing a
service for the four higher religions by providing them "with a
mundane meeting-ground on a worldwide scale," thus causing them
to recognize "the unity of their own ultimate values and beliefs."[417]
If there is to be in the future a political unity of mankind in a World
Commonwealth, it is possible that the exponents of the four living
higher religions may recognize that their seemingly rival systems
were merely alternate approaches to the One True God "along
avenues offering diverse partial glimpses of the Beatific Vision."[418]
Perhaps they will heed the words of protest of the pagan Symmachus against the intolerant victorious Christian Church of the fourth
century A.D.: "The heart of so great a mystery can never be reached
by following one road only."[419]

It should not be surprising that, despite his basic ecumenical
approach to the other higher religions, Toynbee as a Christian
thinker puts a special status and value on Christianity. This is particularly evident in the previously mentioned lecture at Oxford in 1940
on "Christianity and Civilization" which expresses in seminal form
views set forth in the volumes after World War II. If civilization is

the means and religion the end, and if our secular Western civilization perishes, he states, "...Christianity may be expected not only to
endure but to grow in wisdom and stature as a result of a fresh
experience of secular catastrophe."[420] Christian institutions, in his
opinion, are the toughest and most enduring of any known; hence
they are most likely to outlast all secular institutions, including all the
existing civilizations. His view of the historical progress of religion,
which we have earlier mentioned, occurs in this early lecture where
he states that this progress is "represented by the rise of the higher
religions and by their culmination in Christianity."[421] Just as Christianity under the Roman Empire took from the other Oriental religions and philosophies what was best in them, so Christianity may
receive from the present religions of India, the Mahayana Buddhism
of the Far East, and Chinese philosophy new elements to be incorporated into Christianity in the future. Thus Christianity "may be
left as the spiritual heir of all the other higher religions" which in the
middle of the 20th century are "living separate lives side by side with
Christianity and of all the philosophies from Ikhnaton's to Hegel's;
while the Christian church as an institution may be left as the social
heir of all the other churches and all the civilizations."[422] An extreme
statement, but Christian hope and faith perforce paints with bold
colors on the dark horizon of the future.

AFTERWORD

Practitioners in foreign affairs soon learn that some foreign affairs problems, and usually the most important ones, are insoluble; they cannot be solved by the best rational thinking or by ingenious devices; change may mute them and time may erode and even dissipate them. Similarly the great philosophical problems are all insoluble; as long as men think on fundamental issues, they will not go away; they cannot be solved by spinning webs of abstractions which characterize much of contemporary and past philosophy. Authentic philosophy, to my mind, is in effect the making of marginal notes on Reality. This effort seeks to elucidate aspects of reality. The more the marginal notes deal with concrete phenomena rather than abstractions, the closer they are to reality. Time, temporality, is assuredly one of philosophy's insoluble problems. Fifty years ago I was haunted by the philosophical problem of time. Much has intervened since then, and even fundamental aspects of the problem of time may have been altered by changing circumstances and scientific discoveries such as nuclear weapons. Six years ago I set out to endeavor to elucidate aspects of time in a concrete setting. The ontological ultimacy of time I had recognized fifty years ago. During the past six years I came to discern the ontological interrelation of time and rhythm. From Einstein I learned that the concept of periodic occurrence is prior to the concept of time. A periodic occurrence is a rhythm. While rhythm may be conceptually prior to

313

time, rhythm and time are so intertwined in reality that both must be regarded as ontologically ultimate. From Hegel previously I had learned that both the self and time are born of the primordial rhythm of Being. If, as Einstein states, time conceptually is born out of rhythm, must not this rhythm be an expression of the primordial rhythm of Being? Man is a temporal being, but even more: there is no time without the self, without sentient human creatures. Man is a temporal being whose history expresses and reveals the temporal character of reality. Nature and man are bound together, as are the history of nature and the history of man. All the sciences, whether natural or humanistic, are studying reality and seeking to explicate, reveal reality. Since history is the human understanding *sans pareil* of temporal reality, it is the link between the natural sciences and the humanistic sciences, between the history of nature and the history of man, and that only because of the temporal character of reality.

The reader will recognize, I hope, that this book which originated with an attempt to deal with the problem of time is a philosophical effort, and as such, if of value, represents marginal notes on Reality.

NOTES
PART I

1. Jonathan Swift, *Gulliver's Travels* (New York: Alfred A. Knopf, 1925), p. 24-25
2. Lewis Mumford, *Technics and Civilization* (New York: Harcourt Brace, 1934), p. 14
3. G.J. Whitrow, *The Nature of Time* (New York: Holt, Rinehart and Winston, 1973), p. 75
4. Mumford, *op. cit.*, p. 15
5. Galileo Galilei, *Dialogues and Mathematical Demonstrations Concerning Two New Sciences*, Crew and de Salvio translation (New York: Macmillan, 1914), p. 265
6. E.A. Burtt, *The Metaphysical Foundations of Modern Physical Science* (New York: Harcourt Brace, 1927), p. 150
7. Whitrow, *op. cit.*, p. 98
8. G.J. Whitrow, *The Natural Philosophy of Time* (London: Thomas Nelson and Sons, 1961), p. 131
9. *Ibid.*, p. 130
10. *Ibid.*, p. 132
11. Burtt, *op. cit.*, p. 153
12. *Ibid.*, p. 244
13. Alexandre Koyré, *From the Closed World to the Infinite Universe* (Baltimore: Johns Hopkins University Press, 3rd Printing, 1974), p. 161

14. Burtt, *op. cit.*, p. 257
15. J.B. Bury, *The Idea of Progress* (New York: Macmillan, 1932), p. 52
16. *Ibid.*, p. 54
17. *Ibid.*, p. 58
18. John Locke, *An Essay Concerning Human Understanding* (London: Dent, 1961), Vol. I, p. 166
19. Richard I. Aaron, *John Locke* (London: Oxford University Press, 2nd Edition, 1965), p. 307
20. Bury, *op. cit.*, p. 77
21. Whitrow, *Natural Philosophy of Time*, p. 34
22. *Ibid.*, p. 36
23. Koyré, *op. cit.*, p. 235f.
24. Whitrow, *Natural Philosophy of Time*, p. 37
25. G.W. von Leibniz, *Discourse on Metaphysics and Monadology* (Chicago: Open Court, 1927), p. 251
26. *Ibid.*, p. 252
27. Whitrow, *op. cit.*, p. 38
28. Whitrow, *The Nature of Time*, p. 24
29. *Ibid.*, p. 25
30. Albert Einstein and Leopold Infeld, *The Evolution of Physics* (New York: Simon and Schuster, 1938), p. 188
31. L. Marder, *Time and the Space-Traveller* (London: George Allen & Unwin, 1971), p. 23
32. Albert Einstein, *op. cit.*, p. 183
33. L. Marder, *op. cit.*, p. 24
34. Albert Einstein, *Ideas and Opinions* (New York: Crown Publishers, 1954), p. 246
35. Albert Einstein, *Evolution of Physics*, p. 220
36. Albert Einstein, *Ideas and Opinions*, p. 346
37. *Ibid.*, p. 329
38. *Ibid.*, p. 370f.
39. *Ibid.*, p. 371
40. *Ibid.*, p. 295
41. Einstein, *Evolution of Physics*, p. 189
42. Einstein, *Ideas and Opinions*, p. 363
43. Einstein, *Evolution of Physics*, p. 189
44. Einstein, *Ideas and Opinions*, p. 363
45. *Ibid.*, p. 364
46. *Ibid.*, p. 295
47. *Ibid.*, p. 298
48. *Ibid.*, p. 299

49. Alfred North Whitehead, *Science and the Modern World* (New York: Macmillan, 1925), p. 174
50. *Ibid.*, p. 183
51. *Ibid.*, p. 181
52. Einstein, *Ideas and Opinions*, p. 247
53. Whitrow, *Natural Philosophy of Time*, p. 211
54. Einstein, *Ideas and Opinions*, p. 371
55. Whitrow, *Nature of Time*, p. 123
56. *Ibid.*, p. 124
57. *Ibid.*, p. 125
58. Whitrow, *Natural Philosophy of Time*, p. xi
59. Einstein, *Ideas and Opinions*, p. 286
60. *Ibid.*, p. 287
61. *Ibid.*, p. 347
62. *Ibid.*, p. 248
63. *Ibid.*, p. 348
64. *Ibid.*, p. 375
65. *Ibid.*, p. 330
66. Whitrow, *Natural Philosophy of Time*, p. 237
67. *Ibid.*, p. 238
68. Whitrow, *Nature of Time*, p. 138
69. *Ibid.*, p. 139
70. *Ibid.*, p. 140
71. *The Confessions of St. Augustine*, translated by E.B. Pusey (New York: Everyman's Library, Dutton, 1966), p. 259
72. *Ibid.*, p. 261
73. *Ibid.*, p. 262
74. *Ibid.*, p. 276
75. Steven Weinberg, *The First Three Minutes* (New York: Basic Books, 1977), p. 14
76. *Ibid.*, p. 15
77. *Ibid.*, p. 21
78. *Ibid.*, p. 12
79. *Ibid.*, p. 21
80. *Ibid.*, p. 26
81. *Ibid.*, p. 34
82. *Ibid.*, p. 49
83. *Ibid.*, p. 50
84. *Ibid.*, p. 148
85. *Ibid.*, p. 153
86. *Ibid.*, p. 154
87. Whitehead, *Science and the Modern World, op. cit.*, p. 193

88. Gerald Feinberg, *What is the World Made Of?* (New York: Doubleday, 1977), p. 269
89. Adolph Baker, *Modern Physics and Antiphysics* (Reading, Mass: Addison-Wesley, 1970), p. 181
90. *Ibid.*, p. 152
91. Whitrow, *Natural Philosophy of Time*, p. 175
92. Whitrow, *Nature of Time*, p. 92
93. David Layzer, *The Arrow of Time*, Ms. dated July 15, 1975, p. 3
94. Gerald Feinberg, *What is the World Made Of?*, p. 233
95. D.I. Blokhintsev, *Space and Time in the Microworld* (Boston: Reidel, 1970), p. vii-viii
96. Whitrow, *Nature of Time*, p. 158
97. *Ibid.*, p. 159
98. Weinberg, *The First Three Minutes*, p. 29
99. *Ibid.*, p. 112
100. *Ibid.*, p. 113
101. *Ibid.*, p. 75
102. W.C. Saslaw and K.C. Jacobs, Eds., *The Emerging Universe* (Charlottesville: University Press of Virginia, 1972), p. 149
103. *Ibid.*, p. 10
104. *Ibid.*, p. 99
105. David Layzer, "Stellar Evolution," *Encyclopedia of Science and Technology* (New York: McGraw Hill, 1977), Vol. 13, p. 116f.
106. Benjamin F. Howell, Jr., "Earth," *McGraw Hill Encyclopedia of Science and Technology* 1977, Vol. 4, p. 367
107. Clair C. Patterson, "Earth, age of," *Ibid.*, Vol. 4, p. 368
108. Stephen Toulmin and June Goodfield, *The Discovery of Time* (New York: Harper & Row, 1965), p. 143
109. *Ibid.*, p. 144
110. *Ibid.*, p. 145
111. John Verhoogen et al., *The Earth* (New York: Holt, Rinehart and Winston, 1970), p. 12
112. Toulmin, *op. cit.*, p. 170
113. Verhoogen, *op. cit.*, p. 12f.
114. Toulmin, *op. cit.*, p. 162
115. Verhoogen, *op. cit.*, p. 202
116. Toulmin, *op. cit.*, p. 198
117. *Ibid.*, p. 199
118. *Ibid.*, p. 200
119. *Ibid.*, p. 201

120. *Ibid.*, p. 201f.
121. *Ibid.*, p. 202
122. *Ibid.*, p. 203
123. *Ibid.*, p. 207
124. *Ibid.*, p. 208
125. *Ibid.*, p. 209
126. *Ibíd.*, p. 210
127. *Ibid.*, p. 211
128. L.E. Orgel, *The Origins of Life: Molecules and Natural Selection* (New York: John Wiley, 1973), p. 25f.
129. *Ibid.*, p. 125
130. *Ibid.*, p. 129
131. *Ibid.*, p. 130
132. *Ibid.*, p. 131
133. *Ibid.*, p. 203
134. *Ibid.*, p. 158
135. *Ibid.*, p. 175
136. *Ibid.*, p. 35
137. George G. Simpson, *The Major Features of Evolution* (New York: Columbia University Press, 1953), p. 312
138. *Ibid.*, p. 310
139. *Ibid.*, p. 311
140. Harold F. Blum, *Time's Arrow and Evolution* (Princeton: Princeton University Press, 1951), p. 200
141. *Ibid.*, p. 201
142. Bury, *The Idea of Progress*, p. 336
143. Simpson, *op. cit.*, p. 312
144. Blum, *op. cit.*, p. 200
145. Whitehead, *Science and the Modern World*, p. 160

NOTES
PART II

1. Paul Fraisse, *The Psychology of Time* (New York: Harper & Row, 1963), p. 200, n.

2. *Ibid.*, p. 155
3. *Ibid.*, p. 156
4. *Ibid.*, p. 157
5. *Ibid.*, p. 159
6. *Ibid.*, p. 269
7. *Ibid.*, p. 277
8. *Ibid.*, p. 281
9. *Ibid.*, p. 285
10. *Ibid.*, p. 71
11. *Ibid.*, p. 76
12. *Ibid.*, p. 78
13. *Ibid.*, p. 76
14. Henri Bergson, *Time and Free Will* (New York: Macmillan, 4th Edition, 1921), p. 100
15. *Ibid.*, p. 101
16. Fraisse, *op. cit.*, p. 122
17. *Ibid.*, p. 83 (quoted from J.M. Guyau, La Genèse de l'idée de temps, 2nd ed. Paris: Alcan, 1902).
18. *Ibid.*, p. 85
19. *Ibid.*, p. 86
20. *Ibid.*, p. 87
21. *Ibid.*, p. 88
22. *Ibid.*, p. 90
23. *Ibid.*, p. 91
24. Ernst Pöppel, "Oscillations as Possible Basis for Time Perception," *The Study of Time*, edited by J.T. Fraser et al. (New York: Springer-Verlag, 1972), p. 224
25. *Ibid.*, p. 235
26. Fraisse, *op. cit.*, p. 87
27. Eugene Minkowski, *Lived Time*, translated by Nancy Metzel (Evanston: Northwestern University Press, 1970), p. 80
28. Fraisse, *op. cit.*, p. 97
29. *Ibid.*, p. 203
30. Minkowski, *op. cit.*, p. 14
31. Fraisse, *op. cit.*, p. 202
32. *Ibid.*, p. 205
33. Minkowski, op. cit., p. 88
34. Thomas J. Cottle and Stephen L. Klineberg, *The Present of Things Future* (New York: The Free Press, 1974), p. 19
35. Fraisse, *op. cit.*, p. 184
36. Minkowski, op. cit., p. 370
37. *Ibid.*, p. 371

38. Cottle, *op. cit.*, p. 22
39. Fraisse, *op. cit.*, p. 185
40. *Ibid.*, p. 163
41. Minkowski, op. cit., p. 93
42. Bergson, *op. cit.*, p. 9
43. Minkowski, op. cit., p. 101
44. Fraisse, *op. cit.*, p. 192
45. William Ernest Hocking, *The Self: Its Body and Freedom* (New Haven: Yale University Press, 1928), p. 46
46. *Ibid.*, p. 12
47. S.G.F. Brandon, *History, Time and Deity* (Manchester: Manchester University Press, 1965), p. 12
48. Fraisse, *op. cit.*, p. 173
49. Minkowski, op. cit., p. 131
50. *Ibid.*, p. 133
51. *Ibid.*, p. 132
52. *Ibid.*, p. 134
53. Fraisse, *op. cit.*, p. 169
54. *Ibid.*, p. 289
55. *Ibid.*, p. 169
56. Cottle, *op. cit.*, p. 25
57. *Ibid.*, p. 166
58. *Ibid.*, p. 167
59. *Ibid.*, p. 168
60. *Ibid.*, p. 171
61. J.E. Orme, *Time, Experience, and Behaviour* (London: Iliffe Books, 1969), p. 46
62. Cottle, *op. cit.*, p. 172
63. Konrad Lorenz, *Studies in Animal and Human Behaviour* (Cambridge: Harvard University Press, 1971), Vol. II, p. 324
64. Donald R. Griffin, *The Question of Animal Awareness* (New York: The Rockefeller University Press, 1976), p. 97
65. Cottle, *op. cit.*, p. 6
66. Carl Sagan, *The Dragons of Eden* (New York: Random House, 1977), p. 107
67. Fraisse, *op. cit.*, p. 152
68. Griffin, *op. cit.*, p. 50
69. R. Allen Gardner and Beatrice T. Gardner, "Communication with a young chimpanzee: Washoe's Vocabulary," *No. 198— Modeles Animaux du Comportement Humain*, Colloques internationaux du C.N.R.S. (December 1970), p. 263
70. B.T. Gardner and R.A. Gardner, "Comparing the Early

Utterances of Child and Chimpanzee," *Minnesota Symposia on Child Psychology*, ed. by A. Pick (Minneapolis: Univ. of Minn. Press, 1974), 8, p. 20

71. B.T. and R.A. Gardner, "Evidence for Sentence Constituents in the Early Utterances of Child and Chimpanzee," *Journal of Experimental Psychology: General*, 1975, Vol. 104, No. 3, p. 266
72. *Minnesota Symposia, op. cit.*, p. 20f.
73. W.E. Hocking, *op. cit.*, p. 3
74. B.T. and R.A. Gardner, "Comparative Psychology and Language Acquisition," offprint, May 1977
75. Griffin, *op. cit.*, p. 84
76. *Ibid.*, p. 101
77. Sagan, *op. cit.*, p. 122
78. Griffin, *op. cit.*, p. 37
79. Fraisse, *op. cit.*, p. 21
80. *Ibid.*, p. 38
81. *Ibid.*, p. 163f.·
82. *Ibid.*, p. 164
83. *Ibid.*, p. 165
84. *Ibid.*, p. 48
85. J.D. Palmer, *An Introduction to Biological Rhythms* (New York: Academic Press, 1976), p. 23f.
86. G.W.F. Hegel, *Sämtliche Werke*, 20 volumes, edited by H. Glockner (Stuttgärt: Fromann's Verlag, 1927), X, p. 272 (my translation)
87. Charles M. Sherover, *The Human Experience of Time* (New York: New York University Press, 1975), p. 52
88. *Ibid.*, p. 47
89. *Ibid.*, p. 75
90. *Ibid.*, p. 76
91. *Ibid.*, p. 77
92. *Ibid.*, p. 80
93. St. Augustine, *Confessions* (New York: Dutton's Everyman's Library, 1966), p. 271
94. *Ibid.*, p. 273
95. Hegel, *op. cit.*, Vol. II, p. 612 (cf. Baillie's translation, p. 800)
96. *Ibid.*, p. 618 (cf. Baillie, p. 807)
97. Hegel, *op. cit.*, Vol. IX, p. 79 (my translation)
98. B.S. Aronson, "Time, Time Stance, and Existence," *The Study of Time* (New York: Springer-Verlag, 1972), p. 296
99. Fraisse, *op. cit.*, p. 159
100. Minkowski, op. cit., p. 33

NOTES
PART III

1. *Herodotus*, Loeb Library translation by A.D. Godley (New York: G.P. Putnam's Sons, 1926), p. 3
2. *Thucydides*, Loeb Library translation by C.F. Smith (New York: G.P. Putnam's Sons, 1928), p. 3
3. C.F. von Weizsäcker, *The History of Nature* (Chicago: University of Chicago Press, 1949), p. 10
4. H.P. Rickman in Introduction to *Pattern and Meaning in History* by Wilhelm Dilthey (New York: Harper and Brothers, 1962), p. 47
5. J.E. Pfeiffer, *The Emergence of Man* (New York: Harper and Row, 1972), p. 13
6. Brian M. Fagan, *World Prehistory* (Boston: Little Brown and Co., 1978), p. 79
7. *Ibid.*, p. 82
8. *Ibid.*, p. 92
9. *Ibid.*, p. 93
10. Grahame Clark, *Aspects of Prehistory* (Berkeley: University of California Press, 1970), p. 57
11. Pfeiffer, *op. cit.*, p. 53
12. *Ibid.*, p. 158
13. Clark, *op. cit.*, p. 58
14. Ragnar Granit, *The Purposive Brain* (Cambridge, Mass: MIT Press, 1977), p. 54
15. Arnold J. Toynbee, *A Study of History*, abridgement of Vols. I-VI by D.C. Somervell (New York and London: Oxford University Press, 1947), p. 49
16. Clark, *op. cit.*, p. 62
17. *Ibid.*, p. 67
18. *Ibid.*, p. 68
19. Grahame Clark, *World Prehistory*, Third edition (London and New York: Cambridge University Press, 1977), p. xv
20. Clark, *Aspects, op. cit.*, p. 85
21. Robert J. Braidwood, *Prehistoric Men*, Seventh edition (Glenview, IL: Scott, Foresman and Co., 1967), p. 114
22. *Ibid.*, p. 141

23. Clark, *Aspects, op. cit.*, p. 100
24. *Ibid.*, p. 106
25. *Ibid.*, p. 109
26. *Ibid.*, p. 110
27. Pfeiffer, *op. cit.*, p. 304
28. Clark, *Aspects, op. cit.*, 112
29. *Ibid.*, p. 114
30. *Ibid.*, p. 121
31. *Ibid.*, p. 122
32. *Ibid.*, p. 124
33. *Ibid.*, p. 126
34. *Ibid.*, p. 127
35. *Ibid.*, p. 130
36. *Ibid.*, p. 131
37. Clark, *World Prehistory, op. cit.*, p. 374
38. Clark, *Aspects, op. cit.*, p. 130
39. *Ibid.*, p. 127
40. John A. Wilson, *The Burden of Egypt* (Chicago: University of Chicago Press, 1951), p. 13
41. H. and H.A. Frankfort, J.A. Wilson, T. Jacobsen and W.A. Irwin, *The Intellectual Adventure of Ancient Man* (Chicago: University of Chicago Press, 7th Printing, 1972), p. 26
42. Wilson, *op. cit.*, p. 49
43. *Ibid.*, p. 2f.
44. *Ibid.*, p. 48
45. *Ibid.*, p. 3
46. *Ibid.*, p. 4
47. *Ibid.*, p. 53f.
48. *Ibid.*, p. 54
49. *Ibid.*, p. 218f.
50. *Ibid.*, p. 297
51. Henri Frankfort, *Kingship and the Gods* (Chicago: University of Chicago Press, 2nd Printing, 1955), p. 4
52. *Intellectual Adventure, op. cit.*, p. 128
53. *Ibid.*, p. 186
54. E.A. Speiser, "Ancient Mesopotamia," *The Idea of History in the Ancient Near East*, ed. R.C. Denton (New Haven: Yale University Press, 4th Printing, 1967), p. 56
55. *Ibid.*, p. 57
56. *Ibid.*, p. 62
57. *Ibid.*, p. 55

58. Frankfort, *Kingship, op. cit.*, p. 398
59. Frederick W. Mote, *Intellectual Foundations of China* (New York: Alfred A. Knopf, 1971), p. 9
60. Raymond Dawson, *The Chinese Experience* (New York: Charles Scribner's Sons, 1978), p. 75
61. Mote, *op. cit.*, p. 19
62. Joseph Needham, *Science and Civilization in China* (Cambridge, England: The University Press, 1956), Vol. 2, p. 292, Note d.
63. R. Wilhelm tr., The *I Ching* (Book of Changes) tr. from German into English by C.F. Baynes (New York: Pantheon Books, 1950), p. 135
64. *Ibid.*, p. 97
65. *Ibid.*, p. 202
66. Mote, *op. cit.*, p. 21
67. Dawson, *op. cit.*, p. 76
68. Needham, *op. cit.*, p. 290
69. Dawson, *op. cit.*, p. 4
70. *Ibid.*, p. 10
71. *Ibid.*, p. 78
72. Mote, *op. cit.*, p. 58
73. Dawson, *op. cit.*, p. 84
74. Joseph Needham, "Time and Knowledge in China and the West," in J.T. Fraser, ed., *The Voices of Time* (New York: George Braziller, 1966), p. 104
75. *Ibid.*, p. 105
76. S.Y. Teng, "Herodotus and Ssu-ma Chien: Two Fathers of History," *East and West* (Rome: 1961), p. 233
77. Clae Waltham, tr., *Shu Ching: Book of History* (Chicago: Henry Regnery Co., 1971), p. xii
78. *Ibid.*, p. 189
79. Burton Watson, *Ssu-ma Chien, Grand Historian of China* (New York: Columbia University Press, 1958), p. viii
80. Nathan Sivin, "Chinese Conceptions of Time," *The Earlham Review*, Vol. I, (Fall, 1966), p. 90
81. Watson, *op. cit.*, p. 6
82. *Ibid.*, p. viii
83. Needham, *Voices, op. cit.*, p. 108
18. *Ibid.*, p. 133
85. Mote, *op. cit.*, p. 50
86. Frankfort, *Kingship and the Gods, op. cit.*, p. 339

87. Evode Beaucamp, *The Bible and the Universe: Israel and the Theology of History* (Westminster, Md.: The Newman Press, 1963), p. 44
88. G. van der Leeuw, "Primordial Time and Final Time," *Man and Time*. Eranos Yearbook No. 3 (Princeton: Princeton University Press, 2nd Printing, 1973), p. 345
89. William A. Irwin, "The Hebrews," *The Intellectual Adventure of Ancient Man*, H. Frankfort et al. (Chicago: University of Chicago Press, 1946), p. 237
90. Frankfort, *Ibid.*, p. 372
91. Walter Eichrodt, *Man in the Old Testament*, tr. by K. and R. Gregor Smith (London: SCM Press Ltd., 1951), p. 13
92. Frankfort, *Kingship, op. cit.*, p. 278
93. G. Ernest Wright, *God Who Acts* (Chicago: Henry Regnery Co., 1952), p. 43
94. *Ibid.*, p. 48
95. Christopher R. North, *The Old Testament Interpretation of History* (London: The Epworth Press, 1946), p. 171
96. Bertil Albrektson, *History and the Gods* (Lund, Sweden: CWK Gleerup, 1967), p. 115
97. *Ibid.*, p. 119
98. *Ibid.*, p. 121
99. *Ibid.*, p. 120, n. 18
100. *Ibid.*, p. 122
101. Mircea Eliade, *The Myth of the Eternal Return*, tr. by W.R. Trask (Princeton: Princeton University Press, 1974), p. 104
102. Beaucamp, *op. cit.*, p. xi
103. Wright, *op. cit.*, p. 51
104. Irwin, *op. cit.*, 318f.
105. Millar Burrow, "Ancient Israel," *The Idea of History in the Ancient Near East* (New Haven: Yale University Press, 1955), p. 110
106. North, *op. cit.*, p. 34
107. Eliade, *op. cit.*, p. 104
108. Beaucamp, *op. cit.*, p. xv
109. Hans Walter Wolff, *Anthropology of the Old Testament* (Philadelphia: Fortress Press, 1974), p. 88
110. J. Pedersen, *Israel* (Copenhagen: Branner og Korch, 1926), Vol. I, p. 487
111. James Barr, *Biblical Words for Time*, rev. ed. (London: SCM Press Ltd., 1969), p. 144

112. Cecil M. Bowra, *The Greek Experience* (New York: Praeger Publishers, 1969), p. 12
113. *Ibid.*, p. 5
114. *Ibid.*, p. 20
115. Werner W. Jaeger, *Paideia: The Ideals of Greek Culture* (New York: Oxford University Press, 2nd Edition, 1945), p. 74
116. *Ibid.*, p. 314
117. *Ibid.*, p. 148
118. *Ibid.*, p. 125
119. *Ibid.*, p. 254
120. Bowra, *op. cit.*, p. 144
121. *Ibid.*, p. 154
122. *Ibid.*, p. 126
123. *Ibid.*, p. 45
124. *Ibid.*, p. 48
125. Jaeger, *op. cit.*, p. 326
126. *Ibid.*, p. 327
127. Bowra, *op. cit.*, p. 59
128. *Ibid.*, p. 60
129. *Ibid.*, p. 61
130. *Ibid.*, p. 60
131. Jaeger, *op. cit.*, p. 176
132. *Ibid.*, p. 155
133. Bowra, *op. cit.*, p. 179
134. Chester G. Starr, "Historical and Philosophical Time," *History and the Concept of Time*, Beiheft 6 of *History and Theory* (Wesleyan University Press, 1966), p. 27
135. John H. Finley, Jr., *Thucydides* (Cambridge: Harvard University Press, 1942), p. 8f.
136. *Ibid.*, p. 97
137. *Ibid.*, p. 310
138. Jacqueline de Romilly, *Time in Greek Tragedy* (Ithaca: Cornell University Press, 1968), p. 51
139. *Ibid.*, p. 53
140. *Ibid.*, p. 59
141. Robert Nisbet, *History of the Idea of Progress* (New York: Basic Books, Inc., 1980), p. 13
142. *Ibid.*, p. 17
143. *Ibid.*, p. 23
144. *Ibid.*, p. 25
145. *Ibid.*, p. 26

146. Starr, *op. cit.*, p. 28
147. Nisbet, *op. cit.*, p. 27
148. Romilly, *op. cit.*, p. 69
149. *Ibid.*, p. 89
150. *Ibid.*, p. 91
151. *Ibid.*, p. 93
152. *Ibid.*, p. 94
153. *Ibid.*, p. 107
154. *Ibid.*, p. 108
155. *Ibid.*, p. 109
156. *Ibid.*, p. 123
157. *Ibid.*, p. 170
158. Hajime Nakamura, "Time in Indian and Japanese Thought," in *The Voices of Time* (New York: Braziller, 1966), p. 81

Hegel

All translations from German texts are my own, except as indicated.
159. Nisbet, *op. cit.*, p. 176
160. A. Seth, *Hegelianism and Personality* (Edinburgh: Blackwood and Sons, 1887), p. 170
161. G.W.F. Hegel, *Die Vernunft in der Geschichte: Einleitung in die Philosophie der Weltgeschichte*, edited by G. Lasson, third edition (Leipzig: Felix Meiner, 1930), p. 30. To be cited hereon as V.
162. Ralph Waldo Emerson, Essays: First Series (Cambridge: Riverside Press, 1921), p. 3
163. Hegel, V., *op. cit.*, p. 53
164. *Ibid.*, p. 45
165. *Ibid.*, p. 160
166. *Ibid.*, p. 48
167. *Ibid.*, p. 162
168. *Ibid.*, p. 50
169. Hegel, *Die Orientalische Welt*, edited by Lasson, second edition (Leipzig: Meiner, 1923), p. 274
170. *Ibid.*, p. 275
171. *Ibid.*, p. 343
172. Hegel, V., *op. cit.*, p. 178
173. *Ibid.*, p. 179, underlining by me
174. *Ibid.*, p. 231
175. Hegel, *Die Griechische und die Römische Welt*, edited by Lasson, second edition (Leipzig: Meiner, 1923), p. 533

176. W.E. Hocking, "On the Law of History," *University of California Publications in Philosophy*, II, 3 (Berkeley: The University Press, 1909), p. 52
177. Hegel, V., *op. cit.*, p. 93
178. L. von Ranke, *Weltgeschichte*, Vol. II, Pt. IX (Leipzig: Duncker und Humblot, 1888), p. x
179. *Ibid.*, p. xi
180. Hegel, V., *op. cit.*, p. 42, 52
181. *Ibid.*, p. 32
182. *Ibid.*, p. 41
183. *Ibid.*, p. 40
184. A.N. Whitehead, *Adventures of Ideas* (New York: Macmillan, 1933), p. 15
185. *Ibid.*, p. 21
186. Hegel, V., *op. cit.*, p. 158
187. Hegel, *Sämtliche Werke*, 20 volumes, edited by H. Glockner (Stuttgart: Fromann's Verlag, 1927), I, p. 481
188. W.E. Hocking, *The Self: Its Body and Freedom* (New Haven: Yale University Press, 1928), p. 157
189. Hegel, V., *op. cit.*, p. 65
190. *Ibid.*, p. 75
191. *Ibid.*, p. 82
192. *Ibid.*, p. 37
193. *Ibid.*, p. 82
194. *Ibid.*, p. 37
195. *Ibid.*, p. 33
196. Ranke, *op. cit.*, p. 7
197. B. Croce, *On History*, tr. by D. Ainslie (London: Spottiswoode, Ballantine and Co., 1921), p. 102
198. Hegel, V., *op. cit.*, p. 92
199. Croce, *op. cit.*, p. 102
200. *Ibid.*, p. 103
201. Whitehead, *op. cit.*, p. 26
202. J. Burckhardt, *Weltgeschichtlichen Betrachtungen* (Leipzig: Insel Verlag, undated), p. 45
203. Hegel, V., *op. cit.*, p. 46
204. *Ibid.*, p. 38
205. Hocking, "On Law of History," *op. cit.*, p. 63
206. Hegel, V., *op. cit.*, p. 75
207. *Ibid.*, p. 133
208. Hegel, Glockner edition, *op. cit.*, Vol. IX, p. 80
209. *Ibid.*, p. 81

210. *Ibid.*, p. 80
211. Hegel, V., *op. cit.*, p. 134
212. Hegel, Glockner edition, *op. cit.*, Vol. II, p. 613
213. Hegel, *Phenomenology*, tr. by J.B. Baillie (New York: Macmillan), 1931), p. 801
214. *Ibid.*, p. 807
215. Hegel, V., *op. cit.*, p. 42
216. Hegel, Glockner edition, *op. cit.*, Vol. II, p. 620
217. Friedrich Hoelderlin, *Sämtliche Werke* (Leipzig: Insel Verlag, Dünndruck Ausgabe), p. 689
218. Hegel, V., *op. cit.*, p. 102
219. Hegel, Glockner edition, *op. cit.*, Vol. VII, p. 35
220. Hegel, V., *op. cit.*, p. 24
221. Hegel, Glockner edition, *op. cit.*, Vol. XIX, p. 96
222. Hegel, V., *op. cit.*, p. 165
223. Hegel, *Die Germanische Welt*, ed. by G. Lasson, second edition (Leipzig: Meiner, 1923), p. 779
224. Hegel, V., *op. cit.*, p. 281
225. *Ibid.*, p. 200
226. Whitehead, *op. cit.*, p. 3
227. R. Haym, *Hegel und seine Zeit*, edited by Rosenberg (Leipzig: Wilhelm Heim, 1927), p. 5
228. Hegel, V., *op. cit.*, p. 232, 225
229. Ranke, *op. cit.*, Part IX, Vol. II, p. xiii
230. Burckhardt, *op. cit.*, p. 56
231. Hegel, Glockner edition, *op. cit.*, Vol. IX, p. 83
232. *Ibid.*, p. 86
233. *Ibid.*, Vol. XVII, p. 355
234. Martin Heidegger, *Sein und Zeit* (Halle: Max Niemeyer, 1931), p. 431
235. Hegel, Glockner edition, *op. cit.*, Vol. IX, p. 80
236. *Ibid.*, p. 97
237. *Ibid.*, p. 52
238. R. Kroner, "System und Geschichte bei Hegel," *Logos XX*, 2 (Tubingen: J.C.B. Mohr, 1931), p. 255
239. Hegel, Glockner edition, *op. cit.*, Vol. IX, p. 86
240. Whitehead, *op. cit.*, p. 246
241. Hegel, Glockner edition, *op. cit.*, Vol. 286
242. *Ibid.*, Vol. XVII, p. 262
243. Hegel, *Jenenser Realphilosophie*, zig: Meiner, 1931-2), Vol. II, p. 12
244. Hegel, Glockner edition, *op. cit.*, Vol. VI, p. 156

245. A.N. Whitehead, *Religion in the Making* (New York: Macmillan, 1926), p. 92
246. Hegel, V., *op. cit.*, p. 69
247. C.S. Peirce, *Collected Papers* (Cambridge: Harvard University Press, 1931), Vol. I, p. 18
248. Hocking, "Law of History," *op. cit.*, p. 63
249. Whitehead, *Adventures of Ideas, op. cit.*, p. 192
250. R. Peattie, *College Geography* (Boston: Ginn & Co., 1926), p. 3
251. Burckhardt, *op. cit.*, p. 62

Spengler

252. Anton M. Koktanek, *Oswald Spengler in seiner Zeit* (Munich: C.H. Beck Verlag, 1968), p. 332
253. Oswald Spengler, *The Decline of the West*, tr. by C.F. Atkinson (New York: Alfred A. Knopf, 1926), Vol. I, p. xiv
254. *Ibid.*, p. 105
255. *Ibid.*, p. 49
256. H. Stuart Hughes, *Oswald Spengler: A Critical Estimate* (New York: Charles Scribner's Sons, 1952), p. 62
257. Spengler, *op. cit.*, I, p. 24
258. *Ibid.*, p. 40
259. *Ibid.*, p. xv
260. *Ibid.*, p. xiii, my translation from German text, I, p. vii
261. *Ibid.*, p. 104
262. *Ibid.*, p. 21
263. *Ibid.*, p. 106
264. *Ibid.*, p. 47
265. *Ibid.*, p. 21
266. *Ibid.*, my translation from German text, I, p. 28
267. *Ibid.*, p. 26
268. *Ibid.*, p. 27
269. *Ibid.*, p. 31
270. *Ibid.*, p. 5
271. *Ibid.*, p. 4
272. *Ibid.*, p. 105
273. *Ibid.*, p. 109
274. *Ibid.*, p. 110
275. *Ibid.*, p. 5
276. *Ibid.*, p. 39
277. *Ibid.*, p. 107
278. *Ibid.*, p. 41

279. *Ibid.*, p. 39
280. Spengler, *Decline of the West* (New York: Knopf, 1928), Vol. II, p. 446
281. Spengler, I, p. 145; my translation from German text, I, p. 188
282. *Ibid.*, I, p. 129; my translation from German text, I, p. 168
283. *Ibid.*, I, p. 54; see German text, I, p. 72
284. *Ibid.*, I, p. 101
285. *Ibid.*, I, p. 174
286. *Ibid.*, I, p. 41
287. *Ibid.*, I, p. 23
288. *Ibid.*, I, p. 46
289. *Ibid.*, I, p. 59
290. *Ibid.*, I, p. 63
291. *Ibid.*, I, p. 56
292. *Ibid.*, I, p. 100
293. *Ibid.*, I, p. 94
294. *Ibid.*, I, p. 95; my translation from German text, I, p. 127
295. *Ibid.*, my translation from German text, I, p. 128
296. *Ibid.*, I, p. 96
297. *Ibid.*, I, p. 8
298. *Ibid.*, I, p. 9
299. *Ibid.*, I, p. 10
300. *Ibid.*, I, p. 9
301. *Ibid.*, I, p. 10
302. *Ibid.*, I, p. 97
303. *Ibid.*, I, p. 143
304. *Ibid.*, I, p. 146
305. Sophocles, *The Oedipus Cycle*, tr. by Dudley Fitts and Robert Fitzgerald (New York: Harcourt Brace Jovanovich, 1977), p. 9
306. *Ibid.*, p. 55
307. *Ibid.*, p. 61
308. *Ibid.*, p. 65
309. Spengler, *op. cit.*, I, p. 130; my translation from German text, I, p. 169
310. *Ibid.*, I, p. 12
311. *Ibid.*, I, p. 14
312. *Ibid.*, I, p. 174
313. *Ibid.*, I, p. 188
314. *Ibid.*, I, p. 189
315. *Ibid.*, I, p. 174
316. *Ibid.*, I, p. 190
317. *Ibid.*, I, p. 174

318. *Ibid.*, I, p. 79
319. *Ibid.*, I, p. 120
320. *Ibid.*, I, p. 126
321. *Ibid.*, I, p. 127
322. *Ibid.*, I, p. 122
323. *Ibid.*, I, p. 7
324. *Ibid.*, I, p. 8
325. Hughes, *op. cit.*, p. 70
326. Spengler, *op. cit.*, I, p. 140
327. *Ibid.*, I, p. 49
328. *Ibid.*, I, p. 119
329. *Ibid.*, I, p. 118
330. *Ibid.*, I, p. 119
331. *Ibid.*, I, p. 121
332. *Ibid.*, I, p. 129
333. *Ibid.*, I, p. 122

The German text from which my translations were made is as follows: Oswald Spengler, *Der Untergang des Abendlandes* (München: C.H. Beck'sche Verlags Buchhandlung, 1923).

Toynbee

334. Arnold J. Toynbee, *Civilization on Trial* (New York: Oxford University Press, 1948), p. 9
335. *Ibid.*, p. 10
336. Arnold J. Toynbee, *A Study of History*, Abridgement of Volumes VII-X by D.C. Somervell (New York: Oxford University Press, 1957), p. 277
337. *Ibid.*, p. 303
338. *Ibid.*, p. 277
339. Toynbee, *Civilization on Trial*, *op. cit.*, p. 38
340. Toynbee, Abridgement of Volumes VII-X, *op. cit.*, p. 303
341. Arnold J. Toynbee, *A Study of History*, Abridgement of Volumes I-VI by D.C. Somervell (New York: Oxford University Press, 1947), p. 51
342. *Ibid.*, p. 75
343. *Ibid.*, p. 77
344. Times Literary Supplement, "Study of Toynbee: A Personal View of History," *Toynbee and History*, edited by M.F.A. Montagu (Boston: Porter Sargent, 1956), p. 104
345. Toynbee, Abridgement of Volumes I-VI, *op. cit.*, p. 67

346. O.H.K. Spate, "Reflections on Toynbee's *A Study of History: A Geographer's View*", *Toynbee and History, op. cit.*, p. 300
347. *Ibid.*, p. 301
348. Wayne Altree, "Toynbee's Treatment of Chinese History," *Toynbee and History, op. cit.*, p. 254
349. Toynbee, Abridgement of Volumes I-VI, *op. cit.*, p. 77
350. *Ibid.*, p. 11 n.
351. *Ibid.*, p. 189
352. *Ibid.*, p. 199
353. *Ibid.*, p. 211
354. *Ibid.*, p. 212
355. *Ibid.*, p. 273 n.
356. *Ibid.*, p. 279
357. *Ibid.*, p. 363
358. *Ibid.*, p. 190
359. Toynbee, Abridgement of Volumes VII-X, *op. cit.*, p. 312
360. *Ibid.*, p. 313
361. G.W.F. Hegel, *The Phenomenology of Mind*, tr. by J.B. Baillie (London: George Allen, 1910), p. 474
362. Spengler, *The Decline of the West* (New York: Knopf, 1928), Vol. II, p. 363
363. Toynbee, Abridgement of Volumes I-VI, *op. cit.*, p. 549
364. Toynbee, Abridgement of Volumes VII-X, *op. cit.*, p. 87
365. *Ibid.*, p. 88
366. *Ibid.*, p. 89
367. *Ibid.*, p. 57
368. Toynbee, *Civilization on Trial, op. cit.*, p. 16
369. Toynbee, Abridgement of Volumes VII-X, *op. cit.*, p. 287
370. Toynbee, *Civilization on Trial, op. cit.*, p. 39
371. Spengler, *The Decline of the West* (New York: Knopf, 1926), Vol. I, p. 428
372. Toynbee, *Civilization on Trial, op. cit.*, p. 12
373. Toynbee, Abridgement of Volumes I-VI, *op. cit.*, p. 367
374. Toynbee, *Civilization on Trial, op. cit.*, p. 12
375. Toynbee, Abridgement of Volumes I-VI, *op. cit.*, p. 253
376. *Ibid.*, p. 254
377. Toynbee, *Civilization on Trial, op. cit.*, p. 38
378. *Ibid.*, p. 235f.
379. *Ibid.*, p. 236
380. Arnold J. Toynbee, *A Study of History* (London: Oxford University Press, 1954), Vol. IX, p. 224f.
381. *Ibid.*, p. 227

382. Toynbee, Abridgement of Volumes VII-X, *op. cit.*, p. 270
383. Pitirim A. Sorokin, "Toynbee's Philosophy of History," *Toynbee and History, op. cit.*, p. 189
384. Pieter Geyl, "Toynbee as a Prophet," *Toynbee and History, op. cit.*, p. 375
385. Hugh Trevor-Roper, "Testing the Toynbee System," *Toynbee and History, op. cit.*, p. 123
386. Quincy Wright, *A Study of War* (Chicago: The University of Chicago Press, 1942), Vol. I, p. 224
387. *Ibid.*, p. 225
388. *Ibid.*, p. 226
389. Spengler, *The Decline of the West*, Vol. I, *op. cit.*, p. 110 n.
390. Wright, *op. cit.*, p. 231
391. Toynbee, Abridgement of Volumes VII-X, *op. cit.*, p. 281
392. *Ibid.*, p. 284
393. Jose Ortega y Gasset, *Man and Crisis* (New York: W.W. Norton, 1958), p. 51
394. *Ibid.*, p. 59
395. *Ibid.*, p. 60
396. *Ibid.*, p. 65
397. Frank L. Klingberg, "The Historical Alternation of Moods in American Foreign Policy," *World Politics* 4 (January 1952), p. 260
398. Arthur M. Schlesinger, *Paths to the Present* (New York: Macmillan, 1949), p. 89
399. *Ibid.*, p. 90
400. Toynbee, Abridgement of Volumes VII-X, *op. cit.*, p. 285
401. Klingberg, *op. cit.*, p. 265f.
402. Toynbee, Abridgement of Volumes I-VI, *op. cit.*, p. 9
403. *Ibid.*, p. 192
404. *Ibid.*, p. 245
405. *Ibid.*, p. 254
406. *Ibid.*, p. 276
407. *Ibid.*, p. 285
408. *Ibid.*, p. 367
409. *Ibid.*, p. 441
410. *Ibid.*, p. 552
411. Toynbee, Abridgement of Volumes VII-X, *op. cit.*, p. 304
412. *Ibid.*, p. 314
413. *Ibid.*, p. 319
414. *Ibid.*, p. 328
415. Toynbee, Abridgement of Volumes I-VI, *op. cit.*, p. 403

416. Toynbee, Abridgement of Volumes VII-X, *op. cit.*, p. 90
417. *Ibid.*, p. 92
418. *Ibid.*, p. 118
419. *Ibid.*, p. 91
420. Toynbee, *Civilization on Trial, op. cit.*, p. 239
421. *Ibid.*, p. 251
422. *Ibid.*, p. 240

INDEX

Aeschylus, 201, 208, 210, 215, 218, 220, 223, 224, 225
Agis, 248
Alcibiades, 247
Altree, W., 286
Anaximander, 206
Animals
   subjective experience, self-awareness of, 116-127
   evolution of self-awareness from animal to man, 117f., 160f.
   temporal horizon of animals, 117, 121f., 123f.
Anxiety, 106f., 110, 171f.
Authentic philosophy, 313f.
Archilochus, 207, 210
Aristophanes, 231
Aristotle, 9, 111, 139, 204, 213, 218, 227
Augustine, St., 33, 122, 139, 227, 280
Augustus, Caesar, 290

Bachelard, G., 96, 105
Bacon, Francis, 10
Barr, J., 201
Barrow, Isaac, 6, 10
Beaucamp, E., 190
Bergson, Henri, 93, 94, 96, 97, 100, 109,

121, 285, 287, 288, 289
Beria, L., 305
Biology, 59, 65-70
Blokhintsev, D.I., 48
Blum, H.F., 83, 84
Bodde, Derk, 186
Boltzmann, Ludwig, 49
Bourdon, B., 98
Bowra, C.M., 208, 214
Boyle, Robert, 5
Braidwood, Robert, 159
Brezhnev, L., 305
Browning, R., 286
Buffon, Comte de, 59, 66
Bulganin, N., 305
Burckhardt, J., 245, 257

Childe, Gordon, 158
China, 170, 176-186, 195, 200, 210, 213, 217, 226, 231, 233f., 263, 278, 286
   earliest writing, 177
   dualisms in thought, 177
   universe uncreated, a rhythmic organism, 177f.
   Son of Heaven, 180f.
   Tao, the Way, 181
   importance of history, 182f.

337

rhythmic rise and fall of dynasties, 184f.
concepts of time, 185f.
history as revelation, 186
Chou En-lai, 306
Christianity, 203, 218, 239, 253, 256, 257, 287, 291, 292f., 297, 439f.
Cicero, 214
Clark, Grahame, 154, 155, 157, 158, 160, 161, 163, 164
Clarke, Dr. Samuel, 11
Clausius, R., 48
Cleckley, H., 107
Cleomenes, 248
Clocks, 3-5, 20f., 25
   caesium atomic clock, 44
   pulsar clock, 44f.
   radioactive clocks, 45
      decay type, 45
      accumulation type, 46
   clocks in biological rhythms, 129f.
   human perception of time intervals not controlled by biological clock, 132
   human biological clock, 135f., 162f.
Compton scattering, simultaneous wave/particle properties, 42
Comte, August, 218, 219
Confucius, 178, 180, 310
Conjoint concepts
   space-time, wave-particle, 43
   discreteness/continuity of time, 100
   subject-object, 146
   consciousness, self-consciousness, 146
Consciousness, self-consciousness, 138f.
   as conjoint concepts, 146
   relation to history-writing, 147
Copernicus, N., 15
Cosmology, 31
   physical structure of the universe, 32-34
   origin of the universe, 35-40
   world models, 31, 37f.
   standard model ("the Big Bang"), 37f.
   the oscillating universe, 39f.
Courbon, 107
Croce, B., 242

Darwin, Charles, 14, 65f., 118, 126, 145, 155, 281
   influence of Lyell, 65f.
   influence of Malthus, 67f.
   Origin of Species, 68f.
   progress in evolutionary processsess, 84
Dawson, Raymond, 181
Death, 110f., 161f., 171
Delacroix, H., 100, 103
Descartes, René, 58, 227
Dicke, R.H., 38, 39
Diderot, D., 14
Dollo's Law, 83
Doppler, J.C., 35
Doppler effect, 35f.
Dreams, 136
   temporal disorder of, 108f.

Earth
   evolutionary process of, 57
   age of earth, 57f.
   geologic temporal development of, 59f.
Eddington, A.S., 31, 49
Egypt, 159f., 166, 167-172, 175, 176, 177, 181, 186f., 188f., 199, 202, 278, 284
   cultural effect of rhythms of the Nile, of other natural rhythms, 167f.
   sun-God Rē and pharaoh, 168
   absence of time sense, 169
   written and art records, but no history, 170
Eichrodt, W., 191, 192
Einstein, A., 16-31, 138, 313f.
   special theory of relativity, 16-19
   views on the time concept, 20-24
   corresponding views of psychologists, 102
   general theory of relativity, 28-31
   light as particles, 42
Eliade, M., 196
Emerson, R.W., 230
Essen, L., 44
Eternity, 170, 171, 258-261, 262

See also Egypt, Hegel, Spengler, Toynbee

Eudemus, 218
Euripides, 224, 225, 226
Evans-Pritchard, E.E., 114
Evolution, 65-70, 72f.
  natural selection, 73, 78, 80, 81, 157
  mutant variations, 81
  weakness of evolutionary theory, 81
  irreversibility of time in evolution, 82-84
  social and cultural, 156f.
Existence, 147f.

Fagan, Brian, 151
Feinberg, Gerald, 47
Fraisse, Paul, 20, 87f., 91, 94, 96, 99, 100, 101, 103, 110, 121, 122, 130
Frankfort, H.A., 159, 169, 176, 189, 192
Friedmann, Alexandre, 37
Future, 10, 103, 106f., 112, 114f., 122, 123, 141, 147f., 169, 185, 195, 198, 200, 210, 217, 222, 255-258, 272-273, 295f., 309-312
  See also past, present, Hegel, Spengler, Toynbee

Galaxies, 51-53
  formation of, 52f.
  temporal nature of, 53
  chronological and evolutionary ages, 53
Galileo, 5, 6, 60
Gardner, Beatrice and Robert, 120, 123f., 161
Geology, 59-64
  theory of catastrophes, 60f.
  observable cause/effect processes in time, 60f.
  a historical science, 62
  uniformitarianism, 63f.
  effect of geology on biology, 65f.
Geyl, P., 299
God, 7, 8, 9, 12f., 204, 205, 218, 219, 226, 242, 243, 253, 261, 297
  See also Greeks, Hebrews, Toynbee

God-oriented culture, 203, 214, 219
Goethe, J.W., 266, 267, 268, 270, 275, 286
Gothberg, L.C., 91
Granet, M., 180
Granit, Ragnar, 156
Greeks, The, 175, 176, 177, 181, 196, 201-225, 226, 231, 235, 239, 265, 276f.
  geographic and climactic influences on civilization and culture, 201-203
  a man-oriented culture, 203-205
  poets as spiritual leaders, 205-209
  rhythm and metric of Greek poetry, 207
  rhythm at center of Greek understanding of universe and man, 207f.
  Greek religion, 209-212
  Greek philosophy, 212-214
  the art of history-writing, 214-218
  Greek view of time, 201, 218-222
  Greek view of progress, 219f.
  time in Greek drama, 222-225
Griffin, Donald R., 125
Güterbock, H.G., 175f.
Guyau, J.M., 97, 106

Haldane, J.B.S., 73
Haym, R., 255
Hebrews, The, 184, 186-201, 202, 205, 208, 209, 212, 218, 222, 226
  origins in historic experience, 187f.
  historical experience at core of Hebrew religion, 188f.
  God of Hebrews (Yahweh), 188f., 209, 212
    absolute transcendence of God, 191
    as reflexive, self-conscious existence, 191
    will of God, 191f.
    prophets as spokesmen, 194f., 218
  universalism in Hebrew thought, 196f.
  conception of time, 200f.
Hecateus, 206
Hegel, G.W.F., 138, 139f., 185, 186, 200, 203, 213, 217, 226, 227-265, 268, 270, 272, 273, 275, 281, 282, 283, 284, 288, 291, 294, 295, 297, 312, 314

philosophy of history, culmination of his achievement, 227-229

Weltgeist (World Spirit), 229-230

rise and decline of a *Volksgeist* (Spirit of a People), 230-233

efficacy of self-consciousness, 231-233

transition (Uebergang) from one *Volksgeist* to another, 233-234

geography and history, 234-236

self-determination vs. self-consciousness, 236-238

freedom as purpose of world history, 238-240

men as means, 241-245

List der Vernunft (cunning of reason), 242, 244

necessity and possibility in history, 245-248

view of time, 248-252

absolute system vs. individual time-conditionedness, 252-255

eternal spirit as *Macht der Zeit* (power over time), 254

the future, 255-258

time and eternity, 258-261

depreciation of time, 261-265

Heidegger, M., 250, 259, 268

Henlein, Peter, 4

Heraclitus, 222, 259

Herodotus, 147, 167, 182, 199, 202, 206, 210, 211, 214, 219, 223, 226, 277

Hesiod, 206, 212, 219, 220

Hippias of Elis, 211

History, 27, 159, 186, 248, 265f., 268-270, 275, 280, 281, 283f.

of nature, 145f., 314

of man, 146f., 314

link between natural and social sciences, 187, 314

in Mesopotamia as ruling the gods, 174

recurring cycles in Mesopotamian history, 175f.

importance of, in China, 182f.

historical experience basic to Hebrew nation and faith, 188f.

for Hebrews, history as locus of God's activity, 192

Hebrew prophets speak out divine word about history, 194f.

emergence of history based on linear temporality, 194

past, present, future grouped together by prophets, 198

court history of King David as historical narrative, 199

Herodotus and Thucydides, 214-217

for Greeks, not God but Man acts, 218

temporal progression in history is sinusoidal, 222

tragedy and history emerged together in Greece, 223

rhythms in history, 227-312

See also Hegel, Spengler, Toynbee

Hitler, A., 305

Ho Hsin, 186

Hobbes, T., 8, 10

Hocking, W.E., 109, 110, 124, 236, 246, 262

Hoelderlin, F., 252

Homer, 204, 206, 209, 210, 211, 212, 218, 220, 222

Hope, 109f.

Hsun Tzu, 126

Hubble, Edwin, 36

Hubble Constant, 36

Huggins, Sir William, 36

Hughes, H.S., 279

Husserl, E., 97

Hutton, James, 14, 60, 62

Huxley, Julian, 161

Huygens, Christiaan, 5f.

Ikhnaton, 312

India, 234, 263, 277

Jaeger, W., 206, 207, 214

James, William, 99, 102, 135

Janet, P., 27

Jaspers, Karl, 134, 245, 275

Juglar, C., 298

Kamenev, L., 305
Kant, Immanuel, 14, 36, 52, 227, 265, 266, 279
Kelvin, Lord, 5
Kepler, Johannes, 5
Khrushchev, N.S., 305
Kierkegaard, S., 227
Kissinger, H., 306
Klingberg, Frank, 302, 305, 306
Kohler, Wolfgang, 161
Kondratieff, N.D., 298
Korsakov's syndrome, 134
Kosygin, A., 305
Kroner, B., 260

Lamarck, J., 63, 66
Lao-Tse, 310
Lavelle, L., 87, 105
Leakey, Louis, 150
Lee, Dorothy, 113, 115
Leibniz, G.W., 10, 11f., 30, 185, 227, 235, 266, 281
Lenin, V., 304, 305
Locke, John, 10, 14
Lorenz, Konrad, 118
Lyell, Charles, 61, 63f., 65f., 67, 70

Mach, E., 96, 102
Malenkov, G., 305
Malrieu, Ph., 88
Malthus, T., 67
Man, 218, 219, 247f.
    as temporal being, capable of history, 147
    capacity for objectification, 160
    articulate speech, 160f.
    sense of time, 162f.
    capacity to explain, 164f.
Man-oriented culture, 203-205, 213, 218, 219
Marshack, Herbert, 163
Marx, Karl, 217, 227
Mead, Margaret, 114
Memory, 89, 92, 95, 100, 103, 108, 111, 123, 134f., 147
Mencius, 126, 182

Merleau-Ponty, M., 140f.
Mesopotamia, 159f., 166, 171-176, 177, 180, 186f., 192, 196, 199, 202, 226
    anxiety in culture, 171f.
    culture correlated to natural rhythms, 172
    consonant political and religious pattern, 172f.
    assembly of gods, 173f.
    historical events in divine framework, 174f.
    rhythmic regularity in dynastic history, 175f., 184
metathesis, 98
Mewes, R., 301
Michaud, E., 91
Michelet, J., 228
Michelson-Morley experiment, 17f.
Microwave radiation, 33, 37f.
Miller, Stanley, 73, 75, 76
Milne, E.A., 49
Minkowski, Eugene, 103, 105, 106, 107, 109, 110, 141
Minkowski, H., 18, 26
Mitchell, W.S., 297-298
Montaigne, M. de, 109
Montesquieu, C., 14
More, Henry, 8
Mote, F.W., 177, 180
Mounier, E., 197
Mumford, Lewis, 4, 5

Nakamura, H., 226
Needham, Joseph, 177, 180, 184, 185, 186, 200
Newton, Isaac, 7, 8f., 10, 30, 42, 52, 270, 281
Nietzsche, F., 266-268
Nisbet, R., 219, 222, 227
Nixon, R., 306
"Now," The, 148, 259f.

Oparin, A.I., 73f., 77
Orgel, L.E., 74, 76, 78
Origins of Life, 71-81
    first appearance, 71

Oparin's theory of a reducing atmosphere, 73f.
the prebiotic soup, 74
bacterial and primitive plant organisms, 75
replication of macromolecules, 77
development of cell, 79
transition from replicating molecules to reproducing cells, 80
cellular reproductive capability, 80
Ortega y Gasset, J., 302

Past, 114, 122, 141, 147f., 169, 176, 181, 185, 198, 200, 222, 223, 255, 258f.
See also present, future
Pedersen, J., 200
Peebles, P.J.E., 38
Peirce, C.S., 262
Penzias, Arno, 33, 37
Pericles, 205, 217, 221, 247, 290
Periodic occurrence
conceptually prior to time (Einstein), 22
psychologically prior to time, 102
Persia, 233, 263
Pfeiffer, John E., 156
Philip of Macedon, 290
Piaget, Jean, 87, 88, 89, 90, 91
Pieron, H., 100
Pindar, 206, 218, 223, 224
Planck, Max, 43
Plato, 204, 213, 218, 221, 222, 227, 231, 260
Plotinus, 139
Poeppel, Ernst, 102f.
Poincaré, H., 16
Poulet, Georges, 109
Popov, N.A., 134
Prehistory, 149-165
origin of term, 149
temporal span, 149
from hominid to man, 150-153
walking upright (bipedalism), 153f., 157
toolmaking, 154f.,
food eating and sharing, 155

hunting, 155
brain size growth, 155f.
social and cultural evolution, 157f.
factors in its acceleration, 158
domestication of plants and animals, 158f.
village farming community, 159f.
burial, 161
ornaments, early art, 161f.
awareness of time, 162-165
"time-factored and time-factoring" thought, 163
Stonehenge, 163f.
the Mayas, 164f.
Present, 114, 122, 141, 147f., 198, 200, 222, 255, 258f.
See also past, future
Presentism, living only in the present, 107f.
Progress, 10, 14, 219-221, 255f., 265, 284
Protagoras, 204, 220f.
Pythagoras, 207, 218

Quantum theory, 41-46

Ranke, L., 199, 237, 242, 257
Read, Herbert, 162
Reality, 262, 313f.
its temporal character, 115, 146f.
relation to presentness, 147f.
Reflexivity, 138, 141, 147
Relativity See Einstein
Religion, 283f., 292-294, 297, 309, 311f.
as stemming from consciousness of time, 110
See also Egypt, Mesopotamia, Hebrews, Greeks, Toynbee
Rhythm, 23, 207
macroscopic rhythm, oscillating universe, 39f.
microscopic rhythms in waves and particles, 43
rhythmic structures, auditory, 95
importance in perception of succession and duration, 96
linked to perception of time, 96f.

primordial rhythm of reflexivity intrinsic to time, 97
biological rhythms, 128-137
  endogenous, 128, 133, 135
  exogenous, 128
  innate, 128f.
  development of rhythms in children, 131f.
  mitotic, 133
  in nervous system, 133f.
  synchronization, cyclochronism, 134
  adaptation to periodic changes, 136
geophysical rhythms, 128, 136
physical universe is basically rhythmic, 136
rhythms in history, 284, 291f., 296f., 297-307
  See also Hegel, Spengler, Toynbee
Rhythmicity ·
  intrinsic to nature of being, 39f.
  in Hegel's thought, 140
Roberts, M.S., 53
Robertson, H.P., 30
Romero, Francisco, 160
Rosenzweig, F., 257
Rostow, W.W., 297
Royce, Josiah, 109

Sagan, Carl, 120
Schlesinger, Arthur M., 303
Schelling, F., 252
Schopenhauer, A., 228
Scrope, George, 61
Self
  time as construction of the self, 109
  desire and hope as intrinsic to, 109
  as purpose, 109f.
  death as limit to, 110f.
  the self and time, 138-141
  consciousness, self-consciousness, 138f., 146, 232f., 238f.
  the conscious observer, 146
Self-awareness, 158, 160f., 161f., 162, 164f.
  evolution of, from animal to man, 117f., 160f.

Seth, A., 228
Shakespeare, W., 222
Simmel, G., 265
Simonides, 208, 210, 222
Simpson, George Gaylord, 82, 84
simultaneity of events, 18
Slavery, Hegel's and Whitehead's views contrasted, 239f.
Smith, William, 62
Socrates, 204
Solon, 207, 218, 222, 224
Somervell, D.C., 299
Sophocles, 204, 211, 215, 218, 221, 223, 224, 225, 226, 231
Sorokin, P., 299
Space-time, 25-27, 30, 43
Spate, O.H.K., 286
Speiser, E.A., 175
Spengler, Oswald, 226, 265-281, 282, 283, 284, 291, 294, 295, 296, 297, 301
  intellectual origins, 265-268
  relation to Hitlerism, 267
  "*the* philosophy of our time," 269
  cultures as organisms, as basic data of history, 268-272
  phase of civilization, 270-272
  sense of the future, 272-273
  culture as actualization of a soul, 273f.
  separateness of cultures, including even mathematics, 274
  systematic and physiognomic as spheres of morphology, 274f.
  concerning the Greeks, 276f.
  views on time and space, 277-280
  causality and destiny, 279f.
Spinoza, B., 227
Ssu-ma Ch'ien, 182, 183
Stalin, J., 305
Starr, C., 215, 221
Stellar evolution, 54-58
  population types, early phases, main sequence, 55
  from red giant to supernova or white dwarf, 56
  time scale, 56f.
  irreversible nuclear transformations

evidence of unidirectional temporality, 57
Strasser, G., 267
Stratigraphy, 62f.
  worldwide stratigraphic time scale, 64
Su Sung, 4
Subject-object
  as conjoint concepts, 146
Swift, Jonathan, 3, 4, 15

Teggart, F.J., 282
Temporal perspectives in primitive societies, 113-115
Temporality, 20f., 47f., 139, 148, 194, 200, 215, 225f., 252, 262f., 295, 296
Teng, S. Y., 182
Thales, 206, 222, 224
Theognis, 224
Thorpe, W.H., 127
Thucydides, 147, 199, 203, 214, 215-219, 221, 222, 226, 231, 275, 276, 277, 281, 300
Time, 9f., 27, 167, 192, 200f., 215, 221f., 238, 245, 246, 258, 258-265, 277-281, 294-296, 315f.
  as aspect of relation between universe and observer, 30f.
  as protraction of the mind (St. Augustine), 139
  as relative, 16f
    See also Einstein
  as spatial dimension, 6, 92f.
  before God created the world, 7, 33
  before the Big Bang, 38f.
  boredom, as clearest experience of, 105f.
  cyclical view of, 9f., 14, 167f., 172, 185f., 200, 201, 218, 219, 222, 223, 225f., 296
  coexists and coextensive with universe, 33
  conjoint with space, 43
  cosmic time, 31, 32f.
  development of time concept in modern science, 6-15
  direction of, 47-50
    reversal of temporal direction in physics, 47
    time-reversal invariance in microphysics, 47
    directedness of time in macrophysics, 48
    Second Law of Thermodynamics, 48f.
    cosmological expansion, 49f.
  discreteness/continuity of, 100
  enlargement of temporal horizon by geologists, 59f.
  Greek art, poetry, and history as means of defeating time, 209, 219
  Herodotus' unique sense of time, 215
  independent of events (Newton), derived from events (Leibniz), 11
    polemical exchange of letters between Leibniz and Dr. Clarke (writing for Newton), 11-13
  individual and social aspects of the experience of, 105-115
    individual aspects, 105-111
    social aspects, 111-115
  linear continuous advancing, 3, 5, 9f., 15, 186, 200, 201
  linear, mathematical, 6f, 8
  measurement of, 4f., 7, 21, 22, 25f., 44-46, 130, 132, 137f., 139, 163f.
  perception of, linked with rhythms, 96f.
  psychogenetic development of consciousness of, 87-93
    reflex reactions, respondent and operant conditioning, 87f.
    temporal horizon acquired, 88
    temporal horizon and unity of personality, 88
    consciousness of duration, 90
    time independent of change, 91
    intelligence and temporal orientation, 91
    experience of, in relation to space, 92f.
    construction of, 93

conceptual consciousness of time and the self, 93

rhythm as primordial ground of, 23, 138, 141

See also Einstein, Rhythm

succession and duration, 94-98

succession, 13, 91

experience of, irreversibility, 92

simultaneous perception of *before* and *after*, 94

subjective patterning, 95

order of succession perceived, 95

intervals (durations) perceived, 95

duration, 8, 9, 10, 23f., 90f.

experience of an interval, 92, 95

temporal limits, 95

interval of 0.75 seconds, a psychic constant, 97

related to walking, 95

perceived present, 99-104

upper limit of its time-span, 100-102

lower limit, 102

rhythmic processess as basis for time perception, 102f.

role of meaning, 104

structure of time and its historic character, 148

time and motion, 7f., (Barrow), 9 (Newton), 139 (Aristotle)

time-sense

hearing as, 97f.

explained by physiological clock, 136

waiting and expectation as origninal experience of, 106, 109, 224, 225

Whitehead's views, 23f., 255, 260, 261

See also past, present, future, space-time, Greeks, Hebrews, Hegel, Spengler, Toynbee

Tournal, 149

Trevor-Roper, H.R., 299

Toynbee, Arnold, 226, 281-312

intellectual origins, 281-282

investigate *sub specie temporis*, 282, 294

civilizations as smallest intelligible

fields of history, 282-284

"challenge and response" in civilization building, 284-288

role of the individual, 288f.

"breakdown" of civilization, 289f.

abhorrence of war, 290f.

disintegration of civilizations, 291f.

relation between higher religions and civilization, 292f.

views on time, 294-296

rhythm of civilizations, 296f.

minor rhythms in history, 297-306

economic cycles, 297f.

war and peace cycles, 298-301

generation cycle, 301f., 304

alternation of introversion/extroversion in American foreign policy, 302f.

liberal/conservative alternation, 303f.

cycles in Communist regimes, 304-306

future of Western society, 307-310

as a Christian thinker, 311f.

Tyrtaeus, 206

Urey, H.C., 73

Vigny, Alfred de, 109

Voltaire, F., 10

Wallace, A.R., 68, 281

Waltham, Clae, 183

Watch, 4

Watson, Burton, 185

Weinberg, Steven, 37, 38, 39, 51

Weyl, Hermann, 26

Whitehead, A.N., 23f., 41, 84, 127, 185, 239, 240, 244, 255, 260, 261, 262

Whitrow, G.J., 5, 31, 32f., 49

Whorf, B.L., 115

Wilhelm, R., 178

Wilson, J.A., 168

Wilson, R.W., 33, 37

Wittgenstein, L., 119, 122

Wolff, H.W., 200

World-models, 30, 31, 37

Wright, G.E., 193, 198

Wright, Quincy, 299, 301, 302
Wundt, W., 96, 97, 102

Xenophanes, 212

Yerkes, R.M., 119f.
Young, Thomas, 42

Zech, Jacob, 4
Zeitgedaechtnis of bees, 135
Zinoviev, G., 305